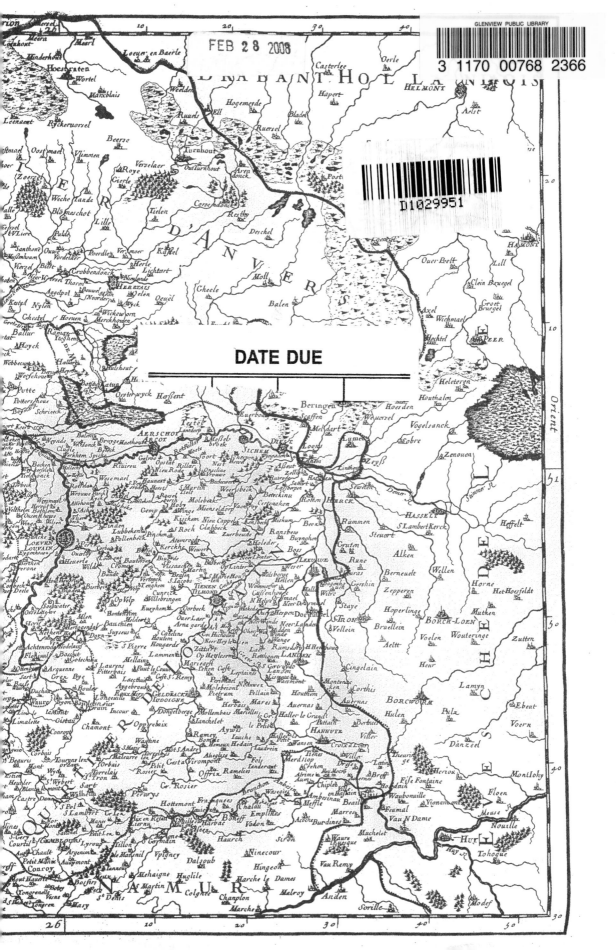

DATE DUE

Flemish DNA & Ancestry

Guido J. Deboeck

Flemish DNA & Ancestry

History of three families over five centuries
using conventional and genetic genealogy

GUIDO J. DEBOECK

Includes
Flanders-Flemish DNA Project

DOKUS PUBLISHING
ARLINGTON, VIRGINIA

Additional copies of this book may be obtained from the author.
This book is available at special quantity discounts for bulk purchases.
To inquire about these discounts contact the author via e-mail.

Guido J. Deboeck
3850 North River Street
Arlington, VA 22207-4650

Email: gdeboeck@mac.com

Website: www.dokus.com

Library of Congress Control Number 2007932645
ISBN No. 0-9725526-7-7

Keywords:
genealogy, genetic genealogy, DNA testing
family history, history of Flemish families
history of Flanders, history of Brabant, history of Brussels
lace, lace making, beer brewing
evolution of prices-, wages-, value of money in Belgium

Cover Design and Photography by G. Deboeck

Published for Dokus Publishing by
Gateway Press, Inc.
3600 Clipper Mill Road, Suite 260
Baltimore, Maryland 21211-1953

www.gatewaypress.com

Printed on acid-free paper.

Printed in the United States of America

Dedication

This book is dedicated to
the memory of my parents

René Corneille Deboeck
1913-1985

Marie-Louise Girardin
1918-2001

My grand parents

Guillaume & Joanne Deboeck-Nobels
Jean & Josephina Girardin-De Maseneer

and

10 generations of ancestors preceding them.

Table of Contents

PART TWO: ESCAPE TO THE UNITED STATES

PART THREE: OUR GENETIC INHERITANCE

List of Illustrations

List of Tables

Foreword

Guido Deboeck, who is part of a new generation of twentieth-century immigrants to the USA, continues an old Belgian tradition of discovering a new world. The first settlers in New York were Belgian entrepreneurs of which some temporarily lived in Holland, and hence were taken for Dutch. Even today there are many Belgian names in New York that remind about the land of origin. Many well-known Americans find in their family history links to Belgium. For example, Theodore Delano Roosevelt, is linked to the Beligan families Lannoy and the Dutch family Roosevelt. In the nineteenth century there was the discoverer, Jacques Moerenhout (1796-1879), who mapped large parts of the American continent. There were also hundreds of thousands of Belgians who settled in the northern part of the USA and Canada where till today they leave their traces (e.g. the Gazette of Detroit).

Guido Deboeck presents his family history in the first place for Flemish-Americans in the USA and Canada. In his work many typical terms and circumstances are elaborated and put in historical context. This provides added value to family history. Writing in this way is however a challenge: the author should be able to transpose himself into the spirit of his ancestors in order to place them in their exact space- and time frame. Often one has to struggle with mountains of data which have to be presented in a well-organized and intelligent manner. Furthermore, the narrative should not fall into a hagiography in which ancestors are placed on a pedestal. This is a huge challenge that Guido Deboeck meets exceptionally well.

His work tells the story of three Flemish families, from whom he and his wife descend, that illustrate the Belgian history of the last five centuries. With a lot of human psychology, and using his own professional education and experience, the author paints marvelously the history of these ancestors from the sixteenth to the twentieth century.

Genealogists approach with caution and hope what new scientific discoveries can bring about the origin of mankind. DNA tests can define the migration route our ancestors have taken out of Africa. The real interest and excitement for the genealogist is, however, when the DNA of family members who have a common ancestor in, say, the sixteenth or seventeenth century, is compared. Do all genealogists dare to test that far? When the DNA of people with common surnames whose genealogical link is not evident is compared, evidence may be found whether a common link exisits. If confirmed, this can stimulate collaboration to find the common ancestor.

Genealogy has just entered a new phase where new tools and approaches create possibilities for new exiting developments. Where written documents fail, genetic and medical science can provide support to genealogy. Guido Deboeck is one of the first of Flemish descent to tread this path; he encourages others to deploy these new tools and approaches in their search of the origin of their families. Are you ready to follow him?

Jan Caluwaerts
Professional Genealogist
Leuven, Belgium

The book I have the pleasure to present here, has many qualities and will interest a large and diverse number of readers. The genealogists, in the first place, will enjoy the book. In the introductory chapter they will find a very useful methodological guide for traditional genealogical research, as far as it is based on historical documents. The following questions are asked: What kind of written sources to look for? Where can they be found? How to analyze historical documents for genealogical purposes? How do you apply the method of "historical critique" on genealogical data?

In the chapters that follow, the author goes beyond the presentation of methodological guidelines. He applies the methodology to the research he undertook on the origins of his family roots. The interested genealogists therefore can follow in detail how the proposed methodology can be used in practice, how a solid scientific basis can be given to family history research.

This book goes beyond traditional genealogical research. The author goes beyond it by integrating genetics into genealogical research. He explains in an accessible way how the modern science of genetics can be deployed as an important, even crucial, complement to the traditional approach. He specifies, for example, how DNA tests can help in verifying or falsifying hypotheses about an assumed ancestry; he clarifies how DNA tests can bring together a number of families who were not aware of their common genealogical origin. The author applies with success the proposed method of genetic genealogy to research on the DNA of Flemish people (including Flemish immigrants in the United States and elsewhere) to enhance understanding of their European roots.

The scope of this book is such that genealogists in general will enjoy reading it and will benefit from its methodological guidelines and practical applications. Descendants of Flemish immigrants into the United States will, of course, have an extra reason for enjoying the book: it offers them an excellent framework for the study of their own genealogical roots and the history of their own immigrating ancestors.

The book will interest still a larger readership as a fine example of European and American family history. In the first place the case-study presents in a vivid way the European history of three families, all connected with the origins of the Deboeck family: firstly the history of the Deboeck family sensu stricto, i. e., the history of the family in its male ancestors line; secondly the history of the Girardin family, tracing the genealogical origins of the author's mother, thirdly the history of the De Zutter family, tracing the genealogical origins of the author's wife.

Next to the genealogical roots of the three families, the author describes the entrepreneurial careers of the European ancestors of the first two families and the civil servant careers of the ancestors of the third family. It's a fine micro-history of nineteenth and twentieth-century Europe, with inter alia interesting stories on family businesses in Belgium during the last two centuries, on life in occupied Belgium and in Germany during the Second World War. In a separate chapter, the author tells the story of his own career as an immigrant in the United States: this story is also well worth reading.

The scope of the book is larger than just a genealogical case-study of a family. Readers interested in business history, in immigration history and in war history will find several chapters very informative, even fascinating.

May this book encourage many who have Flemish roots, including immigrants to the United States, to join the Flanders-Flemish DNA Project, a promising initiative that the author launched and outlined in the last chapter of this book.

Professor Emeritus Herman Van der Wee
'De Hettinghe', Sint Pauwels, Belgium

Genealogy has captured the hearts and minds of humans since the beginning of time… from stories shared by hunter-gatherers around the campfire to researchers chasing down the elusive documentation to prove a rumored familial connection. To the frustration of many avid genealogists, where the paper trail breaks down there is no way to reach across the gulf to the family's deeper history, at least, not until recently.

Now more and more genealogists have discovered a new tool that survives burnt courthouses, surname changes, and dispersions: DNA. Since 2000, Genetic Genealogy has become an increasingly important aid to genealogists and lovers of family history.

Guido Deboeck's journey into Genetic Genealogy began with his own DNA testing followed by his launching of the Flanders-Flemish DNA Project that he helped to grow into this exceptional study. This book gives an intriguing glimpse into Guido Deboeck's journey, both as a genealogist and as a genetic genealogist.

Bennett Greenspan
President & Founder of FamilyTreeDNA
Houston, Texas

This book provides a detailed overview about the possibilities of using recent scientific progress in DNA analysis to prove the results obtained by traditional genealogical research. By using DNA technology it becomes possible to go beyond traditional family tree reconstruction by linking your family roots to other families. I would encourage people interested in genealogic research in Flanders to read this book so that they become aware of the possibilities and pitfalls of DNA testing.

Professor Ronny DeCorte
Department of Human Heredity
Catholic University Leuven

This book incorporates the history of three families. It offers guidance and direction to researchers by providing sources, a brief history of Flanders and Brabant, as well an introduction to that fascinating new avenue of research, genetic genealogy. In recounting his own family's history, Guido Deboeck has drawn on the local atmosphere to pique your interest. To those of us who constantly look for means to learn more about our ancestors and our heritage, this book is very welcome.

Margaret Roets
Genealogical Society of Flemish Americans
Detroit, Michigan

Preface

On my first trip to Japan, when I was 21 years old, I learned about Japanese customs that are thousands of years old. In Taiwan I admired Chinese artworks that are over five thousand years old. On a trip to Australia I learned that Aboriginal people had been around for at least 40,000 years. At the occasion of the opening of the National Museum of the American Indian in Washington, I watched a parade of 23,000 Native Americans and found the multi-media production, 500 Nations (Kevin Costner Explores America's Indian Heritage) that contains the history of Native Americans who lived thousands of years ago, before Columbus "discovered" America.

This book is about traveling back in time! Time travel is the concept of moving backwards or forwards to different points in time, in a matter analogous to moving through space. Some interpretations of time travel suggest the possibility of travel between parallel realities or universes. There are no planes, boats, or busses you can take to travel in time.[1] Only genealogy can take you there!

Spencer Wells wrote that genealogy is the second most popular American hobby after gardening and the second most visited web sites after pornography.[2] Genealogy requires a lot of patience in searching for and finding documents in libraries and archives; persistence in consulting civil- and parish registers, deciphering documents written in old languages. Family histories can be assembled only by patiently linking individual birth, marriage and death records. Journals, photo albums, and possibly interviews of older people, often provide additional important insights. This I consider conventional genealogy.

Less than five years ago, genealogy exploded into genetic genealogy, i.e., the use of DNA tests to explore paternal and/or maternal lineages. Through DNA testing it is possible to verify with whom we are related as well as find information on our deep ancestry. Through DNA testing it becomes possible to find out the path our ancestors followed to get out of Africa (because that is where we all came from). Hence, genetic genealogy enriches conventional genealogy.

In this book I propose to travel back in time to discover the history of three Flemish families who survived close to five centuries. The Deboeck family, whose surname represents one of the oldest and most authentic names in Flanders, struggled for three hundred years to move from a small rural village in Little Brabant to an urban, industrial town near Brussels. After farming, they excelled as entrepreneurs in lace making. My mother's family, the Girardin family, passed ancient traditions of beer brewing from generation to generation, and has brewed beer for the last 125 years. My wife's family, the De Zutter family, has been in civil service for generations.

This book integrates the findings of years of conventional genealogy research with results from genetic genealogy. It includes insights on the deep ancestry of these families. This book also introduces the Flanders-Flemish DNA project, started in 2005 to bring together the DNA from people with Flemish roots.

---

1. Some scientists have argued that we live in an eleven dimensional world; that time travel is quite feasible when enough energy can be applied to move matter through wormholes. See M.J.Duff, editor, *The World in Eleven Dimensions: supergravity, supermembranes and M-Theory,* IOP Publishing, 1999, 513 pp.

2. S. Wells, *Deep Ancestry: inside the Genographic Project,* p.11.

Conventional genealogy tells us about past generations. Genetic genealogy provides insights in the genetic inheritance that will be passed to future generations. Linking the past with the future creates a unique legacy. This book is the start of a knowledge base that future generations can browse to reflect on where they came from.

Somewhere in the back of my mind there is "a dream," that maybe one day, fifty or a hundred years from now, a great-grandson or -daughter discovers this book in a library and updates it so that this knowledge base expands. Maybe another fifty or hundred years later, someone else will update it again. To make this first volume more interesting, I have included many photos. Quite a few of these are over a hundred years old.

A picture is worth a thousand words (or is it a million now)? This book contains many pictures, thus millions of words. Look carefully at these photos, they tell a lot about Flemish families, about their character and spirit, their hard work, their entrepreneurial and artistic skills, their love for language and land. These photos speak volumes about Flemish people who have yet to gain their true independence.

Guido Deboeck
Arlington, Virginia

Acknowledgements

A simple idea of documenting my family history was never supposed to grow into a virtual teamwork among lots of people on two sides of the Atlantic Ocean.

My main collaborators, to whom I owe more than thanks, were Jan Caluwaerts who did the original research on my oldest ancestors; Jos Dermout who traced the Girardin family in France, Jozef Goethals who researched the ancestors of my wife; and Paul Duran who contributed two technical papers and helped to interpret the comments from some reviewers. A few others mailed me important documents: Marcel Stappers about lace making in Vilvoorde, Stanny van Grasdorff about the history of Sint-Amands, Guido Pauwels, about the history of the Girardin brewery, Karel Denys about emigration, and Rick Claessens about the military archives. Several reviewers read my earlier drafts and substantially enriched the final outcome. Among them were Leo van Houtven, Rick Ghesquiere, Adrien Goorman, Rick Claessens, Jos Dermout, Jozef Goethals, Paul Callens, Robert De Boo, and Jim Brown. They all contributed more than they think.

I am grateful to Professor Herman van der Wee for his meticulous comments about the historical parts and to Professor Ronny DeCorte of the K.U.L. for his help with the genetic chapters and the interpretation of DNA results. I am also grateful to Bennett Greenspan who three years ago got me started with DNA testing and always helped with lightning speed when I had yet another question.

Thanks are also due to Margaret Roes, Karel Denys, Elisabeth Khan, and Cheryl Heckla of the Genealogical Society of Flemish Americans for all what they contributed to Flemish American Heritage and the Gazette of Detroit. Regine Brindle, President of The Belgian Researchers serialized one chapter of this book early on in Belgian Laces. Finally a word of thanks to Mieke Ghesquiere, P. van Hindertael and M. Quintyn for their keeping the Washington Flemish Club alife.

Roxanne Carlson patiently corrected my draft and made this text much more readable. Cherie Wood provided the gorgeous layout that merged over a hundred images, twenty tables and a dozen family charts into my text. Ann Hughes, President of Gateway Press, was enthusiastic about this project from the moment she first heard about it. Her encouragements and guidance through the production process were invaluable.

The initial stimulus for this work emerged from regular wine tasting sessions with Otto Raggambi. My wife and companion of almost 40 years fine-tuned her own family history, remained patient all the nights I got up to write, and remains anxious to discover what else I have up my sleeve. In the middle of this project we enjoyed a wonderful wine tasting tour of New Zealand and South Australia. Charing, our friend from over 25 years, continued to take care of all of us, our home, our garden, and all the chores that otherwise needed our attention. At Touch of Asia in Virginia, Tukta relieved most writing stress by her magical stone massages.

This project was undertaken for Toni, Pascal and Nina; their spouses, Olivia and Lynn; our granddaughter, Anastasia, and all future grandchildren. May they learn from this where they came from, what their ancestors went through, and what challenges they face in mankind's continued exploration of earth, space and deep ancestry. To all who have contributed my heartfelt thanks; I owe you and I hope you forgive any remaining mistakes, which are mine.

Guido Deboeck,
August 14, 2007

Chapter 1
Introduction

Why research family history?

Few people take an interest in family history when they are young. As long as grandparents are alive family history is learned by listening to their stories or observing their traditions. When parents and grandparents pass away there are no opportunities anymore to ask questions. The vacuum created by their departure creates a desire to learn more about family history. Lots of people only take an interest in family history when it is much harder to obtain the relevant information. The higher cost is paid because digging into the past can bring back cherished memories.

Learning family history from my grandparents did not occur in my case. I was not that lucky! My paternal grandfather died some twenty-one years before I was born; my maternal grandmother died four years before I was born. My other grandmother died two weeks before I was born. I only got to know my godfather,[1] Jean-Baptist Girardin, who was my grandfather on my mother's side. He died however when I was barely 16 years old. My godfather remarried after his wife died and his second wife outlived him by close to forty years. Hence, of all my grandparents the one I got to know the longest was my step-grandmother.

Neither my father nor my mother paid a lot of attention to family history, although as we will discover later each of them made huge contributions. My father started with filmmaking after the Second World War (WWII), and made about three dozen films about family excursions and trips. All of these were preserved and are still in my possession. They came with a catalogue in his handwriting. He also took thousands of color slides kept in carousels also catalogued. My mother kept photo albums with photos from her youth, her parents, and my grandparents. All of this provided an incredible source of information.

My first interest in family history occurred about twenty-five years ago. Like my parents I was born in Flanders, the Flemish speaking northern part of Belgium.[2] My parents lived in Vilvoorde, about 6 miles north of Brussels. In 1964 I went to the Catholic

---

1. In the Catholic religion the godfather and godmother are people who accept responsibility for the religious education of a child. In Dutch they are called "peter" and "meter". Since this book is about Flemish families, I will occasionally provide the Dutch term to facilitate understanding by those who are not natural English readers.

2. Throughout this book I will often refer to Flemish also as the language spoken by the people of Flanders, although the official language is Dutch.

University of Leuven where I met Hennie De Zutter who became my wife. From 1969 to 1972 I studied in the USA. After earning my Ph.d. we moved back to Europe. Five years later we moved permanently to the USA where we have had our residence for the past thirty plus years.

In 1972 our first child, Toni, was born. Ten years later my dad went to the city hall in Vilvoorde to consult the civil registers. In early 1983 I received from him a letter that contained information about three generations of the Deboeck family. This included my grandparents and great-grandparents. From the letter I learned for the first time about my grandfather, my grandmother, and even my great grandparents. There was no other information in the city hall of Vilvoorde because earlier ancestors were not born in Vilvoorde.

Parish registers were kept much earlier than civil records. By some fortunate coincidence I found that the parish registers of Greater Grimbergen, which is close to Vilvoorde, had been translated from Latin into Dutch and had been issued on a CD ROM.[3] It covered all the parish registers from 1577 to 1900 in Grimbergen and the villages surrounding Grimbergen (including Beigem, Bevre, Borgt, Heienbeek, Humbeek, and Strombeek). The information on this CD ROM enabled me to trace my ancestors back to 1700 without even leaving home.

In August 2005 on a visit to Belgium, I contacted a professional genealogist, Jan Caluwaerts[4] and asked him whether it would be possible to trace my family history back even further. He smiled and hinted that maybe one or two more generations could probably be found... Caluwaerts took a map and drew a circle around Grimbergen and the surrounding villages and told me he would work from there and see what he could find.

Six months later I received a report that surprised me. Caluwaerts found the exact date and location of the birth of Franciscus de Boeck, my oldest known ancestor based on my own research. He was born in Londerzeel, which was not on the CD ROM of Greater Grimbergen. He also found four more generations preceding Franciscus. Hence, Gillis de Bock, born in Sint-Amands circa 1540 became my oldest known ancestor. Sint-Amands is northwest of Brussels in an area known as Little Brabant. So, I am the 13th generation descendant of Gillis De Bock of Little Brabant, which is a small area in the north west of Flemish-speaking Brabant, a province in current day Belgium.

---

3. This CD ROM, made to celebrate in 2002 the 75th anniversary of the David's Foundation (Davidsfonds) in Grimbergen, was a gigantic work accomplished by some 18 enthusiasts of family history. This CD can be found in the Village shop, Prinsenstraat 22, 1850 Grimbergen. The address of Davidsfonds is Kerkplein 5A, Grimbergen. More information on this CD can also be found at http://users.pandora.be/huwa/open/genealogie/genealogie.htm.

4. See http://www.familysearch.be

Prior to going to Belgium in August 2005 I inquired about DNA testing. The idea of DNA testing had been on my mind even before 2000 when for the first time the full human genome had been documented (more on this follows in Quick Introduction to Genetic Genealogy). In early 2005 I talked about it with my son who gave me his strong endorsement. "Go for it, Dad", I recall Toni saying.

In mid 2005 I obtained a few DNA testing kits from FamilyTree DNA Inc (FTDNA) in Houston. Using these I collected several DNA samples from people who immediately understood the relevance during my stay in Belgium. On return these kits were mailed to FTDNA for analysis at the University of Arizona. Eight weeks later I received my first DNA results. This was a couple of weeks before the Second International Conference on Genetic Genealogy held in Washington, D.C. in early November 2005. I participated in the conference, tried to understand all the lectures and the jargon, and got very excited about genetic genealogy.

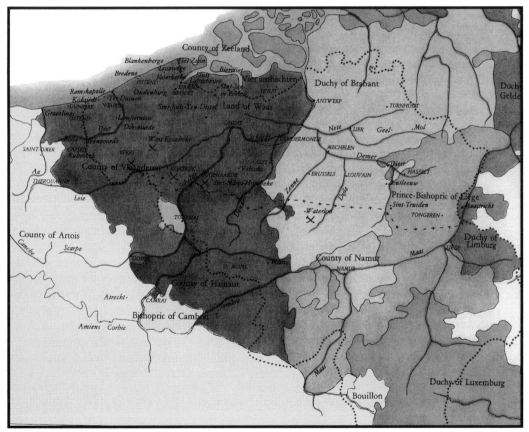

Figure 1.1: Map of the Southern Low Countries in the later Middle Ages, including present-day Flanders (source: Patricia Carson: Flanders in Creative Contrasts, Davidsfonds, Tielt, 1990, p 26).

Months after receiving Caluwaerts' report and this International Conference my interest in genealogy went into even higher gear. In the spring of 2006 a friend of mine published a book about the Goethals-Tavenier family.[5] Another friend, with whom I regularly talked about politics during our Friday afternoon wine tasting sessions, kept telling me that he (who was 77 at the time) should do something about collecting his family history. Without realizing it he kept in fact telling me that rather than arguing about politics, I should collect my family history. Since that conversation, we have talked much less about politics, have enjoyed more wine tasting, and at least I have made some progress in documenting my family history…

Early in the summer of 2006, in Aspen at the Wine and Food Festival, where my wife took me for Father's Day, I decided to write this book that integrates conventional and genetic genealogy. There are plenty of books on the genealogy of different nationalities (British, Irish, Italians, French…) and there are lots of books on the family history of different families. However, there are few books on Flemish families and none so far that includes genetic results. There are plenty of books on how to explore genetic genealogy, but few with actual DNA results. Last but not least, there are no books that I know on the deep ancestry of Flemish families that trace their history back to more than 8 centuries.[6]

This brings us to an important question: why do people want to do research on deceased relatives? A classic fortune cookie reads: Forget about the past there is no future in it! Nevertheless in what follows I will briefly describe some of my main reasons for digging into my past.

My most important reason for doing research about family history is to find out where I came from. Second most important reason is to define or refine my identity. Alex Haley said: "In all of us, there is a hunger, bone-marrow deep, to know our heritage – to know who we are and where we have come from. Without this enriching knowledge, there is a hollow yearning. No matter what our attainments in life, there is a vacuum, and emptiness, and most disquieting loneliness."[7]

Why define or refine identity? We all have a name; identity is sometimes complimented by looks, likes or dislikes, our energy or what drives someone. Identity is also about family, where someone is born or where someone grew up. Or identity can be assigned by nationality. If you are American you often are asked: are you Irish-, Italian-, German-, Latino-, or Native American? I was born in Belgium, Brussels to be precise, grew up in Vilvoorde,

---

5. Jozef Goethals: Goethals, Tavernier-Vanmaele: The Ancestors of August Goethals and Elza Tavernier.

6. The history of one of the oldest families of Antwerp, van de Werve, covers 800 years and was written in 1988 in Les van de Werve : 800 ans d'histoire, (volume I & II) by Yves Schmitz and Alfons Bousse - Waremme, December 1988. See http://www.werve.org/GB/publication.htm

7. Alex Haley, Roots, G K Hall & Co, 1976; paperback June 2007. See also http://www.kirjasto.sci.fi/ahaley.htm

moved to Leuven, studied in New England, worked in Switzerland, spent most of my life in Virginia. What does that make me? I guess you could call me Belgian-American or better yet Flemish-American! Now that I also became an American citizen, I guess that I am also a European-American (in contrast to African- or Latino-American).

We all have multiple identities and none is fixed in stone. On the surface, new identities can be constructed or enhanced. Through DNA testing yet more identity can be discovered. Thus by doing research on my ancestors, by documenting my family history, and by plunging into genetics my identity has expanded. This will become much clearer after you find out about my haplotype, my haplogroup, where I came from, and where I am on the phylogenetic tree of human relations that will be discussed later in this book.[8]

Sometimes finding out where we came from and what our true identity is can take years. Little progress is made for years then suddenly it goes in leaps and bounds. Oftentimes finding out where we came from takes a lot of work. Civil registers are relatively easy to read; old parish registers are more difficult since they were mostly kept in Latin.[9] Often the more detailed information cannot be found without professional help. In addition sheer "luck" in finding things can also play a role. For example, not all parish registers in Belgium have been translated or issued on a CD ROM; those of Greater Grimbergen were.

Another important reason to study family history is the so-called "bragging rights." Anyone who can trace his/her ancestors to the fifteenth or sixteenth century, or even earlier, can obviously be proud to have accumulated so much information about his family. Han van der Voort wrote: "A straight, unbroken line of descendancy from illustrious figures who lived long ago has a great appeal to many people, and I am no exception."[10] Often family histories contain puzzles created by "non-parental events" (a euphemism used in genealogy for referring to children whose father is not known, although all children do have of course a father...) Solving these puzzles can provide great satisfaction and remains a solid basis for bragging rights.

---

8. Josephine Johnson spoke about identity in her talk on "Ethical Issues and Genetic Ancestry" at the Third International Conference on Genetic Genealogy, in Houston in November 2006. I am grateful to her for providing these insights in the different dimensions of identity and how identity can be expanded.

9. Parish registers in Flanders in the seventeenth and eighteenth centuries were written in Latin; before that some were in Old Dutch. In the southern part of the country, in Wallonia, they were in French.

10. Han van der Voort, My reasons, http://home . planet.nl/~voort359/home3int.html

Many people search for family history because they are born discoverers. Columbus for example had an idea that he wanted to test; in the process he came across an entire new continent and various islands that he mistook to be the Far East. Genealogists are discoverers who likewise can come across new findings that are not always properly identified. Genealogists start out on one or more ideas but may discover entire new family branches in the process. They are like detectives. For example, Agatha Christie's most famous creation, the Belgian Inspector Hercules Poirot, is a detective obsessed with solving puzzles. Poirot operates systematically and often advocates the use of "little grey cells." He also loves being theatrical and mysterious, and never seems to part with information until the last moment. Poirot appeared in over 30 novels and over 50 short stories.[11] Other quirky but brilliant fictional detectives with outrageous character, owe a lot to Hercule Poirot, who was the only fictional detective to be given an obituary in the New York Times.

Genealogy is like a virus: anyone who has caught that virus will admit this. What starts with simple recording of birth and death dates of parents and grandparents quickly leads to extensive expeditions to collect information in Family History Libraries on long gone relatives. The satisfaction of finding another generation, of adding another branch to the family tree, of solving puzzles, is like victory in a war! Most likely it is a victory in personal war against ignorance! So many ancestors…so little time to learn about them!

Let us also not forget that anyone who got an advanced degree is "brainwashed" to collect and organize data, test hypotheses, and write. It is especially easy to fall for genealogy because every question solved leads to two more questions… In every family sooner or later there emerges an avid genealogist and you can be sure that older members of the family will know who that person is.

My main reasons for undertaking this study are all of the above. I am eager to find out where I came from, where my ancestors came from. I am intrigued by stories that were handed over from generation to generation. I like to solve puzzles, and was brainwashed to do research. My academic training added a few other reasons for undertaking this work. I wanted to create awareness for advances in genetic genealogy to facilitate the documentation of genetic inheritances. I also wanted to lay a foundation for a more in-depth study of Flemish DNA.

---

11. Critics have claimed that Poirot was based on two other fictional detectives of the time: Marie Belloc Lowndes' Hercule Popeau and Frank Howel Evans' Monsieur Poiret, a retired French police officer living in London. Like Sir Arthur Conan Doyle with Sherlock Holmes, Agatha became tired of her creation. By 1930 she found Poirot "insufferable," and by 1960 she felt that he was a "detestable, bombastic, tiresome, egocentric little creep." Yet the public loved him.

As my ninety-six-year-old uncle, Georges Mergeay, once said: "{you} have quite a capability to generate a lot of work for yourself…" He probably meant "making life more interesting." This is why I want to travel back in time through Flanders, the place where my ancestors came from, where they struggled over five hundred years to survive, and to learn about their struggle of survival, their successes, and the opportunities they created for me to write this book.

Main sources for Conventional Genealogy

Conventional genealogy is based on documents. The etymology of the word genealogy comes from the Middle English genealogie, the French généalogie, from late Latin genealogia. The word genealogy comes from two Greek words genea, meaning "race", "birth", "descent" or "family" and logos. The proper root for -logy is logos meaning word, the word about, or the science of (like theology, the word about theos=god). Genealogy is derived from "to trace ancestry", the science of studying family history.

In the previous section I explained "why" this study was undertaken. Let me now review the main sources that were used.[12] The starting point of my research was the Civil Registry; next, came the Parish Registers, the Orphan Acts and the Meiseniers letters. There were also population censuses and militia records that were consulted. Last but not least, some of the most valuable information came from tax records. All of these sources are discussed next in some detail.

Civil Registry

Four years after France invaded Flanders in 1796 the French imposed French civil law. From 1796 onwards all births, marriages, and deaths in Belgium were recorded in the Civil Registry kept in each municipality. A copy of these records was also kept in each of the Courts of First Instance ("de Rechtbank van Eerste Aanleg").

In the birth certificates we find the name of the newborn, as well as the names, ages and professions of his or her parents; sometimes even the names of the grandparents. This makes finding relationships much easier compared to Anglo-Saxon equivalents. Although marriage certificates did contain this information until the French occupation, parish registers remained very cryptic. Besides the Civil Registry there is also the foundling registers and the population census collected about every ten years.[13] In 1846 the first Belgian census of a scientific nature was organized.

---

12. An excellent guide to doing genealogical research on Flanders has been written by Johan Roelstraete, Handleiding voor Genealogisch onderzoek in Vlaanderen (Handbook of genealogical research in Flanders), VVF, Roeselaere, 1998.

13. Specifically in 1856, 1866, 1876, 1880, 1890, 1900, 1910, 1920, 1930, 1947, 1961, 1970, 1981, 1991, 2001

It was not an ordinary count of inhabitants; it comprised a complete section on agriculture and industry. Since 1846 there have been 15 population censuses in Belgium. The different censuses occurred at intervals of approximately ten years. Although, according to the basic legal texts censuses were meant for purely administrative purposes, all the ones held since 1856 have also inquired about demographic, social, and economic data.

Parish Registers

Prior to the imposition of French civil law and the creation of the Civil Registry, parish priests all over Europe kept records of all baptisms, marriages and deaths. In the Southern Netherlands (currently Belgium) this recording became obligatory in 1564, the year after the Council of Trent (1545-1563).

The Arch Duke Albert and Arch Duchesse Isabella, who ruled Flanders from 1598 to 1621, ordered all aldermen in towns and villages to make copies of all church records. A century and a half later Arch Duchesse Maria Theresia issued an ordinance requiring new copies of all church records up to that time. Most of these records were kept in Latin.

An alderman was a member of a municipal assembly in a town or city with many jurisdictions. The title alderman was derived from the Anglo-Saxon position of Ealdorman, literally meaning "elder man", and was used by the chief nobles presiding over shires.

The parish records of Greater Grimbergen (which have been translated from Latin into Dutch) proved invaluable. In it I found the names, the birth- and baptism dates, the parents, and grandparents (who were often chosen as godparents for the first two children) of my ancestors back to 1700. Records also revealed the profession of the father and/or the parish of origin of the parents.

All parish registers in Flanders and lots of other places in the world were filmed by the Mormons and are kept in a library in Salt Lake in Utah. Any of these films can be consulted in Salt Lake or in a Family History Center of the Church of Jesus Christ of Latter Day Saints (Insert on page 9). Some can also be consulted on the Internet (hereafter also referred to as the worldwide web). A lot of family information reported in this book was found on microfilms in Family History Libraries in Virginia and Maryland.

Orphan Acts

Prior to the Council of Trent and the recording of all births, marriages and deaths by church priests, there was orphan guardianship, which goes back to the fourteenth century.

At the death of one of the parents, children up to 25 years of age were considered to be minor orphans. Within weeks of a death a request for guardianship had to be submitted to the alderman on the Orphan Chamber. This Orphan Chamber appointed two guardians, usually one from each side of the family. In addition an inventory of all personal property and real estate was compiled. Although the surviving parent retained care of the children, the management of the property was the responsibility of the guardians who yearly had to report to the aldermen.[15]

Orphan acts can be a rich source of family information in East and West Flanders; they virtually did not exist in Brabant. Orphan acts reveal the name of the deceased, the name of the surviving parent, the minor children, the grandparents, and the property of the family. They also revealed income from loans, house and land rents, and debts. These orphan acts were written in Middle Dutch, which today can only be read by language specialists.

Looking for information in Family History Libraries.

The process of looking up parish registers on microfilm can be summarized as follows:

On the worldwide web go to www.familysearch.org. Go to "Sitemap" --the tab in the right hand corner-- and pick from the list Search by location (or Search by surname).

Enter a location or surname. This yields a listing of all available microfilms on the surname or location you entered.

Obtain a printable list by clicking on "here" and then go with that list to the nearest Family Center.

At the Center fill in a form to request the microfilm(s) you are interested in. The requested microfilm(s) are then ordered from Salt Lake and will be made available in 3 to 4 weeks.

When the microfilm(s) arrive, you will get a call from the Center. At the Family Center you can then browse the microfilm(s), and make copies of any of the documents you are interested in.

You can order any number of microfilms you wish. You have four weeks' time to consult them or if you need more time you can extend the consultation period. This process for consultation of parish registers also applies for all orphan-, aldermen-, and notary acts.

The nearest Family Center for people living near Washington DC in Virginia is in McLean at 2034 Great Falls Street. Addresses for other Family Centers in the U. S. or abroad are provide on the above website.

Notary Acts and Alderman Acts

All transactions related to properties were registered in order to be legal. These registrations were done via notary and alderman's acts, written by clerks ("stoelklerken" in Dutch). These were notaries that worked for the town hall; several clerks worked together. At the end of each year all documents were bundled into registers. This explains why these registers are not strictly chronological, but chronological by clerk.

---

15. Jozef Goethals, Goethals, Tavernier-Vanmaele, 9.

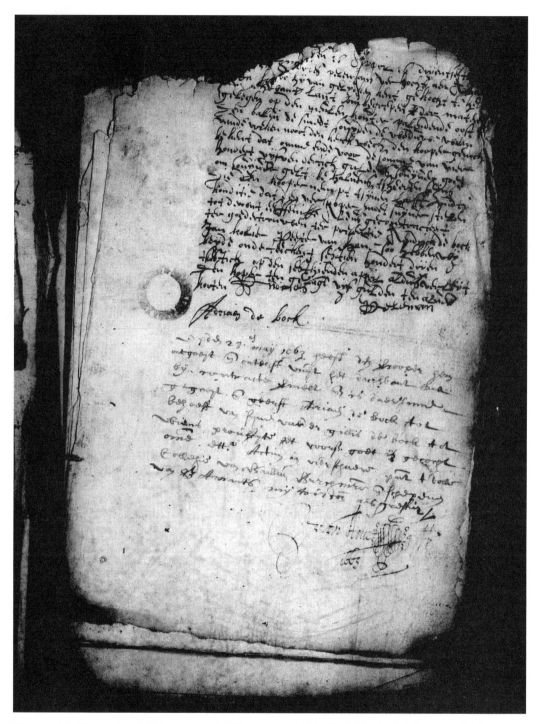

Figure 1.2: Example of Alderman Act ("Schepenakte" in Dutch) of Sint-Amands in Belgium, signed by Adriaen de Bock, circa 1663, found in collection of acts from Sint-Amands from 1622-1796 FHL (Family History Library) Microfilm number 0794075.

Tax records

In the sixteenth century taxes were expressed as penning. Taxes were raised as 100e, 20e, or 10e penning. A 100e penning was a onetime tax on total wealth, a 20e penning or 5% was applied to the sale of all real estate properties, and a 10e penning applied to all other sales and on exports. Let me first explain how these taxes came about, before I elaborate on the currency.

Under the reign of Emperor Charles V in the period from 1542 till 1555, very high taxes were raised, including among others a 10e penning on rented properties. When the Spanish King Philip II tried in 1556 to further increase these taxes, heavy resistance emerged, especially in Brabant. In 1558-1560 the king tried again to raise taxes but failed to get the endorsement of the individual states.

In 1567 King Philip II nominated the Duke of Alva as governor of what then was called the Netherlands. The duke undertook centralization and introduced taxes that provided the king with ample income without requiring the endorsement of new taxes by the states.

The introduction of the 20e Penning and especially the 10e Penning, considered extraordinarily high, was heavily protested. As a compromise Duke Alva accepted that Flanders would contribute annually 650,000 guilders to be collected by a 20e penning on the real estate properties and a tariff of 10 shilling per barrel of wine imported.

In July 1571 a more moderated 10e Penning and 20e Penning was officially declared. The protest against these taxes mounted and again Flanders was requested to contribute 650,000 guilders raised by a 10e and 20e penning on the rent of properties plus a 20e penning on profits. In 1576 these taxes were abolished.

A penning was 1/240th of a Flemish pound because a Flemish pound was composed of 20 shillings – also called schellingen in Dutch -- and each shilling was worth 12 groot or twelve penningen. Some authors referred to groot as groat in Dutch or denier in French.

Besides a Flemish pound there was also a Brabant pound that could be converted into Flemish pounds. From May 15, 1435 onwards one pound Flemish groat was equal to 1.5 pound Brabant groat.[16]

One silver piece ("stuiver" in Dutch or "patard" in French) was equivalent to 2 Flemish groats or 3 Brabant groats. One Brabant guilder was divided into 20 silver pieces (stuivers) or 60 Brabant groats; hence was equivalent to one fourth of a pound Brabant groats or one sixth of a pound of Flemish groats.

---

16. The smallest unit in the Flemish and Brabant money system was "groat" according to H. Van der Wee, but "groot" in the publications of John Munro and others.

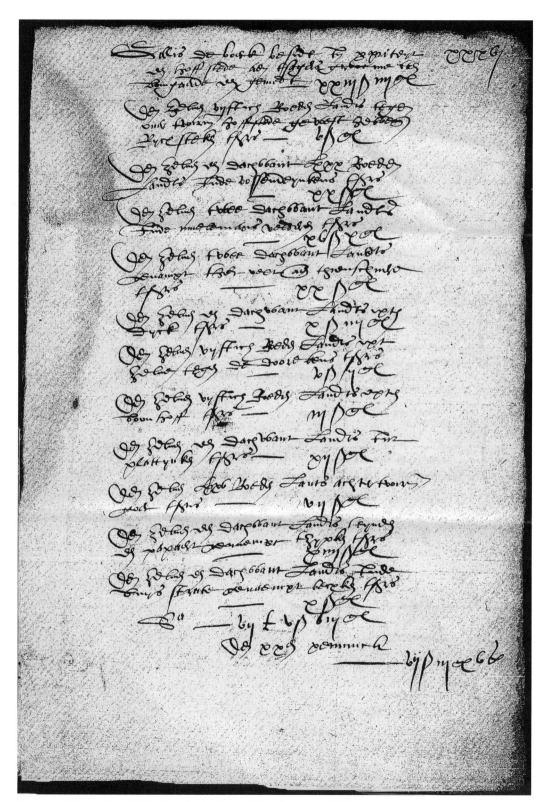

Figure 1.3 Page from 20th Penningkohier of Sint-Amands 1571

To collect the new taxes Penningkohieren were made. A Penningkohier was a list of all people in a village with their properties on the basis of which taxes were raised. These taxes were based on the estimated size of the properties plus the rents that were payed for land or goods in use. In these inventories of properties and rents, the size of land was expressed in bunder, dagwanten, gemeten and in roeden.[17]

Penningkohieren were made in all villages by a local magistrate; they produced a wealth of information on both the people and their land. In the 20e Penningkohier of Sint-Amands made in 1571 that can be found in the city archives of Gent,[18] my oldest known ancestor, Gillis de Bock, is mentioned. This tax document was of particular value since it contained a detailed list of all the properties of my oldest known ancestor (see Chapter 2, Gillis de Bock).

Meiseniers letters

Another important source of information for all those who have ancestors in Brabant are the so-called meiseniers letters. Meiseniers were originally the big landowners, the large farmers in contrast to the small farmers who could employ only a few laborers.

The etymological origin of "meiseniers", mansionarius, is owner and inhabitant of a mansio, or a domain in contrast to someone living in a casa (or hut), a "kossaat" or casatus. The land that belonged to a domain (een "hof" or "hoeve") varied by region.[19]

For centuries big landowners from Brabant went to Grimbergen to prove to the local authorities their land ownership and hence receive their meiseniers letter. To receive such a letter meant to have "meiseniers blood" (just like royalty are said to have blue blood, although no blood test of anyone royal has ever shown blue blood…). Some Brabant families with long histories to this date consider having "meiseniers blood" as an honor.

Caluwaerts wrote in an introduction to Jan Lindemans's book on Meiseniers Blood[20] that the registers of meiseniers,

---

17. One bunder was 13,365 square meters or approximately 3.21 acres (1.3 hectares). A bunder was a traditional Dutch unit of land area. Since the adoption of the metric system in the Netherlands in 1809 the bunder was considered equal to approximately one hectare (2.471 acres). Historically, the unit varied with locality, generally in the range 0.85 to 1.3 hectares. The unit was also used in the southern part of Belgium, and was called the bonnier. One "bunder" was four dagwanten, 300 gemeten or 900 roeden. One roede was 14.85 square meters.

18. Stadsarchief Gent XXste Kohierpenning, 1571, bundle 62/63, microfilm 335, box 128. Original researched by Stanny van Grasdorff.

19. In Brabant and in Grimbergen in particular the land could cover 36 bunder, split into three pieces of land each about two bunder (mansus) or one each in three properties of the community.

20. J. Lindemans, Van Meiseniersbloed (About Meisenier Blood, Flemish Association for Genealogy, Region Flemish Brabant), Vlaams Brabant, 1998.

recorded from the fifteenth to the eighteenth century, show that this etymological meaning of the word changed over time. While the title was first established in 1297 as a result of an agreement between Jan I and the Lords of Grimbergen to counter balance the statute of burghers (see below), the statute of meiseniers became a statute that was inherited. Hence in the seventeenth and eighteenth century one had to prove that one was meisenier by inheritance. Among the many that became meiseniers were not only big landowners, but also craftsmen, civil servants and smaller land-owners.

In reality meiseniers became a term to indicate a class of people who had certain privileges in Brabant.[21] The most important privilege they obtained was to be free from the Dead Hand, meaning they could only be brought before their own aldermen, whichever the mischief or indictable offense that had occurred.

Meiseniers letters from the end of the sixteenth century onwards provided precise information on descendants including the name of the parents, sometimes the grandparents, the location of birth and residence, and the relationship with the two sponsors or witnesses. All of this was very beneficial in expanding my family histories.

Jan Lindemans collected for several years the meiseniers letters from small villages like Buggenhout, Londerzeel and Grimbergen. He published alphabetical lists of these letters in Eigen Schoon & De Brabander from 1944 to 1956. After the publication of the last edition, the entire collection was published in a book that in 1998 was reedited and reprinted.

In Jan Lindemans' book I found on page 21 to 23 that in the period from 1559 till 1792 some 59 meiseniers letters were handed out to persons with the last name "de bock" or "de boeck." Among these 59 were several "de bocks" who are my ancestors. Hence I can proudly claim to have meiseniers blood, which was inherited from several of my ancestors. To have meiseniers blood, I actually consider, more honorable than to have "blue" blood because no one born in royal families has ever had to prove anything…

In Vilvoorde there were the "burghers" ("poorters"). Before France annexed the southern part of the Netherlands (roughly present day Belgium), several classes of residents existed: men were either "poorter" (burgher), "keurboer" (gentleman-farmer), "vrijlaat" (serf under franchise), or "laat" (serf). Women were "poorteresse" (female burgher), "keurzuster" (gentlewoman-farmer), "vrijlatesse" (female serf under franchise), or "latesse" (female predial serf). The term "vreemde" (stranger or foreigner) and "gediende" (servant) could apply to either a man or a woman.

To free themselves from serfdom country people left the rural areas and moved to the cities. After living in a city for a

---

21. According to Marcel Stappers the rights and privileges of meiseniers can be found in two book volumes "Costuymen van Brabandt" published in 1682.

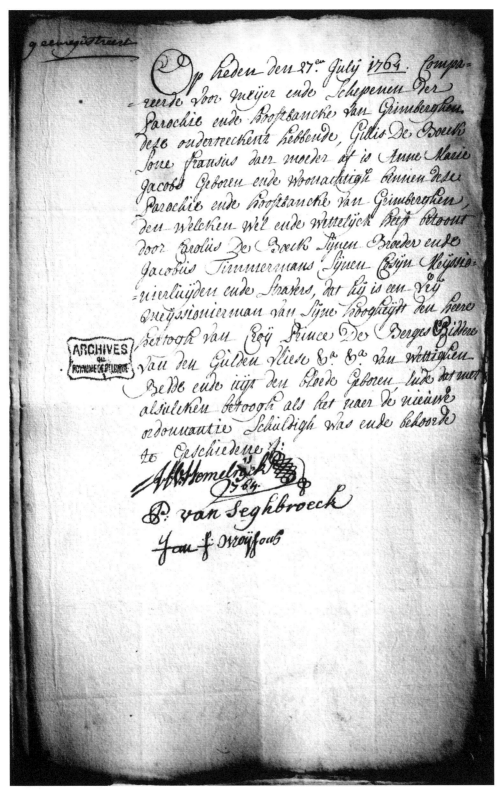

Figure 1.4 Meiseniers letter of Gillis de Bock, July 27, 1763

minimum of time (usually one year and a day) one could apply to become a burgher, which was like obtaining a passport, but for a city. In Vilvoorde one had to pay between 3 and 6 gilders to become a burgher.[22] Once the status of burgher was obtained, it could be inherited. The lists of burghers contained the names of those who became burghers in a particular period.

Once the status of burgher was obtained the rural lord had no further claim. Burghers were under the jurisdiction of the city they lived in and received the privileges of "poortershap"; hence were named "poorters" which translated in French was bourgeois. Those who lived outside the city could still become burghers but they would be "buiten-poorters" or outside burghers.[23]

The way to become a burgher was different from town to town and city to city; some cities required registration and payment of a fee. Burghers had certain privileges. For example, business could be conducted, city jobs could be obtained, goods could not be confiscated, and a burgher's house was his castle, it could not be violated.

Others who did not reside in the city could still obtain some of these privileges by becoming outer burghers ("buiten-poorters"). In present day terms we would call it non-residents.[24] To be a burgher meant to be of some social standing in the community. This status was not reserved to those of high society. Besides the parish priest, the noble men and women, there were farmers and regular folks who became burghers.

In sum, various sources from civil registries, foundling acts, population censuses, parish records, orphan acts, meiseniers letters provided invaluable information to assemble the histories of the families in this book.

Quick Introduction to Genetic Genealogy

In spite of the numerous sources and vast amount of documented information that can be found, we should not forget that documents can contain errors, may have been written to mislead or hide the truth; or may have been destroyed either on purpose or by accident (e.g. by fire, floods or earthquakes). Additionally, some relationships may never have been recorded. This is why conventional genealogy can only go as far as the research of documents allows.

---

22. Lists of burghers from Vilvoorde for the period 1680-1767 still exist although a great deal were destroyed in the disaster that occurred in 1489.

23. The VVF periodical Vlaamse Stam of July-August 1992 contains an interesting article on the registration of burghers in the County of Flanders. John Roelstraete's Handleiding voor genealogisch onderzoek in Vlaanderen (Manual for genealogical research in Flanders).

24. For example, non-residents are foreigners that work for international organizations or remain in a country on a special visa status as long as they are employed; also foreign students and diplomats.

To go beyond the constraints of the paper world, there is genetic genealogy. Genetic genealogy relies on DNA which all of us have, does not change, cannot be destroyed, and is never wrong.

DNA testing complements conventional genealogy through the analysis of the sequence of chemicals that defines each human being. Through DNA testing one can tell if two people are related (even though one cannot tell the exact nature of the relationship), verify or potentially correct genealogical information extracted from documents.

To get a better understanding of the potential of DNA testing I provide in this section a quick introduction to genetic genealogy. A more in-depth introduction is provided in Chapter 8. Concrete examples and uses of DNA results are provided in Chapter 9 and 10.

The DNA of human beings contains the blueprint of life, i.e., all the instructions that build and control the day-to-day functioning of our cells in our body. This blueprint life with its instructions is passed from parent to child with few or minor changes.

DNA stands for DeoxyriboNucleic Acid. It is structured as a double-stranded helical molecule. Think about a ladder with rungs or sides that are twisted: the rungs are composed of chemicals held together with a sugar backbone, somewhat like table sugar. These chemicals are called nucleic acid bases, or nucleotides; they are the building blocks of every DNA molecule. The four nucleotides contained in every DNA molecule are Adenine, Cytosine, Guanine, and Thymine, which are simply labeled as A, C, G, and T.

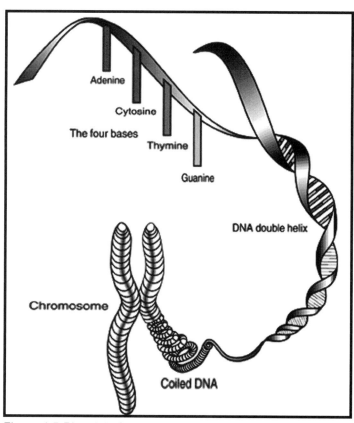

Figure 1.5 Pictorial of nuclear DNA structure (source: Charles F. Kerchner Jr. Genetics and Genealogy, http://www.kerchner.com/)

A section of the long, double-stranded helical DNA molecule is a gene. A gene contains instructions for some specific functions such as making a protein. Some genes are responsible for physical characteristics.

There are about 30,000 genes but they constitute less than five percent of all DNA. The rest is commonly called "junk DNA" although some parts of this DNA determine the structure of the chromosome.[25]

Genes are packaged in 46 chromosomes that are arranged in 23 pairs that define the human genome. In sum, the complete human genome contains billions of bits of information. Children inherit copies of their parents' DNA. This genetic hand-off is repeated from generation to generation. In copying DNA there may on occasion occur some mistakes, for example, the substitution of a C for G or a T for an A.

Think about monks in a medieval monastery who copied manuscripts and on occasion made some mistakes (maybe after finishing their daily ration of five liters beer, see Chapter 5). Despite the efforts of even the abbot of the monastery, who proofread all pages that the monks copied, there may remain spelling mistakes in the final document.

The same happens when proofreading a book: several mistakes may be removed but despite my best efforts some mistakes still remain. In genetics, such mistakes are called mutations. These mutations provide variation or the evolution of the basic building blocks. However, mutations occur at a low rate, maybe 50 changes per generation in billions of nucleotides that make up the human genome.

How can this evolution in the building blocks be useful to genealogists? The DNA in the nucleus of a cell contains 23 pairs of chromosomes. One pair determines the gender. Males receive or inherit a Y chromosome from their father and an X chromosome from their mother. Females inherit two X's. Hence, males with the same Y chromosome have a common ancestor. Y chromosome analysis (Y-DNA) can verify or help to investigate the paternal lineage of an individual. Investigation of the X chromosomes in a female can verify her paternal lineage only if X's common between two sisters also is the same as the X chromosome of their father.[26]

Outside the nucleus of a cell there are many small organelles, called mitochondria. These are the power stations of a cell as they are structures in which energy is produced and stored. Mitochondrial DNA (mtDNA) is the small amount of DNA found in the mitochondrion. mtDNA is passed on via the egg cell of a

---

26. Advanced testing offered by FamilyTreeDNA now includes X-STR DNA Panels. There are two X-STR panels available. Males have an X and a Y chromosome, and females have two X chromosomes. Therefore, these tests are available to both males and females. The male receives his X chromosome from his mother, and the female receives one X chromosome from her mother and one from her father. These tests can be used for closely related family testing.

25. As the saying goes, one man's junk is another man's treasure; this "junk" DNA contains the story of our ancestors!

mother, hence only females can pass mtDNA to their offspring. In consequence, an analysis of the mtDNA in males or females can provide valuable information to verify or help investigate the maternal lineage of an individual.

In this way genetic genealogy can identify paternal lineage via Y chromosome analysis and identify the maternal lineage via mtDNA analysis. By testing males for both Y-chromosome and mtDNA, one can trace their paternal and maternal lines. By testing females for mtDNA, one can trace their maternal lines. The information obtained through these analyses can determine the specific branches via which an individual comes from the evolutionary tree of human relationships. DNA testing complements conventional genealogy. Both conventional and genetic genealogy can contribute to a more comprehensive family history.

The first complete sequence of the human genome was completed on June 26, 2000, meaning it was only seven years ago that the all 3 billion units that make up our genes were documented. On June 26, 2000, President Bill Clinton recognized in the East Room of the White House, Francis Collins, a physician who led the Human Genome Project, and Craig Venter, a private entrepreneur. According to Clinton these pioneers created "the most important, most wondrous map ever produced by humankind."

History of Flanders and Brabant

Conventional and genetic genealogy are used in this book to document the history of three families from Flanders.[27]

Flanders, which is the Dutch-speaking part of Belgium, includes five provinces, namely Antwerp, East- and West Flanders, Limburg, and Flemish-Brabant. Brussels, the capital of Belgium, is administratively separate from Flanders. Brussels is the capital of Flanders, Belgium and Europe.

One of the families in this book came from Little Brabant, a small area in Brabant. Another family came from Pajottenland, an area southwest of Brussels. The third family is from Flanders. Before I jump to the history of these three families let's learn about Flanders and Brabant, the area and history of the place where these families came from.

1 History of Flanders

Flanders covers 5,221 square miles, i.e., 13,522 square km, which is less than half the size of Maryland, or roughly the size of Connecticut. The current population of Flanders is over 6.02 million, which is less than the population of Virginia (currently 6.79 million). The density of people in Flanders is however five

---

27. Besides numerous books, the following pages on the worldwide web provide additional sources for information on the history of Flanders and the Spanish Netherlands:
http://www.theotherside.co.uk/tm-heritage/background/flanders.htm.

times higher than in Virginia (it is 886 per square mile in Flanders versus 160/square mile in Virginia).

In 862 the county of Flanders was formally established by Charles the Bald (Karel de Kale) as a feudal fief. He was the first king of France, Francia occidentalis. After passing into the hands of the dukes of Burgundy, following the marriage in 1384 of Margaret III (Margareta van Maele) with Philip the Bold (Filips de Stoute), the county of Flanders became part of a union with neighboring provinces, including successively the county of Namur, the duchies of Brabant and Limburg, the counties of Hainaut, Holland and Zeeland, and the duchy of Luxembourg. Ultimately this union became the Seventeen Provinces.

With the death in 1482 of Mary of Burgundy, who married Maximilian of Austria, the era of the Burgundian Netherlands gave way to that of the Habsburg Netherlands, during which the union of all seventeen provinces under Habsburg rule was completed. Other important developments during that era were the cession of sovereignty in 1529 of the counties of Flanders and Artois by France to the Holy Roman Empire. In 1548 the seventeen provinces were set up as a single administrative unit called the Burgundian Circle, within the Holy Roman Empire and the Habsburg possessions. The decision was made that succession in all of the provinces would be governed by the same rules so as to ensure that all the provinces would be inherited by the same monarch.

Upon the abdication of Charles V, the Habsburg realms were divided between his son Philip II, who became King of Spain, and his brother Ferdinand I, who became Holy Emperor. In 1556 the Seventeen Provinces, which were allocated to Philip II, became the Spanish Netherlands.

As a result of serious conflicts with Philip II, which led to the Eighty Years' War (1568-1648), the Northern provinces separated from the Spanish Netherlands and set up the independent United Provinces in 1581. Through the Treaty of Munster in 1648 (Peace of Westphalia) the north was officially recognized as an independent country. As a result the Spanish Netherlands came to coincide with the Southern Netherlands.

In 1598, Philip II granted the Spanish Netherlands formal independence from Spain to be ruled by his daughter Isabella and her husband Albert of Austria. Since they remained childless, the Spanish Netherlands returned in 1621 under Spanish rule.

Under the Treaty of Utrecht of 1713, ending the Spanish succession war, Spain ceded the southern Netherlands to Austria, inaugurating the era of the Austrian Netherlands. Rebellion against the centralizing policy of the Austrian rulers led the provinces of the southern Netherlands in January 1790 to establish the United States of Belgium as an independent federated republic. Austrian rule was however restored by the end of 1790.

Following conquest by France in 1794, the southern Netherlands and the Prince-Bishopric of Liege were annexed to the French Republic in 1795.

The county of Flanders and the other constituent counties and duchies, with their local autonomy and privileges, were abolished and replaced by departments in the framework of a unitary state with centralized powers. Subsequently, with the advent of the imperial regime in France in 1804, the southern Netherlands became part of the French Empire.

Successively Prussia, Austria, and the newly created Kingdom of the Netherlands (northern Provinces) exercised provisional authority over the southern Netherlands after the defeat of Napoleon's army (at Leipzig in October 1813) and the departure of the French (in February 1814).

The claims of the Kingdom of the Netherlands on the southern Netherlands were accepted by the major European powers in June 1814. The final act of the Congress of Vienna in July 1815 confirmed the establishment of the United Kingdom of the Netherlands under William of Orange, uniting the north and the southern Netherlands.

An uprising of the southern provinces in 1830 led to the creation of the newly independent Kingdom of Belgium. The constitution adopted in 1831 provided for a unitary state with a parliamentary system of government. Between 1970 and 1993, through four revisions of the constitution, the unitary state was transformed in an ad hoc federal state, with three regions responsible for territory-related matters and three communities responsible for personal matters. The issue of the residual powers between the federal government, the regional and the community governments remains unsettled.[28]

In a nutshell, the history of Flanders[29] is a sequence of periods (see below) in which Flanders was dominated by the Spanish, the Austrians, the French, and the Dutch, before it gained independence in 1830. The unitary state created in 1830 was turned into a federal state with three regions and three communities through the constitutional change in 1992. Regional elections held in 2004 brought about a Flemish government that for the first time is composed differently than the federal government.[30]

28. The complexity of the Belgian federal model is described by Professor J. Van Ginderachter in
http://www.ecsanet.org/conferences/ecsaworld2/Ginderachter.htm

29. Summarized in collaboration with Paul Duran.

30. The history of Belgian Federalism is provided at
http://www.flandersonline.org/news/123/953

History of Flanders: successive periods

County of Flanders	862-1795
Burgundian Netherlands	1384-1482
Habsburg Netherlands	1482-1556
Spanish Netherlands	1556-1713
Austrian Netherlands	1713-1789 and 1790-1794
United States of Belgium	1790
French Republic	1795-1804
French Empire	1804-1814
French Monarchy	1814-1815
United Kingdom of Netherlands	1815-1830
Kingdom of Belgium (unitary state)	1830-1992
Flanders (as federal region and community)	1993 - present

2 History of Brabant

Brabant was the name given over time to an area of variable size under different administrative entities. Between the ninth and eleventh centuries Brabant was a Carolingian shire (pagus Bracbatensis) located between the rivers Schelde and Dijle. After the decline and collapse of the Frankish Carolingian Empire Brabant emerged as a feudal duchy out of the former duchy of Lower Lorraine. The latter was split up into Brabant, Luxembourg, Hainaut, Namur and other small feudal states.

In the twelfth century Brabant was a landgraviate, i.e., the part of the shire between the rivers Dender and Dijle. For a long time the territory covering the current Dutch province of North Brabant and the Belgian provinces of Brabant and Antwerp, plus the capital Brussels, formed the Duchy of Brabant.

The German Emperor Frederick Barbarossa created the title Duke of Brabant. Henry I of Brabant, Warrior of the House of Leuven, was the first to get the title of Duke of Brabant in 1190. Three generations of his heirs ruled relatively peacefully.

In 1283 John I of Brabant bought the Duchy of Limburg from Adolph V of Berg and secured his acquisition by defeating and slaying his competitor Henry of Luxemburg at the Battle of Worringen on June 5, 1288.

After that battle and in exchange for the financing of military and court expenditures, the Dukes of Brabant had to guarantee the rights and privileges of various local lords and burghers. Through the charter of Cortenberg in 1312 Duke John II entrusted the imposition of taxes to a council of burghers and nobles, who also oversaw the maintenance of justice and the equal application of the laws.

John III, Duke of Brabant, was a shrewd diplomat who strengthened the Duchy by advantageous marital alliances with neighboring principalities. When his daughter Johanna and her husband, Duke Wenceslas of Luxembourg acceded to the Duchy of Brabant, they granted the charter of rights known as the Blijde Inkomst[31] (The Happy Entry, or La Joyeuse Entrée in French) on January 3, 1356. This charter gave Brabant an exceptional position among the feudal states of the Low Countries and allowed it to play an eminent role in later centuries in the resistance against absolutist rulers.

After Wenceslas's death, Johanna continued to rule Brabant and Luxembourg, but was challenged by the sister of her husband, Louis II. She had to rely for aid on the House of Burgundy. The financial situation of Brabant turned into a catastrophy with high debt. Johanna called in the help of a young branch of the Burgundy kings who first as regents and later as dukes governed. Among them were Anton of Burgundy (1404-1406), Jan IV (1415-1427) and Philip of St. Pol (1427-1430). After the death of Philip the family line died out, and inheritance passed to Philip III, also known as the Good of Burgundy. Philip the Good reigned over Flanders, Brabant, Hainaut, Luxemburg and Namen. This ended the independence of the duchy of Brabant. The subsequent history of Brabant is part of the history of the Seventeen Provinces.

The Brabant Revolution of 1789-90 was an unsuccessful armed resistance to the abrogation of the Blijde Inkomst by the Austrian Emperor Josef II.

The French occupation of the Southern Netherlands in 1795 dissolved the Duchy of Brabant. The territory was reorganized in "les départements des Deux-Nèthes (present province of Antwerp) et Dyle" (the later province of Brabant), which after the independence eventually became part of Belgium.

The influence of Brabant's democratic and constitutional traditions is still reflected in the Belgian flag that uses red, yellow and black. The title of Duke of Brabant has been revived as the title bestowed to the eldest son of the King of Belgium.

---

31. The Blijde Inkomst has been viewed as an equivalent of the Magna Carta that established for England the rule of law. It is the only other medieval document with claims to comprise a written basis of governance, an early successful example of a nation-state. The actual effectiveness of the Magna Carta and its functioning significance was exaggerated by the Romantic historians of the nineteenth century.

The Brabant Revolution of 1789-1790 and the United States of Belgium.

The southern Netherlands was ruled by the Austrian Habsburg Dynasty from 1713 onwards. The southern Netherlands was economically important, but strategically poorly located from an Austrian perspective. During the many wars of the eighteenth century, in which Austria and France were enemies, Austria was mostly incapable of defending the southern Netherlands. The French occupied most of the southern Netherlands.

In 1784-1785 Emperor Joseph II tried to swap the southern Netherlands for parts of Bavaria, but this plan did not materialize. Joseph II was adamant about political reforms that he regarded as enlightened. These reforms included the closure of numerous monasteries and the cancellation of regional privileges. The century old privileges of the Estates of Brabant, the Blijde Inkomste, was cancelled on June 18, 1789, the year of the French Revolution.

Administrative reforms implemented two years earlier whereby the Council of Brabant was replaced by a supreme court, led to a resistance movement called the Statists. This movement was led by H.C.N. Van der Noten, a lawyer of Brussels. Another faction, originally supportive of the reforms, was lead by Jan-Frans Vonck, and was called the Vonckists.

Poor harvests and subsequent famine contributed to the revolutionary mood. The revolution in Brabant was politically more directed against the reforms by Joseph II, while the revolution in Liège was more directed against the Ancien Regime.

The cancellation of the Blijde Inkomste on June 18, 1789 alienated the Vonckists, who acted in cooperation with the Statists. In October 1789, the Manifest of the People of Brabant was published, proclaiming independence. The Habsburg forces were expelled. The Estates General met on January 11, 1790 and proclaimed The United States of Belgium (Etats Belgique Unis).

Emperor Joseph II died in February 1790. The Brabant coalition of revolutionaries broke up. The Vonckists were chased out and persecuted. Prussia promised not to support the revolutionaries. On December 3, 1790, Austrian troops occupied Brussels, and thus ended the short-lived United States of Belgium.

Source: Post M.J.H. "De Driebond van 1788 en de Brabantse Revolutie," Bergen op Zoom, 1961. Wrappers, 142 pp. Doctoraatsthesis, Universiteit van Nijmegen.

Objectives and layout of this book

You recall why this study was undertaken, what sources were used, and what approaches were employed. The goals of this book are to employ conventional and genetic genealogy to achieve the following specific objectives:

1. Document the family history of three families from Flanders using document research. Provide historical backgrounds on the times and places where these families lived.

2. Describe the occupations of each of these families including the history of embroidery and lace making, and beer brewing.

3. Discuss the main trends in Flemish emigration, particularly in the nineteenth and twentieth centuries; their underlying causes,

and the contributions Belgian immigrants made (especially to the United States).

4. Provide an introduction to genetic genealogy and demonstrate how genetic genealogy can be used to investigate paternal and maternal lineages.

5. Provide concrete illustrations of DNA results; show how DNA results should be interpreted and used to solve family puzzles. Demonstrate how genetic genealogy can complement conventional genealogy.

6. Provide a summary of what is currently known about the deep ancestry of my paternal and maternal ancestors and hence the deep ancestry of lots of Flemish people.

7. Introduce the Flanders-Flemish DNA project, a geographic project that I started a few years ago to bring together the DNA from people who have or believe to have roots in Flanders.

To achieve these objectives this book is organized as follows. Chapters 2 to 6 provide the family histories of three families from Flanders. These families are the Deboeck family, which is my father's family; the Girardin family, which is my mother's family; and the De Zutter family, which is my wife's family. Each chapter provides brief historical backgrounds on the places each of these families lived.

Chapter 2 starts off with the origin of the "de bock" family and follows this family as it moved from Sint-Amands in Little Brabant to Grimbergen and from rural occupations to urban industrial work.

Chapter 3 expands on what this family undertook in an urban town where they became pioneers and entrepreneurs. The chapter contains the history of lace making in Flanders and how the family got involved in mechanical embroidery and lace making.

Chapter 4 is focused on the Girardin family. This family from Pajottenland lives southwest of Brussels. The family has brewed beer for 125 years and still brews beer today. The chapter includes the history of beer brewing in Pajottenland and in particular the unique beers made around Brussels. These beers are based on traditions that are 400 years old.

Chapter 5 traces the history of the De Zutter family, who is from West Flanders close to the North Sea. The family moved from Blankenberge to Nieuwpoort where they still reside today. Since my wife's mother came from former East Germany, I also traced my wife's grandparents back in Germany.

Chapter 6 is about Flemish emigration. This chapter describes the migration trends and the motivations of Flemish people who moved overseas.

Chapter 7 tells the story of how the 13th generation descendant of the Deboeck family migrated to the USA and how the family branched out in the USA.

Chapter 8 provides an in-depth introduction to genetic genealogy, including how to take a DNA test, what to expect in terms of the results, and how to interpret DNA results. The chapter provides concrete illustrations of the DNA test results of the author and his wife and thereby defines the genetic inheritance of the Deboeck children.

Chapter 9 illustrates common uses of genetic genealogy. It includes a discussion of how to compare DNA results, how to resolve family puzzles, and how to participate in surname and/or geographic projects.

Chapter 10 introduces the Flanders-Flemish DNA project that brings together in one place on the worldwide web, DNA from people who have or believe to have roots in Flanders.

My epilogue weaves together reflections from the past with the future and focuses on the promise of life extension and genomics. The medical applications of DNA testing that are not covered in this book provide new challenges and advantages for substantial extension of life. Genomics will make genealogy even more challenging in the future.

This book can be read in a number of different ways. Those interested in the history of any of the three families covered in this book can immediately skip to the relevant chapters: read Chapters 2, 3 and 7 for the Deboeck family; Chapter 4 for the Girardin family; Chapter 5 for the De Zutter family. If your surname is not one of these names you may find the genetic genealogy material in Chapters 8 to 10 more interesting. If you are mainly interested in Flemish-American heritage you should read Chapter 6, which provides the history of Flemish emigration and Chapter 7, which talks about the migration of my family to the USA. You may also be interested in Chapter 10, which discusses the Flanders-Flemish DNA project. Finally, if you are mainly interested in historical aspects, you can browse through this book and find brief histories on Flanders in general, Brabant and West Flanders in particular, or Brussels, Blankenberge, Nieuwpoort and a few other places. You can also find in this book the histories of lace making and beer brewing.

The annexes to this book contain a series of more technical papers. I have included an annex on the other branches of the Deboeck family. There is also a brief on distance, land measurements and land prices in the sixteenth century. A real paper prepared by Paul Duran provides the evolution of prices, wages and the value of money in Belgium over the past six centuries. Paul Duran also provided a note on the value of investments in Belgium in current U. S. dollars. The last annex puts in historical context the question whether Leopold I, the first King of Belgium, may have been the father of Franciscus-Alexius Girardin. At the end of this book you can find a glossary, some useful links to information on the worldwide web, and detailed subject- and name indices to facilitate quick searches.

In the future a "virtual museum" will be established on the worldwide web that contains more photos and memorabilia about Flemish families than could fit in this book. In addition, the Flanders-Flemish DNA Project will continue to provide a source for information about Flemish DNA and ancestry.

Chapter 2
De Bock family of Little Brabant (1540-present)

The De Bock family of Little Brabant is one of *the oldest and most authentic families in Brabant.* This according to J. Lindemans who in 1952 wrote about this family in "Oude Brabantse Geslachten" (Old Brabant Families), which appeared in *Eigen Schoon en De Brabander,* a local genealogical journal titled *Own Beauty and the Brabander.*[1] Over time the spelling of this name has changed and there are many variants of this name. The name has evolved from *de Boucq, de Bock, de boeck, to deboek.* In Belgium there are at present over 8,800 persons with this name or its most common variants.[2]

My ancestors can be traced back to Gillis de Bock who was born circa 1530-40 in Sint-Amands, a small village in Little Brabant. Sint-Amands is in the center of the triangle between Brussels, Gent and Antwerp. Other branches of the family can be traced back to many other villages in Brabant or Antwerp. Some of these branches will be covered in Annex 1.

The *de Bock* family of Little Brabant was a very prominent family already in the sixteenth century. This is evident from records that have been found that document the land they owned and the Meiseniers letters they obtained.

In this chapter I will discuss first the origin of this surname. Next, visit the birthplace of my oldest known ancestor from Sint-Amands and its surroundings. Next, provide the pedigree of 15 generations of the *de Bock* family of Little Brabant.

Origin of the family name

The surname De Bock already appeared in old documents of the twelfth century. For example, in Puurs in 1157 it appeared in *Arnoldus Hircus el filius suus Boidinus* and in *Gozuinus Hircus.*[3] The name also appeared in 1162 in *Arnoldus Boc en avunculus suus Arturus de Puderce.*[4] The name appeared again in 1262 in *Arnoldus Rufus Hyrcus, Arnolddus Boc, Gosuin Boc;* and it appeared in Grimbergen in 1280 in *Henricus Bouc villicus* (meier) *de Grimbergis.* It

---

1. J. Lindemans, "Oude Brabantse Geslachten" (Old Brabant Families), *Eigen Schoon en De Brabander,* Year 34, number 5-6, 1952, p.176-187.

2. Based on the information at familienaam.be there are 8,841 persons with the name de boeck, Deboeck or de bock in Belgium.

3. Cartularium of Grimbergen, hs Hoevenarts number 7

4. ibid number 9

also showed up in 1286 in *Henricus dictus Boch*.[5]

De Bo(e)ck is the Brabant version of a name that in Flanders is common. M. J. Vandenweghe wrote in *Hallensia* in 1935 (freely translated) *"this name is widespread in several communities in Brabant, among others in Dworp, Lembeek, Sint-Pieters-Leeuw, Gooik as well as outside Brabant."*[6]

Vandenweghe found in the accounts of Halle en Kenast[7] that in 1538 *Anthone le Boucq* bought half of a house called "Spanje" from the widow Sidrachus van Ittre. Two years later, he is named again *"De Anthone le boucq, dit Carnin, pour l'arrentement de la maison despaigne rendue a nouvelle loy"* (for renting of the house 'despaigne' returned new loy).

There probably was a family of royal descent known as *le boucq de Carnin* that lived in the neighborhood of Valenciennes.[8] If so *Anthone le Boucq dit Carnin* must have been family of *Pieter de Bouck,* who is the oldest known ancestor of the *de Boucq* family from Halle. Pieter le Boucq was married to Barbara De Stryckere. They had seven children including four sons: Pieter, Arnold (Anthone), Joos and Jan. A chart of the descendants of the family le Boucq from Halle, based on the work of Vandenweghe is shown in Annex 1.

Vandenweghe concluded that the name had many spellings, *De Boeck, de Boucq, De Bouck, De bocq, de bock, de boec, de boucq, Du Bouck, De Boucq, Bocx, Boecx, De Bouche, sboekxc among others* and was widespread. It was *"if not the oldest, certainly one of the oldest family names in Halle".*

There are few families whose name can be found back for six centuries in the same community. This does not mean that all families with this surname have a common ancestor. In 1935 no one could have guessed that based on DNA testing it would become possible to determine whether they have a common ancestor. This shall be discussed in Chapter 8 and 9 when I talk about genetic genealogy and surname projects.

Over time the spelling of the family name changed. Prior to 1200 people in Flanders (like in the rest of Europe) had only one name. Everyone was called by a first name. The growth of the population, the increasing trade, and the emergence of cities in the twelfth century imposed the need to distinguish better between individuals and different generations. Circa 1300 it became insufficient to simply add "young" or "old", "junior" or "senior" after a first name.

---

5. ibid numbers 230 and 252

6. M.J. Vandenweghe: "De Familie De Boeck" (the family De Boeck), Hallensia III, Oude Reeks No III, 1935, p 73-75

7. See *Domeinen van Halle en Kenast,* number 9632

8. There is a site on the internet http://boucq.chez-alice.fr/Nom.htm that describes Boucq as a village of Meurthe and Moselle. The name of the village may come from the Latin *Boconis Villa*, village in the woods.

Officially there were no family names yet, but unofficially family names became more and more popular. When there was more than one "Jan" in a village then all of them got an additional name based on some physical features. For example, Jan with blond hair became "Jan de Witte" ("witte" is Flemish for blond); Jan who was tall became "Jan de Grote" ("grote" is Flemish for tall).

When people died these additional names disappeared but when the population kept increasing, such names were more and more inherited. The official use of family names varied from one area to another.

In the late Middle Ages the second name became a name that was inherited from father to son. From August 23, 1794, onwards it was no longer permitted to use a name other than the one on the baptism certificate. From that date onwards everyone had to use the family name of his/her father.

On August 18, 1811, Napoleon ordered everyone to adopt a family name. Many people did not take this seriously and adopted a silly name assuming that after Napoleon they would get rid of it. Some simply ignored the decree of the Emperor. The period to adopt a family name was extended to January 1 of 1814.

King Willem I of the Netherlands, who ruled from 1815 till 1830 signed a royal resolution on November 5, 1825 that ordered everyone to adopt a family name. Those who did not were punished.

How the spelling of family names changed.

The change in spelling of the name "de Bock" had something to do with the adoption in 1804 of the "Siegenbeek" spelling in the Netherlands. With the spirit of the French Revolution pervading all areas of thought, attempts were made to unify spelling and grammar. Matthijs Siegenbeek, professor at Leiden was asked in 1801 to draw up a uniform spelling; the priest Petrus Weiland was asked to write a grammar book. A few years later Siegenbeek published his treatise on "Nether" Dutch spelling (nether means "lower", i.e. belonging to "the lower countries near the sea") to promote uniformity ("Verhandeling over de Nederduitsche spelling ter bevordering van de eenparigheid in dezelve") in 1804 and a Dictionary for the "Nether" Dutch Spelling (Woordenboek voor de Nederduitsche spelling) in 1805. The government of the Batavian Republic officially brought in the spelling "Siegenbeek"[9] on 18 December 1804 but Siegenbeek's spelling never achieved real popularity.

In the Dutch speaking areas the Siegenbeek spelling was always unpopular. After Belgium declared independence in 1830 the spelling was denounced as "Hollandish" and "Protestant". The spelling situation was quite chaotic with much discussion about whether to use 'a' or 'ae', 'oo' or 'oó', 'ee' or 'eé', 'ei' or 'ey', 'ui' or 'uy', 'ambt' or 'ampt', 'u' or 'ue', and about the spelling of verbs.

In 1836 the Belgian government offered a reward for a proposal for a new spelling. In the end the jury, headed by Jan Frans Willems, produced their own suggestion in 1839, which remained quite close to the Siegenbeek spelling in use in the Netherlands. They retained their own spelling of a few words such as kaes (cheese), ryden (to ride) en vuerig (fiery). The Willems spelling was given royal approval on January 9, 1844.

The ordinance to register family names only came in 1811 in the Netherlands; many Flemish names kept their old spelling including the use of "oe", "ck" etc. The registration of names in the Netherlands transformed the spelling of many names into modern versions. Hence, de bock evolved to de boeck and eventually was spelled in one word, deboeck.[10]

Family names were made up based on various attributes. Common sources of family names include the following: First, there are the *names derived from the first name* of the father or mother: *patronimen or matroniemen.* For example, the son of Jan became Jans-zoon or Jans-seune, which later was written as Janssen(s). The son of Michael became Michiels, Matthias, or Mahieu.

Secondly, there were *names derived from place names or rivers.* For example names referring to an area, city or village, such as De Lille, DeRoubaix, Van Aken, Van Parijs. There were also the names that received an addition such as "–laar" or "-man(s)". For example, Brusse-laar(s), Ceule-mans, Goor-man, Meys-mans. There were also names derived from where a person was from. For example, De Vlaeminck, Vlamincx, De Waele, De Kempenaar. There were names based on rivers: Van der Schelde, Van Mandele, Van der Mandere. Some names were derived from local place names such as -biest, -bogaerd, -broek, -dijk, -heide, -meerch etc. Examples are Van Daele, Vander Biest, Vander Beke, Opdebeek, Ackerman, Beeckman, Van der Ven, Vereecken.

Third, there are the family *names that derive from a profession, occupation or title* that people obtained. Examples of names derived from a profession are De Backer, Schoenmakers, De Zutter, Dem(o)(u)lder, De Snyder, De Metser, De Sm(i)(e)t, De Wulf (a wulf is a vault, hence the vault keeper). Examples of names derived from a title are: De Prins, Deconcinck, De Graeve, De Leenheer, Rentemeester, De Coster.

---

9. Siegenbeek thought that the spelling should reflect refined Dutch pronunciation, taking into account the uniformity, etymology and analogy. From the Siegenbeek spelling we get the modern Dutch ij, called "lange ij" (long y) as distinct from ei, which has identical pronunciation and is called the "korte ei" (short ei). The word for iron " ijzer" used to be written yzer. Other spellings from Siegenbeek include: berigt (modern Dutch: bericht / report), blaauw (blauw / blue), Dingsdag (dinsdag / Tuesday), gooijen (gooien / to throw), magt (maagd / virgin), kagchel (kachel / stove), koningrijk (koninkrijk /kingdom), muzijk (muziek / music) and zamen (samen / together).

10. In 1954 a political agreement was reached at the highest levels between the Netherlands and those speaking Dutch (or Flemish) in Belgium. This Dutch language agreement ("Taalunie") produced the "Dictionary of the Dutch Language" ("Woordenlijst Nederlandse taal"). As a result the spelling of Dutch in both the Netherlands and in Flanders is uniform, which has remained so till today. Recent rather limited spelling differences in Dutch are part of this language agreement. Variants between Dutch spoken in the Netherlands and Dutch spoken in Flanders may occur in vocabulary and/or expressions that are used. These variants are labeled in the "great Van Dale" dictionary as AZN ("Algemeen Zuid-Nederlands") or common south Dutch in Belgium. Source: Dirk De Zutter, teacher and expert in Germanic languages.

Family names could also be derived from physical features, moral standing, or comparison with animals or plants. For example, physical features could have been the source of family names like De Groot(e), De Grijze, De Staercke, De Vuyst. Moral standings could have been the source of names like De Soete, De Taeye, De Vriendt, De Wilde. Based on comparisons with animals, family names like De Wolf, De Cock, Valcke, Vincke, could have emerged.

The name 'de Bock' may have been based on the name of a plant. Just like Verlinde, Populier, Peereboom, Eeckhout, Van Eecke, or Abeels. Vandenweghe's research suggests that the first appearance of this name may have been in the area of Halle. The *Halderbosch* (a wood near Halle) contained beech woods ("beuke bomen"). Vandenweghe therefore suggests that the name could have been derived from "beech wood".

Ann Marynissen, who is a professor and specialist in Flemish language and names, does not think so. She wrote: "when {this} name would be derived from a tree, it should have been in the form 'Van de beuk', which is not the case."[11]

Another possibility is that the name is a reference to an animal. In Flemish a "bok" is a male deer or goat (buck in English). This view is based upon the explanation that is supported by the explanation given by Dr. Frans Debrabandere in his authorised dictionary.[12]

Another possibility, my preferred one for reasons not difficult to guess, is that the name 'de Bock' could have been a nickname for a family who was persistent, steadfast or even overly stubborn (in Flemish, "een harde kop", "een stijfkop"). When we reivew the lives of several members of this family it will become clear why this explanation of this surname is certainly a plausible one.

The birthplace: Sint-Amands and surroundings

Sint-Amands was the birthplace of my oldest known ancestor. Sint-Amands is located about 18.7 miles (i.e. 30 km) from Antwerp at the river Scheldt. Joined with municipalities of Lippelo and Oppuurs it is situated in the southwestern corner of the current province of Antwerp, and is part of what is called Little Brabant, an area enclosed by two rivers, the Scheldt and the Rupel.

The oldest mention of Sint-Amands is *Baasrode-Sancti-Amandi.* The oldest Latin name of Sint-Amands in "Orbis Latinus" is *Amandi burgus of Amandi oppidum.*[13] The town was the central

---

11. Professor Dr Ann Marynissen, Institut für Niederländische Philologie, Koln, personal communication, July 18, 2006.

12. Frans Debrabandere "Woordenboek van de familienamen in België en Noord-Frankrijk" (Dictionary of familynames in Belgium and North France). L.J. Veen Amsterdam/Antwerpen, 2003, page 147.

13. See Stanny van Grasdorff: "Geschiedenis van Sint Amands," at http://www.stanny-van-grasdorff.com

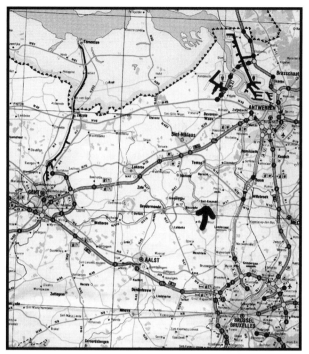

Figure 2.1 Map of Little Brabant showing Sint-Amands in the center; Antwerp in the northeast; Gent in the west; and Brussels in the south.

part of the Carolingic domain Baceroth (Baasrode) and was given by Lodewijk The Pious to the abbey of Saint-Amand (Elnone) in North France. The abbots of Elnone were considered as the chieftains of Sint Amands. From the eleventh century until the end of the Middle Ages, the influence of the Berthouts was strongly present. In the fifteenth century members of Vilaind and Halewijn succeeded the Berthouts.[14] In 1789 Sint-Amands had about 2,300 souls. There were 521 houses in Sint Amands. Forty years later Sint-Amands counted 2,904 people; by the beginning of the first World War (WWI) in 1914 population had grown to 3700. At present, the population of Sint-Amands is approximately 7,683.

Since 1776 the power over Sint-Amands was in the hands of Adriaan de Walckiers, with his "baljuw" (a represenative of the Duke) Ignatius Sarens. The mayor was Petrus Joannes Rollier who was the baljuw before Sarens.

Sint-Amands is near Lippelo and Oppuurs.[15] Lippelo[16] belonged to the "meierij" (a local administrative unit) of Merchtem in the quarter of Brussels. Local governors were the gentlemen of Grimbergen.[17] Together with Liezele and Malderen, Lippelo formed one jurisdiction of aldermen or magistrates. The parish of Lippelo belonged to an old foundation of a residential church,

14. Sint-Amands was a part of the land of Dendermonde. From ecclesiastical perspective the area gravitated, however, towards Brabant. In the Middle Ages Sint-Amands was part of the diocese of Kamerijk and of the main deanery ("aartsdekenij") of Brussels. With the foundation of the new dioceses, Sint-Amands first belonged in 1560 to the archbishopric of Mechelen, later to the diocese of Gent, deanery of Dendermonde. After the Council of Trent the parish of Sint-Amands was added to the archbishopric of Mechelen.

15. In 1977 a merger between cities results in Sint-Amands expanding to actually include the villages of Lippelo and Oppuurs.

16. In the old days Lippelo was called Lippinclo, after the Germanic "Lippinga" (people of Lippo) and "lauha" (a small wood on a high sandy soil).

17. Jacques Ferdinand de la Pierre, baron du Faey, Frans Albert van Croij en de Wild- en Rijngraaf van Salm

which probably came into possession of the abbey of Affligem in the twelfth century.

Oppuurs[18] is the higher situated part of the emerging Puurs. The family Van der Calsteren, originally from Leuven, possesed a large property in the fifteenth century. Later Oppuurs was pawned to Joost Snoy. In 1664, under Jan Karel Snoy, it received the title of Lordship. In 1818 the king appointed Idisbalda-Ghislain Snoy as mayor of Oppuurs.[19] Oppuurs belonged to the parish of Puurs. It was also the main place of a kanton to which Sint-Amands belonged, together with Bornem, Hingene, Lippelo, Liezele, Mariekerke and Weert.

Fifteen generations of the family

The previous section described Sint-Amands, the village where my oldest known ancestors came from. I shall now trace the history of the *de Bock* family. The oldest so far known ancestor of the de Bock family was born circa 1530-1540 in Sint-Amands in Little Brabant. His name was Gillis de Bock.

The descendants of Gillis de Bock moved from Sint-Amands to Vilvoorde. From Sint-Amands the family moved to Lippelo (see map below), then to Manderen, next to Londerzeel. From there they moved to Grimbergen and then to Vilvoorde. In this section I describe the itinerary followed by the de Bock family, all the way to Vilvoorde. In Chapter 3 I shall describe the business that the family established in Vilvoorde. After discussing emigration I will reveal in Chapter 7 how one descendant of this family made it to the USA.

The itinerary outlined on the map below, is remarkable in several ways. The distance from Sint-Amands to Grimbergen is less than 12.5 miles (20 km). The distance from Grimbergen to Vilvoorde is 2.5 miles (4 km). In some 400 years the de Bock family moved about 15 miles! Then, the thirdteenth generation descendant moved over 3000 miles away from Brussels…

Few genealogy studies contain details about ancestors that lived so long ago. This book even contains descriptions of the properties my ancestors owned in the early sixteenth century. Usually this is only found in books about people of royal descent. In the case of the de bock family, I was able to trace back the history of twelve generations, the itinerary the family followed, the properties they owned, as well as the titles they received. This was thanks to the support of a professional genealogist, several friends, and the worldwide web.

---

18. The oldest reference to Oppuurs was Oppuedersel in 1414.

19. Duke Snoy d'Oppuurs, former Minister for Economic Affairs who passed away, signed the historical pact of the European Union in Rome for Belgium.

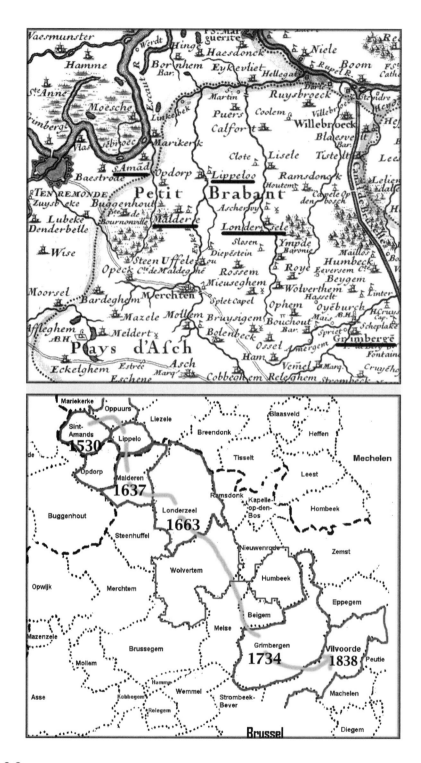

Figure 2.2
Map of Little Brabant (macro photo of map of Spanish Netherlands) and itinerary of the
de bock / deboeck family from 1530 to 1838. The descendants of Gillis de Bock moved
from Sint-Amands to Vilvoorde via Lippelo, Manderen, Londerzeel and Grimbergen.

Successive generations of the de Bock / de Boeck family[20]

I. **Gillis DE BOCK,** born circa 1540.

II. **Matheus DE BOCK,** born ca. 1565 in Sint-Amands.

III. **Amandus DE BOCK** born in 1608 in Lippelo, died in 1681.

IV. **Egidius DE BOCK** born in 1637 in Malderen, died in Londerzeel in 1700.

V. **Joannes DE BO(E)CK** born in 1663 in Londerzeel and died ca. 1720 in Londerzeel.

VI. **Franciscus DE BOECK** born in Londerzeel in 1700 and died in 1775 in Grimbergen.

VII. **Egidius DE BOECK** born in 1734 in Grimbergen and died in 1770.

VIII. **Egidius DE BOECK** born in 1765 in Grimbergen and died in 1829.

IX. **Joannes-Baptist DE BOECK** born in 1815 in Grimbergen and died in 1880.

X. **Everard De Boeck** born in 1838 in Vilvoorde and died in 1909

XI. **Guillaume De Boeck** born in 1874 in Vilvoorde and died in 1925.

XII. **René Deboeck** born in 1913 in Vilvoorde and died in Vilvoorde in 1985.

XIII. **Guido Deboeck** born in Etterbeek, Brussels in 1946.

XIV. **Toni, Pascal and Nina Deboeck,** born in Worcester (Mass) in 1972, Fairfax (Virginia) in 1980 and Fairfax (Virginia) in 1983, respectively.

XV. **Anastasia Gabriella Deboeck** born on November 14, 2006 in Mishawaki, Indiana.

What follows is a detailed description of each of these generations. If your surname is not De Bock or Deboeck or one of its other variants, you may want to skip the details of this family and move to Chapter 3 where I describe what profession they adopted in the early part of the twentieth century. You may however be interested in reading first about my oldest ancestor himself, simply because of the information that was retrieved from tax records from the sixteenth century. The information from those records

---

20. This is based on a Note from J. Caluwaerts received in the Spring of 2006 in which he documented the history of the De Boeck family of Little Brabant, complemented with my own research that was based on the parish registers of Great Grimbergen and with research done by my dad in the civil registers of Vilvoorde.

was transposed into today's terms. In what follows the link between successive generations will be indicated by roman numbers in bold e.g. *(see generation I below)*.

I. Gilles de Bock was born ca. 1530-1540. This was derived from a reference to his name in the 20th Penningkohier of Sint-Amands of 1571. Gillis was probably 35 to 45 years old at the time of this submission for the tax records.[21]

He was probably the son of Amandt de Bock and *Johanna Boonaerts* who from 1560 onwards were *outer burghers* ("buitenpoorters") of Aalst, a town 16 miles northwest of Brussels. The status of outer burghers was described in Chapter 1.

The 20th Penningkohier of Sint-Amands (the definition of a penningkohier was provided in Chapter 1) contained the following description of the properties of Gillis de Bock.

> "Folio (or number of the document) 21: Als pachter huurde Gillis van Marie Van Assche twee dagwanden weide gelegen in "Het Meynhout".
>
> Filio 67: Als eigenaar bezat Gillis in Sint-Amands: een hofstede aan het Sagers, groot met een boomgaard een gemeten; verder nog 50 roeden land tegenover de storm, een dagwant en 30 roeden land in de Vossendycken; twee dagwant land in de Moelemansvelden; twee dagwant land genaamd het Heetveld tegen de Schelde; een dagwant land op den dijck; 50 roeden land op het zelfde, tegen de Doorekens; 50 roeden land op het Boonhof; een dagwant land in het Plattijnken; 26 roeden land achter het voornoemde goed; een dagwant land op het einde van de Papaert, genaemd Het Zijpken; een dagwant land in de Buysstrate, genaemd Beeksken".

The 20th Penningkohier of 1571 of Sint-Amands, kept in the city archives of Gent, indicates that Gillis was a large farmer who rented land from Marie Van Assche, land that was located in "Het Meyenhout" and that he owned a farm at the Sagers and several other properties that in total may have been the equivalent of 5 hectares or 12.35 acres (1 ha = 2.47 acres). He clearly was either the biggest or one of the bigger landowners in Sint-Amands.

E. De Wever wrote about rents and the prices of land, in the period 1550 till 1800. The land prices in Zele, which is close to Sint-Amands, can be found in his work. From it data was extracted that contains rents and selling prices of arable land in currency of those times (see Annex 2). Arable land around 1570 sold according to De Wever for 47 pound Flemish groats per hectare which translaties into 70.5 (47x1.5) pound Brabant groats.[22] To obtain

---

21. J. Caluwaerts, second report on the De Bock family of Little Brabant, 2006

22. Based on prices provided in E. De Wever, "Rents and Selling Prices of Land at Zele," in H. Van der Wee and E. van Cauwenberghe, eds., *Productivity of Lands and Agricultural Innovations in the Low Countries (1250-1800),* Leuven, Leuven University Press, 1978. pp.55-63. A detailed table of rent and land selling prices can be found in Annex II.

the equivalent in groats, these pounds need to be multiplied with 240, hence 70.5 pound Brabant groats corresponds with 17,040 (71x240) Brabant groats.

What is 17,040 Brabant groats in 1571 worth today? A detailed study of the evolution of prices, wages and the value of money in Belgium over the past six centuries prepared by Paul Duran explicitly for this book (see Annex 3) permits us to calculate the answer to this question. Table 1 in Annex 3 shows that for the period 1551-1575, the value of 1 Brabant groats was equal to 0.5 Euros of 2006. Hence 17,040 Brabant groats would correspond with 8,520 (17,040x0.5) Euros in 2006.

If the land that Gillis de Bock declared in 1571 was approximatley 5 hectares and if all the land was arable land and of the same quality of the land in Zele (on the basis of which the rents and prices of land was estimated by E. De Wever) then the value of his land could be estimated at 42,600 (8,520x5) of 2006 Euros.[23]

Figure 2.3 *Map of Sint-Amands of 1785 which shows the* Cuytelgem street just under the Molen Cauter. *Source: Geschiedenis of Sint-Amands (History of Sint-Amands), Yolande Hertens, 1987.*

23. See Annex III, P. Duran, "The evolution of prices, real wages and the value of money in Belgium over the past six centuries."

II. Matheus de Bock who was a son of Gilles **(see Generation I above)**, was born ca. 1565, he died possibly September 10, 1625, in Sint-Amands.[24] He married around 1590, *Johanna van Praet*. Johanna was the daughter of Nicolaes van Praet who lived in the Cuytelgem street in Sint-Amands. A map of Sint-Amands of 1785 shows the Cuytelgem street under the Molen Cauter (in the northwest corner). Matheus and Johanna had six sons and two daughters. Their children were

1. Joannes (Jan) was born ca. 1590, he died in Malderen September 10, 1669. He was "meier" of Opdorp. He married *Joanna*

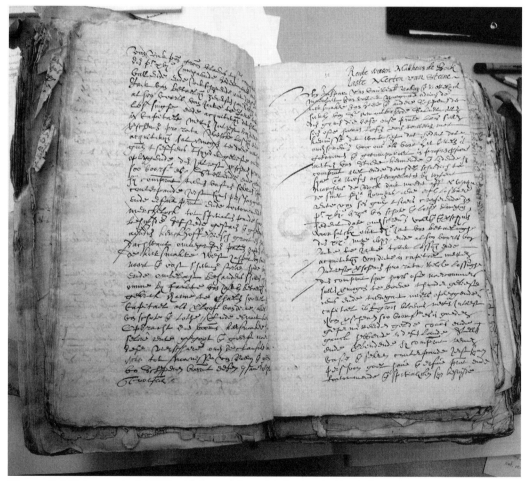

Figure 2.4 Notary act of 1636 which mentions Matheus de Bock (upper right hand corner).

24. In the City Archives of Antwerp there is a notary act of October 1623 in which the inheritance of Matheus de Bock is provided. There are also acts of 1634 and 1636 in which the inheritance of the younger Matheus married to Catherine de Smet was listed. Finally in the act of July 29, 1641, written by notary Geeraert of Paesschen in Liezele (register 2864), a compostion of the family Matheus de bosck is provided. This act was written in connection an authorization granted for an act in Dendermonde.

Rogmans on November 6, 1611. Joanna died in Malderen on April 2, 1669. Their children can be traced back in Opdorp which at the time was part of the parish of Malderen. They were the parents of nine children all baptised in Malderen but born in Opdorp. *Note that godfather and godmother names where available are shown after "'pm,'" which is Dutch for "peter en meter".*

i. Philippus, born December 23, 1614 (pm: Philips de Prince and Johanna Rogmans standing in for Anna Verhagen)

ii. Egidius (Gielis), born September 24, 1617 (pm: Rutgert van Marselaer[25] and Johanna van Praet)

iii. Mattheus, born January 3, 1621 (pm: Mattheus de Bock and Anna Rogman)

iv. Johanna, born April 21, 1624 (pm: Judocus Rogman and Amanda de Prince)

v. Elisabeth, born August 20, 1627 (pm: Judocus Rogman and Elisabeth de Bock), buried in Malderen on April 8, 1631

vi. Judocus (Joos), born January 28, 1631 (pm: Judocus Rogmans and Catharina Joos). He married Maria Van Assche in Malderen on November 8, 1652.

vii. Johannes (Jan), born February 4, 1635 (pm: Joannes Joos and Catherina de Smet), who became Meisenier in 1658.

viii. Adriana, born February 25, 1638 (pm: Henricus de Bock and Anna Rogman)

ix. Adrianus, born July 19, 1639 (pm: Adrianus Rijnckens and Anna Rogman).

3. Hendrick, born circa 1595, married Catharina Verstappen on May 12, 1619 in Sint-Amands. In 1658 he was a witness by the signing of an act by which his nephews became Meiseniers. He is mentioned as their uncle.

2. Egidius (Gillis) was born ca. 1595. He married in Sint-Amands on October 24, 1618, *Catharina Joos.* She became first godmother in Malderen in 1631 and later was godmother also for the children of Joos De Bock and Maria van Assche in 1655. The children of Joos and Catherina included:

---

25. Rutgert van Marselaer was the Lord of Opdaorp, in important figure who did not become godfather of everyone.

i. Adriaen married on November 3 in Malderen, Joanna Van Doorslaer. He became Meisenier in 1658.[26]

ii. Jan married in Sint-Amands on July 1, 1670, Maria Segers. He became Meisenier in 1696.

iii. Matheus born in 1628, married in Sint-Amands on June 14, 1659, Maria Meert and became Meisenier in 1658.

iv. Henricus (Hendrick), born in 1630; became Meisienier in 1658. In 1663 he was mentioned as a witness in a notary act through which his brother Adriaen bought land for their father Gillis.

v. Joanna, born in 1634. She became Meisienier in 1658.

vi. Adriana. He became Meisenier in 1658.

vii. Catherina, born in 1639.

viii. Maria, born in 1644.

4. Elisabeth, born ca. 1597, married Joannes van Grootven in Sint-Amands on November 17, 1619.

5. Maria, born ca. 1599, married Jan Joos in Sint-Amands on July 9, 1623.

6. Pieter (Petrus) was born circa 1600.

7. Amandus, born in 1608. *(See Generation III below).*

8. Matheus who married on August 1, 1621, Catharina De Smet, daughter of Romanus "Romeyen" and Maria "Mayken" Abeloos. Romanus was a magistrate in Sint-Amands. They had two children: Romanus, born January 11, 1623 (pm: Romanus de Smet and Johanna van Praet) and Maria, born in Sint-Amands on May 8, 1625 (pm: Johannes de Bock and Maria Abeloys). Maria became Meisenier in 1698 and married Jan de Budt.[27]

According to J. Caluwaerts, Matheus De Bock may have been the brother of Huybrecht de Bock who was married to *Ursula Verstap-*

---

26. Several of Egidius's children became Meiseniers. Evidence to this can be found in J. Lindemans, Van Meiseniersbloed (Of Meiseniersblood), VVF, 1998, page 21, next to 1658. The supporters for these letters were Jan and Hendrick de Boeck, uncles of Egidius's children.

27. Evidence to this can be found in J. Lindemans, Van Meiseniersbloed (Of Meiseniersblood), VVF, 1998, page 22, next to 1698.

pen and who died in Malderen on May 19, 1628. The parish registers of Sint-Amands start only in 1614 but there are other sources on Sint-Amands that potentially could confirm this relationship.

III. Amandus "Amant" de Bock, fifth son of Matheus de Bock was born in 1608 in Sint-Amands and died in Lippelo on March 22, 1681. His death certificate was exceptionally detailed for the period. It mentioned that he was buried "in navi ecclesiae" (the nave of the church in Lippelo) close to the Sint Stephanus altar, under a stone and that the year of his birth was 1608. This stone may no longer be there because it was not described in a study of the history of the parish of Lippelo.[28]

Amant de Bock was an educated person; his signature was found on a notary act of 1641.

Amant married three times and had in total at least twenty children. Given that he was educated and that he married the daughter of De Smet-Biesens, we can with some certaintly claim that he belonged to the better classes of the area in his time.

Amant first married *Catherina de Smet,* in Lippelo on September 3, 1627. Catherina was the daughter of Jan and Maria de Smet-Biesens. Maria Biesens was the daughter of Leonard Biesens en Johanna de Rijcke, descendant of the gentlemen of Marselaer and inheritors of the foundation "De Doorne Croone". In the parish of Lippelo there is still a stone of Jan de Smet-Biesens and family. (see Van Elsen, page 258). Amant and Catherina had seven children

1. Joannes was born in Sint-Amands on October 3, 1628 (pm: Joannes de Smet & Joanna van Praet)

2. Petrus was born in Sint-Amands on March 15, 1630 (pm: Petrus Coliers & Magdalena de Smet)

3. Maria born in Sint-Amands on October 10, 1632 (pm: Joannes de Bock & Maria Abeloys). She married Jan De But

4. Anna born in Sint-Amands on April 14, 1635 (pm: Joannes Joos & Anna Smet)

5. Egidius born in Lippelo on March 2, 1637 (pm: Egidius van Waerbeke & Maria de Smet). He married twice as we shall show below *(see Generation IV below).*

6. Henricus born in Lippelo on January 28 in 1640 (pm: Maria de Prince & Henricus de Smedt)

7. Joachim born in Lippelo on February 1, 1642 (pm: Joachim Zeeberch & Joanna de Clercq)

28. J.A. Van Elsen, Geschiedenis der parochie Lippelo (History of the parish of Lippelo) in Eigen Schoon & De Brabander, 1932.

Amant married a second time with *Elisabeth Verstappen* in Lippelo in May 1645. Together they had ten children.

1. Joanna was born in Lippelo on January 9, 1646 (pm: Joannes Biesman & Joanna Broeckmans)

2. Petronella was born in Lippelo on January 6, 1647 (pm: Franciscus Gerarts & Petronella de Smedt) and died in Malderen on September 24, 1714. She married in Lippelo on January 24, 1666 Paschasius "Passchier" van Nuffel (born in Malderen June 10, 1640, died January 18, 1717), son of *Peeter and Catharina van den Bossche*

3. Philippus born in Lippelo on February 4, 1648 (pm: Philippus Verschueren & Jacoba van Wemmel)

4. Judocus born in Lippelo on July 28, 1649 (pm: Judocus Rogman & Anna vander Stappen)

5. Adrianus born in Lippelo on November 8, 1650 (pm: Adrianus vanden Bossche vicepastor & Catharina Verstraten)

6. Philippus born in Lippelo on July 27, 1653 (pm: Philippus Verschueren & Maria de Bock)

7. Joannes born in Lippelo on February 10, 1655 (pm: Joannes van Paschen & Maria de Somer)

8. Joannes born in Lippelo on July 19, 1656 (pm: Joannes van Paschen & Maria Waerbeeck)

9. Franciscus born in Lippelo on February 13, 1658 (pm: Franciscus Brijs & Joanna Peeters)

10. Elisabeth born in Lippelo on August 19, 1659 (pm: Joannes Meert & Elisabeth Zeebroeck)

Amant married a third time, circa 1664, *Joanna Mehauden,* born in Zarlardinge, who died in Lippelo on September 1, 1693. She was the sister of pastor Petrus Mehauden from Puurs and connected to pastor Dominicus Mehauden in Londerzeel. Amant and Johanna had three children:

1. Catharina born in Lippelo on February 2, 1664 (pm: Romanus de Smet & Catharina Meert)

2. Jacobus born in Lippelo on December 1, 1665 (pm: Jacobus van Nuffel standing in for *dominus* Petrus Mehauden pastor in Puurs & Catharina Boydens)

3. Susanna born in Lippelo May 11, 1668 (pm: Reverendus Dominus Petrus Mehauden pastoor in Puurs & Susanna Davidts)

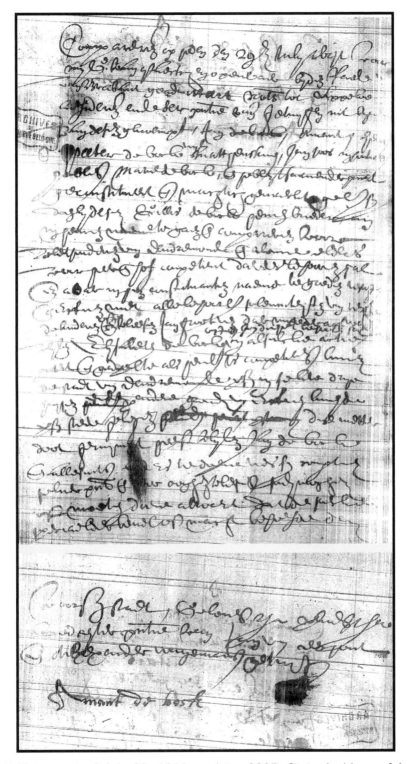

Figure 2.5 Notary act of July 29, 1641, register 2865, State Archives of Antwerpen, made by Notary Geeraert van Paesschen, in Liezele, Includes Signature of Amant De Bock made when he was 32 years old in 1641

Transcription of original text of the Notary Act from July 29, 1641 written in old Dutch and translated by J. Caluwaerts.

Comparerende op heden den 29e july 1641 voor mij G. Van Paesschen openbaer bij den Rade van Brabant geadmitteert notaris tot Lippelo residerende ende ter presentie vande getuygen int eynde can dezer genoempt, Jan De Bock, Amant, hen(rick) & Peeter de Bock, wijlen Mattheus kinderen, Jan Joos in huwel(ijck) hebbende Marie de Bock & hebben tsaemender handt geconstitueert & machtich gemaeckt gel(ijck) sij doen bij dezen Gilles de Boeck hennen brueder, om in hennen naem te gaen & compareren voir (de) wethouderen van Dendremonde & alomme elders voir heer & hof competent da...behhoirl(ijck) sal en(de aldaer in hen constituanten naeme te goeden en (de) erffven met alle behoirl(ijcke) solemniteiten van rechte de kindern & wees [van] Jan Grootven daer moeder aff was wijlen Elisabeth de Bock in alsulcke actie paert & gedeelte als henl(ieden) is competerende binnen de stadt Dendermonde v(v00r)schr(reven) in sekere drije huysen ende andere gronden & erffen vinnen de v(oor)sch(reven) stede gelegen ---[doorgehaald] die metter door geruympt heeft wijen jan de Bock & allesints weders te doene... sijn compt...selver p(rese)nt & twee ooghen wesen & souden moghen oft moeten doene alsvoere dat de...(saeke) speciaele der bevel oft macht behobve den voorsh(reven) staret, geloven(de) etc(etera) gedaen ter p(rese)ntie van Jan van den hove & Alexander Wagemans, getuygen. [Handtekening] Amand de Bock.

Abbreviated English Translation of Notary Act from July 29, 1641

On July 29th, 1641 appeared before G. Van Paesschen, official of the Court of Brabant, registered notary of Lippelo...the witnesses Jan De Bock, Amant, Hen(rick) and Peeter de Bock, who are children of Mattheus, Jan Joos who married Marie de Bock and ....provided authorization to Gilles de Boeck their brother, to buy in their name...

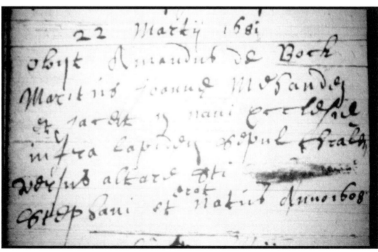

Figure 2.6 Death certificate of Amandus DE BOECK, 1681, buried in the church of Lippelo.

IV. Egidius 'Gillis' de Bock, fourth son of Amandus DE BOCK and Catherina de Smet, was born in Lippelo on March 2, 1637. He died in Malderen on April 4, 1700.[29] He married twice. His first marriage was with Marie Verheyden on June 11, 1660 in Malderen. Maria Verheyden died fourteen years later on April 26, 1674 in Malderen. Together they had four children. The first one was stillborn on September 7, 1661. Then followed:

1. **Joannes** born on January 27, 1663 (pm: Henricus de Bock & Joanna Mehouden standing in for Catharina Joos), Meisenier since 1705 *(see Generation V below).*[30]

2. **Anna** born on November 30, 1666 (pm: Matthias van Dorslaer and Anna van Laken), godmother in 1692, Meisenier since 1705, in Ramsdonk.

3. **Gerardus** born on March 10, 1672 (pm: Paschasius Verheyden standing in for Gerardus van Dorslaer) – died in Malderen June 28, 1674.

Five months after the death of Maria, Gillis married Catherina Goossens on September 11, 1674 in Londerzeel. Catherina was the daughter of Christophorus and Barbara *Verlinden*. Witnesses were Paschasius van Nuffel (brother-in-law of Gillis) and Matthias Goossens. Catherina was born on November 8, in 1643 and died January 20, 1721. Gillis and Catherina had at least five children. They were:

1. **Philippus** born in Malderen on June 26, 1675 (pm: Philippus de Bock & Petronilla de Bock). He married on November 4, 1702, Maria WALSCHAP

2. **Catharina** born in Londerzeel April 28, 1677 (pm: Guilielmus Mertens & Catharina de Boeck)

3. **Romanus** born in Londerzeel on February 12, 1679 (pm: Romanus van Gucht & Anthonetta Segers)

4. **Antonetta** born in Londerzeel on August 31, 1681 (pm: Philippus vanden Voorden and Antonette van Linthaudt)

---

29. A notary act made by notary Vandendriessche on June 20, 1703, provides the inheritance of Gillis de Bock. This act is referred to in another notary act of December 24, 1709, in which Jan de Boeck sells to his son-in-law, Jan van Assche, a piece of land located in Lippelo, that was called "Het Belleveldeken". This piece of 28 roeden (415 square meters) was inherited by Jan de Bock from his parents Gillis de Bock and Maria Verheyen. Source: J. Caluwaerts, private mail of October 1, 2006.

30. Evidence to this can be found in J. Lindemans, *Van Meiseniersbloed* (Of Meiseniersblood), VVF, 1998, page 22, next to 1705.

5. Franciscus born in Londerzeel July 11, 1683 (pm: Franciscus de Boeck & Barbara Goossens)

Figure 2.7 Birth Certificate of Egidius de Bock (1637), baptised by pastor Antonius Fleurquin.

V. Joannes "Jan" de Bo(e)ck, first born son of Egidius DE BOCK, was born in Malderen on January 27, 1663 (hence three years older than he was estimated in 1702) and died in Londerzeel in 1717 or 1721. He became Meisenier (see Chapter I) in 1705.[31] The people who supported him to get his Meisenier's letter were Jan van Gròotvrint (read: van Grootven) and Passchier van Nuffel. Jan was a brewer and pub keeper. He lived in Londerzeel in the pub called *De Croon.*

In 1710 Jan was called "Jan de Bock sone Gillis" (Jan de Bock son of Gillis). This facilated his identification because in Londerzeel there were several Jan de Bocks.[32]

Jan married in Londerzeel on August 5, 1692, *Catharina de Bie,* who was born in Londerzeel on April 16, 1655, and who died on April 10, 1738.[33] She was already twice a widow before she married with Jan. She had previously been married with Jan Mertens (married on October 23, 1678, and had three children) and with Egidius van Assche (who she married on June

---

31. Evidence to this can be found in J. Lindemans, Van Meiseniersbloed (Of Meiseniersblood), VVF, 1998, page 22, next to 1705.

32. Namely Jan de Bock, husband of Jacoba Doms.

33. In a notary act of July 19, 1706, Jan de Boeck and Catherine de Bie declare that on July 8, 1706, they sold to Franciscus Abeloos a farm called De Croon located in Londerzeel, the size of which was 12 "roeden" (about 178 square meters). They also sold a horse, three rabbits, two pigs, and ten tons of beer. They received 2000 guldens for this.

27, 1685, and with whom she had two children). She was the daughter of Engelbertus de Bie (magistrate in Londerzeel) and Maria *Segers.*[34] In spite of Catharina's age – she was 37 years old when she married Jan -- she and Jan had still three children, all born in Londerzeel. They were:

> **1. Anna** born on August 16, 1693 (pm: Engelbertus de Bie namens Egidius de Bock and Anna de Bock). She married in 1725, Jan van Assche (parents from among others Joannes Baptista van Assche, died in Londerzeel in 1728, and became Meisenier; was called upon several times to support the Meiseniers applications of his family).[35]

> **2. Petronella** born March 24, 1697 (pm: Reynerus van Eeckhoudt & Petronilla de Boeck)

> **3. Franciscus** born December 22, 1700 (pm: Franciscus van Assche & Joanna van Sande), who continues the family history in Grimbergen *(see Generation VI below)*

In the City Archives of Brussels in bundel 536 there is a population count of Londerzeel taken in 1702. On page 6, family 27 is mentioned as follows:

Jan de Boeck (pachter [doorgehaald] brouwer/ aut 36 jaeren
Cathelijn de Bie sijne huysvre. aut 46 jaeren
Marie Mertens sijne schoondochter / aut 18 jaeren
Catharina van Assche sijne schoon/dochter aut 10 jaeren
een halff ploegh [doorgehaald][36] */ een peerdt / een vercken [doorgehaald]/ twee coyen / drije renders / een calff / een vercken /*

VI. Franciscus de Boeck, first son out of the marriage of Jan DE BOCK and Catherina de Bie, was born in Londerzeel on December 22, 1700. He died in Grimbergen on August 8, 1775.

He became Meisenier on July 31, 1772 (the "stavers" or supporters for his Meisenier's letter were Carel de Boeck & Joannes Baptista van Assche). He married with *Anna Maria Jacobs* in Grimbergen on May 16, 1724. Anna Maria was born in Grimbergen on March 14, 1700 and died in Grimbergen on October 3, 1764. She was the daughter of Jan and Hermelindis de Cré. Franciscus and Anna Maria had seven children all born in Grimbergen. They were:

---

34. L. Lindemans, Genealogie de Bie uit Londerzeel, in: L'Intermédiaire des Généalogistes, nr. 297 (May-June 1995), p. 161. Catharina's ancestors were from father to son involved in the city administration.

35. A "straver" is a witness or supporter for the new Meiseniers, usually a family member already a Meiseniers.

36. A "halve ploeg" is a measurement of land on which Jan was taxed.

1. Carolus born on May 9, 1725 (sub conditione, pm: Carolus Jacobs & Catharina de Bie). Recognized as Meisenier of Grimbergen since June 2, 1750; supporters were Martinus de Cree and Jacobus Timmermans.

2. Maria Anna born on June 23, 1727 (pm: Henricus de Cré & Maria Mettens). Received her Meisenier's letter on April 23, 1762. Supporters were her brother Carel and Jacob Timmermans "cosijn germeyn.'"

3. Anna born on March 27, 1732 (pm: Hendricus Jacobs and Anna de Boeck)

4. Egidius 'Gillis' born on July 3, 1734 (pm: Egidius de Keyser and Maria Timmermans). *See Generation VII below.*

5. Anna Catharina born on July 27, 1736 (pm: Judocus van Asch and Anna de Boeck) died on May 13, 1738

6. Maria born on January 22, 1739 (pm: Anthonius Admiraels & Maria Sloors)

7. Maria born on September 22, 1740 (pm: Joannes van Humbeeck and Maria van Roy) died on October 22, 1740.

The information that follows came mainly from the civil registers in the City Hall of Vilvoorde.

VII. Egidius 'Gillis' de Boeck, second son of Franciscus De BOECK and *Anna Maria Jacobs* was born in Grimbergen on July 3, 1734. He died on February 14, 1770. He became Meisenier on July 27, 1764 (see Figure 1.5). His supporters were his brother Carel and Jacob Timmermans. He married *Anna Maria van Dongelbergh* in Grimbergen on August 7, 1764. She was born in Grimbergen on May 24, 1742 and was the daughter of Carolus & Catharina *van den Bergh.* Gillis and Anna Maria had three children all born in Grimbergen. They were:

1. Egidius born in Grimbergen on September 13, 1765, and died there on October 4, 1829 *(see Generation VIII below).*

2. Corneille (Cornelius) was born on August 24 and died nine days later on September 2, 1767

3. Corneille (Cornelius) was born in Grimbergen on August 26, 1768 and died two years later on March 10, 1769.

VIII. Egidius de Boeck first son of Gillis DE BOECK and *Anna Maria van Dongelbergh* was born on September 13, 1765 in Grimbergen and died there in October 4, 1829. He married *Anne Doms* who was born on November 11, 1769. They had seven children:

1. Franciscus was born in Vilvoorde on April 8, 1792 and he died eleven months later on March 5, 1793.

2. Everardus was born on April 1794; he died June 5, 1839. He married Therea Germus, with whom he had one son, Carolus.

3. Cornelius was born on July 30, 1796.

4. Maria-Elizabeth was born in in 1798; she died young when she was six years old, on December 8, 1804.

5. Maria Therese was born on October 30, 1803.

6. Pierre was born in Borgt on September 10, 1806 and died 27 days later on Ocober 7 1806.

7. Jean-Baptiste (Joannes) was born in Grimbergen on October 18, 1815 and died May 27, 1880 *(see Generation IX below)*

IX. Jean-Baptist (Joannes) de Boeck, fifth son of Egidius DE BOECK and *Anna Maria Jacobs* was born on October 18, 1815 in Grimbergen and died May 27, 1880. He married *Anne Maria Francisca Van Herp* on November 8, 1837 in Grimbergen. Anne Maria Van Herp was born on July 1, 1810 in Humbeek and died in Vilvoorde on June 23, 1886. Together they had four sons:

1. Everard was born in Vilvoorde on December 12, 1838; he died in 1909 *(see Generation X blow)*

2. Cornelius was born in Vilvoorde on January 3, 1846. He married Afiana Joanna VerVonck (born 1847 and died 1917). They had one son called Franciscus.

3. Joseph was born in 1842

4. Guillaume was born in 1849.

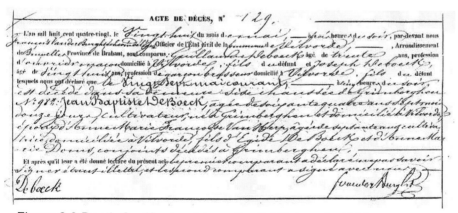

Figure 2.8 Death Certificate of Jean-Baptist Deboeck, 1886

X. Everard Deboeck, oldest son of Jean-Baptist and Anna Maria Jacobs, was the first to be born in Vilvoorde. He was born on December 12, 1838. He died on September 10, 1881 in Vilvoorde. He married with *Gertrude Verhaegen* on May 2, 1864 in Vilvoorde (See marriage certificate on page 53). Gertrude was the daughter of Guillaume Verhaegen and Josine Hoedemaekers. Gertrude was born in Vilvoorde on February 1, 1840. At the time of the wedding Everard could not write; he signed with a cross. The newlyweds lived at Quai du canal ("Kanaal kaai") number 3. They had five children.

1. Caroline, born in Vilvoorde on October 23, 1864. Caroline died one year, ten months and six days later on August 29, 1866.

2. Anne-Marie was born in Vilvoorde on August 2, 1869. She married Guillaume Debulpaep.

3. Jozef, was born in Vilvoorde on November 5, 1871

4. Guillaume, born in Vilvoorde on May 17, 1874 and died on April 12, 1925. He married Joanne Nobels who was born January 29, 1876 and died May 4, 1942 ***(see Generation XI below).***

5. Victor, was born on April 26, 1877 and died in 1949. A brief introduction to the life and profession of Victor can be found in Chapter 3.

XI. Guillaume Deboeck, oldest son of Everard and *Gertrude Verhaegen,* born in Vilvoorde on May 17, 1874 and died on April 12, 1925. On December 20, 1896 he married in Vilvoorde *Joanne Nobels* who was born January 29, 1876 and died May 4, 1942. Joanne was the oldest daughter of Guillaume Nobels and Josephine Moens. Their marriage act showed that both Guillaume and Joanne were working in a factory ("ouvrier de fabrique"). The life of Guillaume and Joanne will be described in Chapter 3. Together they had four children:

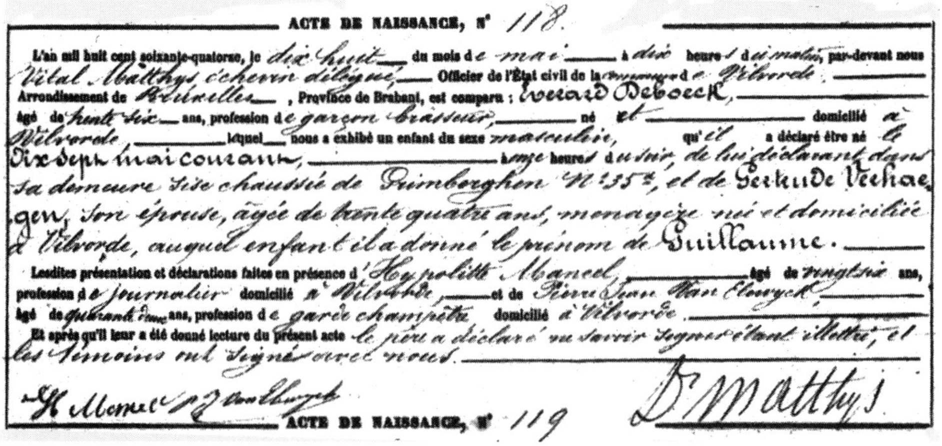
ACTE DE NAISSANCE, N° 118.

L'an mil huit cent soixante-quatorze, le dix huit du mois de mai à dix heures du matin, par-devant nous Vital Matthys échevin délégué, Officier de l'État civil de la commune de Vilvorde. Arrondissement de Bruxelles, Province de Brabant, est comparu : Everard Deboeck, âgé de trente six ans, profession de garçon brasseur, né et domicilié à Vilvorde, lequel nous a exhibé un enfant du sexe masculin, qu'il a déclaré être né le dix sept mai courant, onze heures du soir, de lui déclarant dans sa demeure sise chaussée de Grimberghen N° 35, et de Gertrude Verhaegen, son épouse, âgée de trente quatre ans, ménagère née et domiciliée à Vilvorde, auquel enfant il a donné le prénom de Guillaume.

Lesdites présentation et déclarations faites en présence d'Hypolitte Mancel, âgé de vingt six ans, profession de journalier domicilié à Vilvorde, et de Pierre Jean Van Elewyck, âgé de quarante deux ans, profession de garde champêtre domicilié à Vilvorde.

Et après qu'il leur a été donné lecture du présent acte le père a déclaré ne savoir signer étant illettré, et les témoins ont signé avec nous.

H Mancel P J Van Elewyck D Matthys

ACTE DE NAISSANCE, N° 119

Figure 2.9 Birth Certificate of Guillaume Deboeck, may 17th, 1874

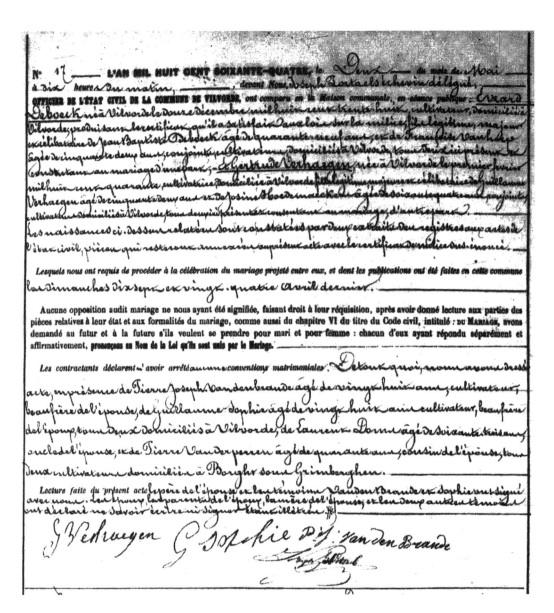

Figure 2.10 Marriage certificate of Evrard Deboeck and Gertrude Verhaegen, May 2, 1864, Vilvoorde

Figure 2.12 Guillaume Deboeck and his oldest son Joseph born in 1898 Photo taken around the turn of the century

Figure 2.13 Joanna Deboeck-Nobels and her oldest daughter, Josephine born 1897 (photo taken around the turn of the century)

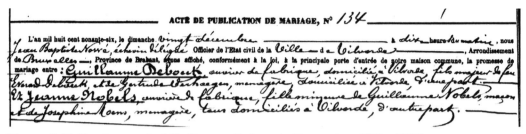

Figure 2.11 Marriage act of Guillaume Deboeck, December 20th, 1896.

1. Josephine born in Vilvoorde on May 20, 1897, died in Vilvoorde on September 27, 1970. She remained single throughout her life. Guillaume was 23 and Joanne was 21 when Josephine was born, five months after their marriage.

2. Joseph born in Vivoorde on December 6, 1898 and died in Schaerbeek in May 31, 1980. He married (when he was 51 years of age) on February 14, 1950 with *Lea Norga* who was born in Schaarbeek on July 28, 1911. She was the daughter of Gustaaf Norga and Anne-Marie Solberg who married February 5, 1903. Gustaaf was born on December 9, 1875 and died August 5, 1945. Anne-Marie Solberg was born in Maaseik on September 11, 1874 and died in Schaarbeek on November 23, 1943. Joseph and Lea had two daughters: Anne-Marie and Jeannine.

2.1 Anne-Marie (Josephine, Pierre) was born in Etterbeek on September 6, 1951. She married on December 22, 1973, Roland Desmeth born on July 19, 1951. After the death of Roland she remarried in Braine l'Alleud on February 25, 1989, Jens-Pieter Myllerup, born January 25, 1937.

2.2 Jeannine (Paula, Renée, Marie) was born on November 3, 1952 in Etterbeek. She married in Schaarbeek on September 9 1977, Luc Abts born August 10, 1948. They had two daughters: Marie-Aurèle, born in Ukkel on March 15, 1979 and Anne-Cécile born in Ukkel on March 14, 1980.

3. Pieter (Petrus) was born on October 5, in 1900 and died of a heart attack on August 24, 1955 in Vilvoorde. He married Jose De Cat, born on May 7, 1915 in Mechelen. They lived in an apartment on the Henri 1 lane, no 131 in Vilvoorde.

4. René Corneille was born in Vilvoorde on August 25, 1913. He married *Marie-Louise Girardin* on August 25, 1943 in St Ulriks Kapelle. He died on July 6, 1985. On April 8, 1954 he became a Knight in the Order of Leopold II[37] ("Ridder in the Order of Leopold II") for his services contributed to Belgian industry as shareholder of the PVBA Deboeck Brothers *(see Generation XII below).*

XII. René Corneille Deboeck, youngest son of Guillaume and Joanne Nobels, was born in Vilvoorde on August 25, 1913. He married *Marie-Louise Girardin* on August 25, 1943 in St. Ulriks Kapelle. He died on July 6, 1985. Rene Corneille and Marie-Louise Girardin had two sons:

1.Guido Jean-Baptist, born on January 6, 1946 in Etterbeek *(see Generation XIII).*

2. Marc, born on November 15, 1947.

XIII. Guido Jean-Baptist Deboeck, oldest son of René Corneille and Marie-Louise Girardin was born in Etterbeek on January 6, 1946. He married Hennie Irma De Zutter on May 14, 1969 in the cityhall of Leuven and on August 14, 1969 in the Chapel of the Castle of Heverlee in Leuven. Hennie is the daughter of Daniel De Zutter, born October 15, 1916 in Blankenberge and Irmgard Burkhardt, born on March 1, 1923 in Braunichswalde in former East Germany. Daniel De Zutter died on June 14, 1990. The history of the

Figure 2.14 Marriage booklet of René-Corneille Deboeck and Marie-Louise Girardin, August 25th, 1943, Sint Ulriks Kapelle.

37. The Order of Leopold II is a military order of Belgium and is named in honor of King Léopold II. The decoration was established in 1900 by Léopold II as king of the Congo Free State and was in 1908, upon Congo being handed over to Belgium, incorporated into the Belgian awards system. The order is awarded for bravery in combat or for meritorious service to the benefit of the Belgian nation. It can be awarded to both Belgians and foreigners. The order has become a long service order and is awarded alternatively with the Order of the Crown as the Order of Leopold is awarded under rare circumstances. The Order currently stands third after the Order of Leopold (1st) and the Order of the Crown (2nd) in the Belgian honors hierarchy.

De Zutter family will be discussed in Chapter 5. Hennie and Guido have three children:

Toni Francis born in Worcester, Massachusetts, on June 9, 1972.

Pascal René, born in Fairfax, Virginia, on April 15, 1980.

Nina Maria, born in Fairfax, Virginia, on April 8, 1983.

XIV.1 Toni Francis

Deboeck oldest son of Guido Deboeck and Hennie De Zutter, was born on June 9, 1972 in Worcester, Massachusetts. He married on October 7, 2006 Olivia Yvonne Lopez in La Porte, Texas. Olivia is the daughter of John and Minnie Lopez of La Porte, Texas.

XIV.2 Pascal René Deboeck, second son of Guido Deboeck and Hennie De Zutter, was born on April 15, 1980 in Fairfax, Virginia. He married Lynn Marie Duesterhaus on October 1, 2005 in South Bend, Indiana. Lynn is the daughter of Judie and Richard Duesterhaus of Vienna, Virginia.

XIV.3 Nina Maria Deboeck, daughter of of Guido Deboeck and Hennie De Zutter, was born on April 8, 1983 in Fairfax, Virginia.

XV. Anastasia Gabriella Deboeck, first born daughter of Pascal and Lynn Deboeck, born on November 14, 2006 in Mishawaka, Indiana.

Chapter 7 provides more details about the 13th, 14th and 15th generations of the Deboeck family.

Table 2.1 shows some interesting statistics about the successive generations of the de Bock family. From it the following observations can be made:

• *The average age at death* of the first five generations of the de Bock family was relatively high; it was 63.5 years.

• It dropped in the next three generations to 61 years, mainly because Egidius "Gillis" de Bock lived only till he was 35 years old (he was born in 1734 and died in 1764). At age 30 he married and had three sons before he died five years later!

• In the nineteenth century two generations of the family died early: Everard died when he was 42 years old and Guillaume died when he was 50 years old. In 1848 there was a potato scarcity in Flanders, which may have caused undernutrition. Guillaume's death may have more to do with heart failure although his death notice did not specify the nature of his short painfull illness.

• In the twentied century Josephine died at age 73, Joseph at age 82, Pierre at age 54, and René at age 71; hence the average increased to 70.

• *The average number of children* for the first 12 generations of the family was 6.6 of which 4.2 were boys and 2.2 were daughters. This average was however raised by Amandus "Amant" de Bock who married three times and had 20 children and by Egidius "Gillis" de Bock who married twice and had 9 children.

• *The average age at marriage* of the Deboeck family taking into account all those who married as of the 14th generation was 25.6 years.

• Francois de Boeck was the l*ongest married* (so far). He married at age 24 and lived until 1724 when he and Anne Maria Jacobs were 50 years married.

Apart from these statistics, this chapter pointed out that there are more than 8,800 people in Belgium who have the name Deboeck or one of its variants. I traced the history of only one branch of this family, the one that started ca. 1530-1540 in Sint-Amands with Gillis de Bock of Little Brabant. There are many more branches that still need to be documented. Some are discussed in Annex 1.

There is so far no firm evidence that all the branches that are mentioned in Annex 1 are related or even have a single ancestor.[38] To explore which branches are or are not related, much more genealogical research will be required. Alternatively, if current day descendants of various Deboeck family branches are willing to take a DNA test, it may be feasible to determine via DNA records, who is related to whom. This will be discussed in Chapter 9 that provides an introduction to the Surname Project Deboeck and an example of how DNA records can be compared. For further information on this Surname Project see

http://www.familytreeDNA.com/public/Deboeck.

---

38. Genetic testing may eventually determine whether there was one common ancestor or whether there were multiple.

Table 2.1 Fifteen generations of the de Bock family of Sint-Amands: some statistics

Gen	Ancestor	Born	Died	Estimated Age at Death	Married on	Spouse	# Children	#Sons	# Daughters	infant deaths**	Age upon first marriage	Years married
	------ 16th century ------											
1	Gillis de Bock	1540										
2	Matheus de Bock	1565	1625	60	1590	Johanna van Praet	8	6	2		25	35
	------ 17th century ------											
3	Amandus "Amant" de Bock	1608	3/22/1681	73	9/3/1627 5/x/1645 1664	Catherina de Smet Elisabeth Verstappen Joanna Mehauden	7 10 3	5 7 1	2 3 2		19 37 56	18 19 17
4	Egidius "Gillis" de Bock	3/2/1637	4/4/1700	63	6/11/1660 9/11/1675	Maria Verheyden Catherina Goossens	4 5	2 3	2 2	1	23 38	15 25
5	Joannes "Jan" De Bo(e)jck	1/27/1663	1717 or 1721	58	8/5/1692	Catherina de Bie	3	1	2		29	29
	------ 18th century ------											
6	Franciscus De Boeck	12/22/1700	8/8/1775	74	5/16/1724	Anna Maria Jacobs	7	2	5		24	50
7	Egidius "Gillis" De Boeck	7/3/1734	2/14/1770	35	8/7/1764	Anna Maria van Dongelbergh	3	3	0	2	30	5
8	Egidius "Gillis" De Boeck	9/13/1765	10/4/1829	64	1791 ?	Anne Doms	7	5	2	2	26	38
	------ 19th century ------											
9	Jean Baptist "Joannes" De Boeck	10/18/1815	5/27/1880	64	11/8/1837	Anne Marie Francisca Van Herp	4	4	0		22	42
10	Everard De Boeck	12/12/1838	9/10/1881	42	5/2/1864	Gertrude Verhaegen	5	3	2	1	26	16
11	Guillaume De Boeck	5/17/1874	4/12/1925	50	12/20/1896	Joanne Nobels	4	3	1		22	28
	------ 20th century ------											
12	Rene Corneille Deboeck	8/13/1913	7/6/1985	71	8/25/1943	Marie Louise Girardin	2	2	0		30	24
13	Guido Deboeck	1/6/1946	na		8/14/1969	Hennie De Zutter	5	2	1	2	23	38*
14	Toni Deboeck Pascal Deboeck Nina Deboeck	6/13/1972 4/15/1980 4/8/1983	na na na		10/7/2006 10/1/2005	Olivia Lopez Lynn Duesterhaus	0 1	0 0	0 1		34 25	1* 2*
	------ 21th century ------											
15	Anastasia Deboeck	11/14/2006	na									
	Average/ancestor->						6.4	4.1	2.2	1.3	25.6	25.6

* as off October 2007
** includes miscarriages, stillborns and infant deaths upto 2 years

60   *Flemish DNA & Ancestry*

Figure 2.16 Views of Vilvoorde in the old days: left to right starting at the top: Our lady of Hope Church of Vilvoorde, Avenue J-B. Nowe, the market place of Vilvoorde, the Burned Bridge, the New Lane with monument W. Tyndall (just opposite from where I was brought up) and the Avenue Henry 1st.

Descendants of Gillis de Bock

Gillis DE BOCK (1530 -)
b. 1530-1540, Sint-Amands

└ Matheus DE BOCK (1580 -)
  b. 1580, Sint-Amands

    └ Amandus DE BOCK (1608 - 1681)
     b. 1608, Sint-Amands
     d. 1681, Lippelo

       └ Egidius DE BOCK (1637 - 1700)
        b. 1637, Lippelo
        d. 1700, Malderen
        & Maria VERHEYDEN
        & Catharina GOOSSENS

          └ Joannes DE BOECK (1663 - 1717)
           b. 1663, Malderen
           d. 1717, Londerzeel
           & Catherina DE BIE

             └ Franciscus DE BOECK (1700 - 1775)
              b 1700
              d. 8 Aug 1775, Grimbergen
              & Anne Marie JACOBS (1700 - 1764)
              b. 14 Mar 1700, Grimbergen
              d. 3 Oct 1764, Grimbergen
              m. 16 May 1724, Grimbergen

                └ Egidius DE BOECK (1734 - 1770)
                 b. 3 Jul 1734, Grimbergen
                 d. 14 Feb 1770, Grimbergen
                 & Anna VAN DONGELBERGH (1742 -)
                 b. 24 May 1742, Grimbergen
                 dp. Grimbergen
                 m. 7 Aug 1764, Grimbergen

                   └ Egidius DE BOECK (1765 - 1829)
                    b. 13 Sep 1765, Grimbergen
                    d. 4 Oct 1829, Grimbergen
                    & Anne DOMS (1769 -)
                    b. 11 Nov 1769, Grimbergen
                    bp. Grimbergen
                    m. 8 Jan 1792, Vilvoorde

Figure 2.15 Family tree of the de Bock/De Boeck family 1530-1540 till present.

Descendants of Gillis de Bock
(continued)

Jean-Baptiste DEBOECK (1815 - 1880)
b. 18 Oct 1815, Grimbergen
d. 27 May 1880, Vilvoorde
& Anne Marie Francisca VAN HERP (1810 - 1886)
b. 1 Jul 1810, Humbeek
d. 23 Jun 1886, Vilvoorde
m 8 Nov 1837, Grimbergen

    Evrard DEBOECK (1838 - 1909)
    b. 12 Dec 1838
    d. 1909
    & Gertrude VERHAEGEN (1840 - 1917)
    b 1 Feb 1840, Vilvoorde
    d. 30 Jan 1917
    m 2 May 1864, Vilvoorde

        Guillaume DEBOECK (1874 - 1925)
        b. 17 May 1874
        d. 12 Apr 1925, Ukkel
        & Joanna NOBELS (1876 - 1942)
        b. 29 Jan 1876
        d. 4 May 1942, Vilvoorde
        m. 20 Dec 1896, Vilvoorde

            Rene DEBOECK (1913 - 1985)
            b. 25 Aug 1913, Vilvoorde
            d. 6 Jul 1985, Vilvoorde
            & Marie-Louise GIRARDIN, (1918 - 2001)
            b. 17 Feb 1918, Sint-Ulriks-Kapelle
            d. 6 Feb 2001, Jette
            m 25 Aug 1943, Sint-Ulriks-Kapelle

                Guido DEBOECK, (1946 -)
                b. 6 Jan 1946, Etterbeek
                & Hennie DE ZUTTER (1946 -)
                b. 29 Aug 1946, Blankenberge
                m. 14 May 1969, Leuven

                    Toni DEBOECK, (1972 -)
                    b 9 Jun 1972, Worcester, Mass

                    Pascal DEBOECK, (1980 -)
                    b 15 Apr 1980, Fairfax , Va

                    Nina DEBOECK, (1983 -)
                    b. 8 Apr 1983, Fairfax , Va

Chapter 3
Deboeck Brothers: Entrepreneurs in embroidery and lace making (1875-1968)

Everard De Boeck, my great-grandfather, was born in 1838, the year a peace treaty was signed by the great European powers that confirmed Belgium as an independent state. Belgium had declared its independence in 1830 but the Dutch did not recognize Belgium till 1839.

Everard, the oldest son of Jean-Baptist and Anna Maria Jacobs, married Gertrude Verhaegen in 1864. They had five children including three sons: Jozef, Guillaume and Victor. A chart of all the descendants of Everard De Boeck is shown in Figure 3.1.

Guillaume was my grandfather. He married Joanne Nobels in December 1896, five months before the birth of Josephine, their first child. Guillaume probably got to know Joanne while he (and possibly she) was working in an embroidery factory in Vilvoorde. Just after the turn of the century Guillaume stopped working for someone else and launched his own embroidery factory. The enterprise that he started survived the next fifty years.

Guillaume died in 1925, a month before reaching his fifty-first birthday. Joanne Nobels and her children continued the enterprise; she kept it alive until her children were ready to take over. In 1941 Joanne's children formally established the Deboeck Brothers Ltd. (Gebroeders Deboeck PVBA), which they managed for some 30 years.

This company produced mechanical lace for curtains and furniture decorations, which was sold in Belgium as well as in several European countries. Guillaume's enterprise grew into a sizable and profitable company that sustained three families over several decades.

In this chapter I trace back the life of Guillaume De Boeck, his wife Joanne and their children. I focus on the founding father, his sons and their descendants. I will also briefly outline the business that Victor, his brother, started. To understand the context in which mechanical lace making was started it is useful to first learn, if you do not already know, the history of lace making in Flanders.[1]

---

1. An earlier draft of this chapter has been published in Belgian Laces, the official quarterly bulletin of The Belgian Researchers, Belgian American Heritage Association in Indiana. The first part of this chapter appeared in volume 29 #111, January 2007.

Descendants of Everard De Boeck

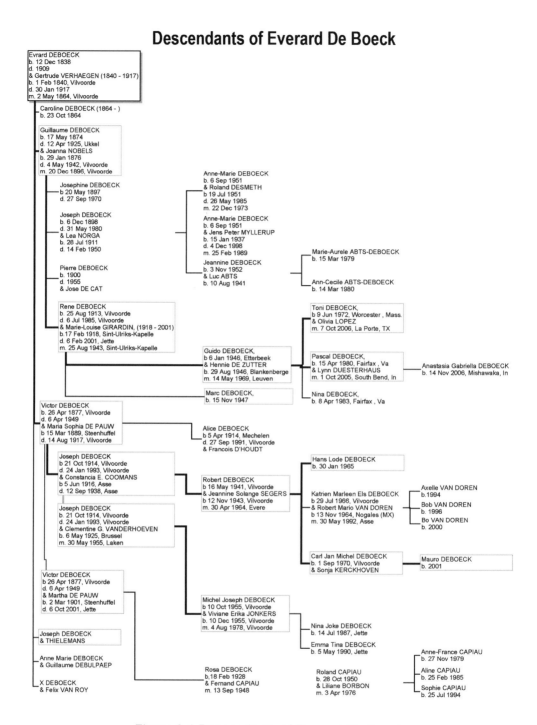

Figure 3.1 Descendants of Everard De Boeck

Brief History of Lace making in Flanders

According to Pat Earnshaw, the word "lace" is derived from the Latin *laqueus,* meaning a noose or a hole outlined by a rope, string or thread.[2] So the term "lace" covers a great variety of ornamental openwork fabrics formed by the looping, plaiting, twisting or knotting of threads of flax, silk, gold, silver, cotton, mohair or aloe; whether done by hand or by machine.

The origin of lace is unclear. Some authors suggest that the manufacturing of lace started during ancient Rome. This is based on the discovery of small bone cylinders in the shape of bobbins. The ancient Persians, Greeks, Chinese, and Egyptians made a kind of lace, but little is known about its appearance. The arts of drawn thread work and netting practiced by the ancient Egyptians were completely lost for centuries. They were rediscovered in the 15th century in Italy.

The first references to lace can be found in the Milanese Sforza family in 1493.[3] The earliest specimens of Italian lace were produced in convents. Nuns had the time, patience, and skill to produce these works of art.

In the sixteenth century, Emperor Charles the Fifth decreed that lace making was to be taught in schools and convents. During the Renaissance and Enlightenment, the making of lace was firmly based in the domain of fashion. Lace was designed to replace embroidery so that with ease one could transform dresses to follow different styles of fashion. Unlike embroidery, lace could be removed from a costume or dress and be replaced.

The history of lace making in Flanders that runs from the mid sixteenth to the mid twentieth century[4] is long because craftsmen and designers adapted to constantly changing styles and techniques.

Why did lace making develop in Flanders? Flanders provided all the essential ingredients to make lace: it had mainly sandy soil, skilled labor and capital.

The sandy soil of Flanders was perfect for growing flax, the oldest and strongest vegetable fiber, ideal for lace making. Flanders

2. Pat Earnshaw, *The Identification of Lace,* Shire Publications Ltd, Buckinghamshire, UK, 1980.

3. Sforza was a ruling family of Renaissance Italy, based in Milan. The dynasty was founded by Muzio Attendolo, called Sforza (from *sforzare,* to exert or force) (Cotignola, 1369 - near Pescara, 1424) a condottiere from the Romagna serving the Angevin kings of Naples. He was the most successful dynast of the condottieri. His son Francesco Sforza ruled Milan for the first half of the Renaissance era, acquiring the title of Duke of Milan from the extinct Visconti family in 1447. While there were many good rulers in the family, there were also a number of despots, many of whom were mentally unstable. This family would later join with the Borgia Family, through the arranged marriage of Lucrezia Borgia to Giovanni Sforza (who was the son of Galeazzo Maria Sforza).

4. Margaret Vincent, *A Delicate Art: Flemish lace* 1700-1940; L. Paulis, Pour connaitre La Dentelle.

was long known for producing the best quality flax thread in the world.

In the 1700s one fourth of the population in Flanders was involved in growing flax, spinning linen threads, and weaving linen fabrics. Anne Marie Claeys wrote that during the sixteenth and seventeenth centuries when lace making knew its biggest growth, many Flemish lace makers were sent abroad to teach other women the art of lace making. Nuns traveled with their lace pillows to India and China; others emigrated to America, Canada, New Zealand or Australia. This is why Flemish lace is nowadays being made in India and China where they continue to make lace based on Flemish techniques.[5]

Flanders had plenty of skilled labor as well as capital. It also had good communications, especially with Spain, which from 1516 onwards claimed Flanders as part of the *Spanish Netherlands.*

The earliest lace dated from the mid sixteenth century and evolved from embroidery.[6] *Embroidered laces* that have a woven fabric base[7] appeared primarily on the seams, cuffs and collars of garments. This can be seen on many portraits painted by Flemish and Dutch painters. The Spanish dictated the form of early Flemish braided laces.

Late in the sixteenth century, Flemish lace was identifiable according to the place it was produced. Flanders abandoned embroidery in favor of braiding (which is like twisting three or more threads into a thick cord). As the threads were wound on bobbins, the technique was called bobbin lace.

Bobbin lace[8] is related to braided work: several threads are secured at the top of the pattern and are twisted by hand to create a design. The pattern rests on a pillow into which controlling pins are pushed. The excess threads are wound on long thin bobbins. There are two kinds of bobbin lace: continuous or straight and non-continuous bobbin lace. *Continuous bobbin lace* uses one set of threads which stretch the entire length of the work. Both the patterned areas and the background are created simultaneously. Non-continuous bobbin lace is created in two stages. The design elements are made first, and then linked together with net or with braids.

Bobbin lace is different from needle lace, which originated in Italy. Needle lace is developed from embroidered lace. Over time, greater amounts of ground were removed, leaving larger areas open. Ultimately, the entire ground fabric was dispensed with

---

5. Claeys, Anne-Marie: "In Brugge herleeft het kantklossen" (In Bruges lace making is reviving), *Libelle-Rosita,* no. 22, June 4, 1982.

6. There are important differences between embroidery and lace: the latter is worked on the basis of a paper pattern, on a net (tulle), or on a combination of both.

7. If this fabric ground does not have natural holes, then certain threads are cut or pushed aside to form gaps. Needlework embellishments are added either to the woven fabric or as fillings between the gaps.

8. Charlotte Kellog, *Bobbins of Belgium.*

so that the needlework was grounded only by a cord, temporarily or tacked to the paper pattern.

The differences between the bobbin and the needle lace categories come down to the following: needle lace is made with one thread and one needle; bobbin lace can be based on many threads and many needles.[9] The Flemish braided laces stayed in fashion for 75 years.

In the seventeenth century, the wealthy Dutch steered away from the stiff collars and adopted falling collars. Jan Vermeer (1632-1675), a Dutch painter, painted "The Lace Maker," (see Figure 3.2) which shows a lady bent over a cushion with her fingers moving the bobbins.

In the latter half of the century, fashion shifted to France and the court of Louis XIV. Flemish lace makers experimented with less geometric forms, barely patterned webs, and designs that resembled a traditional woven fabric.

In Binche, a town in Hainaut province near Valenciennes, a continuous bobbin lace was made with designs that include barely recognizable flowers and tiny leaf patterns. It was called *Binche lace.* It was usually two inches wide with straight edges on a ground that is often based on what was called a *snowflake* stitch.

Another continuous bobbin lace made near Antwerp consisted of symmetrical designs mainly of potted flowers. This type was called *Pottenkant* ("potten" is Flemish for pots) and was heavier than Binche lace.

The Dutch closed the river Scheldt in 1585, which effectively halted the production of Pottenkant; manufacturing of lace in Binche continued. Then after the French were defeated and the Treaty of Utrecht was signed in 1713, Flanders was put under Austrian control and renamed *the Austrian Netherlands.*

Binche lace designs made in Valenciennes evolved in the eighteenth century to a distinct type of lace called Valenciennes. This is a continuous bobbin lace based on a woven background surrounded by a row of tiny pinholes, but no cordonnet ("traceerdraad"

Figure 3.2 Above: "The Lace Maker" (De Kantwerkster) by Jan Vermeer, Dutch painter 1632-1675. Louvre, Paris; Below: two lace makers in Brugge.

9. In addition to the above main categories of lace there is imitation lace, which mimics embroidered, needle or bobbin laces, but uses newer techniques. Included in this category are crocheted lace, tatting, tape lace, appliqué work, and all machine made laces. Source: Margaret Vincent, *A Delicate Art: Flemish Lace, 1700-1940.*

in Dutch). The ground developed a characteristic round or diamond shape mesh. The records of Valenciennes show that the eighteenth-century lace industry moved steadily into the industrial age.

Women and young girls made lace. Some women helped with the agrarian work, but when there was little to do on the land they worked on spinning, weaving, and lace at home to provide additional income.

Lots of farmers in the first half of the eighteenth century had a weaving loom at home. These looms could occupy four to five people who each produced four to five *ell* per day (an ell is 27 inches). Many young girls who lived in charity institutions learned lace making from nuns; they worked long days for hourly wages that were miserable.

In Mechelen and Brussels new forms of lace developed. Mechelen, which is *Malines* in French, produced *Mechlin,* a continuous bobbin lace made with designs that include complex floral arrangements on a ground. Mechlin uses a wide variety of stitches according to traditional patterns, but with no original designs, meandering vines and assorted textures.

A variation of Mechlin is *Point d'Angleterre*,[10] also a continuous bobbin lace. From the back, the ground threads are visible as they pass unused under the toile (background) work. Other variations came from Lille in France. *Lille lace* is similar to Mechlin; it generally uses a simple background; and appears slightly fuzzy.

Mechelin, Point d'Angleterre and Lille laces were well suited for narrow edgings, lappets,[11] sleeve ruffles, and neckties, which were part of the fashion in the eighteenth century.

In Brussels and Brabant, non-continuous lace developed. *Brussels lace* is very loosely woven toile, grounded by either mesh or braids that link individually created small ornaments, and woven motifs such as flowers or leaves.[12]

---

10. Both the art and the fine materials for lace making were limited in England. In 1662 such huge sums of money were going out of the country for the material that Parliament prohibited its importation. This posed a problem for merchants who had to fill large orders for the court of Charles II. They began smuggling the choicest Brussels lace into England and selling it as "English point." Today Brussels lace is still called *point d'Angleterre.* Source: In *Britannica Student Encyclopedia.* Retrieved July 18, 2006, from Encyclopædia Britannica.

11. A lappet is a decorative flap or fold in a ceremonial headdress or garment. They were a feature of women's headgear until the early twentieth century. They remain strongly associated with religion. Each bishop's mitre contains two lappets. The most famous usage of lappets occurs on the Papal Tiara.

12. Brussels lace or ribbon lace is lace that today is manufactured on a larger scale. It is a very strong lace used for house linen, such as tablecloths, napkins, place mats, doilies, runners, etc. Again the pattern is drawn on paper. First the lace maker will sew the ribbon onto the paper following the design. Then she will fill up the empty spaces with a needle using a variety of stitches. The paper is not pierced; the result being that

By the end of the eighteenth century and the turn of the nineteenth century, social and political upheavals changed the dress code. Women wore silk and cotton dresses embellished with embroidered muslin rather than lace. There was instability in Flemish lace production and lace making came under the threat of machines. Inventors and engineers had experimented since the mid eighteenth century with machines that simulated the motions of a hand knitter. More about the machines that were invented can be found in the next section.

The Flemish lace making industry would not have survived were it not for a turning point in 1830 when Belgium became independent. New nationalism emerged and local industries revived. Flemish lace makers created two new types of lace: *Duchesse and Point de Gaze.*

Duchesse lace, also called *Pointe de Flandre* is widely regarded as the most beautiful of the pillow (or bobbin) laces.[13] It is pure white and has a graceful rhythmic pattern. The designs consist of leaves, flowers, and scrolls. It emerged from the eighteenth century Brussels lace: it is a non-continuous bobbin lace; toile woven in whole and half stitches embellished with rolled work; generally grounded with braids.[14] Since one could purchase single elements, Duchesse lace became available to a wide segment of society. Bridal veils of the Flemish Duchesse lace are often heirloom treasures.[15]

---

only the paper and the ribbon are attached to one another. Finally, when all the empty spaces are filled in, the tacking thread is cut on the back of the paper; the item of lace is removed and the paper pattern can be used again. The result is a finished item of lace, a corner, border, or centre piece, which may be then applied on Flemish linen to finish tablecloths, place mats, handkerchiefs, and a variety of other pieces.

13. Duchesse lace is manufactured on a "carreau" or cushion, taken from the Flemish word "kussen," on which the paper pattern is pinned. This pattern is the design to be realized in lace. The lace maker generally works with 22 bobbins ("klosjes" in Dutch), two of which are called the conductors. The more complicated the design, the more bobbins have to be used. For a Binche "Point de Fée" up to 200 bobbins have to be utilized. The conductors are woven from left to right, and from right to left. The end of the row having been reached, the thread is held in place with a pin. The conductor's threads form the weft of the work, while the other bobbins form the *warp,* or the vertical threads of the design. To make the corner of a handkerchief, the lace maker will have to work for about three days, depending upon her level of skill.

14. It could have been named after Marie-Henriette, wife of King Leopold II, also Duchesse of Brabant.

15. Duchesse or Princess lace is still manufactured today and is mainly used for wedding veils, christening dresses, mantillas, and other ceremonial occasions. Nowadays, the net is made by machine. The flowers, stalks, and leaves are applied on the net by hand with a needle. In former times the net was also handmade, either by needle or by bobbins. This handmade net was given the Dutch name "Drochel."

Point de Gaze lace is more original and more impressive than Duchesse. It is a needle lace; toile of various Alençon filling stitches, surrounded by a cordonnet; a ground of needle made loops; various floral designs, including the typical tiered rose pedals. It was made in great quantities and contained Victorian elements.

Late in the nineteenth century, related to Duchesse lace and the English Honiton or bobbin lace was *Rosaline,* a non-continuous pillow lace based on toile of whole or half stitches with some rolled work and with crinkled edges; sometimes embellished with small needle made rings.[16]

The designs of Rosaline consist of a random assortment of poorly drawn flowers and leaves linked together by haphazard braids. It was named after the Italian needle lace with the similar look. Despite its lack of style, Rosaline became a very popular lace, which survived into the twentieth century.

The end of Flemish lace making as an art came as a result of the deterioration of style in Duchesse and Point de Gaze and the tremendous popularity of mediocre Rosaline. Advanced technology, which I will discuss in the next section, allowed mechanical duplication of the most complex styles.

Today, two main techniques are still practiced in Flanders. The first, a needle lace, is still manufactured in the region of Alost (Aalst). It is called Renaissance or Brussels lace because it is mostly sold in Brussels. The second type, the bobbin lace, is a specialty of Bruges. This is a very expensive type of lace and is therefore no longer manufactured for commercial purposes. There are no lace factories anymore in Brussels or Bruges but some individuals still make lace.

Some examples of Flemish laces are shown in Figures 3.3 to 3.5. Pedigrees of the various kinds of lace discussed are shown in Figure 3.6.[17]

---

16. Rosepoint or Rosaline lace is made with a needle. It is considered to be the most delicate and precious of all laces. The pattern is first designed on paper, often reinforced with a piece of tissue, on which the design is realized. The design usually represents a rose or some other flower. To start, the lace maker elaborates the flower's outline with a thicker thread, so to add relief to the work. The next stage is to fill in the interior of the flower design with much finer thread and a variety of different stitches. A fine handkerchief medallion takes three days' work. To produce larger pieces, all the medallions are sewn together with a thread that is so fine that it can only be detected by the eye of an expert. A certificate dating from 1922 states that the veil made for Queen Elizabeth required 12,000 hours of work and is made up with 12,000,000 stitches.

17. For more details on types and techniques of lace making see: Heather Toomer, *Antique Lace, Identifying Types and Techniques;* Emily Reigate, *An Illustrated Guide to Lace;* Marian Powys, *Lace and Lace Making;* Ernest Erick Pfannschmidt, *Twentieth Century Lace;* J Coene, "Lace Lexicon," Waasmunster (http://users.belgacom.net/coene) July, 2002.

Figure 3.3 Example of *Flemish Rococo lace:* a flower arrangement composed of little flowers with small threads. Made in the 19th and 20th century mainly in Bruges, Brussels, Alost and Tielt (from Deboeck Personal Lace Collection).

Figure 3.4 Example of *Duchesse Lace of Bruges:* very fine lace with flower motives connected with threads. Typical flower in the middle surrounded by detailed motifs composed of flowers and leaves around it. Originated in 1850 under the guidance of Maria-Hendrika, wife of Leopold II, who was Duchesse of Brabant (from Deboeck Personal Lace Collection).

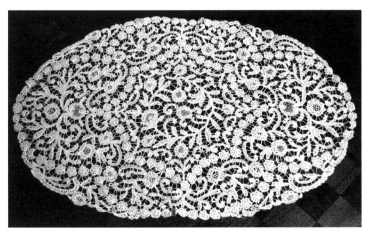

Figure 3.5 Example of *Brussels Rosaline Pearl Lace:* late 19th century handmade lace in rococo style containing small figures connected with irregular threads. Made in Alost, Erpe-Mere and Liedekerk. Called "Brussels" Rosaline, because it mainly was sold in Brussels at the Market Place (from Deboeck Personal Lace Collection)

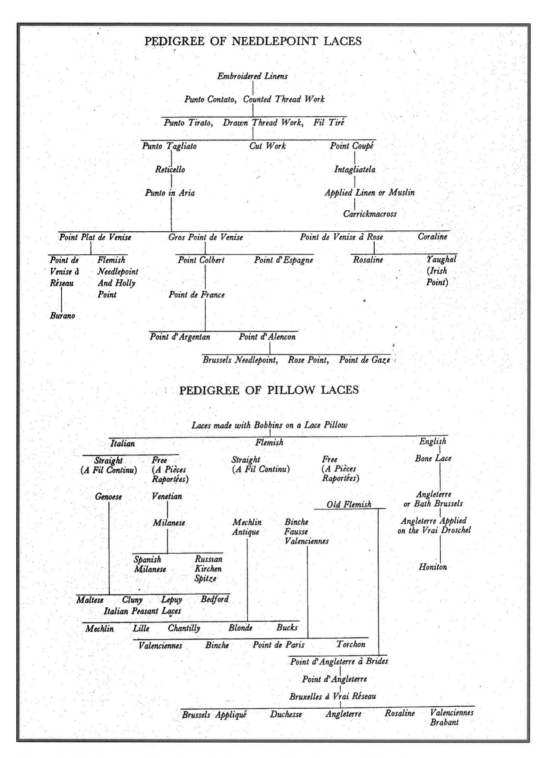

Figure 3.6 Pedigree of Needlepoint Laces and Pedigree of Pillow Laces.
Source: Marian Powys: *Lace and Lacemaking,* Dover Publications, New York, 1982

Guillaume Deboeck launches embroidery and mechanical lace factory

Guillaume De Boeck died in 1925 before his fifty-first birthday. The death notice of Willem (Guillaume) De Boeck read: husband of Joanna Nobels, born in Vilvoorde on May 17, 1874, and deceased on April 12, 1925, provided with the Holy Sacraments after a short but painful sickness in Ukkel, Institut des deux Alice.[18] The notice mentioned Joanna Nobels, his widow, his four children, Josephina, Joseph, Pieter and René, and the families De Boeck and Nobels.

What can one write about a grandfather who died twenty-one years before I was born? There was no chance to get to know him. Guillaume did not write books or perform great deeds that attracted the attention of historians. So how can one capture his life?

It is amazing what one can find once one starts doing research. There is the basic data that can be extracted from birth-, marriage-, and death certificates. There are the stories that were told about the deceased. There are shoeboxes or photo albums with pictures, unfortunately not always labeled.[19] Assembling what can be found often leads to an impression of the life of a deceased. If in addition one reads about the history of the time when someone lived and/or the profession he/she was involved in, then one can put together an image of what his/her life was.

In what follows an attempt is made to reconstruct some parts, maybe milestones, in the life of Guillaume De Boeck who lived around the turn of the century and was a pioneer in lace making and in many other ways, at least that is what his grandson thinks.

You recall that Guillaume was the son of Everard De Boeck and Gertrude Verhaegen (see Figure 3.7) who both were born in Vilvoorde. Guillaume's father was thus the first De Boeck who made it to the town.

Guillaume married Joanne Nobels in December 1896. They had their first child at a young age: Joanne was 21 years and Guillaume was 23 when Josephine was born on May 20, 1897. Eighteen months later, Joseph was born. He was born on December 6, a day that in Europe is called Saint

Figure 3.1 Gertrude Verhaegen, mother of Guillaume De Boeck (1840-1917)

---

18. Sometimes death notices provide indications of the cause of death, for example in this case "a short painful sickness." As we shall see later this is important information that can help to establish a medical pedigree.

19. Sometimes there are homemade films. Our children and grandchildren may in the future be interested in them as well as in our computer files, CDs, bookmarks, blogs, and websites that were created.

Nick ("Sint Nikolaas") day. Two years later another son was born who was named Pieter, but throughout his life was called Pierre. Then thirteen years later they had another son, René Corneille, born on August 25, 1913. The age difference between Josephine, Joseph and Pierre on the one hand and René on the other hand is an important fact that will explain a great deal of what happened fifty years later.

No information about the education of Guillaume was found but it is not unreasonable to assume that he finished primary school. Guillaume probably attended a Catholic primary school from 1880 to 1886.[20] There was only one municipal school, one Catholic school and nine private schools in Vilvoorde.[21] Nuns of the order of Ursulinen ran Our Lady of Consolation ("Onze Lieve Vrouw Ten Troost") that was located right across from where Guillaume lived. However, this school was for girls only. In 1879 another Catholic school opened in Vilvoorde; it was the "Institut Notre Dame". This was the precursor of Our Beloved Mother High School ("Onze Lieve Vrouw College") that in 1905 was expanded to include secondary education.[22]

Since secondary education was only added in 1905, it is unlikely that Guillaume attended high school. His sons, Joseph, Pierre and René completed high school. I attended classes at the same school; started primary schooling in 1951 and completed high school in 1962. The first three years of secondary education I attended at the Our Beloved Mother High School, the Flemish name of what used to be the Institut Notre Dame; thereafter I completed high school in Saint Peters High School (Sint Pieters College) in Jette, Brussels. So, the *Institut Notre Dame* trained quite a number of Deboecks.

---

20. In 1842 the central government of Belgium, the new independent kingdom, set out to reorganize primary education. It recognized the need for a compromise between the desires of the state and those of the church. In 1879 the "School Strife" broke out, an open warfare between the state and the church. This was the result of a new law passed by the "liberal" majority government, which wanted complete control of education by the state. As a result so-called "free schools" organized by the church to provide education with religious content were no longer permitted. The municipal councils appointed the teachers who held a diploma from the "Royal Normal School" for teacher training. In 1884, a newly elected Catholic government canceled the earlier law and returned the situation to where it was after 1842. This school battle continued until 1958 when all parties compromised and agreed to the "School Pact."

21. A.L.E Verheyden, "Vilvoordse scholen vroeger en nu", 1974.

22. Secondary education in Vilvoorde actually started with the establishment of an agricultural ("tuinlandbouw") school in 1864 and a technical drawing school in 1883.

Figure 3.8 Guillaume Deboeck and Johanna Nobels on their wedding day, December 20, 1896.

Early in his life Guillaume worked in an embroidery factory in Vilvoorde. There were several at the time: L. A. Legrand, J. B. Vanden Breeden, and Marcelis. The history of all three of these can be found in Jos Lauwers.[23] A summary of the history of L. A. Le-Grand, the largest of all three manufacturers, is provided below.

Lace making in Vilvoorde from Coosemans to Legrand

The industrialization of embroidery and lace making started in the nineteenth century. The production of mechanical tule (a transparent background used for lace making) became possible through a machine invented in the U. K. by Heatcothe in 1806.

In 1817 Dendermonde became the first city to produce mechanical tule, which was comparable with the manual made tule used in Chantilly and Lille lace. This tule made by André Coosemans in Dendermonde, was used for embroidery.

Joshua Heilmann from Mülhausen invented in 1834 automatic embroidery. He tried to export his machine to France, but finally sold it to Rittmeier from Sant Gallen in Switzerland.

In 1846 Louis-Alexander Legrand established in Brussels an enterprise to produce tule. In 1862 André Coosemans brought his tule operation to Vilvoorde.

In 1874 Louis-Alexander Legrand became a partner of "Coosemans and Cie" and was nominated head of the firm. Four years later this firm was renamed Etbs L. A. Legrand, also called, "Het kantfabriek van Vilvoorde" (The lace factory of Vilvoorde).

Louis-Alexander introduced mechanical production of embroidery in Belgium in 1880. Because of the popularity and the demand, his firm made a rapid expansion and was imitated by other firms in Vilvoorde; among others, Guillaume De Boeck et Enfants. Louis-Alexander died in 1905 but left behind ten children of which three sons, Alexander, Louis and Henri, who already in 1893 succeeded their father. His sons developed new industry branches for the production of lace on tule to be used for curtains.

In 1895 the firm became a collection of enterprises and in 1912 got the legal status of a "Naamloze Venootschap" which is like incorporation (Inc.) in the States. Soon the staff was composed of 689 employees. Each of the three sons of Louis-Alexander took charge of a separate branch of the company. It was Louis Legrand, the second son of Louis-Alexander, who took over the production of embroidery and macramé lace.

Swiss stitching and Schiffli machines were deployed. The first 9 yards Schiffli machines were introduced in 1905. In 1911 another revolution happened with the introduction of Jacquard machines. The first were bought in 1923. By 1928 the offices and workspaces of the firm in Vilvoorde and Bevere covered 4 hectares and employed 750 people.

In 1939 it was Henri, a son of Louis Legrand, who continued the embroidery and macramé lace making. Around 1965 there was another modernization through the procurement of six new Zangs looms which could produce simultaneously two pieces of 15 yards (or two of ten yards). The embroidery still worked till 1976 after which lace making by Henri Legrand, was stopped.

The third son of Louis-Alexander, Henry Legrand, passed his company to his son Joseph, who established the N. V. Manufacture J. Legrand that is still in business today. Under the direction of Roger Legrand and his son Vianney, their factory on the Withernstraat 41 in Vilvoorde, concentrates on the distribution and production of custom made curtains and bedcovers.

Source: E. Van Noten, Het Kantfabriek van Vilvoorde, Vlaamsche Drukkerij, Leuven, 1907.

---

23. Jos Lauwers, Van Lakenweverij tot kantwerk en wanttapijten, binnen de driehoek Brussel-Leuven-Mechelen.

Sometime in the early 1900s Guillaume started a business of his own. An old photo of unknown date shows a factory called "G. De Boeck et Enfants, Vilvoorde," in other words, G. De Boeck and Children.

Another photo shows the entire family, except René who was not born yet in 1913. The date of this photo can be derived from the Holy Communion dress worn by Josephine. Holy Communion in the Catholic Church is performed at age 12; Josephine was born in 1897, hence the photo is from circa 1909.

Judging from the suite, the dress and the jewelry (the watch of Guillaume and necklace worn by Joanne), this family photo demonstrates that in 1909 Guillaume and his family were well off. I therefore derive that Guillaume was already in a business of his own by 1909.

Figure 3.9 Factory in Vilvoorde called "G. De Boeck et Enfants"

Figure 3.10 Guillaume De Boeck and family, circa 1909. From l. to r. Joseph (oldest son), Guillaume, Josephine (oldest daughter), Joanne Nobels (wife of Guillaume) and Pieter (Pierre).

Further evidence that Guillaume was in business of his own can be derived from several photos that were first found in 2005. One photo showed Guillaume and family in a factory.[24] The photo (see Figure 3.11) shows the entire family: Guillaume at the *pantograph* (see below), Joanne showing off an embroidery piece, Josephine behind a thread machine, and the boys in front. One of the boys is holding an oilcan to oil heavy machinery. This is Pierre who would later in life turn out to become the technical "engineer" who would take care of the machinery. He was also the one who later in life would help my brother and me build many things.

This kind of total family involvement in the enterprise prevailed for more than half a century. The enterprise launched by Guillaume would involve only the immediate family; no one else would get a role, a function, or even shares in the company. This was strictly a family enterprise (a decision that much later would prove to be fatal)!

This photo of the family at work also provides proof that Guillaume must have started his own business at pretty young age. If this picture is from circa 1907-1910, then it shows that at age 33 Guillaume was already a few years in business.

Figure 3.11 Guillaume in the embroidery factory. Front: Joseph and Pierre and unknown worker; back row: Joanne Nobels, Josephine, unknown worker and Guillaume. Photo circa 1907-10.

---

24. By sheer accident, in 2005 in a box among many other old photos, kept by Anne-Marie Deboeck, daughter of Joseph I found a photo that shows Guillaume, his wife, their daughter and their two sons at work.

The enterprise that Guillaume started was one of making *macramé lace.* This is a coarse lace made of twine, used to decorate windows and furniture.[25] Macramé lace was made mechanically. Mechanical embroidery and lace making relied on technology that emerged in the late 1800s and became available around the turn of the century.

Guillaume probably started with two Schiffli machines,[26] which is all that could fit in the workplace ("ateliers") his enterprise occupied in the Nieuwelaan in Vilvoorde. In 1910, the first "continuous thread" frames with shuttles appeared. The production principle was not the same anymore. Instead of using the hand embroidering technique, it worked according to the sewing machine technique. The design was driven by a punch card, called *jacquard.* The working of a Jacquard loom, as well as the process of producing macramé lace with Jacquard machines is explained on page 83.

A postcard dated March 2, 1925,[27] contains the following:

"Mijneer Jacqard, Joseph et Consort, Aucun autre n'y appartient, ce qui vraiment fait exception en Belgique, et du materiel compossé de métiers jacquard. Zorg maar dat ge voor zooveel jacquards werk hebt, daar twyfel ik aan, want de commerce gaat heel slecht, en er is een grote crisis op handen. Vele groeten aan mijnheer Joseph Jacquard"

---

25. Definition taken from *The Nuttall Encyclopædia,* edited by the Reverend James Wood (1907).

26. The development of machine embroidery took place in the 1800s. Joshua Heilmann from Mulhouse in Switzerland worked on the design of a *hand embroidery machine.* The first machines were *arm frames:* an embroidery arm frame is a frame that reproduces exactly the movement of an embroiderer's hand. This allows the production of very fine work. It is made of a vertical frame on which an embroidery textile is stretched. The frame is mobile and is moved by a lever, called *pantograph,* activated by a worker according to a drawing on a board.

This revolutionized the embroidery industry. The *shuttle embroidery* and the *chain stitch embroidery* methods quickly followed Heilmann's invention. The beginnings of shuttle embroidery dates back to the 1860's when Isaac Groebli, from St. Gallen, Switzerland, was inspired by the work produced on the sewing machine. Around 1870's there were fourteen companies manufacturing embroidery machines in Switzerland. The looms used multiple needles and were an unbelievable improvement over the age-old process of stitching by hand. They were, however, powered manually.

Immediately afterwards, Issac Groebli of Switzerland invented the first practical Schiffli embroidery machine. This machine was based on the principals introduced by the newly invented sewing machines. Groebli's machine utilized the combination of a continuously threaded needle and shuttle containing a bobbin of thread. The shuttle itself looked similar to the hull of a sailboat. "Schiffli" means "little boat" in the Swiss dialect of the German language, so his machine came to be known as a *schiffli machine.*

27. Addressed to Etbs. G. De Bouck, Bureau 187-189, Nouveau Boulevard. Ateliers 9,11, Rue de la Coline, Vilvoorde,

It is not immediately clear what to derive from this postcard written in 1925 partially in French and partially in Dutch. The Dutch sentence clearly expresses reservation of deploying Jacquard machines because of the "big (economic) crisis that is coming." The other sentence translated from French means "It really is an exception in Belgium, if anyone can make good use of all the functions provided by Jacquard looms." This could mean that Jacquard looms created such a wide variety of possibilities that only a few in Belgium could realize (or see) their full potential.[28]

Thirty years later, René Deboeck wrote to his brother Joseph (who handed over the day-to-day operations to him) that "in all honesty, I have respect for your persistence displayed after the death of our father, who hesitated about signing the contract for the modernization of the Schiffli machines...."

This provides evidence that Schiffli machines were used in the enterprise and that around 1925 Jacquard machines were considered. Guillaume reluctantly signed the contract for the modernization of the Schiffli machines before he died. This is how several Jacquard machines were bought in 1925, just two years after Legrand, who was the major competitor of De Boeck et Enfants enterprise, had introduced the same machines. Shortly after signing the contract for the Jacquard machines Guillaume died at age 50, most likely of a heart problem.[29]

Figure 3.12 The early Jacquard machines installed at the De Boeck factory in the Rue de la Colline (Hellingen straat)

28. If Guillaume Deboeck saw the potential of Jacquard machines while others did not, he must have been my grandfather because in the late seventies I saw the potential of personal computers while many could not imagine that eventually we all would use them for a wide variety of applications.

29. His sons Joseph, Pierre and possibly René also died from heart related problems. Pierre died in 1955 of a stroke; Joseph had several heart attacks in the late sixties and seventies. René suffered from high blood pressure and hypertension until he died on July 6, 1985. The importance of this will be discussed in the Epilogue of this book.

The Jacquard loom

The Jacquard loom is a mechanical loom, invented by Joseph Marie Jacquard in 1801, which used the holes punched in pasteboard punch cards to control the weaving of patterns in fabric. The loom enabled even amateur weavers to weave complex designs. Each punch card corresponded to one row of the design and the cards were strung together in order.

Each hole in the card corresponds to a "Bolus" hook, which can either be up or down. The hook raises or lowers the harness, which carries and guides the warp thread so that the weft will either lie above or below it. The sequence of raised and lowered threads is what creates the pattern. Each hook can be connected via the harness to a number of threads, allowing more than one repeat of a pattern. A loom with a 400 hook head might have 4 threads connected to each hook, giving you a fabric that is 1600 warp ends wide with four repeats of the weave going across.

It was the first machine to use punch cards to control a sequence of operations. Although it did no computations based on them, it is considered an important step in the history of computing hardware.

The ability to change the pattern of the loom's weave by simply changing cards was an important conceptual precursor to the development of computer programming. Specifically, Charles Babbage planned to use cards to store programs in his Analytical engine. At first sight this may seem unremarkable but it was a clear turning point in the ability to store and re-use machine instructions. Whilst Babbage did not live to see that his ideas were viable, they have since been proved to work reliably.

The term "Jacquard loom" is a misnomer. It is the "Jacquard head" that adapts to a great many dobby looms such as the "Dornier" brand that allow the weaving machine to then create the intricate patterns.

Jacquard looms, whilst relatively common in the textile industry, are not as ubiquitous as dobby looms, which are usually faster and much cheaper to operate. However unlike jacquard looms they are not capable of producing so many different weaves from one warp. Modern jacquard looms are computer controlled and can have thousands of hooks. And inevitably, unlike Jacquard's original invention there is now no need for the use of punched cards - instead the patterns are literally computer controlled.

The threading of a jacquard loom is so labor intensive that many looms are threaded only once. Subsequent warps are then tied in to the existing warp with the help of a knotting robot, which ties each new thread on individually. Even for a small loom with only a few thousand warp ends the process can take days.

The full process of producing macramé lace with Jacquard machines is as follows:
1. Designing the model: The very first step is to design a model, which means drawing on paper a design of the macramé lace. The drawing will be enlarged six times, to be able to be encoded by punching a hard paper roll. This step is called in French "la mise en carte".
2. Encoding the model: Once the design is made the drawing is placed on a punching machine. When the punching is done, each embroidery stitch is encoded (punched) according to the jacquard system on a hard paper roll.
3. Embroidery production: The punched band is then placed on the embroidery machine. It is the model's program. The punched roll contains the codes directing the big frame inside the machine. The needle always pricks at the same place. The macramé lace production takes a long time since thousands of embroidery stiches are necessary. The realization of a 60 cm wide item can sometimes take a whole day.
4. Removal of the background: The macramé lace must hold together without its textile support, which will be disintegrated by heat. It is that process that will give the transparency characteristic of macramé lace. For this the whole embroidery is bathed in a chemical and then put through an oven where the textile support is burned away.

5. The finishing touches: Before eliminating the supporting textile, repairs need to be done by hand. Imperfections due to the breaking of a spool or shuttle thread are removed. These finishing steps are very important in order to obtain a faultless quality product. Once the supporting textile is disintegrated different supporting strings are cut by hand. Sometimes there is also a need to do some finishing touches, such as coloring, by hand.

Today, Jacquard looms can still be seen in operation in the Cazé-Ducamp embroidery factory in Villers-Outréaux in France. See http:://www.authentic-macrame.com

There was another dimension to Guillaume's entrepreneurship in lace making. Pictures taken around the turn of the century show Guillaume with friends smiling and joking as he lifts a glass. It is unclear whether the photos shown in Figure 3.13 were staged or whether they show an interest in acting or theater. What is clear, however, is that his son René had a keen interest in theater; my brother and me, when we were teenagers, enjoyed a lot of theater shows together; and two of my children have been active in drama performances during their high school years. What does this tell us about the personality of Guillaume in Figure 3.13 ?

Figure 3.13 Guillaume De Boeck in two comic scenes taken around the turn of the century. In the left hand photo he is the first on the bench; in the right hand photo he is the one standing to the right lifting a glass. Note the hats worn in both pictures. As his grandson I must admit that I like collecting and wearing fancy hats.

Guillaume's enterprise was continued after his death and ended up supporting several families in the next fifty years. In his short life he achieved a lot, given that he only attended primary school. Through establishing a business in embroidery and mechanical lace making he created employment opportunities for his entire family and educational opportunities for the next generations. *Should it then surprise anyone that my grandfather, whom I have never met, has become one of my heroes?*

Figure 3.14 The original family home at Franklin Rooseveltlaan in Vilvoorde which connected to the workplace that gave out in the Hellingen straat

Figure 3.15 Guillaume Deboeck 1874-1925

Brother Victor also started a business

Guillaume's brother, Victor was born in 1877 and married on November 17, 1912, *Maria-Sophia De Pauw,* of Steenhuffel (born March 15, 1889). Together they had two children: Jozef and Alice.

Jozef married first, *Constancia Elizabeth Coomans* (September 13, 1938), with whom he had one son: Robert. Jozef remarried on May 30, 1955, *Clemintine Ghislaine Vanderhoeve,* with whom he had another son: Michel Joseph.

After Maria-Sophia De Pauw died on August 14, 1917, Victor married her sister *Martha De Pauw,* who was born March 2, 1901. Together they had one daughter, Rosa (Rosetta).

Victor was known for his energy and as a man who knew what he wanted. He was real entrepreneur. In the early 1900s he started a lemonade factory on the Grimbergse steenweg 32 in Vilvoorde (Kassei). Between the First and the Second World Wars, probably around 1932, he moved to the Schaarbeeklei 150 where he occupied a larger house with a big storage area.

Figure 3.16 Victor Deboeck 1877-1949

Next to a covered garage there was a kind of lab in which he kept different ingredients and fluid sugars for the production of lemonades. There was also a workplace where there was a bottle washing and filling machine.

In the beginning of the twentieth century, deliveries were made by horse drawn wagons. The story that was passed on to generations was that sometimes at the end of the deliveries, Victor fell asleep on his wagon but the horse always knew how to bring him home. Figure 3.17 shows Victor Deboeck and his lemonade business. Victor is second from the right on his carriage. In the 1930s the horse drawn wagon was replaced by a pickup truck.

Victor was well known for his lemonades in marble bottles ("knikkerfles"). When the bottle was filled the marble would automatically rise and close the bottle. This kind of bottle was popular with the young people; many bottles were smashed to obtain the marble.

Victor produced many different kinds of lemonades, including white, yellow, and green lemonades. Victor delivered in Vilvoorde and its surroundings, all the way to Asse, Wemmel, Merchtem, Nieuwroode and Eppegem. This vast region was according to Robert probably the result of marketing techniques "avant la lettre", meaning marketing that was way ahead of its time. He distributed at the fairs free lemonades to the children who loved the marble in the bottles.

After the death of Victor in 1949, it was his oldest son Joseph who continued the lemonade business. In the 1950s, with rising competition from big foreign names, such as Coca Cola, Royal Crown and Cécémel, and the emergence of bonded cafés (cafés where only certain trademarks could be sold), the production was gradually slowed down and stopped. The business of other lemonades and beer continued till the mid 1970s when Joseph retired.

There are interesting parallels between the character and drive of Guillaume and Victor. Both were men who knew what they wanted, both had the courage to start an enterprise in the early 1900s; they worked hard (Victor falling asleep at the end of a long day of deliveries) and were innovative (marble bottles and marketing techniques practiced by Victor and the latest embroidery machinery bought by Guillaume); they knew

Figure 3.17 Victor Deboeck and his lemonade business. On this picture Victor third from the right.

where they were going, both were true "entrepreneurs". Maybe from Guillaume's and Victor's stories we can imagine what Everard De Boeck must have been like…

Guillaume's wife and children continue the enterprise

The history of what happened after Guillaume died is not well documented. Joanne Nobels, who was 49 when Guillaume died, continued the enterprise first under the name *De Boeck Widow,* later under the name *De Boeck Widow and Children.*[30]

---

30. Anne-Marie Deboeck suggested that Joanne Nobels was not the one who continued Guillaume's business; that instead it was her father Joseph Deboeck. This is contradicted by several documents: Joanne's identity card (which is like a passport for all Belgians) specified that Joanne was an industrialist ("nijveraarster" in Dutch); if she had no profession her identify card would state "homemaker." References were also found in the book cited on the next page on employment in the early part of the twentieth century in Vilvoorde. In it was mentioned that Joanne was the "CEO of the De Boeck workplace." I also found name cards of Joanne Nobels indicating she was in charge of the enterprise established by her husband Guillaume. Joseph may have had an important role in convincing his father to modernize the machinery but all documented evidence shows that it was Joanna who ran the business after Guillaume's death. Later on as the name of the enterprise was changed, the children may have played a more important role.

Figure 3.18 Joseph, Pierre and René in the factory (photos circa 1928-1929)

In a book on companies and employment in the twentieth century,[31] I found that De Boeck started a workplace "for the unwinding of thread on bobbins ("spoelen") and that later on they moved over to mechanical embroidery."

From 1925 till 1929, still under the name *Guillaume Deboeck et Enfants,* an average of six people were employed. Thereafter, under the name *Deboeck Widow,* the enterprise, located on the Franklin Rooseveltlaan, number 189 (formerly called Nouveau Boulevard or Nieuwelaan), produced embroidery from 1930 till 1935 and employed on average 12 people in that period; it reached a maximum of 20 employees in 1935.

From 1936 till 1950 Guillaume's enterprise was called *De Boeck Widow and Children,* located on the Mechelese steenweg 6 in Vilvoorde. The Mechelse steenweg is just across from the Franklin Rooseveltlaan. For a while workspace was rented across from the place where the enterprise was started and work was performed at both locations, but during the war plans were made to build a factory at the Mechelse steenweg 6. In the early 1950's all machinery was moved from the workplace at the F. Rooseveltlaan to the Mechelse steenweg, the new location for the production.[32] The main activity of the Deboeck enterprise became mechanical embroidery on flannel. The average employment increased to 30 and reached 49 by 1950.

---

31. *Bedrijven en werkgelegenheden gedurende de XXst eeuw in Vilvoorde* (Companies and employment in the twentieth century in Vilvoorde).

32. The new Jacquard machines were so long that they reached all the way to the pedestrian path on the Hellingstraat (Rue de la Colline, 7-11). This caused problems with City Hall and hence the planning and move to the new location.

From 1940 onwards there are much better records. Detailed accounting, balance sheets, and profit and loss statements, permit us to reconstruct the history of the firm. In addition, there are official notices in notary acts, reproduced in the Official Gazette ("Staatsblad"). There are also letters during the early years of the Second World War (WWII) and reports on what happened right after WWII. All these provide evidence from which the development of the firm can be derived. In the next section I review first the establishment of the company, secondly the growth of the company in first ten years, thirdly the changes in the fifties and the sixties, and finally the decline and final liquidation of Guillaume's original enterprise.

The establishment of a company

The official establishment of the company as a limited liability company ("PVBA" in Dutch) occurred only in 1941. Hence from the day Guillaume started up the enterprise in the early 1900s till 1925, when he died, and from 1925 till 1941, when Joanne was running the enterprise, there was no legal structure except maybe a sole proprietorship. Before it actually obtained a legal structure some rather remarkable events occurred. Here in a nutshell are the incredible developments in the early 1940s.

On May 10, 1940 at four o'clock in the morning, German troops invaded Belgium. The country mobilized and fought back. My father, the youngest son of Guillaume and Joanne, who was 27 years old at the time, was mobilized and fought against the German invasion. Eighteen days later, King Leopold III, head of the Belgian army sur-

Figure 3.19 Joanne Deboeck-Nobels, widow of Guillaume Deboeck (photo of 1942)

rendered. The 18-day campaign took the lives of 8,000 Belgian soldiers and 12,000 civilians; Germany occupied Belgium for the next four years.

A few days after the surrender of the Belgian army, my father was arrested in Gent. German soldiers arrested him; claimed that the arrest would be of short duration; a few days to verify his papers. My father was still in Belgian military uniform. After his arrest he was deported to Germany like many others and became a prisoner of war (POW). While my father has never spoken about this, some 20 years after his passing away, I found that he was a prisoner in Stalag XI B, a Nazi POW camp near Fallingbostel.[33] He became POW number 37013, who was detailed to work on a farm.

His family, however, did not know his whereabouts. He had disappeared after the surrender. Joanne became seriously sick and was in need for surgery. She refused to go for surgery as long as she did not know the whereabouts of her youngest son. This is when "the bottom felt out" according to Jeannine Deboeck, youngest daughter of Joseph. She wrote: *"the youngest son was taken prisoner, he worked at a farm in Germany. Dad (Joseph) did everything possible... used his contacts in Germany (i.e. suppliers of materials to the factory), to obtain a permit to travel to Germany. This was one of the biggest mistakes he made in his life! His trip through enemy country angered the local people who used the occasion of his absence to break in and put the factory on fire. He lost on both ends: in Germany he was considered as a spy and as a result had to hurry back and in Belgium he was considered as a collaborator."* [34]

From a letter written by my father that was dated August 18, 1940 and mailed to his mother, sister and brothers, I learned that my father was doing well in Germany, was working on a farm on the harvest, had no complaints about his treatment, and that he "expected not to be there very long...." In other words, he expected to be transferred or released soon.

The Flemish National Alliance[35] (VNV) who tried to recruit Flemish men to fight as soldiers in the German army (possibly against the Russians) pleaded with Hitler to release Flemish POWs who fought in the Belgian Army. Flemish soldiers were released in 1940 from POW camps on the order of Hitler. This is a unique gesture in the history of warfare. The released POWs were allowed to return to Belgium. Among these POWs was my father.

On August 29, 1940, prisoner 37013 received a release letter ("Entlassungsschein" in German, see Figure 3.20). Signed

---

33. A complete list of POW camps in Germany can be found at http://www. pegasus-one.org/pow/frames.htm. Pictures of Stalag XI B are shown on http://www.pegasus-one.org/pow/frames.htm

34. Jeannine Deboeck: private letter November 15, 2006. The friction that emerged between Joseph and René (that will be discussed later) was probably caused by these events at the beginning of the war. Nevertheless, as will be demonstrated later the company continued after the war to rely heavily on German expertise for the design of macramé lace (see reference to Robert Schmidt).

35. The Flemish National Alliance, the Flemish Nationalist Party recruited actively for the SS labeled "Foreign Legions." They created the "Waffen SS Legion Flandern" and used the VNV to recruit it. See: http://conservative-reality.blogspot.com/2006_03_01_conservative-reality_archive.html

by Leutnant Hische, commandant of Stalag XI B, this letter ordered that the released prisoners should return to their home village and immediately report to the local police, and refrain from any unfriendly action against Germany or the German army. The military clothes and the weapon in their possession had to be immediately returned to the police in Belgium.

On September 3, 1940, my father returned by train via Berlin to Vilvoorde and reported to the police station (which recorded the deposition of his weapon). Other Flemish POWs who were not freed were not so lucky. My father-in-law stayed four years in prison and suffered through unspeakable times.

Five months after my father's return from Germany, the Deboeck brothers established a limited liability company! Next to launching a business around the turn of the century, the establishment of a limited liability company months after the beginning of another war, is just the most incredible move the Deboeck family ever made. Were they convinced the occupation would not last long? Or were they thinking like the Rockefellers who maintained that the best time to invest is when there is blood in the streets?

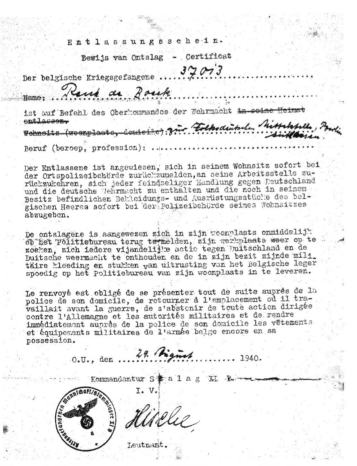

Figure 3.20 Release letter of POW number 37013, August 29, 1940

In a supplement to the Belgian Official Gazette of Ministerial Decisions ("Staatsblad der Ministeriële Besluiten") of February 9, 1941 under number 1368, I found the official notice of establishment of the company. The notary act signed on January 29, 1941 in front of Mr Jean Matthys in Vilvoorde, established a company under the name

"Etablissementen Weduwe Guillaume Deboeck en kinderen; Deboeck, gebroeders, Opvolgers", personenvennootschap met beperkte aansprakelijkheid PVBA ("Firm Guillaume Deboeck Widow and Children, Deboeck Brothers, Successors. Ltd")

The company was established for a period of 30 years starting on January 1, 1941 and was given the number 345615 in the commerce registry.[36] The purpose of the company was to perform "any transactions directly or indirectly related to the production and selling of any kind of embroidery or similar articles."

The original capital of the company was established at 440.000 Belgian Francs (BF). Translated into 2006 US dollars the original capital was $14,912. Each shareholder subscribed to 110 shares of 1000 BF each, which is the equivalent of $3,728 in current US dollars.[37]

There were only four shareholders in the company: Josephina, Joseph, Pieter and René-Corneille. Only the men were nominated to be administrators ("beheerders"); Joseph was appointed as Chairman ("beheerder-voorzitter").

After full subscription of the initial capital by the original four shareholders, Joanne Nobels, who was not a founding partner, brought in 240,000 BF ($8,135) on February 15, 1941. This additional capital was distributed as shares to the original four shareholders. Each received 60 additional shares. Shortly thereafter Joanne died on May 4, 1942. Josephine assumed the caretaker role of her mother and provided for her three brothers. She would continue in this role for a long time since Joseph married only in 1951.

Some fifteen months after the death of Joanne, my father married on August 25, 1943 Marie-Louise Girardin, in St-Ulriks-Kapelle (see Figure 3.22). The marriage took place on his birthday. More about his marriage follows in Chapter 4.

The first couple of years, the young married couple lived in the house at the F. Rooseveltlaan. After the completion of the factory on the Mechelse steenweg they moved to a private apartment above the factory.

---

36. It was formally deleted from the commerce registry on June 21, 1973 when all activities had stopped.

37. See Annex 4 on Investments in Belgium in 1935-85 in US dollars of 2600.

Figure 3.21 Front of the Deboeck Brothers factory on Mechelse steenweg 6 in Vilvoorde. The two large garage doors gave access to the factory in the back; the white door gave access to the private apartment on the second and third floor. This location became the sole address of the factory after the move from the Hellingen straat in the early 1950s.

In May 1950, the name of the company was changed, and the capital was increased. The Official Gazette of May 10, 1950, reports that in a notary act by Robert Philips (signed in Koekelberg on April 18, 1950) the name of the company is changed to "Ets. Deboeck Gebroeders" (Deboeck Brothers Ltd). The original capital of 440,000 BF augmented by 240,000 BF brought in by Joanne was increased by another 570,000 BF and thus became 1,250,000 BF (25,000 US dollars in 1950 or $209,500 in current 2006 dollars).

Figure 3.22 Marriage of Marie-Louise Girardin and René Deboeck, August 25, 1943 Sint-Ulriks-Kapelle (Dilbeek), Belgium.

In 1956, after the death of Pieter, Josephine Deboeck is nominated to be an "administrator". It is interesting to note that while Josephine was a shareholder from the beginning and nominated to be administrator in 1956 that the name of the company remained "Deboeck Gebroeders" (and not Deboeck Brothers and Sister")

On April 18, 1950 Josephine added 380,000 BF ($7,600); Joseph, Pierre and René were given each 80 additional shares. The same day each of them subscribed to an additional 63 shares ($1,260).

At the death of Pierre in 1955, his wife José De Cat signed off on all her rights to her husband's 313 shares, and his shares were distributed among the remaining shareholders. Josephine received 106 shares, Joseph 103 shares and René 104 shares. This shows again that this family did not allow others to participate in the company. Even the wives of the original shareholders were never allowed to own stock or play any management role in the company.

The net result of these share allocations was that from 1955 onwards the company is owned by three shareholders, Joseph owned 417 shares; Josephine owned 416 shares; and René had 416 shares. Although there was an almost equal distribution of shares and thus of voting power in the company, it will turn out that the death of Pierre shifted the power balance in the company towards Joseph and Josephine, which were of approximately the same age and 17 years older than their youngest brother.

Conducting business during and after the war: the first ten years.

The early years after the startup of the company were not easy: there was a war going on; Belgium was occupied by Germany; getting materials for the production was restricted. At one point during the war official permission was asked to travel to France to procure the necessary thread for continuation of the embroidery production.

Nevertheless the company kept producing during the war years and steadily increased total sales and gross revenues. Starting in 1947 it also started exporting. Total sales went from 994,726 BF in 1941 to 7,606.830 BF in 1950, an annualized 22% increase.

Earnings in the first couple of years were positive but small. In 1941 the company made 14,630 BF profit; in 1942 it made 8,685 BF profit; in 1943 it made 21,948 BF profit. In 1944 and 1945 losses were made to a tune of 432,732 BF cumulative. Some of these losses were amortized with the profit made in 1946, but it was not until 1949 that the company again got into the black. In 1950 on the basis of 7.6 million BF of gross revenues 1.7 million of profit (22%) was made. In the same year exports of embroidery and lace represented some forty-seven percent of total sales.

The company struggled through difficult times. It kept expanding and kept people employed during the war years. In an article of De Strijd, a paper of the Brussels Federation of the Communist Party, published in 1946, anger is expressed about the fact that the Deboeck company kept building; that so much stone and cement was used to build new workspaces ("enough to actually repair all the houses that had been damaged in Vilvoorde during the war"). The paper questioned whether a proper building permit had been obtained or if there was one, on whose advice it had been granted. The war created a lot of friction and suspicion among the people. Some paid a price for it with their life, others got their reputation badly damaged, yet others absorbed losses even after the end of the war and climbed back up.

Figure 3.23 Photos of the Deboeck Brothers factory in early 1950s: from left to right starting at the top: Jacquard machines; second row: punch machine and punch card rolls driving the Jacquard machines; third row: workspace with stitching machines for finishing lace and view of the office of René Deboeck

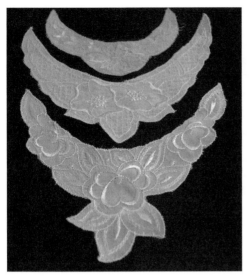

A letter written on the eve of Christmas of 1947 shows the appreciation the employees had for the management. The letter written by a representative addressed to the management expresses the feelings of the employees for all the sacrifices. Freely translated the letter reads as follows:

"...We {the employees} consider it our duty to express our sincere feelings of admiration and want to express our thanks for the way you keep handling the heavy burdens that the current social laws are imposing on you. We can hardly imagine the financial burdens that this must have imposed on you.

Figure 3.24
Sample of embroidery made during the war years by Deboeck Brothers. This kind of embroidery was used for women's lingerie. As during the war there was less demand for this kind of embroidery, most was made to keep the employees at work, at great expense to the company.

...We are really proud about the new workspaces that are under construction, the adequate lightening, proper ventilation and the broadminded thinking that went into the design of these workspaces, which we will be the first beneficiaries of. Even the huge capital expenditures that these new buildings required have not scared you from providing us with these improved working conditions. ...We hope that by our steadiness and adaptability to the tasks at hand, we can reassure you that our thanks will not be in vain, because we realize that our social wellbeing depends on the growth and expansion of the company. ...On behalf of the entire staff, we offer you this present with our sincere best wishes for 1948. May the Deboeck company be blessed by many more brilliant years. Your success and prosperity will be our success and welfare ('Uwe roem en voorspoed is onze roem en welvaart'). Long live the Deboeck company."

Figure 3.25
Employees
of the
Deboeck
Brothers,
photo
circa 1953

The growth of the company in the fifties and sixties

The evolution and growth of the company in the fifties and sixties can best be summarized in a single table. The table below shows the gross revenues, the realized profits, profit as a percentage of gross revenues, and the employment in the fiscal years 1954 to 1966.

Gross revenues climbed from 7.6 million BF in 1950 to 13 million BF in 1964-65, growth of 3.6% per year. Profits hovered around 1 million BF a year with the exception of 1955 and the years after 1963. They reached a peak in fiscal 1957-58. Profit as a percentage of gross revenues averaged about 9.5% per annum with highest percentage 16.4% achieved in 1954-55. The company provided steady employment to about 60 women and 4 men. It also supported the families of Joseph, Pierre and René Deboeck as well as Josephine who stayed single.

In sum, Table 3.1 shows the good years of the Deboeck Brothers! Note however that while gross revenues in 1966 were about the same as in 1958, the profits as a percentage of gross revenues dropped to 4% as compared to 15% in 1957-58. These were the signs that clouds were appearing on the horizon…

Year	Gross Revenues (GR) Millions BF	Profit Millions BF	Profit as % of GR Percent	Employment Women	Men
1954-55	9.55	1.58	16.42	60	3
1955-56	8.87	.015	1.69	58	4
1956-57	9.98	1.14	11.23	60	4
1957-58	11.31	1.70	15.01	68	4
1958-59	8.23	.83	10.02	59	4
1959-60	8.60	.94	10.85	54	4
1960-61	10.59	1.24	11.65	54	3
1961-62	10.69	1.39	13.00	52	4
1962-63	10.73	1.19	11.02	53	4
1963-64	11.43	.25	2.21	49	4
1964-65	13.03	.99	7.56	53	4
1965-66	11.42	.45	4.07	52	4

Source: Report on the Status of the Company as off October 19, 1966, prepared by R. Deboeck.

Table 3.1 Gross Revenues and Profits of the Deboeck Brothers Ltd; Employment provided in the period 1954-1966.
(Exchange rate 50 BF=1 dollar)

The decline and liquidation of the company

Starting in June 1965 there was a decline in orders for lace coming from Belgium, the Netherlands and Germany. The French producers offered prices that were substantially lower. On top there was increasing competition from East Germany. In contrast Sweden and Portugal asked for representatives to be designated and were stepping up orders.

Another problem that continued to affect the company was the rapid increase in social liabilities. Between June 1965 and June 1966 there was a 4.6% increase in the consumer price index. Salary increases resulting from this index increase, could not be passed on to the customers since product prices had been fixed in the beginning of the year. The expenditures for social security (the R.M.Z or "Rijksmaatschappelijke Zekerheid"), were adding 30.4% to employees' salaries.

Increasing price competition and rapid escalation of social charges affected the bottom line. Profits in 1966 were merely 4 % of the gross revenues compared to 7.5% in the previous year.

All these problems were summed up in a report made by my father and submitted on October 19, 1966 to the Chairman of the Board who was not happy about these developments. For weeks and months that followed the submission of this report he ignored addressing the issues.

When in addition financial difficulties emerged in regard to the payment of creditors in April 1967 the Chairman called a General Assembly meeting for May 22, 1967. On the agenda for the first time was a discussion of the liquidation of the company. The meeting of May 22, 1967 did not take place but another one was scheduled for May 29, 1967. Before the meeting my father wrote a letter to the Chairman to express his surprise and dismay about the agenda for the meeting.

On June 5, 1967 the Board met again and voted in favor of the liquidation of the company: two shareholders voted "for" (Joseph and Josephine) and one shareholder (my father) vote "against" the liquidation!

Attempts were still made in June 1967 to call on the Prime Minister of Belgium to protect the lace industry. In August Prince Albert (currently King Albert II of Belgium) was invited to visit the factory, but he refused because "operations of the company had ceased...." Prince Albert was at the time in charge of promoting Belgian businesses!

Why did Deboeck Brothers close and what happened?

The simple answer to this question is that the Board of Directors voted to liquidate the company. The underlying causes were more complex. There was increased competition in lace making from abroad (dumping prices applied by the French and by Eastern Europe); there was less demand for lace in Belgium; social welfare contributions were huge (30% of salaries) and kept increasing. There was also a delay in the granting of a work permit by the government for the replacement of an essential designer who was about to retire and was responsible for the production.

When the government finally granted the work permit, the company was already closed.

Other reasons for the closing of the company are more speculative, but are part of the paper records regarding the liquidation. Two shareholders became disinterested in the continuation or the extension of the company's life. Remember that the company had been set up for 30 years in 1941 and hence needed to be extended in 1971. Joseph, Chairman of the Board was 69 and Josephine was 70 years old. Friction between the shareholders that had accumulated for years came to a boiling point.[38]

In 1968 on a vacation in Montreux in Switzerland, the Chairman of the Board had a heart stroke; this paralyzed him for quite a time.[39] As a result he completely withdrew and handed all responsibilities to my father.

There was also a lack of successor(s) for the company: Josephine remained unmarried; Joseph married at advanced age; he had two daughters that were 17 and 16 years at the time while my father had two sons but neither was interested in stepping in (they went to the university and developed totally different interests). Maybe my interests were not that different, except that the long hours that my dad put into running the enterprise strongly discouraged me from taking over the company. In the end, I ended up as an entrepreneur (just like my dad) of introducing technology innovations in a large international organization in Washington, DC (as will be discussed in Chapter 7). The day I received my offer for employment at the World Bank, in early December 1975, was probably the happiest day in the life of my dad.

There is a Flemish saying that says *als het regent dan kan het gieten* ("when it rains it pours"), when something starts going wrong, a lot can go wrong for various reasons. To pinpoint why the Deboeck Brothers closed is not easy. Friction between the older shareholders and the one that was 17 years younger were certainly part of the problem. There are the obvious facts, a vote in the General Assembly meeting of June 5, 1967 and there are the surrounding factors that are subject to interpretation.

What is undeniable, however, is that the company had gone through some money losing years right after it had been founded and after the Second World War, but it had never folded. In spite of all the difficult years from startup till after the war the company had survived through creative management. In the mid

---

38. Joseph bought a car for personal use and charged it to the company; he withheld regular distributions (which was like a salary) to his brother. Through the intervention of his wife this was in 1968 corrected.

39. This was not the first time Joseph had health problems. At the end of the 1930s he was hospitalized in Leuven for what then was considered a total burn out. At the end of the 1940s he again had some problems that nevertheless did not prevent him from continuing to work. This is based on private mail of November 15, 2006 from Jeannine Deboeck.

1960s new challenges arose. Profits were down but there were no losses. This could hardly have caused the closing of the company. The fundamental reason for the closure therefore was the lack of succession planning on the part of the aging shareholders. This may have been the result of the stubborn beliefs of the Chairman of the Board in keeping the company a strictly "family enterprise." It was his stubborn beliefs that prevented the firm, which was the creation of his father and my grandfather, from taking a path that would have allowed it to survive into the twenty-first century.

Financial and Economic impact

What did Deboeck Brothers achieve in 30 years?

In the records of the firm we found an estimate of the value of the company shares as of June 30, 1966. The calculation made at the time was based on a simple average of the value of the shares on June 30, 1965 and the value one year later.

On June 30, 1966, the value of each share was estimated to be 8,117 BF (or $162.34 at the exchange rate in 1966). Hence, 417 shares, held by each shareholder in 1966, were worth 3,384,789 BF ($67,695).

In 1941, each shareholder had contributed 110,000 BF or the equivalent of $3,728. Additional capital brought into the company by Joanne and Josephine was distributed to the other shareholders. Only once did all shareholders bring in about 63,000 BF ($1,260) of new capital. The bulk of the increase in the number of shares from 110 to 417 came from redistributions of the shares of Pierre and from gifts made by Joanne and Josephine in the early years of the company.

In consequence, the increase from $3,728 to $67,695 between 1941 and 1966 can be considered as capital gains. These capital gains represent an 18.15 fold nominal increase over the value of shares in 1941. Since the cost of living increased by 2.48 times, the net increase in value of all shares was 7.3 fold (18.15 divided by 2.48).

A 7.3 fold increase in the period 1941 till 1968 represents a rate of return on capital of 7.4% annualized over 27 years.[40] Note this is limited to the period starting with the establishment of the Ltd and does not take into account that Guillaume De Boeck started the business some 30 to 35 years earlier (without which Joanne could not have made her contribution in 1941).

To put this return into proper perspective it should be compared with yields on long-term government bonds in Belgium (because the alternative of investing in the firm would have been to invest it in long-term bonds). In Belgium in the period 1950-59 the average nominal yields on long-term government bonds was 4.96%; in the period 1960-69 the yields were 6.15%; and in the period 1970-79 the yields were 8.26%. In real terms, these yields were 3.11%, 3.49% and 1.43% for the respective periods.

If 7.4% annualized return achieved by the Deboeck Brothers over 27 years is compared with real yields of long-term bonds, varying between 1.4% and 3.4%, then *we have to conclude that Deboeck Brothers did pretty well financially. The value added of return on capital versus real long-term bond yields ranged from 4% to 6% per year over close to 30 years. This is after payment of salaries and bonuses to all shareholders.*

What probably was of even greater importance to the Deboeck Brothers was the steady employment they provided to approximately sixty employees (employment that was sustained through the war years).

Finally, they also made the windows of Flanders and in many other European countries a little bit more beautiful by gorgeous macramé lace. Given the history of lace making in Flanders this was the continuation of a long "Flemish tradition."

---

40. A detailed explanation of how these numbers were derived can be found in Annex 4.

After the decision to liquidate was made, the activities of the company slowed down and came to a full stop. The assets of the company, including seven Jacquard machines, an embroidery machine, the stock of unsold lace, and all the equipment were sold. In the end also the buildings were sold. Employees were paid a closing premium plus all social benefits. The company ceased all activity and closed permanently in mid 1973, the year my father became 60.

The rapid decline of the company in the second half of the sixties, and the disagreements around liquidation, caused a painful struggle between the older and younger shareholders. Jozef had a first heart attack in April 1968, which forced him to take it easy.[41] He suffered two more heart attacks in 1973 and 1980. He was an addicted cigar smoker, who throughout his life enjoyed good eating and drinking. After the liquidation of the company Jozef traveled for the first time by plane to Rome (i.e. in 1975 when he was 77 years old). He spent the rest of his days in Knokke where he died on May 31, 1980 at age 82. He died ten years after Josephine, who passed away in 1970 at age 73.

Once the liquidation was decided, my father took charge of letting all employees go, selling all the assets and closing the books. In this period he started traveling extensively. He traveled to many countries, focused on his hobbies and his personal investments. It was in this period that he for the first time traveled to the United States where he came to visit my wife and me in Worcester and attended my Masters graduation at Clark University in 1970.

Figure 3.26 The Deboeck brothers shown from left to right: Joseph, Pierre two foreign technicians (who helped to install and move the Jacquard machines, names unknown), and René-Corneille.

---

41. Subsequently, he changed his opinion about the liquidation. He wrote: "the company had been liquidated because all activities had ceased...," although activities did not cease until the liquidation decision was taken!

.Figure 3.27 Macrame Lace produced by Deboeck Brothers in the 1960s.

Private investments

After the death of Pierre in 1955 my father became for all practical purposes the CEO of Deboeck Brothers.[42] He managed production, sales, and finances. He maintained all communications with clients and visited them regularly.

Through self-schooling he learned to read and write in French and German. Late in life when he started traveling, he also learned some English. He communicated with clients mainly through letters that he often wrote by hand in draft and then typed himself on an old fashion typewriter.

Figure 3.28 René Deboeck doing accounting in the early days of the company.

His management was focused squarely on obtaining factory orders and maintaining good relations with clients. He monitored the production process by walking around the factory, recording machine cycles, keeping detailed track of productivity.[43]

---

42. The family lived in an apartment above the factory. To get to work my father had only to go down stairs. This did not contribute to a clear separation between work and private life as many who work from home have found out. At the factory there were two shifts: the first shift of women started at 6 am and worked till 2 pm; the second shift worked from 2 pm till 10 pm in the evening. Every morning at 6 am my father opened the doors of the factory for the first shift of women to come in; and at ten pm he closed the doors after the second shift left.

43. Total cycles achieved, and cycles lost due to maintenance or temporary stoppages. His report of October 1966 contained such a detailed analysis of the total number of machine cycles per year.

When the production of orders would run late or deadlines for the delivery had to be met, he helped to pack and prepare shipments; many times packages were brought by him to the train station or delivered in person to clients.[44]

My father's main interest was however economic and financial management. He read daily a couple of newspapers, kept up with economic and social developments, as well as financial markets.[45]

The financial developments were of particular interest also because of his private investments. Detailed records, kept

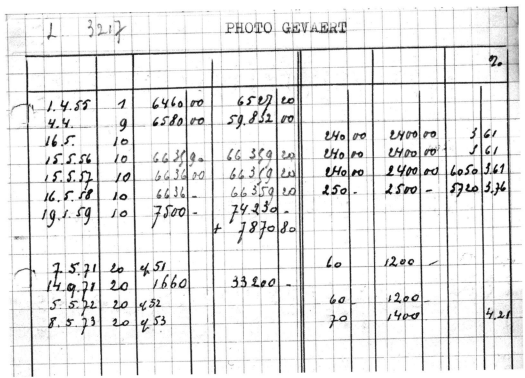

Figure 3.29 Pages from my father's investment accounting. Columns show from left to right: the date of purchase or sale, the number of shares, the unit price, the total price paid/received, the dividend per share, total dividends received, the percentage rate of the dividends.

---

44. I remember that on several Saturday trips to Knokke we would stop in Bruges for delivering of finished lace packages to a client and obviously have a meeting with him. This always delayed our arrival at our weekend getaway.

45. His favorite newspapers were "La Libre Belgique" and "Echo de la Bourse", at least until Flemish equivalents appeared, such as "De Standard" (The Standard) and "De Financieel Economische Tijd" (The Financial Economic Times).

meticulously through the years, showed that he invested in the stock market as early as the mid 1950s.[46]

The records about his investments showed that these were not aimed at speculation at price increases; shares were held five, ten or even fifteen years. The main purpose was collecting dividends. His investment portfolio moved from all stocks to a more diversified portfolio of stocks and bonds over the years.[47] The evolution of the stock prices in the seventies on the Brussels Stock exchange (see Figure 3.30) shows that the All Shares Index of Belgian stocks increased by 4.6% until the mid sixties but from 1972 till 1982 moved barely.[48]

Private investments in the stock and bond market were a way to stay in touch with the economic and financial developments. My father read a lot, cut out and copied articles from the newspapers and assembled his own knowledge base. He collated books of economic and financial articles.

The fiscal conservatism that shines from the records of his investment management suggests that he was not speculating on the markets.[49] The Brussels exchange in the fifties and sixties

---

46. The earliest records show that he bought shares and kept a portfolio of oil (Petrofina, Canadian Petrofina), mining (Auxiliare des Mines), utilities (Gaz et Electricite de Hainaut), and technology (Photo Gevaert) shares. He also got involved with Belgian Congo via investments in Belgo Katanga. The rapid decline of Belgo Katanga stock, after the independence of Congo in 1960, may have stimulated his interest in greater diversification. Starting in 1971, René's portfolio included several banks, holding companies, real estate companies, metal-, chemical- and other industries. He also invested abroad (France, Netherlands and Luxembourg) and in companies in South Africa.

47. The bonds that were held were mainly long-term government bonds, loans for constructions of highways (e.g. autoweg E3), utilities (E.B.E.S); even I.B.R.D. loans. Finally, there is also participation in mutual funds like KB Income Fund, Unifonds etc.

48. In the period from 1955 till 1964 (the first period for which financial records of the portfolio are recorded), the All Shares Index of Belgian stock prices increased an average by 4.68% annually. In the period from 1972 till 1982 the same index barely moved. It actually lost 0.08% annually. Long-term government bonds as well as bonds issued by utility companies yielded in that period 7.5% to 8.5%. Hence, there was good reason to diversify into bonds. It is only in the last few years of my father's life that he enjoyed higher rates of return. In the period from 1980 till 1983 the increase of the All Shares Index of Belgian stocks was 17.7% annualized. The financial records show that in 1983 his total portfolio return was 10%. It was the first year for which total return was computed based on both realized gains and unrealized increases resulting from price changes. Three years before his death, my father handed the management of his portfolio over to me.

49.I found in the records that instead of buying and selling rapidly, shares were held for long periods; instead of focusing on growth companies,

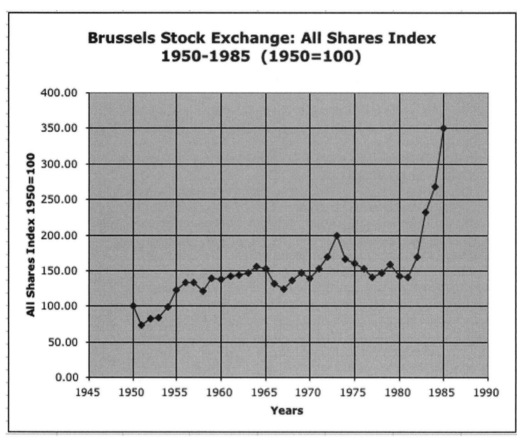

Figure 3.30 Evolution of the All Shares Index of the Brussels Stock Exchange from 1950-2000. Source: Geert De Clerq, Ter Beurze, Geschiedenis van de aandelenhandel in Belgie 1300-1990, page 319

was understood by only a few, just like day trading or timing the markets is not well understood by many today. The market was not accessible to many people. His fiscal conservatism in private investments complemented the prudent management that he pursued in running Deboeck Brothers.

Personal hobbies

René Deboeck had many "hobbies" including filmmaking, photography, collecting post stamps and traveling.

---

shares were held in what today would be called "blue chip" companies; and instead of speculating on price increases the main intent was collecting income through dividends. Putting all this together the investing approach that was followed comes closer to the one of Warren Buffet's than to growth-oriented, rapid turnover investment approach of William O'Neil.

Some time before the Second World War he met George Mergeay who later became his brother-in-law since George married the sister of my mother. They probably met in Café Luminor on the market place in Vilvoorde, which was their regular Café ("stamkafee" in Dutch). When George became 95 years in 2005 a special celebration was organized in Café Luminor, because George had been client in the same café for 75 years, thus he had started going to that café in 1930.

Together George and René belonged to a film club. Already during the war years they would make 16 mm black and white films. They made film titles and undertook film editing by cutting and pasting together filmstrips. I do not know how many films George made but in the period from 1946 to 1973, my father made some 30 films. All of them were kept on large wheels, properly catalogued, with descriptions of each film. The earlier films were mainly about family events and excursions; later documentary films were made about the places we visited.

As technology evolved the 16 mm films became 8 mm, the black and white became color, and George even experimented with sound films.

The most remarkable film that was catalogued was a black and white film from August 1943, probably made by George, that documented the wedding of René with Marie-Louise Girardin. On this black and white film one sees the assembly of the family and guests in Vilvoorde; the trip to Sint-Ulriks-Kapelle.

Figure 3.31 Messrs Robert Schmidt and René Deboeck, photo taken on March 25, 1972, on the 80th birthday of Robert Schmidt, who was the key lace designer at Deboeck Brothers. Robert was also a close friend of René. He died in Aachen-Haaren on May 26, 1991, at the age of 99 years.

Then following those car trips there is this procession of fourty horse drawn carriages moving guests to the church. In the church the images are dark and barely visible but they show clearly the taking of the vows. After the church the procession of carriages goes back to the farm. Finally at the farm there are images of a reception and a dinner for a large number of family and guests. This film, which has been converted from 16mm into digital form and VHS format, provides incredible images of a marriage that took place in the middle of the second World War, while Belgium was occupied by Germany, in a small village just 15 miles from the center of Brussels.

Another hobby of René Deboeck was photography. Originally he produced black and white pictures that were kept in several albums.[50] After my dad's death my mother preserved all these photo albums. She too collected quite a number of albums. After her death in 2001, all of these photo albums made it to the States. In the past years a serious attempt has been made to label as many photos as possible. Proper labeling of photos with dates, subject and names of the persons on the photo ought to be a discipline instilled from early age on....

After the paper photos came the 35mm slides that were collected in slide carousels; some 3000 slides document the various times and places we visited.[51]

René Deboeck also collected stamps. In 1954 the family bought an apartment[52] in Knokke, which brought them more often to Bruges. It was in Bruges that he started a stamp collection. He bought his first album for collecting Belgian stamps. Later on he expanded his collection to other countries as well as other subjects, e.g., stamps related to space adventures (which his grandson took over). His collection of Belgian stamps grew rapidly and is one of the most beautiful and most valuable stamp albums left from those days.

---

50. All these photo albums were preserved by my mother, after my dad's death. She also collected quite a number of albums. After her death in 2001, all of these photo albums made it to the States. In the past years a serious attempt has been made to label as many photos as possible. Proper labeling of photos with dates, subject and names of the persons on the photo ought to be a discipline instilled from early age on....

51. These were stored in rectangle carousels, which only played on European slide projectors. In recent years all of these slides have been moved to plastic sheets that were added to my own slide collection, already over 7000 slides.

52. The apartment was in a building called Gulfstream on the Zeedijk in Knokke. The apartment was bought in 1953 for 322,000 Bfr and notary costs added 44,110 Bfr. (in total this is $7,322 based on 50 Bfr per US dollar in 1953 or about $55,383 in current dollars). It was used mainly for weekend excursions and was rented out in July and August for many years.

All these hobbies have a few things in common: they require skills, persistence and a lot of patience! Through self-schooling my father learned to write in French, German and some English; through daily reading of newspapers he acquired considerable understanding of financial markets and investments. His holding onto shares for five, ten, sometimes fifteen years was the same as what some well-known investment gurus advocate still today. All of his hobbies also required endurance. In today's hectic life we often forget that "Rome was not built in one day." Even writing a book with a word processor takes time…. To achieve valuable results one needs ideas, a plan, some teamwork, and a lot of persistence!

After my father died on July 6, 1985, a thank you note was sent to all those who expressed sympathy. That note included the following:

"The courage of life is often a less dramatic spectacle than the courage of a final moment; but it is no less a magnificent mixture of triumph and tragedy."　　　John F. Kennedy

Figure 3.32 René Deboeck three years before he died on July 6, 1985.

Chapter 4
The Girardin Family:
Brewers of Lambic and Gueuze (1882-present)

It was at a dance in Pajottenland in the early forties that René Deboeck first met Marie-Louise Girardin. She was a gorgeous looking blond, oldest daughter of Jean-Baptist Girardin who was the mayor of Sint-Ulriks-Kapelle, a small village on the outskirts of Brussels. My father was at the time in his late twenties. He was always impeccably dressed, elegant, quiet and polite. There was a war going on; traveling was not easy, but they got to know each other and fell in love. He proposed, she accepted and they married on August 25, 1943, his thirtieth birthday!

In this chapter I trace the ancestors of Marie-Louise Girardin, my mother. Her father was the popular mayor of Sint-Ulriks-Kapelle, who was also a brewer. He was the youngest son of Franciscus-Alexius Girardin, born in 1847 in Sint-Joost-ten-Node (a part of Brussels) who started the Girardin brewery in 1882. The birth certificate of Franciscus-Alexius did not mention who his father was; hence he assumed the last name of his mother, Augustine Girardin. His mother was born in Brussels but her ancestors were from Nevers in France.

Our travel back in time begins in Pajottenland, which is nowhere on any map, then moves to Brussels and the history of this city that is the capital of Flanders, Belgium, and Europe.

The history of the Girardin family is tackled in two parts: first the ancestors of Augustine Girardin are reviewed; second, the descendants of Franciscus-Alexius are listed. This chapter ends with the history of beer brewing around Brussels that leads to the history of 125 years of the Girardin Brewery.

Figure 4.1 Marie-Louise Girardin 1918-2001

Where is Pajottenland?

If you Google for Pajottenland you immediately find that it is the *Tuscany of the North*. If you search for it on a map, even an old map of Belgium, you are not likely to find it. It is not mentioned on any map nor does it appear in any documents.

Under the nickname Franciscus Twyffeloos, F. J. de Gronckel assembled in 1852 a collection of stories that appeared under the title *Pajottenland*. In his work he tried to convince the readers of the heroism of the people of Pajottenland.[1] The term contains *pajot or payot*.

According to Dr. Mon de Goeyse *pajot* was first used during the Brabant Revolution of 1789-1790 (see Chapter 1).[2] It was the term used for soldiers originally from the Southern Netherlands, hired by the Austrian army. *Payot* was the opposite of *patriot*, i.e., the freedom fighters who resisted the occupation by the Austrians. Payot was therefore the name given to those who supported the Austrians.

In 1899 a newsmagazine was published under the name *Het Pajottenland te Gooik*. In 1911 Arthur Cosyn published a book, *Le Brabant inconnu* (the unknown Brabant), in which he wrote *"'t Pajottenland, the country of the 'pays' or comrades."* The same year a genealogical periodical was published under the name *Eigen Schoon* (Our Beauty) that regularly contained contributions about Pajottenland.

In 1977 *Pajottenland* was defined in the Encyclopedia Larousse as follows *"Pajottenland is the area that stretches from the Heuvelstreek and the Brabant lime area to the southwest of Brussels, between the Senne valley in the east and the river Dender in the west; in the north bordering with Little Brabant and in the south with the lime area of Hainaut. It is 290 square kilometers with rolling rural landscape without cities and few main roads."*

Pajottenland is thus an area of some 111 square miles southwest of Brussels. It is a beautiful rural area of rolling hills and small villages. The horizon of Pajottenland covered with trees is dotted with church spires of villages that go back to the 14th century. Those churches still have stained glasses that are relatively intact.

Twyffeloos wrote in 1852: *"no one will ever leave this region {Pajottenland}, these picturesque hills, these fertile valleys without shedding a tear when saying good-bye."*[3] It was in Pajottenland, the *Tuscany of the North,* where my mother was born and where she grew up.

---

1. Frans Jozef De Gronckel, *Payottenland, gelijk het van oudtyds gestaen en gelegen is* (Pajottenland as it existed in the old days). *Gedenkboeksken voor alle die deze contry vry en vrolyk beleven* (a book of memories for all those who in this country live free and happy) by Franciscus Twyffeloos, Doctor in Philosophy, laywer and payot, first edition, Brussels: 1846; third edition, 1852.

2. Dr. Mon de Goeyse: "De Liederen van de Brabantse omwenteling van 1789" (songs of the Brabant Revolution of 1789), doctoral dissertation of 1933.

3. See http://home.tiscali.be/pajottenland/eng/namepaj/nampaj.htm

Brief History of Brussels

Northeast of Pajottenland is Brussels, originally an unassuming village in the marshy valley of the river Senne. The name "Brussels" derives from the old Flemish "broec" and "saal", broadly meaning "settlement in the marsh". Brussels was situated at the crossroads of two major trade routes: the one from England to Germany and the other joining northern to southern Europe.

Around 1100 a defensive wall was built around the town. In 1229 Duke Henry I of Brabant granted the people of Brussels a charter guaranteeing a number of rights. Brussels developed into an important textile center in the Duchy of Brabant.

From the thirteenth century onwards the development of Brussels began to accelerate and the town steadily expanded. The protection provided by the first fortifications became insufficient; between 1357 and 1379 a second city wall was built.

During the fourteenth century the textile industry enjoyed its greatest period of prosperity. Brussels together with the rest of the Duchy of Brabant came in 1430 under the rule of the House of Burgundy. Duke Philip the Good stayed in the *Coudenberch* Palace in Brussels from time to time. Artistic achievements in the fourteenth century included the development of the Brabant gothic style of architecture and the mystical writings in medieval Dutch of Jan van Ruusbroec. Born in a Flemish town between Brussels and Halle, van Ruusbroec became the curate of Saint Gudule in Brussels. In March 1349 he became the prior of a community of canon regulars living the Rule of Saint Augustine.

Father Karel Denys wrote: "van Ruusbroec is the greatest fourteenth century Flemish writer of the Rhenish school of mysticism. He has left a dozen treatises no less remarkable for their piety than for the profundity that earned the titles of 'Admirable' and 'Doctor Divinus' for their author. His thoughts are of a speculative nature but his writings reveal the secret of the authentic experiences of union with God and he invites the reader to follow him along that path."[4]

van Ruusbroec was called "the Father of Netherlandic Prose" because he wrote his works not in Latin but in the language of his own people, in the "Dietse taal" as the Netherlandic language was called those days, with a Brabant flavor.

The rich tide of artistic achievements continued in the fifteenth century. Roger vander Weyden was appointed official painter for the town of Brussels, while Jan van Ruysbroeck became *"meester vanden steenwerke van den torre van der stad raithuse op de merct"* (master mason for the spire of the Brussels Town Hall in the Market square). He completed the spire between 1449 and 1454.

---

4. The best known works of Jan van Ruusbroec are his "Adornment of Spiritual Nuptials" and "The Book of the Twelve Beguines", Karel Denys, Flemish American Heritage.

In 1482 the Low Countries came under the rule of the Habsburgers after the extinction of the Burgundian dynasty. During the reign of Charles V, Brussels became the capital of the wide-reaching Habsburg Empire. From 1531 onwards the ducal household and central administration remained in Brussels. Woodcarving and tapestry weaving reached new artistic heights.

In the sixteenth century until 1531, first Mechelen and then Brussels was *the Princely Capital of the Low Countries,* the home of many adherents of the Reformation. Enraged at the religious fanaticism of the Spanish king, deep resentment arose in which Brussels joined the general rebellion against the Spanish domination. Prince William of Orange celebrated his *Blijde Inkomst* in Brussels.

While the northern Low Countries went their own way in 1585, the southern Low Countries (roughly present-day Belgium) continued under Spanish Habsburg domination until 1713 when they were passed to the Austrian branch of the Habsburg dynasty.

Brussels remained the capital throughout, and was frequently affected by wars. It suffered its harshest ordeal in August 1695 when Louis XIV ordered the bombardment of the city. Countless buildings and works of art were destroyed and many documents were lost from the archives.

In 1793-94 the French invaded Brussels. In 1795 the entire Low Countries were incorporated under the French Republic. From 1793 till 1815 systematic *gallicisation* was enforced. After Napoleon's army was defeated at Waterloo in 1815, the Allies—in particular England—wanted a buffer zone against the French. Consequently the southern and northern Low Countries were reunited under King Willem I of the Netherlands.

Willem I tried to bring the South up to the level of prosperity enjoyed by the North but ran into resistance from Catholic bishops in the South; they were suspicious of the Protestant king. The newly emerged middle class demanded the right of participation in the government.

In 1830 a revolt broke out in Brussels against the Dutch; both Brabant and Hinault (Hennegouwen in Dutch, a province of Belgium) protested against the high taxes. This revived the long-standing hope of the French for annexation of the southern Low Countries. The English were firmly opposed to this and thus supported an independent state. Belgium became an independent country.

On July 21, 1831, the first King of Belgium, Leopold I, ascended the throne (Annex 5 provides the pedigree of Leopold I). Brussels became the capital of the new kingdom of Belgium.[5] After the independence struggle rebuilding of the city started. New enormous buildings were built; the city walls were demolished.

---

5. Dr Paul De Ridder: "History of Brussels, Linguistic usages in Brussels before 1794"; and Brussels, *history of a Brabant city.* See also Paul Belien: *A Throne in Brussels.*

The city expanded. Several international congresses were organized; scientific organizations founded; foreign artists, philosophers, and scientists found their way to Brussels (including Karl Marx, Victor Hugo, Proudhon and others).

Two world wars in the early twentieth century did not stop the further development of Brussels. After WWII Belgium was divided into semi-independent regions, Flanders and Wallonia and Brussels became a region with its own government. Brussels became the capital of Europe and NATO decided to make Brussels its headquarters.[6]

Growing up in Vilvoorde just six miles north of Brussels, I spent a lot of time in the capital. The market place of Brussels remains my favorite. This market place has changed a lot over time as Figure 4.2 shows but many restorations have made the buildings even more beautiful. The market place of Brussels remains one of the most gorgeous market places in the world.

Figure 4.2 Above: Brussels market place in the 1900s; below: views of 2005. Photos by GJD.

6. There are many good books about the history of Brussels, but one of the nicest ones is Jean Stengers et. al., Brussel, *Groei van een hoofdstad* (Brussels growth of a capital).

The ancestors of Augustine Girardin

Franciscus-Alexius was the son of Augustine Girardin, who was born in Brussels, but her ancestors came from France. A chart of the ancestors of Augustine Girardin is provided in Figure 4.3.

The oldest known ancestor of Augustine Girardin was Eustache Girardin. The surname Girardin came, according to the House of Names, from the personal name Gerard, which was derived from old German *Gerhard,* which means spear-brave.[7]

Eustache had two sons, André and Eustache, who were born in Nevers. Nestled in the heart of Bourgogne, the Auvergne, in central France, is Nevers, two hours' drive south of Paris. André and Eustache were brothers; the godmother of the son of Eustache was the wife of André.

André was a blacksmith.[8] André married Marie Geoffroy (godmother of Michel) in 1725. The couple first lived in Poiseux, thereafter in Cigogne. They had two children. Maria Geoffroy died in Cigogne in 1743.

André remarried in 1744, Anne Nandrot, daughter of Charles Nandrot and Helene Chauffournier (from the parish of Saint Jean in Nevers). After Anne Nandrot died, André married a third time, Françoise Amiot in 1753 .

Out of the marriage with his second wife there was a son named Franciscus-Alexius Girardin, who was born on May 23, 1745 in Nevers. He was baptized in the parish of Cigogne (now the Commune de Fermeté). His godfather was François Perreau, Notary Royal; his godmother was Gabrielle Rigny, wife of Edmonde Pillet of the parish of d'Azy (now Sint-Benin d'Azy).

Franciscus married Maria Josepha Marcq on April 7, 1766 in Brussels. Franciscus and Maria Josepha lived in de Montagne de la Cour (number 819) in Brussels. They had ten children:

1. **Pierre Joseph Emanuel** born December 24, 1766
2. **Maria Philipinne Josephe** born July 9, 1769
3. **Jean Francois** born April 3, 1770
4. **Jean-Baptist** born April 22, 1774
5. **Pierre Joseph** born February 19, 1776
6. **Jacobus Josephus,** born April 3, 1778
7. **Pierre Jacques** born October 22, 1779
8. **Josephus Jean** born October 26, 1781
9. **Maria Josepha** born November 1, 1783
10. **Michael Henricus** born November 13, 1786.

---

7. Based on House of Names, http://www.houseofnames.com/xq/asp.c/qx/girardin-coat-arms.htm

8. There were quite a number of iron mines and a lot of metal industry in the region, especially in Imphy and Guerigny where the Royal Ironworks of the French Navy were.

Ancestors of Franciscus-Alexius Girardin

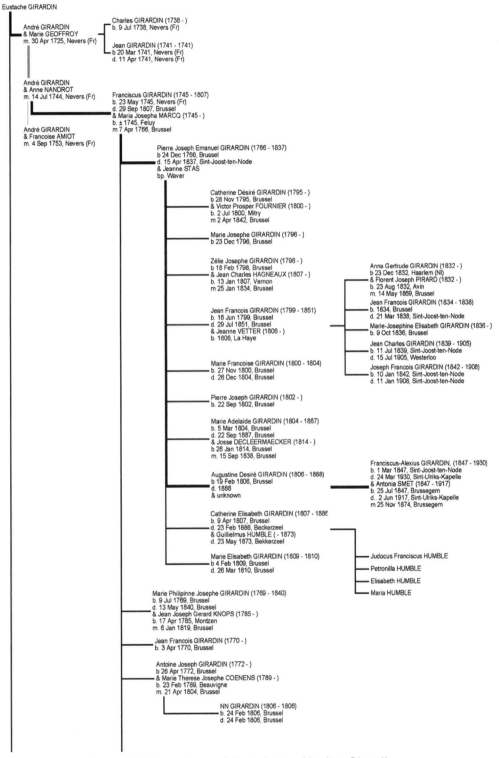

Figure 4.3 Ancestors of Franciscus-Alexius Girardin

Ancestors of Franciscus-Alexius Girardin (continued)

Jean Baptiste GIRARDIN (1774 - 1838)
b. 22 Apr 1774, Brussel
d. 18 Dec 1838, Brussel
& Marie Agathe VANDENBERGHEN (- 1859)
d. 29 Nov 1859, Brussel
m 22 Nov 1795, Brussel

Aldegonde Marie Francoise GIRARDIN (1796 - 1801)
b. 27 Dec 1796, Brussel
d. 5 Jun 1801, Brussel

Antoine Philippe GIRARDIN (1798 -)
b. 14 Oct 1798, Brussel

Marie Josephine GIRARDIN (1801 - 1838)
b. 23 Jan 1801, Brussel
d. 19 Feb 1838, Brussel

Aldegonde Marie GIRARDIN (1803 -)
b. 19 Apr 1803, Brussel

Charlotte Josephine GIRARDIN (1805 -)
b. 28 Apr 1805, Brussel

Pierre Jacques GIRARDIN (1807 - 1807)
b. 12 Jan 1807, Brussel
d. 8 Apr 1807, Brussel

Jacques Eduard GIRARDIN (1808 - 1808)
b. 18 Jan 1808, Brussel
d. 5 May 1808, Brussel

Antoine Marie Eugénie GIRARDIN (1809 -)
b. 8 Sep 1809, Brussel
& Barbe DEWAEGENEER

Francois GIRARDIN (1841 - 1848)
*. 21 Sep 1841, Brussel
+. 8 Mar 1848, Brussel

Auguste Marie GIRARDIN (1811 - 1813)
b. 11 Oct 1811, Brussel
d. 7 Aug 1813, Brussel

NN GIRARDIN (1812 - 1812)
b. 25 Aug 1812, Brussel
d. 25 Aug 1812, Brussel

Marie Agathe GIRARDIN (1814 -)
b. 14 May 1814, Brussel
& Joseph Francois BOUR (1808 -)
b. 22 Jan 1808, Montzen
m. 22 Sep 1849, Brussel

Jean Baptiste Emile GIRARDIN (1818 -)
b. 8 Dec 1818

Pierre Joseph GIRARDIN (1776 - 1816)
b. 19 Feb 1776, Brussel
d. 25 Apr 1816, Brussel
& Marie Claire HOMBLE (1760 - 1855)
b 15 Feb 1760, Leuven
d. 15 Dec 1855, Brussel

Jacobus Josephus GIRARDIN (1778 - 1778)
*b 3 Apr 1778, Brussel
d. 3 Apr 1778, Brussel

Pierre Jacques GIRARDIN (1779 - 1823)
b 22 Oct 1779, Brussel
d. 5 Aug 1823, Brussel
& Marie Elisabeth PITET (1780 -)
b 13 Jul 1780, Brussel
m 13 Dec 1809, Brussel

Marie Louise GIRARDIN (1810 - 1814)
b. 28 Oct 1810, Brussel
d. 13 Nov 1814, Brussel

Josephus Antoine GIRARDIN (1812 - 1826)
b. 4 Jun 1812
d. 16 Sep 1826, Brussel

Michel Francois GIRARDIN (1815 -)
b. 4 Jan 1815, Brussel

Marie Francoise Desire GIRARDIN (1818 -)
b. 17 Feb 1818, Brussel

Joseph Maria GIRARDIN (1821 -)
b. 3 Jul 1821, Brussel
& Marie Adele VAN DOREN (1825 -)
b. 16 Feb 1825, Brussel
m. 6 Nov 1850, Brussel

Josephus Jean GIRARDIN (1781 -)
b. 26 Oct 1781, Brussel

Maria Josepha GIRARDIN (1783 - 1862)
b. 1 Nov 1783, Brussel
d. 16 Jan 1862, Brussel

Michael Henricus GIRARDIN (1786 - 1862)
b. 13 Nov 1786, Brussel
d. 20 Jan 1862, Brussel
& Maria Josepha MALFAIRE (1799 -)
b. 18 Mar 1799, Gemappe
m. 26 May 1828, Brussel

Eustache GIRARDIN
& Michèle BILLOT
m. 2 Aug 1733, Nevers (Fr)

Thérèse Eleonore GIRARDIN (1820 - 1892)
b 25 Nov 1820, Brussel
d. 8 Feb 1892, Brussel
& Jean Baptist VIAL (1813 -)
b. 28 Feb 1813, Saint Didier Sur Rochefort

Michel GIRARDIN (1739 - 1739)
b. 18 Jan 1739, Nevers (Fr)
d. 24 Jan 1739, Nevers (Fr)

Marie GIRARDIN (1738 - 1739)
b. 1738, Nevers (Fr)
d. 25 Jan 1739, Nevers (Fr)

Franciscus died at the age of 62 in Brussels in 1807. Pierre Joseph Emanuel, his oldest son, married Jeanne Stas (sometimes written Stasse)[9] who was from Waver. Together they too had ten children:

1. **Catherine Désiré** (1795-)
2. **Marie Josephe** (1796-)
3. **Zélie Josephe** (1798-)
4. **Jean Francois** (1799-1851)
5. **Marie Francoise** (1800-1804)
6. **Pierre Joseph** (1802-)
7. **Marie Adelaïde** (1804-1887)
8. **Augustine Desiré** (1806-1888)
9. **Catherine Elisabeth** (1807-1886)
10. **Marie Elisabeth** (1809-1810)

Pierre died on April 15, 1837, at age 70 in Sint-Joost-ten-Node. The eighth child of Pierre Joseph Emanuel and Jeanne Stas was Augustine Desiré Girardin, born in Brussels in 1806.

Augustine was born at 10 am on February 19, 1806, in Rue de Villa Hermosa (number 782, seventh section); the witnesses were Joseph Delloije and Jean Francois Heineau. Augustine remained single but gave birth on March 1, 1847 in Sint-Joost-ten-Node (at age 41) to a son named Franciscus-Alexius (the name of her grandfather).

The birth certificate of Franciscus-Alexius that is shown on next page contains interesting information.

Figure 4.4 Photo presumed to be Augustine Girardin (photo date unknown). Note the dress, the jewelry and the hair cover. If this was indeed Augustine Girardin, then this shows a young lady that was not a commoner.

9. Pierre and Jeanne lived in the Rue Montagne de Victoire after they married, and until their second child was born. Thereafter they lived in the Rue Bonnet Rouge and finally in Rue Villa Hermosa.

Figure 4.5
Birth certificate of Franciscus-Alexius contains the following

ACTE DE NAISSANCE, N° 37 (birth certificate number 37)

L'an mil huit cent quarante-sept, le deux du mois Mars, à onze heures du matin, par devant-nous Roch Vangoutshoven, échevin Délégué, Officier de l'Etat civil de la Commune de Saint Josse Ten Noode, Arrondissement de Bruxelles, Province de Brabant, est comparu Vetter Jeanette, âgé de quarante-un ans, profession de garde coucher, né à La Haye domicilié à Saint Josse Ten Noode laquel le nous a présenté un enfant du sexe masculin né en cette commune, le premier de ce mois à sept heures du matin, Rue des Pierres numéro dix-huit, de Augustine Girardin, fille de boutique, âgée de quarante un ans, née à Bruxelles, domiciliée en cette commune, auquel enfant elle déclare que la volonté de la mère est de donner les noms et prénoms de Francois Alexis Girardin.

Lesdites déclaration et présentation faites en présence de Girardin Jean François, âgé de quarante sept ans, profession de marechal ferraud, domicilié à Bruxelles et de Dekoninck Charles Leopold, âgé de cinquante. sept ans, profession de Louageur, domicilié à Molenbeek Saint Jean et ont la comparante et les témoins signés avec nous le présent acte, après qu'il leur en été donné lecture.
S.
J.F. Girardin   C. DeKoninck   R. VanGoedtsnoten.
Johanna Vetter

The original document, obtained years ago from the city hall in Sint-Joost-ten-Node, is transcribed in French; parts are discussed after the transcription.

Transcription of the birth certificate

From this transcript we can derive that Jeanette Vetter was the sister-in-law of Augustine Desiré; Jean Francois, the witness, was the brother of Augustine and was married to Jeannette Vetter.

The birth certificate of Franciscus-Alexius does not provide the name of his father. Finding who was the father is not easy. After years of research it remains a puzzle, but speculations continue. If one were to go by *popular beliefs,* stories passed on from generation to generation then the response to the question: who was the father of Franciscus-Alexius would be Leopold I, the first King of Belgium. This popular belief is so strong that 160 years after his birth, Franciscus-Alexius is still considered by the local people as the son of Leopold I. If one were to investigate *the circumstantial evidence* such as the fact that Leopold loved a lot of women, had many relationships, even had children out of extramarital relationships, then all *circumstantial evidence* would support this popular belief. If one analyzes Leopold's love life (e.g. the age differences between Leopold and the women he had affairs with) then certain patterns reinforce the case to believe that Leopold I may have fathered Franciscus-Alexius.

None of this has so far been proven by documents; however the absence of documents does not prove that a relationship did not exist. In at least one other case where Leopold I had a relationship with a woman all documents were destroyed (see Annex 5).

The private lives of the royalties in Belgium are still heavily guarded. Paul Belien in his book, *A Throne in Brussels,*[10] has done more than anyone else to unveil some of their private lives (or secrets, maybe?).

An attempt to solve the puzzle about who was the father of Franciscus-Alexius is addressed in this book through DNA testing. The subject will first be introduced in Chapter 8 after which actual DNA test results are discussed in Chapter 9. Before

Figure 4.6 Photos of Augustine Desire Girardin: left photo taken on September 1, 1867; right photo taken closer to her death in 1888 (the back of these two photos contained her name). Although there is a significant age difference with the photo shown in Figure 4.4., there is some resemblance between these two photos and the one in Figure 4.4. Note in particular the position of the hands in all three images.

---

10. Paul Belien A Throne in Brussels, Britain, the Saxe-Coburgs and the Belgianisation of Europe, imprint-academic.com, Exeter, UK, 2005.

Descendants of Franciscus-Alexius Girardin

Franciscus-Alexius GIRARDIN
b. 1 Mar 1847, Sint-Joost-ten-Node
d. 24 Mar 1930, Sint-Ulriks-Kapelle
& Antonia SMET
b. 25 Jul 1847, Brussegem
d. 2 Jun 1917, Sint-Ulriks-Kapelle
m. 25 Nov 1874, Brussegem

Marie Elisabeth GIRARDIN
b. 2 Sep 1875, Sint-Kwintens-Lennik
d. 26 Sep 1875, Sint-Kwintens-Lennik

Justine GIRARDIN
b. 12 Sep 1876, Sint-Kwintens-Lennik
d. 14 Jan 1943, Merchtem
& Arnold VAN DEN HOUTE
b. 1 Apr 1873, Merchtem
d. 22 Sep 1954, Merchtem
m. 11 Feb 1904, Sint-Ulriks-Kapelle

Maria GIRARDIN
b. 23 Feb 1878, Sint-Kwintens-Lennik
d. 22 Nov 1943, Groot-Bijgaarden
& Jozef Alois DE RIJCK
b. 7 Dec 1877, Heist op den Berg
d. 4 Mar 1963, Asse

Louis GIRARDIN
b. 2 Sep 1879, Sint-Kwintens-Lennik
d. 12 Sep 1935, Ternat
& Philomena WIJNS
b. 15 Jun 1878, Halle
d. 6 Oct 1963, Ganshoren

Henriette GIRARDIN
b. 17 Nov 1881, Sint-Kwintens-Lennik
d. 17 Apr 1968, Sint-Martens-Bodegem
& Zacharias CARLIER
b. 27 Oct 1877, Sint-Kwintens-Lennik
d. 18 May 1951, Sint-Martens-Bodegem
m. 13 Jan 1912, Schepdaal

Maria Elisabeth GIRARDIN
b. 23 May 1883, Sint-Ulriks-Kapelle
d. 7 Nov 1946, Asse
& Theophiel DE DONCKER
b. 14 Sep 1884, Asse
d. 11 Dec 1962, Asse

Pelagie GIRARDIN
b. 4 Oct 1884, Sint-Ulriks-Kapelle
d. 24 Jun 1958, Sint-Ulriks-Kapelle

Florentine Antoinette GIRARDIN
b. 11 Apr 1886, Sint-Ulriks-Kapelle
d. 31 Mar 1887, Sint-Ulriks-Kapelle

Jean GIRARDIN
b. 9 Jan 1888, Sint-Ulriks-Kapelle
d. 17 Feb 1962, Brussel
& Josephine DE MASENEER
b. 11 Oct 1893, Sint-Ulriks-Kapelle
d. 20 Dec 1945, Sint-Ulriks-Kapelle
m. 20 Aug 1915, Sint-Ulriks-Kapelle

Jean GIRARDIN
b. 9 Jan 1888, Sint-Ulriks-Kapelle
d. 17 Feb 1962, Brussel
& Lisette BEJAER
b. 22 Oct 1900, Asse
d. 29 May 2000, Sint-Ulriks-Kapelle
m. 8 Nov 1947, Sint-Ulriks-Kapelle

Figure 4.7 Descendants of Franciscus-Alexius Girardin (reduced to include only the male lineage that continues to the present day).

Descendants of Franciscus-Alexius Girardin (continued)

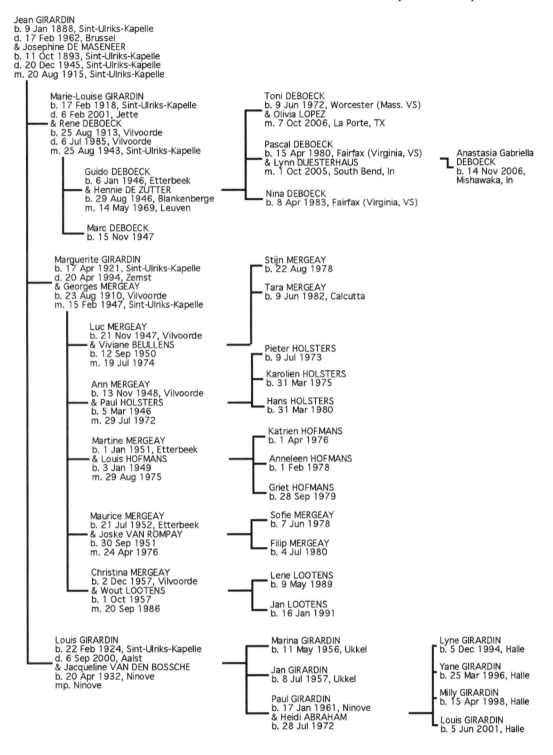

Jean GIRARDIN
b. 9 Jan 1888, Sint-Ulriks-Kapelle
d. 17 Feb 1962, Brussel
& Josephine DE MASENEER
b. 11 Oct 1893, Sint-Ulriks-Kapelle
d. 20 Dec 1945, Sint-Ulriks-Kapelle
m. 20 Aug 1915, Sint-Ulriks-Kapelle

Marie-Louise GIRARDIN
b. 17 Feb 1918, Sint-Ulriks-Kapelle
d. 6 Feb 2001, Jette
& Rene DEBOECK
b. 25 Aug 1913, Vilvoorde
d. 6 Jul 1985, Vilvoorde
m. 25 Aug 1943, Sint-Ulriks-Kapelle

Guido DEBOECK
b. 6 Jan 1946, Etterbeek
& Hennie DE ZUTTER
b. 29 Aug 1946, Blankenberge
m. 14 May 1969, Leuven

Marc DEBOECK
b. 15 Nov 1947

Toni DEBOECK
b. 9 Jun 1972, Worcester (Mass. VS)
& Olivia LOPEZ
m. 7 Oct 2006, La Porte, TX

Pascal DEBOECK
b. 15 Apr 1980, Fairfax (Virginia, VS)
& Lynn DUESTERHAUS
m. 1 Oct 2005, South Bend, In

Nina DEBOECK
b. 8 Apr 1983, Fairfax (Virginia, VS)

Anastasia Gabriella DEBOECK
b. 14 Nov 2006, Mishawaka, In

Marguerite GIRARDIN
b. 17 Apr 1921, Sint-Ulriks-Kapelle
d. 20 Apr 1994, Zemst
& Georges MERGEAY
b. 23 Aug 1910, Vilvoorde
m. 15 Feb 1947, Sint-Ulriks-Kapelle

Luc MERGEAY
b. 21 Nov 1947, Vilvoorde
& Viviane BEULLENS
b. 12 Sep 1950
m. 19 Jul 1974

Ann MERGEAY
b. 13 Nov 1948, Vilvoorde
& Paul HOLSTERS
b. 5 Mar 1946
m. 29 Jul 1972

Martine MERGEAY
b. 1 Jan 1951, Etterbeek
& Louis HOFMANS
b. 3 Jan 1949
m. 29 Aug 1975

Maurice MERGEAY
b. 21 Jul 1952, Etterbeek
& Joske VAN ROMPAY
b. 30 Sep 1951
m. 24 Apr 1976

Christina MERGEAY
b. 2 Dec 1957, Vilvoorde
& Wout LOOTENS
b. 1 Oct 1957
m. 20 Sep 1986

Stijn MERGEAY
b. 22 Aug 1978

Tara MERGEAY
b. 9 Jun 1982, Calcutta

Pieter HOLSTERS
b. 9 Jul 1973

Karolien HOLSTERS
b. 31 Mar 1975

Hans HOLSTERS
b. 31 Mar 1980

Katrien HOFMANS
b. 1 Apr 1976

Anneleen HOFMANS
b. 1 Feb 1978

Griet HOFMANS
b. 28 Sep 1979

Sofie MERGEAY
b. 7 Jun 1978

Filip MERGEAY
b. 4 Jul 1980

Lene LOOTENS
b. 9 May 1989

Jan LOOTENS
b. 16 Jan 1991

Louis GIRARDIN
b. 22 Feb 1924, Sint-Ulriks-Kapelle
d. 6 Sep 2000, Aalst
& Jacqueline VAN DEN BOSSCHE
b. 20 Apr 1932, Ninove
mp. Ninove

Marina GIRARDIN
b. 11 May 1956, Ukkel

Jan GIRARDIN
b. 8 Jul 1957, Ukkel

Paul GIRARDIN
b. 17 Jan 1961, Ninove
& Heidi ABRAHAM
b. 28 Jul 1972

Lyne GIRARDIN
b. 5 Dec 1994, Halle

Yane GIRARDIN
b. 25 Mar 1996, Halle

Milly GIRARDIN
b. 15 Apr 1998, Halle

Louis GIRARDIN
b. 5 Jun 2001, Halle

going to these results it may be of interest to read Annex 5 that provides the historical background on Leopold I.

Augustine did not raise Franciscus-Alexius. He was nursed and brought up by a family without children, probably the sister of Augustine, Catherine Elisabeth Girardin who was married to Guillelmus Homble (or Humble). Augustine died at age 81 in 1888.

The Humble family lived on a farm, called a kam. A *kam* was a farm and brewery, which also produced its own malt. It is from his foster parents that Franciscus-Alexius learned the family tradition of farming and brewing. He married Antonia Smets; together they first lived on a kam on the Tuitenberg in Lennik, later in Sint-Ulriks-Kapelle.

The descendants of Franciscus-Alexius Girardin

Franciscus-Alexius, also known as Frans in Sint-Ulriks-Kapelle, was born in Sint-Joost-ten-Noode on March 1, 1847. He married Antonia Smet on November 25, 1874. Antonia Smet was the daughter of Dominicus Smet and Catharina Van Roy. Antonia was born on July 25, 1847; she was just five months younger than he was. They married in Brussegem, where she was from. They had nine children. A chart of the descendants of Franciscus-Alexius and Antonia is shown in Figure 4.7. If you are not interested in the details of the family history of the descendants of Franciscus-

Figure 4.8 Family of Franciscus Alexius Girardin with in the middle his youngest son Jean (Joannes Baptist). Photo circa 1895. This photo does not include Marie Elisabeth born in 1875 nor Florentine Antoinette born in 1886, both of whom died in infancy.

Alexius Girardin, you can skip right to the next section in which I will discuss what role he and his son played in the community.

1. Marie Elisabeth was born on September 2, 1875 in Sint Kwintens Lennik; she died twenty-four days later on September 26, 1875.

2. Justine (official first name was **Justina**) born on September 12, 1876 in Sint-Kwintens-Lennik; she died at the age of 66 on January 14, 1943. She married Arnold Van den Houte on February 11, 1904 in Sint-Ulriks-Kapelle. Arnold was born on April 1, 1873 in Merchtem and died when he was 81 on September 22, 1954. Together they had eleven children:

> **a. Franciscus Arnoldus** (1905-1975)
> **b. Georges** (1906-1987)
> **c. Louis** (1907-1956)
> **d. Maria Josephina** (1908-1991)
> **e. Henrica Josephina Maria** (1910-
> **f. Rene** (1911-1986)
> **g. Emiel** (1913-1968)
> **h. Louise** (1914-1956)
> **i. Albert Frans** (1916-1998)
> **j. Pelagie** (1918-1998)
> **k. Jozef** (1920-2002)

Justine Girardin married Arnold a second time on August 4, 1904 in Merchtem, presumably because the first marriage was declared not valid.

3. Maria (official first name **Ivonna Maria**) born on February 23, 1878 in Sint Kwintens Lennik; she died in Groot Bijgaarden on November 22, 1943 when she was 65. She married Jozef Alois De Rijck who was born on December 7, 1877 in Heist op den Berg and who died at age 85 on March 4, 1963. They had two children, Rene (1915-1975) and Maurice (1918-1981). Maurice became a priest.

4. Louis (offical first name **Ludovicus Josephus**) born on September 2. 1879 in Sint Kwintens Lennik and died in Ternat on September 12, 1935, when he was 56 years old. He married Philomena Wijns, born on June 15, 1878 in Halle. She died in Ganshoren at age 85 on October 6, 1963.They had three children:

> **a. Joanna** (1904-1993)
> **b. Margareta** (1906-)
> **c. Madeleine Irma** (1908-)

5. Henriette (offical first name **Henrica Josephina**) born on November 17, 1881 in Sint Kwintens Lennik. She died in Sint Martens Bodegem on April 17, 1968 at age 86. She married Zacharias Carlier who was born on October 27, 1877 in Sint Kwintens Lennik and died at age 73 in Sint Martens Bodegem on May 18, 1951. They had five children:

a. **Judo Frans** (1913-1994)
b. **Alice** (1915-1999)
c. **Justina** (1917-)
d. **Jeanne** (1919-)
e. **Eduard** (1921-1997)

6. Maria Elisabeth born on May 23, 1883 in Sint-Ulriks-Kapelle; Maria died in Asse at age 63 on November 7, 1946. She married Theophiel De Donker, who was born in Asse on September 14, 1884 and died in the same place on December 11, 1962. He was 78 years old. They had eight children:

a. **Germaine** (1912-1986)
b. **Pelagie** (1914-1991)
c. **Albert** (1916 -)
d. **Renaat** (1918-)
e. **Maurice** (1919-)
f. **Jan Gabriel** (1920-1938)
g. **Cyriel** (1923-)
h. **Louis** (1927-)

BID VOOR DE ZIEL VAN ZALIGER

MIJNHEER

FRANCISCUS-ALEXIUS GIRARDIN

WEDUWENAAR VAN

MEVROUW ANTONIA SMET

Oud-Burgemeester van Sint-Ulrich-Capelle, vereerd met de Burgerlijke Eereteekens van 1e klas voor 25 en 35 jaren trouwen dienst, Lid van den Bond van het H. Hart

geboren te St-Joost-Ten-Noode, den 1 Maart 1847, godvruchtig overleden te Sint-Ulrich-Capelle, den 24 Maart 1930, voorzien van de HH Sacramenten der stervenden.

7. Pelagie (offical first name **Pelagia**) was born on October 4, 1884 in Sint-Ulriks-Kapelle. She died at age 73 on June 24, 1958

8. Florentine Antoinette (official first name **Florence Antonetta**) was born on April 11, 1886 in Sint-Ulriks-Kapelle. She died less than a year later on March 31, 1887.

9. Jean (official first name was **Joannes Baptist**) was born on January 9, 1888 in Sint-Ulriks-Kapelle. He died (most likely of cancer) on February 17, 1962 in Brussels at age 74. He first married Josephina De Maseneer born on October 11, 1893 in Sint-Ul-

Figure 4.9 Death Print
(Doods prentje)
of Franciscus-Alexius Girardin, 1930.

Figure 4.10 Photo: Jean (Joannes Baptist) Girardin and Josephina De Maseneer
August 20, 1915

riks-Kapelle. Josephina died at age 52 on December 12, 1945.

Franciscus-Alexius Girardin died on March 24, 1930.
Jean and Josephina had three children:

1. Marie-Louise (first names Francisca Maria Louise) was born in Sint-Ulriks-Kapelle on February 17, 1918 and died on February 6, 2001. As was indicated before, she married Rene Corneille Deboeck on August 25, 1943, and together they had two sons: Guido and Marc Deboeck (see Chapter 2 and 7).

2. Marguerite (first names Margaretha Justina Ludovica) was born on April 17, 1921 in Sint-Ulriks-Kapelle and died (of cancer) in Zemst at age 73 on April 20, 1994. She married Georges (Jean Emile) Mergeay, son of Albert Joseph Eugene Mergeay (1876-1958) and Maria Therese Van Wayenbergh (1878-1960). Georges was born August 23, 1910. In 2005 he celebrated his 95th birthday. Georges and Marguerite had five children:

> a. **Luc** (1947-)
> b. **Ann** (1948-)
> c. **Marine** (1951-)
> d. **Maurice** (1952-)
> e. **Christine** (1957-)

3. Louis (first names Lodewijk Frans Alexis) was born on February 22, 1924 in Sint-Ulriks-Kapelle. He died of a major heart stroke in the hospital (Onze Lieve Vrouw Ziekenhuis) in Aalst on September 6, 2000 when he was 76 years old. He married Jacqueline van den Bosssche who was born on April 20, 1932 in Ninove. They had three children

> a. **Marina** born on May 11, 1956 in Ukkel
> b. **Jan** born on July 8, 1957 in Ukkel
> c. **Paul** born on January 17, 1961 in Ukkel. He married Heidi Abraham who was born on July 28, 1972.
> They have four children:
> > i. **Lyne** (1994 -)
> > ii. **Yane** (1996 -)
> > iii. **Milly** (1998-)
> > iv. **Louis Jr.** (2001-)

Josephine De Maseneer, my grandmother that died days before I was born, became the honorary chairwoman of the Gilde of Farmers Women ("Boerinnengilde"), died on December 20, 1945. Her death notice read: She was a caring mother, a faithful companion and strong supporter of her husband. She lived for her children: their happiness was hers. Her compassion for the

Figure 4.11 Photo: Marie-Justine De Maseneer (left) in 1997 at her 100th birthday celebration, and shown on the right with the local governing council.

poor and those in need was well recognized. She lived simply, was careful with her words, and was loved by everyone who knew her.

Josephine De Maseneer had a sister, Marie-Justine who was born on February 28th, 1897 in Sint-Ulriks-Kapelle and who married Frans De Mesmaeker. Justine celebrated her 100th birthday in "De Verlosser," a retirement home in Sint-Ulriks-Kapelle. After many speeches and flowers from the local governing council (see Figure 4.11), she invited the family to a luncheon. On her 100th birthday celebration that I attended in Sint-Ulriks-Kapelle, she stood up at the luncheon, made a speech and sang for all the family. She thanked family members for the support she had received over many years. Justine died a few months later on May 7, 1997.

After Josephine De Maseneer passed away, Jean Girardin married Lisette (Isabella) Bejaer, who was born on October 22, 1900. Together they were a niece couple; she supported him in his career as brewer as well as mayor (see next section).

Jean Girardin, my grandfather, died on February 17, 1962 in the hospital of Sint Remi in Brussels. He received several acclamations for his service as mayor ("Burgelijke medaille van 1ste klas en Lid van de Bond van het H. hart"). He also helped in the works of Don Bosco.

Lisette Bejard died just before her 100th birthday in Sint-Ulriks-Kapelle on May 29, 2000. She had one sister, Julienne, who was married to Robert Spanhoghe, an inspector of schools and educational programs in Belgium.

Figure 4.12 The children of Jean-Baptist Girardin and Josephine De Maseneer: from l. to r: Marie-Louise, Louis and Marguerite. Photo ca. 1936

Two Catholic Mayors of Sint-Ulriks-Kapelle

Franciscus-Alexius and his son Joannes-Baptist were brewers but they were also mayors and contributed in many ways to the community.

As a devoted Catholic, Franciscus-Alexius Girardin played an important role in several local societies. He was a member of the Society of the Sacred Heart of Jesus *(Bond van het Heilig Hart)* and became the Chairman of the Society of Saint Jozef in 1903.

A speech made at his inauguration as Chairman of the Saint Jozef Society stressed that Farmer *(Pachter in Dutch)* Girardin had a good heart, brought up his children in the Christian faith; worked hard, spared no effort to encourage his children; and that they all worked together and never wasted any time. Again we encounter this notion of a family enterprise, in the case of the Girardin family, however, it lasted several generations. Till to-day the Girardin family seldom relied on hired labor; almost all the work on the farm and in the brewery is done by the family.

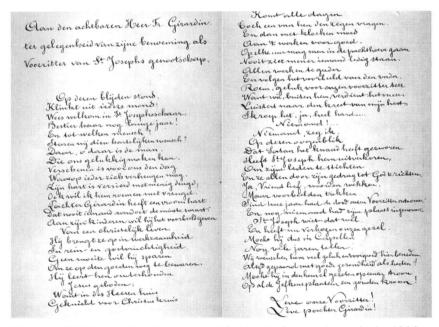

Figure 4.13 Photo: Front cover and full text of speech made in 1903 at the occasion of Franciscus-Alexius becoming Chairman of the Society of Sint Jozef.

In 1904 Franciscus-Alexius was elected mayor of St Ulriks Kapelle. Local beliefs were that mayors were elected on the basis of who gave the most beer to the local cafés. In the case of Franciscus-Alexius it was probably his standing in the community and in the Society of Saint Jozef that brought him to public service.

In the period from 1914 till 1918 Belgium was occupied by Germany. Figure 4.14 shows Franciscus-Alexius as mayor with his city council in exile.

Franciscus-Alexius received various acclamations and two decorations for his civil service as mayor ("Burgelijke Eereteekens van 1e klas voor 25 en 35 jaren trouwen dienst, en Lid van den Bond van het Heilig Hart").

In 1912 when Franciscus-Alexius was 65, he and his wife donated the Girardin Brewery to their youngest son Joannes-Baptist(a) Girardin. In a notary act of July 11 prepared by notary Fernand Wijnants of Opwijk, it is written that Joannes-Baptista received 79.65 *are of land* (one are is 100 square meters and is equivalent to 1.9 acre, one are=0.0247 acre) that was valued at that time at BF 6,212, plus the brewery valued at that time at BF 14,787. His sister Pelagie received four parcels of land, which together totaled 257.41 are of land (equivalent to 6.35 acres), valued at that time at BF 13,000. Hence land prices in Sint-Ulriks-Kaplle were about BF 50.50 per 100 square meters in 1912.[11]

Through this notary act I found from whom Franciscus-Alexius Girardin had bought the land and the brewery. The act states that the brewery was bought in 1898 from Joanna Catherina Janssens, widow of Joseph Wauters in Bekkerzeel, as recorded in a notary act of April 18, 1898 prepared by notaries Ectors and De Tiége.[12]

In consequence, there is some mystery about the startup of the brewery. While Franciscus-Alexius bought the brewery in 1889 according to this notary act, to this date the startup date of the brewery is claimed to be 1882.

Documents obtained from The Registry of Properties ("Kadaster" in Belgium) show that long before that date a brewery existed on the Lindenberg in Sint-Ulriks Kapelle. The earliest reference to a brewery was found in a plan that contained the state of

11. According to P. Duran 1 BF of 1912 is worth 4.554 EUR of 2005. Based on it the land received by my grandfather in 1912 was worth EUR 28,289; the brewery was worth EUR 67,340 in 2005. The total converted to US$ using today's EUR/US$ exchange rate adds up to US$ 73,560 (EUR 95,629/1.3). The land given to Pelagie was worth EUR 59,202 or US$ 45,540 in current dollars.

12. There were four purchases made which were recorded in the notary acts made by Ectors and De Tiége, on April 18, 1898. Joanna-Catharina Janssens, widow of Wauters-Janssens had become the owner of this property via the notary acts prepared by 1/ notary Verbruggen in Jans-Molenbeek on May 14, 1857, May 22, 1847 and April 24, 1858; 2/ notary Crick in Ass, on February 23, 1871; 3/ notary Maes in Brussels on January 25, 1865.

the brewery in 1823. The first owner of the brewery was Stephen Petrus. In 1842 the ownership of this brewery was handed over to Janssens Leon; it then became property of Joanna Janssens before it became the property of Simon Wauters-Janssens.[13]

After he donated the brewery to his youngest son in 1912, Franciscus-Alexius and Antonia continued to live at the brewery. Franciscus-Alexius remained mayor till 1927. He died three years later on March 24, 1930 at age 83.

In 1938 Joannes-Baptista Girardin was elected mayor of Sint-Ul-riks-Kapelle. He remained mayor till 1958 when the Liberal party took over from the Christian-Democrats. Joannes-Baptist, who was my beloved godfather, died on February 17, 1962 at age 74.

Figure 4.14 Photo: Mayor Frans Girardin with his city council during the war. The sign reads: In exile. Photo circa 1914-

Figure 4.15 Joannes-Baptist (also called Jean-Baptist) Girardin, mayor of Sint-Ulriks-Kapelle 1938-1958.

13. Jaak Ockeley, editor of *Eigenschoon en de Brabander,* wrote that in the ledger by Popp (the earliest records of property taxes in Belgium called *Kadastraal*) he found "fabyken, trafyken en andere gebouwde eigendommen: brouwerijen 1 geschat op 38 F" (in other words the value of the brewery for tax purposes was estimated at 38 F) and under article 346 Janssens Joanna Catharina, Cappelle-Sint-Ulric he found "perceel sectie B no 317 brouwery oppervlakte 1 are 50 centiare, klasse 1, belastbaar inkomen de grond 1.08 F, het gebouw 38 F (in other words the land identified as section B no 317 that contained a brewery was 1 are and 50 *centiare* great – 1 are =0.0247 acre – and the property tax on the land was 1.08 BF and on the brewery was 38 BF). Personal e-mail from J. Ockeley, March 2, 2007. His information was confirmed by Guido Pauwels, Inspector Director of Kadastraal, in a letter to me of March 8, 2007.

Beer brewing around Brussels

Before I describe 125 years of brewing by the Girardin family, a few words about beer brewing around Brussels. In and around Brussels beer has been brewed for centuries. Not just any beers but *lambic, gueuze, kriek, framboise and faro,* i.e., beers that are unique to the area of Pajottenland.

Lambic is a traditional beer with a rich somewhat sour flavor. It is made of spontaneous fermentation with at least 30% of wheat. Young lambic (platte, joenk or vos in Dutch) is dry, sour, cloudy and similar in taste to cider. Aged lambic is more mellow and settled. Old lambic has greater acidity. Some lambic is sold as such but most is used to produce gueuze. Since 1880, Lambic has been bottled to simplify transport but also for conservation properties; this gave the birth to Gueuze.

Gueuze: Gueuze is a blend made of 2/3 young Lambic and 1/3 old Lambic. The right ratio young/old is depending on the maturation degree (end attenuation) of each of them. The bottles filled with this blend of wild spontaneous fermented Lambics, are re-fermented in the bottle in a cool cellar following the *Champenoise method* (meaning beer is fermented in the bottles, which are turned regularly and eventually opened to extract the yeast, similar to the way Champagne is fermented). After 6 months the Gueuze obtains a golden color and provides a cider-y, wine-y palate, reminiscent of dry vermouth with a more complex and natural flavor. Beside the traditional Gueuze there are more commercial Gueuzes that dominate the market; these are filtered, pasteurized and have a sweet taste.

Kriek: In origin, this sweet-acid drink was obtained by adding fresh black cherries to a barrel of 6 months aged Lambic. The addition of fruits provokes a new fermentation in the oak barrels. After another 8 to 12 months, only peels and stones of cherries are left and the Kriek-Lambic is ready to be filtered and bottled. The residual sugar can be adjusted with straight-on fruit juice to give a re-fermentation in the bottle. This traditional type of fruit beer is more acid and less fruity.[14]

Framboise, Peach and other fruit beers: Using the straight juice-method these fruit beers are the result of blending young with old Lambic and pure fruit pulp. The result is a fresh, fruity drink with the background of the rich bouquet of Lambic.

---

14. Because of the limited availability and high price of fresh black cherries (they are only available in the beginning of August and are grown less and less) some breweries have developed a unique natural method that uses pure cherry pulp from unfrozen cherries. This creates a fruity and less sour Lambic. This straight cherry pulp is blended with selected Lambic of different ages. Kriek has a pink-red color and a delicious taste of sparkling cherry champagne.

Faro: Faro is a version of Belgium's wild-fermented wheat beer, which is the result of blending Lambic of one summer with old Lambic and candy sugar. Faro is an intriguing balance of wine and sweetness. This was probably the beer depicted in Breughel's painting of *Flemish Village Life.*

Since all of these beers rely on lambic that is made using spontaneous fermentation, meaning the micro bacteria in the air, none of these beers can be made elsewhere than around Brussels. It is the air of Pajottenland and of the many cherry trees in that area that produce the unique flavors of these beers.

These unique beers have been brewed according to methods and traditions that are 400 years old. The history of beer brewing and especially of these unique beers was first published in 2001 by the author in *Un'beer'ably Delicious, Cooking with Artisan and Craft beers.*[15] For those who are interested an abbreviated version follows.

In Belgium, archeological findings from the 3rd and the 4th century show a Roman villa with many add-on buildings where beer was brewed.[16] After 800 AC the term *brewery* appears regularly in documents, although the name brewery differs from area to area and across time.[17]

In the early Middle Ages beer brewing became popular in monasteries and abbeys. In the 6th century the Saint Benedict monks were ordered not to depend on local people; water was contaminated; monks had to learn to brew. In 816 St Gallen in Germany became a real brew center.

The main reason for monks to become interested in beer brewing was to improve the nutritional quality of their own food intake, especially during lent. In fact only during lent was the consumption of a richly brewed beverage allowed.

Each monk was allowed to consume up to *five liters of beer per day;* drinking water was not safe. The monks deciphered the manuscripts used in Egypt and from it brewed beer as a solution to the unsafe water problem. The role played by monasteries and abbeys in the transfer and improvement of knowledge of beer brewing was colossal! Monks were well educated, their social

---

15. Copies of this book can be obtained from DokusPublishing in Arlington or ordered on line via http://www.e-magiantivegifts.com (click on Holiday Gifts/Cookbook) or via http://www.dokus.com.

16. Among the findings were pots and beer glasses, which contained inscriptions that clearly referred to beer. In the museum of Arlon in Belgium there are archeological findings from the 3rd century that show a working cervisiarii. From all of this we can derive that during the Gaul and Roman times, beer was being produced.

17. In the 9th century the term camba and also braxina shows up. In the 13th century the term changes to cambe of bressine (on Romain territory); to *bruwers huse or panhus* (in German territory).

infrastructure and the equipment available to them made monasteries and abbeys the centre of beer brewing and –experience.[18]

Monks have been brewing beer since the 12th century and beer was consumed in abbeys in Belgium, North Germany, Netherlands, England and Ireland. Beer was also brewed in French abbeys in the Champagne region.[19]

While originally only for own consumption, monks after a while started brewing for others. Their production was sold originally only in the pubs of abbeys but after it became popular also to the public. The clerical world made the art of brewing the most respected business! With it came the introduction of the first taxes, as a result of which many clerical breweries closed.[20]

After book printing was invented information on the process of brewing was easily distributed. In 1516 a German decree *(das Rheinheitsgebot)* established for the first time that only barley (later malted barley) and hops and water could be used in producing beer. The use of yeast was not yet known at that time.

In 1693 a French King created the title of *Master Brewer of Flanders, Henegouwen and Artesia,* which were provinces in the kingdom. The brewers who received the honor title of Master Brewer obtained a monopoly for beer production, whereby pub owners were no longer allowed to brew their beer. To make sure that regulations were followed, civil servants were appointed as tasters.

In the 17th century De Rance introduced *La Trappe,* a reformation that was so severe that it became famous. This lifestyle for monks was soon imitated in other abbeys and the new followers were called *Trappists.* There are six Trappist monasteries in Belgium that still brew beer (Achel, Chimay, Orval, Rochefort,

---

18. Some documents from the 9th century show that abbeys could have up to three breweries: one for brewing weak beer mainly for beggars; another one for brewing beer that the monks would drink and which they also would share with pilgrims; and a third one that would brew strong beer that would be served for special guests, like when the bishop would visit. Hence each brewery produced its own beer: the *prima melia of celia* was made for beggars; the *cervisia,* was made for the daily consumption by the monks; and the third, *cervisia mellia,* which resembled mead or honey beer, was made for special occasions. The monks liked *cervisia mellia* so much that the Council of Worms in 868 limited the drinking of it to the festive days.

19. The ruins of the abbey of Villers-la-Ville still show one of the most beautiful abbeys of those days, where between 1270 and 1278 beer was brewed.

20. The discovery of hops for favoring beer, was an important contribution made by a Benedictine nun. Hildegarde van Bingen, the abbess of Diessenberg and an herbalist, was the first to write in the 11th century about the effects of hops on beer and how hops could absorb some of the negative effects of fermentation. She pointed out that adding hops preserves the beer longer. Hops were used as medicine, as a sedative, and also to counter kidney stone problems.

Westmalle, and Westvleteren).[21] The name Trappist is a trademark that can only be used by them; other similar beers are called *Abbey beers.*

In the 14th to 16th century, other beer styles, like *wheat beers,* originated. Wheat beer uses more spices including coriander and orange zest. Beer consumption and production were reflected in the paintings of Brueghel, Teniers, Rubens and other painters.

The invention of the steam engine in 1765 started the industrialization of beer brewing.[22] Scientific progress during the industrial revolution allowed master brewers to refine beer recipes and to improve the quality of various products. During the industrial revolution there was quite a bit of improvement in beer brewing techniques. The thermometer was introduced in 1760; the hydrometer in 1805; refrigeration and control of temperature allowed beer brewing to become independent of seasons.

From the second half of the 18th century and especially in the 19th century dramatic improvements occurred. With the railways distribution was expanded and supplies could be transported. Still, very little was known about the chemical transformation processes that occured during fermentation.

Louis Pasteur, a chemist, born in the Jura in France demonstrated in 1857 that fermentation occurs only in the presence of living cells. His belief that yeast played some role in the process of making alcohol was not original. He was however able to demonstrate that fermentation is due to yeast and that undesired substances (such as lactic acid or acetic acid) made beer and wine sour (due to the presence of additional organisms such as bacteria).[23] Subsequently, the German chemist Eduard Bucher discovered that a cell-free extract of yeast causes alcoholic fermentation. The ancient puzzle was solved; the yeast cell produces the enzyme and the enzyme brings about fermentation.

Brewing benefited enormously from the discoveries of Pasteur. As a result it became possible to produce stable, high quality beers. Over time the production of malt and beer became a real science. A lot of research was done on the appearance of the beer: the head, the bitter qualities of hop, the aging of beer, the aroma and appreciation level of beer, the color and caramelized and burned aromas, the taste of bottled beer. The malt and brewing industry brought many scientific discoveries.

---

21. Jef van den Steen: Trappist: Het Bier en de Monniken (Trappist, the beer and the monks), Davidsfonds, Leuven, 2003.175 p.

22. In 1784 steam engines were first introduced at the Whitbread Brewery. It became possible to produce beer in large quantities.

23. The souring of beer and wine had been a major economic problem. Pasteur contributed to solving the problem: he showed that bacteria are removed by heating the starting sugar solution to a high temperature. Pasteur formulated the fundamental tenets of the germ theory of fermentation, which led to his pasteurization process of sterilization.

From the 18th to the 19th century there was a tremendous increase in the number of breweries. In contrast, in the 20th century there was a drastic reduction in the number of breweries.[24] Brewing became a large industry. Modern breweries emerged that use stainless steel equipment, computer controlled automated operations, and packaging of beer in metal casks, glass bottles, aluminum cans or plastic bottles. The preference of consumers changed to lager beers.

Pilsner, originally brewed in 1842 in current day Czech Republic, was the first pale, lager beer. During WWI Pilsner was introduced in several countries, and became the dominant type of beer that was consumed. During WWII the number of breweries dropped substantially. The Germans confiscated all copper for military purposes and restricted the brewing of beer to the production of beers with low gravity.

Since spontaneous fermented beers require three years of maturing, this did not affect the immediate consumption. The stocks of lambic for producing gueuze were, however, depleted by the end of the WWII. For a couple of years after the war, there was less lambic available for producing gueuze, kriek and framboise. After some difficult periods in the early 90's, the production of special beers remained important and was again on the rise in the beginning of the twenty-first century.

125 years of Girardin Brewery

In 2007 the Girardin Brewery had been in business for 125 years (at least if we accept that 1882 was the year that Franciscus-Alexius started this enterprise). The Girardin Brewery remains to this date a family-owned and family operated brewery. All these years it was Girardins who brewed beer, with very little or no help from any hired labor.

The Girardin Brewery is located on the *Lindenberg* in Sint-Ulriks-Kapelle, which in recent years merged with Dilbeek. Sint-Ulriks-Kapelle is near Groot Bijgaarden, a small village with an old church on the market place, a city hall from the sixteenth century, a castle from the Middle Ages and cafés on every corner. Only seven miles from the center of Brussels in the direction of Asse just past Groot Bijgaarden is Sint-Ulriks-Kapelle. The Brewery is on the Brusselsestraat, the first street to left (after the sign for Sint-Ulriks-Kapelle). This leads to the Lindenberg, one of many hills in Pajottenland. On top of the Lindenberg is the Girardin Brewery built in 1845 but used as a brewery since 1882.[25]

---

24. In 1900 there were 3,223 active breweries in Belgium. This dropped to 1546 in 1930, halved again by 1950 and dropped to 232 by 1970. it gradually decreased to 126 in 1990 and is at present approximately just 100.

25. The attentive reader will have noticed that while the brewery was founded in 1882 as reflected on all labels of the beers made at the brewery, the notary act referred to above indicates that Franciscus-Alexius

The trademark of the brewery can be found right outside the gate: it consists of three barrels with on it Lambic, Gueuze and Kriek (see Figure 4.16). An aerial view of the brewery is shown in Figure 4.17. The building shows a typical layout of a *kam* (an integrated farm and brewery): the right hand side of the building contains the living quarters of the family; next to it are the cellars where the lambic matures in large barrels for three years in dark, damp, environment. The right hand side of the building is the brewery where there is a wooden mash tank, the grain storage and the recently added modern, of copper made, boiling tank. The front is for the stables where horse, cows and pigs were kept (at least in the old days).

Figure 4.16 Trademark of the Girardin Brewery.

This family-operated brewery survived four generations, solely on local demand. Only a small fraction of the production of Girardin beers is exported. It is only since last year that Girardin Geuze could be found in Washington, D.C.; until then all production was for local consumption or export to countries neighboring Belgium.

To understand how the Girardins survived, one needs to know the history of beer brewing, the Flemish culture, and the character of the people in Brabant.

In the beginning of the previous century there were as many breweries in Belgium as there were villages. In 1900 there were 3,223 breweries, and per capita consumption was 220 liters per person per year.

Almost every village had a brewery and it was the mayor of the village who usually owned it. In this Catholic dominated country the mayor was usually Catholic and thus supported the Christian Democratic party. Hence, the mayor in each village brewed the beer and controlled the supply of the beer to the cafés. The opposition, represented by the Liberal party, had to set up a competing brewery in order to gain ground on the Catholic mayor.

In some villages in Flanders there were two competing breweries that produced ten different kinds of beer for a village population of often less than 500. Today, Belgium has a population of approximately 10 million (or twice the number of people in Maryland) but produces 400 to 600 different kinds of beer!

The Girardin brewery was one of those village breweries in the late nineteenth century and early part of the twentieth cen-

---

only bought the property in 1898. This is another part of a puzzle that to this date has not been solved.

Figure 4.17 Farm and brewery on the Lindenberg, Brussels-estraat 12, Sint-Ulriks-Kapelle, above aerial view and below front view.

tury. Franciscus-Alexius Girardin who started the business grew wheat and barley, used the wheat for brewing beer, and used the remainder from the brewing to feed the animals on the farm. Farming and brewing were fully integrated. Brewing was mainly done during the late fall and winter season, never during the summer when the main work was on the land. During summer it was too hot to brew and especially too hot for the beer to ferment.

The origin of the practice of farming and brewing goes back to earlier times. The Duke of Brabant and Limburg, Jan IV, who was the founder of the Catholic University in Leuven (1426), forced all brewers in Brabant in 1420 to use wheat in order to improve the quality of beer. This kind of beer would later be called *lambic*.[26] In the days of Jan IV brewers already belonged to guilds. In 1522 the first brewer house was opened in Brussels. In Antwerp the first one opened in 1553. In 1559 Remi le Mercier of Halle reminded the brewers that everyone should at least use 16 *razieren* (a weight measure of those days) of grain, including 6 *razieren* wheat and 10 *razieren* barley to brew beer. It was clear from this ingredients mix that already in those days lambic was being brewed.

---

26. A lot has been written about the origin of this name, but the most likely explanation is that lambic came from beer from Lembeek, a small village in Pajottenland, not far from Sint-Ulriks-Kapelle.

Each region had its own specific beer: in Flanders it was primarily the sour and brown beers; in Hoegaarden near Leuven it was wheat beers and in the Senne Valley and Pajottenland near Brussels it was lambic.

Franciscus-Alexius who married Antonia Smet, had five daughters and two sons. The youngest son born on January 9, 1888, was named Joannes-Baptista (later called Jean-Baptist, or simply Jean).

While Jean was given the brewery in 1912, he waited until 1930 (when he was 42 years old) to formally take charge of the brewery. Jean was like his father, a hard working, quiet man, devoted to his family, who loved to smoke his own rolled tobacco. He went early to

Figure 4.18 Photo: Jean Girardin with first-born daughter, Marie-Louise (born February 17, 1818) on her first horse ride in April-May 1918.

bed every day and got up long before dawn to feed the animals, plough the land, and start his working day before breakfast. At breakfast, according to story passed on for generations, he would drink a *jenever*,[27] a strong alcoholic beverage that warmed him up.

There is a saying that *the early birds catch all the worms;* this habit of starting early in the morning is still a practice that is engrained in the Girardin family and their descendants.

Figure 4.19 Delivery truck in the days of Jean-Baptist Girardin. Photo circa 1934-37

---

27. Jenever, also known as Genever or Jenever, is juniper-flavored, strong alcoholic liquor of Flanders and the Netherlands from which gin has evolved. Traditional jenever is still very popular in Flanders. Jenever was originally produced by distilling malt wine (moutwijn in Dutch) to 50% alcohol by volume (ABV). Because the alcohol didn't taste very nice due to lack of refined distilling techniques, herbs were added to enhance the flavor. The juniper berry (Jeneverbes in Dutch, which comes from the French Genievre) was best for that, hence the name Jenever (and the English name Gin). Hasselt in Belgium and Schiedam in the Netherlands are famous for their jenever.

Each year on All Saints Day (November 1) when the entire family gathered at the brewery, Jean tapped lambic direct from a barrel[28] (*"van het vat* in Dutch). Barrels of young and old lambic could be found in the dark and cold storage cellars behind the house.

With his son, Louis, and sons-in-law, René and George (who married the sister of Marie-Louise) he would play card games such as "Wiezen" always sitting with his back to the stove in front of the large kitchen window. He looked out on his land and used to say "the cows on his land provided an eternally changing painting, therefore I do not have to go anywhere."

The same kind of scene would replay every New Year's Day when the family gathered, the only difference then was that all grandchildren would read their New Year's letters with wishes to grandpa (in my case godfather) and grandma (my step grandmother). It is a scene that is hard to forget and that should have been digitized, if only there had been digital cameras around in those times.

Figure 4.20 Jean Baptist Girardin and Lisette Bejear

At these family gatherings that included all three of Jean-Baptist's children, Marie-Louise, Marguerite and Louis, and ten grandchildren, a sumptuous dinner would be served always cooked by Jean's second wife, Lisette. Her dinners usually included rabbit made in cherry beer, white and black sausages (black pudding or pensen) with applesauce, and homemade bread. Desserts include a variety of pies and pudding *("rijstpap")*.

Lisette Girardin-Bejaer was a very energetic, lively character who played an important role in the political campaigns and the career of Jean. She had a sharp sense of what was right and wrong, was always well informed about politics (local, domestic, and international), and could talk about anything. She was kind and always treated the grandchildren of Jean as her own.

---

28. Most barrels were from Brussels, each containing 250 liters; there were also pipes (*pijpen* in Dutch) containing 600 to 700 liters. The bigger barrels called *founder* contained 3000 liters. Rows and rows of these were stacked in the dark cellars at the brewery on the Lindenberg, under lots of cobwebs.

Jean remained mayor until 1958, when the World Exhibition was held in Brussels. He managed the Girardin brewery till he died on February 17, 1962. Louis, his only son, took over the brewery and continued the tradition of brewing lambic. In 1984 Louis Girardin said: "the goal is not to expand, but just to survive!" Many local breweries had already closed. What kept the Girardin brewery alive was the production of a high quality lambic and gueuze, faithful customers, and hard work. Louis pointed out: "never be sick because then all goes wrong".

The family performed all the work in the brewery. Louis was the master brewer. His sons Jan and Paul did the brewing while his wife Jacqueline took care of the accounting and the sales. Jan was the first son to study brewing technology; Paul studied electronic engineering.

While Louis was alive his sons would weekly load a truck, drive around and make deliveries to the local cafés. To this date, apart from local deliveries and cases that individuals buy directly at the brewery, when they visit over the weekend, there is little done for marketing. When a few years ago a journalist visited the brewery and asked Paul what was his marketing strategy, Paul replied "here we brew beer, we don't do marketing!"

Louis and Jacqueline liked to take vacations in Germany or Switzerland. On one of those vacations Louis found an old brewery that was for sale. Louis and sons went back to Germany and bought a second-hand copper brew kettle. They spent a month in Germany dismantling it, then fitted it on a truck, and drove it themselves back to Belgium. It took months to assemble, but today it is the pride of the Girardin brewery. It is installed in an annex that was added specifically for the new brew house. The old brew house that is still in use has a cast-iron, open mash turn and bricked-in kettle. The new brew house is fully electrical and automated.

Louis Girardin, just like his father, never retired. He brewed until September 2000, when at age 76 he died from a heart attack. The biggest accomplishments of Louis were to run the brewery from 1962 till 2000 without outside help; to install a modern copper brew house, a bottling machine from Italy; and to diversify the production of lambic by making also a lager beer (called "Pils") and a lemonade. He continued the tradition of his grandfather and brewed lambic to produce gueuze according to the traditional methods that are hundreds of years old!

In October 2000, Paul and Jan took over the Girardin Brewery. Jacqueline Girardin initially continued to do the accounting, but has since handed over the work to Heidi, the wife of Paul. Together they continue the family tradition.

The Girardins are in business because of the quality of their beers, their hard work, their stubbornness and their single minded focus on satisfying the customers. As the brewery diversified the dependency on the sale of lambic beers decreased. After the death of Louis, and the passing away of Marie-Louise, his sister, the family took recluse in the fragility of life, the importance

Figure 4.21 Photo of Louis Girardin Jr., 2001

of children, and simply the realization that work alone should not be the sole priority.

As to the future: Jan is not married, he lives together with his girlfriend. Recently Jan had a severe heart attack; he is taking it somewhat easier, although Jef van den Steen said "there is one thing we know for certain about Jan: he does nothing to improve his health." Maybe his recent accident will change that. Paul is married to Heidi Abraham. They have three daughters (Lynn, Yana and Milly) and one son, Louis, who was born June 2001. It will take another twenty years to know who will become the fifth generation of Girardin brewers.

In sum, the Girardin Brewery remains unique. The Girardin family has brewed for 125 years. Four successive generations of the same family have produced lambic, gueuze, kriek and framboise. The Girardin family continues to use traditional methods to produce unfiltered lambic and gueuze (identified by black labels) as well as filtered versions (identified by white labels). They produce a high quality kriek and framboise, which the Director of the Regional Product Center in Halle called: "best value for money." The brewery has been modernized by the addition of a fully automated brew house and has diversified into the production of a

Pils and lemonades. The Girardin Brewery has over time adapted to changing trends although all brewing is still done without external help. It remains a closed family operated enterprise whose owners care about the quality of their beers more than growth or expansion. *Armand Debelder, Chairman of the High Commission for Artisan Lambic Brewers, called the Girardin brewery the Chateau d'Yquem of Lambic breweries in Belgium.*

Figure 4. 22 Reflection of the landscape of Pajottenland in the Brewhouse of the Girardin Brewery

The Girardin approach to investing[29]

Fanciscus-Alexius and Jean Girardin mainly invested in land, their farm, and brewery. Marie-Louise, daughter of Jean, retained the same interests. She only invested in real estate, never in stocks.

She grew up on the brewery but wanted to become a fashion designer, collected fashion books and had an interest in sketching and design. She undertook some painting, but her father did not let her continue her studies after she finished high school in 1936. She was quite unhappy about this.

After she married an industrialist in 1943 (see Chapter 4) she moved to Vilvoorde. For a few years Marie-Louise lived with the brothers and sister of her husband in the house on the Franklin Roosevelt avenue in Vilvoorde. When the apartment above the lace factory was completed they moved in 1950s to the Mechelsesteenweg, number 6.

She never got used to the pollution in Vilvoorde.[30] She liked the fresh air of Pajottenland, and later of Knokke. For years she was a home keeper focusing on preparing food, washing, ironing and cleaning; this left her unsatisfied. She had plenty of energy and wanted to run a business. Marie-Louise wanted to be involved in the lace firm, but the Deboeck family kept her out. She tried to open a shop to sell curtains and embroidery but her plan never materialized.

Weekly she drove to Pajottenland, the place of her birth, to spend a few hours with her family. When her father died in 1962, she inherited land, a few small houses, and a café. She borrowed money from a notary to turn the small houses into rental properties; transform the café into rooms to rent to students; and to build a villa in the shadows of the brewery where she grew up.

For many years my parents had made plans to build a villa in Meise; land had been purchased, a fence was built; even an orchard had been planted. In the end the plan to build a villa in Meise never materialized. Hence the villa my mother built (with her inheritance) was a reduced version of the plans made for Meise. The design of her villa gave away that it was her hope that we all would use this villa as a second home…

To pay back her debts my mother juggled several jobs: for several years she prepared food in the kitchen of SABENA (the now defunct airline company of Belgium); she was also a supervisor of cleaning crews working at night through the offices of major corporations in Antwerp; she kept a small farm with sheep, geese,

---

29. This section was written on May 14, 2006 in honor of Mother's Day.

30. Right across the Mechelsesteenweg was Entreprises Chimique et Electrique (ECE), a chemical plant, in the Marius Duchéstraat. Until 1959 they produced gelatin based on leftover bones and meat from local "abatoires" (butcheries). Weekly a truck with bones would pass by the house and leave a stench that often would stay around for a day or two.

chickens and rabbits. All of this and many other things she did without help, *Girardin style*.

In the late sixties she moved back to Sint-Ulriks-Kapelle. The decision to liquidate the Deboeck Brothers Ltd. in 1967 precipitated her move. Living in Vilvoorde had become too stressful for her.

Figure 4.23 Francisca Girardin, 1918-2001. (Photo September, 2000)

In her hometown she adopted her middle name, Francisca. She concentrated on real estate investments, just like her father and grandfather always had. Like her father and grandfather; she bought and sold land to buy new properties; upgraded old houses to serve as rental properties. She dealt with renters and students who rented rooms in the house next to her villa. Some students have over the years caused her a lot of grief. To those who were good to her she was a caring, but tough landlady.

In 1992 my mother, who had never flown before, came to visit my wife and me in Washington (see Chapter 7). She had talked about this trip for a long time with her sister, but kept postponing it.[31] In the end it was her sister who challenged her to make the trip. My mother was 74 when for the first time she came to the U.S. The ten days in Washington were not easy for her: she did not speak English, could not communicate with her grandchildren (except with Toni who learned the mother tongue of his parents); and felt uncomfortable in a different world, a world she was not used to. Our way of living and thinking had become so different. After ten days, my mother was happy to return to Belgium.

When my mother died in 2001, days before her 83rd birthday, she had grown a small capital that she inherited to a sizeable fortune. Distrust in banks prevented her from leaving any

---

31. Her sister Marguerite traveled a lot; her husband, George Mergeay became a member of the Rotary Club and attended the international meetings of the Rotaries. Marguerite would often accompany her husband on these trips. They also traveled a lot for pleasure, especially to Portugal.

significant amounts in bank deposits. Instead, she kept investing and gradually paid back all her debts. She fought the bigotry of the early 1900s against women acquiring professional skills; the barriers against women borrowing money; the monopoly of notaries; the government's excessive regulations, its biases against entrepreneurship, and Belgian's high taxes. Belgium remains a country where taxes on income and properties are so high that they create strong disincentives towards entrepreneurship and risk taking.

Francisca gained her financial freedom through hard work, saving every penny, managing rental properties, and savvy management of real estate. She would have loved to read the story of Donald Trump's life and successes. *There are many ways for women to gain their financial freedom but some paths are easier than others...Hers was not the easiest.* The struggles my mother went through in her life were not what many women would be able to do.

Chapter 5
De Zutter Family of West Flanders

In the fall of 1964 I started studying economics at the Catholic University of Leuven. The first exams were held in January 1965. It was after these exams, at a carnival ball, that I first met Hennie De Zutter, a gorgeous looking blond (does this sound familiar…). She was bright, had a lovely smile, was sociable, and full of energy. She was from Lombardsijde (now Westende) but was born in Blankenberge in West Flanders.[1]

I got to know Hennie via a friend, Albert Cluckers, who had the misfortune of introducing us to each other… Another friend, Eddy Van Avermaet, with whom I spent five years in Leuven, got to know Hennie,[2] wanted to marry her but was too much a "gentleman." He missed out on seducing this young lady that would become my wonderful wife, friend, and life companion.[3]

On carnival, i.e., on Fat Tuesday, the night before Ash Wednesday, we went dancing in "den George," a favorite dance saloon in Leuven. From then onwards we hardly could be separated.

The first two years in Leuven we attended the same classes, helped each other during exam periods, went out a lot, including to many beer club evenings. In those first two years we both studied commerce; thereafter I switched to economics.

In the summer of 1966, after the announcement of our exam results of our second year, Hennie for the first time met my parents. My father was delighted meeting Hennie; my mother was surprised that we already had known each other for more than a year.

After the second academic year I went on trips (during the summer) to the USA, Japan and Israel. These trips will be discussed in more detail in Chapter 7.

In the spring of 1968 I proposed to Hennie. We got engaged in June that year and went together during the summer to London. We married almost a year later on May 14, 1969 in the City Hall of Leuven and on August 14, 1969 in the little chapel at the Castle of Heverlee.

---

1. I remembered Blankenberge vaguely because my parents took me there when I was young and pictures show that I played there on the beach before my parents settled on an apartment in Knokke (see Chapter 3).

2. Because we both rented a room in the Frederiklintstraat in the house of Maurice and Madeleine Noël, where Hennie came many times…

3. Eddy Van Avermaet, a Professor of Psychology at the KUL, has been Head of the Department of Psychology in Leuven(1988-94). He wrote *Inleiding tot de Pyschologie (Introduction to Psychology)* with Willy Lens and Paul Eelen, University Press, Leuven, 1996.

In this chapter I describe the ancestors of Hennie De Zutter. The genealogical findings reported here are based on a report prepared by Jozef J. Goethals,[4] who researched the De Zutter family under contract using the parish and civil registers of Moerkerke, Lapscheure and Blankenberge. He consulted these records on microfilms in the Family History Center (of the Church of Jesus Christ of Latter Day Saints) in Maryland. The starting base for his research was four generations of Hennie's ancestors obtained from family records kept by Hennie's mother.[5]

Hennie De Zutter was born on August 29, 1946, in Blankenberge. She is the daughter of Daniel De Zutter and Irmgard Burkhardt. While her father was from Blankenberge, her paternal grandfather and six generations before him were born in Lapscheure. The oldest known parental ancestors of Hennie were however born in Moerkerke.

Lapscheure and Moerkerke are about eight miles east of Bruges; nine miles north of Bruges is Blankenberge. From Blankenberge the family moved to Koksijde, Nieuwpoort and Lombardsijde. All of these moves were the result of the military career of Daniel De Zutter. Hennie's mother and her maternal grandparents are from Braunichswalde in former East Germany.

This chapter starts off with some historical sketches of West Flanders, a province of Flanders that is remarkably different from Brabant. It is different in terms of geography, demographics, history, and last but not least, the mentality of the people![6] Next, I introduce some highlights of the history of the main places where the De Zutter family came from: Moerkerke, Lapscheure, and Blankenberge. After these historical notes comes the pedigree of ten generations of De Zutter family of Blankenberge. The last two sections of this chapter summarize the life of Irmgard Burkhardt and Daniel De Zutter who met during WWII (1940-1945) in Braunichswalde.

---

4. Jozef J. Goethals is a genealogist who has published several books including: *A forgotten family: The Flemish Roots of General George Washington Goethals* (1858-1928), and *Goethals: Tavenier-Vanmaele: Family History*. Goethals's address is: 318 Rossiter Avenue, Baltimore, Md 21212-4419. His e-mail is goetpat@comcast.net

5. Jozef J. Goethals: "The Ancestors of Hennie De Zutter," December 2006, 30 pages plus charts.

6. Over the years I have learned that when in company of West Flemish people it is better to listen than to speak, because West Flemish are great storytellers and have an enormous eagerness to talk. It is by listening to the stories of West Flemish that I came up with the idea of writing about my ancestors of Little Brabant, so as to introduce to them another part of Flanders that has played a key role, as we learned earlier, in the history of Flanders.

From Moerkerke and Lapscheure to Blankenberge

West Flanders is the westernmost province of Belgium. It extends inland from the North Sea coast and is bounded by France on the west and south and by Hainaut, East Flanders, and The Netherlands on the east. It covers an area of 1,214 square miles (or 3,145 square km), has a population of slightly over 1 million people, and is divided into eight administrative *arrondissements.*[7]

West Flanders can be divided geographically into the coastal area and the interior plain. The coastal area (and the polders or land reclaimed from the sea) consists of a straight, 42-mile (68-km) coastline with broad sandy beaches backed by a rampart of sand dunes that reach as high as 100 feet (30 meters) and are one mile (1.6 km) wide in places. These sand dunes are planted with *marram* grass and conifers to help stabilize the sand. This line of dunes is broken only at the mouth of the Yser River near Niewpoort, also at Ostend, and near Zeebrugge, and at the mud-covered inlet of the former Zwijn estuary.[8] Behind the dunes lies a flat plain, the Flemish polders, which are seamed with drainage channels and which extend for 6–10 miles (10–16 km) inland. Bruges (Brugge) is the capital and the largest town in West Flanders. Part of the Flemish textile industry—mainly cotton and linen in Kortrijk, Roeselare, and Menen—is located in the Leie river valley, in the southeast. Bruges is the best known to foreigners as the *Venice of the North* and as a center of lace making (see Chapter 3).

Zooming in on the surroundings of Brugge and in particular on the road from Maldegem to Knokke, we find Moerkerke and Lapscheure, birthplaces of the oldest parental ancestors of Hennie De Zutter (see Figure 5.1).

The history of Moerkerke goes back to 1110. The name "Moerkerke" means church in a marsh, but in the beginning there was no church in the village, but a chapel. This chapel fell under the authority of the church of Oostkerke, as did so many other ones in the region. Moerkerke probably became an independent parish after the construction in the twelfth century of a sea dike

---

7. Veurne, Ostend, Bruges, Tielt, Roeselare, Kortrijk, Ypres, and Diksmuide.

8. The silted-up Zwijn estuary has been made a bird sanctuary.

9. West Flanders is Belgium's leading agricultural province. Along the edge of the dunes, the sandy soils grow potatoes and carrots. In the fertile polders, grass, oats, and fodder crops support the raising of extensive livestock (horses, cattle, pigs). Farther inland, the sand and clay alluvial deposits of the interior plain produce wheat, oats, malting barley, sugar beets, potatoes, tobacco, flax and fodder crops for dairy herds. In the coastal area tourism is the chief source of income, based on a string of seaside resorts, notably Ostend (a cross-Channel ferry port), Blankenberge, Knokke-Heist, and De Panne. Fishing has also gained some importance in Ostend, Niewpoort, and Zeebrugge. The polders are thinly populated, with only a few small market towns, such as Veurne.

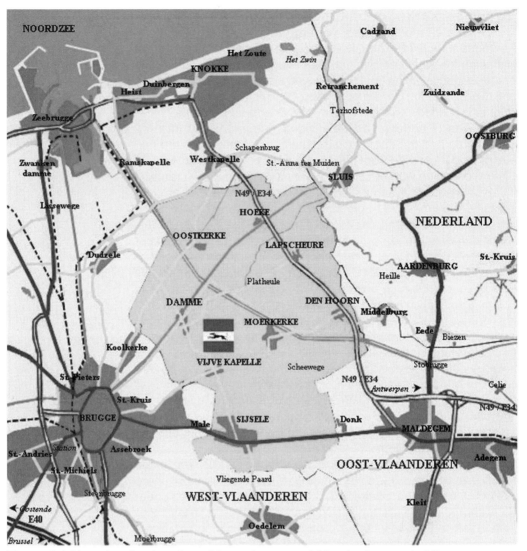

Figure 5.1 Map showing location of Lapscheure and Moerkerke, east of Brugge

between Damme and Den Hoorn. The present church was consecrated in 1870; its patron saint is Saint Dionysius. In the beginning
of the fifteenth century, repairs were carried out. In 1547, the tower
collapsed and was rebuilt two years later. In 1600, the church was
destroyed. The reconstruction was completed in 1654. Eventually,
the church was replaced by the present one.

The castle of Moerkerke, the pride of the village that has
been restored after years of decay, is not the only one on the territory of the village. Not far from the road to Vivenkapelle, there's
the castle of Altena. In the midst of the fields between Moerkerke
and Sijsele there used to be the convent of *Sarepta*. In 1468,
the sisters of Saint Elisabeth settled down here. A century later,
the sisters abandoned their convent because of the threat of the
Geuzen (protestant religious fighters). In 1586 the *Geuzen* burnt

the structures of the convent to the ground. The stones of the old church of *Sarepta* were used in 1923 to erect the chapel of Sarepta. This chapel was bought and cleaned up a few years ago by the local heritage circle.[10]

There used to be seven mills in Moerkerke; not even one remains. The quarter *"het Molentje"* owes its name to a mill that used to be there till 1922. It was a wooden standard mill that was used during more than 150 years by the same family. *"De molen van Schuts"* (named by the villagers, after the name of the last miller) initially was a wooden mill too, but was rebuilt in stone in 1858. This mill was set on fire by Canadian tanks in 1944, to prevent the Germans from using it as a lookout post. The most notorious page in the history of Moerkerke is however not a pleasant one. In 1944, a fierce battle took place known as the battle for "het Molentje". At the end of the Second World War, the tower of the church was shot down by German grenades, fired from artillery placed on the other side of the canals (see details in box). After the war, the tower was rebuilt.[11]

The battle for "het Molentje"

"Het Molentje" is a quarter of Moerkerke, situated on the north of the Leopold and Schipdonk canals.[12] In this peaceful hamlet, the bloodiest battle in Moerkerke's history took place in September 1944. After the landing in Normandy the allied troops advanced rapidly in the direction of Germany. A large part of Belgium had already been liberated. On September 13, 1944, Canadian infantry attempted to cross the Leopold and Schipdonk canals in the area around "Het Molentje" in order to secure the area. The plan was for engineers to construct a steel bridge over the canals, so that allied tanks could penetrate the enemy lines and reach the port of Breskens to free the left banks of the Schelde estuary. This operation, planned for the night of 13 to 14 September 1944, was crucial for the allied forces to use the port of Antwerp. Straight from Adolph Hitler's headquarters came the order to stand ground at all cost alongside the Leopold canal. Reinforcements were brought in including 20mm cannons, antitank weapons and grenade launchers; sharp shooters' holes and machinegun nests were dug out. The *Wehrmacht* made all the necessary arrangements to receive the rapidly approaching Canadian liberators. In the morning of September 10, Germans blew the bridges over the canals; shortly thereafter the locks were opened and slowly the low-lying meadows inundat-

---

10. See http://www.zwinrechteroever.be/

11. Through marriage, the manor Moerkerke passed from the family "van Moerkerke" on to the family "van Praet". The reputation of the stronghold is closely related to the name "van Praet", an old noble family.

12. Moerkerke is surrounded by lots of greens that provide for beautiful walks alongside the canals (Leopold canal and Schipdonk canal), locally nicknamed the "Blinker" (clean one) and "Stinker" (smelly one).

ed (an old tactic in the region that was used also in WWI.) German artillery, placed on the other side of the canals, shot down the tower of the church to prevent the church from being used as an observation post. Armored vehicles coming from the direction of Vivenkapelle announced the arrival of the Canadians. Allied tanks shot the mill of "Schuts" until it burned, thinking that the Germans would use the mill as an outpost. Tanks rolled into the center of the village. Moerkerke was liberated. On Wednesday, September 13, the first shots fell. Grenades were fired from heavy field artillery batteries along the two sides. The Canadian ones were around Sijsele; the German ones on the North Sea coast. When the evening fell, assault boats were put in the water; a total of 440 Canadian infantry soldiers crossed the canal to secure the bridgehead. In the meanwhile, at a few hundred meters from the canal bridge, parts were assembled. The tanks were ready to go. The middle part was relatively easily captured. Once the infantry crossed the second canal, things started to go wrong. The liberators encountered an unexpectedly strong German defense. Errors in orientation and the lack of radio contact isolated small groups of Canadian soldiers. The Germans closed in. They all ended up in house-to-house, even man-to-man fights. Civilians that were not evacuated were killed. Lots of them were hiding in the basements of their houses. The Canadians tried to hold the bridgehead during 17 long hours. Persistent German artillery and machinegun fire made it impossible to even attempt the assembly of the bridge. The liberators were running out of ammunition, the fight continued with knives, bayonets and captured weapons. The Canadians found themselves in a hopeless situation and had to retreat. The Germans successfully held ground; the Canadians never succeeded in liberating the rest of Belgium via this route. The Canadians tried again between Strobrugge and Moershoofde, a bit further east. This was the beginning of what was called operation *"Switchback."* The attack began on October 6; it took till October 19 before their position was secured. The advance to Breskens could finally be continued. By October 19, the zone around "Het Molentje" was cleared and the German lines were pulled back to the "Damse Vaart", where German soldiers in the evening of October 22 blew up the church tower of Oostkerke. The region north of the Leopold canal remained occupied for another six weeks after the battle of "Het Molentje." It was only on November 3, 1944, that the liberation was completed. A modest monument has been placed on "Het Molentje" in memory of the tragic events in the night of 13 to 14 September 1944 when a lot of soldiers and civilians were killed. A street in Moerkerke has been named to honor the Canadian regiment that fought here: the *Algonquinstraat*.

Source: Adapted from Damme-online http://www.damme-online.com/gb/artandculture/uilenspiegel.htm.

Moving further north we find Lapscheure.[13] The name refers to a barn, belonging to a farmer named *Laepe*. In 1110 Balderik, the bishop of Doornik, donated to the abbey of Saint Quinten, the patronage of the church from Oostkerke, together with the chapels from Lapscheure, Moerkerke, and Wulpen on the isle of Cadzand and Waescapelle. In 1240 a church, dedicated to Saint Christian, was built on top of the remains of a former chapel. During the 80-year war (1568-1648) in 1583, Sluis rebels pierced the dikes of the Zwin, destroying the church and the village. In 1652 the present church was built with reusable materials of the destroyed church. It is the only church in the diocese, dedicated to

13. About a thousand years ago, the village was called Lapiscura; in the twelfth century it was Lappescura. In the thirteenth century, Lapscura; in the fourteenth and the fifteenth centuries, Laepscure, also Laepscuere; in the sixteenth century, Laepschuere and since the seventeenth century, Lapscheure.

the Holy Trinity and has as patron Saint Christian (as did the former church). The broken dikes created the *"Lapscheurse Gat"*, a creek that forms the border between Belgium and the Netherlands.

During the 80-year war, Lapscheure found itself literally on the frontline between the Northern and Southern Netherlands. This explains the number of fortresses that were constructed, including the fortress of Saint Donaas, the fortress Frederik and Saint Job. In 1704, Lapscheure was conquered by the Dutch and added to the Dutch territory in 1715.[14] On the territory of Lapscheure, not far from the canal *(Damse Vaart),* there still is on old brickyard, a piece of industrial heritage that provided work for many people in the region during the last century. Lapscheure is an agricultural village that, thanks to its isolated position, is a true oasis of tranquility. The remains of the medieval creeks are omnipresent, which attracts a wide variety of birds and animals. Moreover, in walking distance from the village center, there is a nature reserve.

Northeast of Moerkerke and Lapscheure is Blankenberge, a municipality with a population of 18,135, on a total area of the 17.41 square km (hence a population density of 1,042 inhabitants per square km). Blankenberge has a sandy beach and a structure unique along the Belgian coast: a 350-m long pier. Blankenberge is a lively seaside resort. Along the renovated marina, with moorings for nearly 1,000 boats, there is always something to see or experience. In this renovated marina attention is paid to Blankenberge's maritime past.[15]

In 1815 there were only 1,980 people living in Blankenberge. Fast population growth in the nineteenth century brought the population of Blankenberge to 5,048 in 1900. From 1830 onwards Blankenberge evolved from a fishing village to a tourist resort (see Figure 5.2).

The first hotel on the sea dike was Hotel Godderis. Other hotels included Hotel des Bains et des Familles, Grand Hotel, Hotel Pauwels-D'Hondt, Hotel de Venise, Hotel Continental. In 1859 a casino was added. Gradually Blankenberge became known as a sea resort. Tourism went from 725 "foreign" guests in 1852 to 10,113 in 1872; 17,082 in 1882; 22,781 in 1892.

Tourists had to be fetched from the railroad station and brought to the hotels. In the old days the station was called "statie des ijzeren wegs" or the station of the iron roads. Tourists were

---

14. Since then it returned to Belgium.

15. The Scute is an authentic seaworthy replica of an old Blankenberge fishing boat. Currently a historic pilot cotter is being replicated. You can watch activities in the yard during a walk around the marina. The maritime fleet completed in the autumn of 2005 includes also an authentic shrimp boat. On the quay near the "embarcadero" there is also "half" a fishing boat. In the marina-linked industrial zone, near the Bevrijdingsplein, a ship shed has been erected in which old historic boats will be built or renovated.

picked up at the station with "chars à banc" (coaches). A picture published by Elie Bilé in 1971 in his book on Blankenberge, shows Pieter Bernardus De Zutter, the great grandfather of Hennie (see figure 5.4) as a coach driver picking up tourists at the railway station.[16]

Figure 5.2 Postcard from Blankenberge in the 1930's followed by present day views.

16. Elie Bilé: *Blankenberge: een rijk verleden en een schone toekomst* (Blankenberge a rich past and nice future), page 64.

The De Zutter family of Blankenberge

This section outlines the ancestors of Hennie De Zutter (Figure 5.3). The surname De Zutter has over time had many variants including among others the following: De Sutter, De Suttere, De Zuttere.

The information in this section has been extracted from parish and civil registers.[17] To save space this outline only focuses on direct ancestors (except for the last two generations). A more complete genealogical study of the De Zutter family can be found in the report of Jozef Goethals.[18]

If your family name is not De Zutter or you are not interested in the details of the history of this family, you can skip to the next section in which I will discuss the life of Irmgard Burkhardt.

First Generation: N. N. DE ZUTTER.

An analysis of the baptismal records in which godparents and marriage witnesses are mentioned, leads to the conclusion that the following are siblings and children of an unknown N. N. De Zutter born ca 1615 in Moerkerke.

i.   **Jacoba** was born ca. 1638, she married Petrus Vercruysse, on 27 August 1663.
ii.   **Mattheus** (died circa 1705)
iii. **Maria**
iv.   **Cornelius** (ca 1647-1720)
v.   **Joannes**
vi.   **Jacobus.**
vii. **Carolus.**

Second Generation: CORNELIUS DE ZUTTER was born ca 1647; he married on February 11, 1670 when he was 23, *Maria Vandewiele,* in Moerkerke. He died in Lapscheure on November 7, 1720 when he was 73. They had the following children:

i.   **Joannes** (1671-1720)
ii.   **Rolandus** (-1724)

---

17. The specific parish records consulted for Moerkerke included 1603-1796 (FHL 1142472); 1603-1709 (FHL 0293083), 1603-1728 (FHL 1218126) and 1706-1780 (FHL 0293084). The parish records that were consulted for Lapscheure included 1693-1796 (FHL 1142465 and 1218111). The Civil records for Lapscheure included: 1789-1800 (FHL 1231469), 1810-1831 (FHL 1231470), 1809-1842 (FHL 1349208), 1832-1870 (FHL 121471), 1871-1900 (FHL 1383336). The civil records of Blankenberge included 1872-1890 (FHL 1383078), 1890-1899 (FHL 1383079), 1899-1900 (FHL 1383090) and 1877-1890 marriage records (FHL 2003411). FHL refers to the microfilm number of the Family History Library).

18. Jozef J, Goethals: "The Ancestors of Hennie De Zutter," December 2006, 30 pages plus charts. This study that was contracted is available on request from H. Deboeck-De Zutter.

Ancestors of Hennie De Zutter

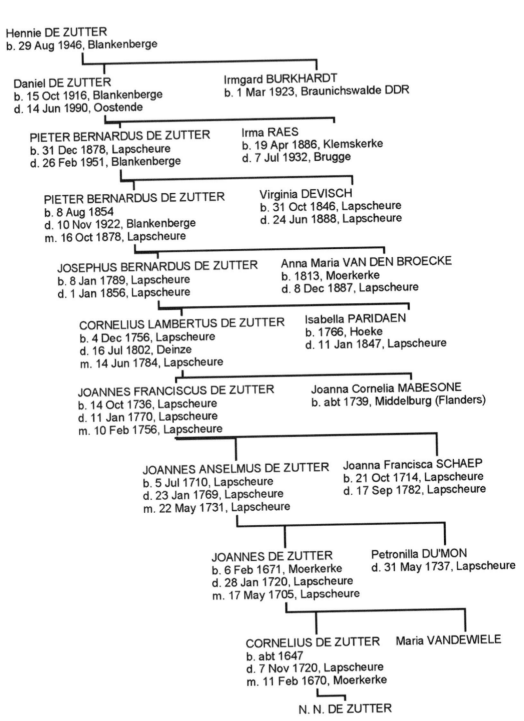

Hennie DE ZUTTER
b. 29 Aug 1946, Blankenberge

Daniel DE ZUTTER
b. 15 Oct 1916, Blankenberge
d. 14 Jun 1990, Oostende

Irmgard BURKHARDT
b. 1 Mar 1923, Braunichswalde DDR

PIETER BERNARDUS DE ZUTTER
b. 31 Dec 1878, Lapscheure
d. 26 Feb 1951, Blankenberge

Irma RAES
b. 19 Apr 1886, Klemskerke
d. 7 Jul 1932, Brugge

PIETER BERNARDUS DE ZUTTER
b. 8 Aug 1854
d. 10 Nov 1922, Blankenberge
m. 16 Oct 1878, Lapscheure

Virginia DEVISCH
b. 31 Oct 1846, Lapscheure
d. 24 Jun 1888, Lapscheure

JOSEPHUS BERNARDUS DE ZUTTER
b. 8 Jan 1789, Lapscheure
d. 1 Jan 1856, Lapscheure

Anna Maria VAN DEN BROECKE
b. 1813, Moerkerke
d. 8 Dec 1887, Lapscheure

CORNELIUS LAMBERTUS DE ZUTTER
b. 4 Dec 1756, Lapscheure
d. 16 Jul 1802, Deinze
m. 14 Jun 1784, Lapscheure

Isabella PARIDAEN
b. 1766, Hoeke
d. 11 Jan 1847, Lapscheure

JOANNES FRANCISCUS DE ZUTTER
b. 14 Oct 1736, Lapscheure
d. 11 Jan 1770, Lapscheure
m. 10 Feb 1756, Lapscheure

Joanna Cornelia MABESONE
b. abt 1739, Middelburg (Flanders)

JOANNES ANSELMUS DE ZUTTER
b. 5 Jul 1710, Lapscheure
d. 23 Jan 1769, Lapscheure
m. 22 May 1731, Lapscheure

Joanna Francisca SCHAEP
b. 21 Oct 1714, Lapscheure
d. 17 Sep 1782, Lapscheure

JOANNES DE ZUTTER
b. 6 Feb 1671, Moerkerke
d. 28 Jan 1720, Lapscheure
m. 17 May 1705, Lapscheure

Petronilla DU'MON
d. 31 May 1737, Lapscheure

CORNELIUS DE ZUTTER
b. abt 1647
d. 7 Nov 1720, Lapscheure
m. 11 Feb 1670, Moerkerke

Maria VANDEWIELE

N. N. DE ZUTTER

Figure 5.3 Paternal ancestors of Hennie De Zutter.

iii.	**Mattheus** (1673-)
iv.	**Paulus,** who was born on July 20, 1675 in Moerkerke.
v.	**Martina** was born on September 6, 1676 in Moerkerke. Martina died in Moerkerke on April 3, 1723; she was 46. On May 3, 1703 when Martina was 26, she married Joannes De Bouvere, in Moerkerke.
vi.	**Maria** was born on October 31, 1679 in Moerkerke. Maria died when she was 66. On October 29, 1709 when Maria was 29, she married Joannes Delmotte, in Moerkerke. He was born ca. 1678 in Moerkerke. Joannes died in Moerkerke on 3 September 1746 when he was 68.
vii.	**Anna** was born on 23 June 1683 in Moerkerke.

Third Generation: JOANNES DE ZUTTER was born on February 6, 1671 in Moerkerke. He first married Maria Degoe who was born ca. 1683 in St Catherina (Damme). Maria died in Lapscheure on April 19, 1703 when she was 20. They had one child.

i.	**Maria** who died on April 14, 1703 in Lapscheure.

Joannes married a second time, *Livina Van Hoecke* who was born ca. 1658 in Lapscheure. Livina died in Lapscheure on December 19, 1704 when she was 46.

When Joannes was 34, he married a third time on May 17, 1705, *Petronilla Du'Mon,* in Lapscheure. Petronilla died on May 31, 1737 in Lapscheure. Joannes and Petronillia had the following children:

i.	**Joanna Philippa** (1706-1753)
ii.	**Petronella** was born on January 20, 1708 in Lapscheure. Petronella died in Lapscheure on July 21, 1711 when she was 3.
iii.	**Joannes Anselmus** (1710-1769)
iv.	**Carolus Jacobus** was born on March 26, 1712 in Lapscheure; he died in Lapscheure on November 9, 1714 when he was 2.
v.	**Philippus Jacobus** was born on September 25, 1713 in Lapscheure; he died in Lapscheure on September 9, 1744 when he was 30.
vi.	**Petronella Francisca** (1716-)
vii.	**Petrus Joannes Bernardus** was born on July 24, 1718 in Lapscheure; he died in Lapscheure on September 27, 1733 when he was 15.

Joannes De Zutter died in Lapscheure on January 28, 1720 when he was 48. Petronella Du'Mon remarried on 27 April 1723 to Ludovicus Van den Broecke in Lapscheure.

Fourth Generation: JOANNES ANSELMUS DE ZUTTER was born on July 5, 1710 in Lapscheure. When he was 20, he married Joanna Francisca Schaep on May 22, 1731, in Lapscheure. She was born on October 21, 1714 in Lapscheure; she died in Lapscheure on September 17, 1782 when she was 67. They had the following children:

i. **Joanna Francisca** (1732-1781)
ii. **Isabella Francisca** (1733-1789)
iii. **Petrus Joannes** who was born on May 29, 1735 in Lapscheure; and who died in Lapscheure on June 14, 1735 when he was less than 1 year old.
iv. **Joannes Franciscus** (1736-1770)
v. **Petronella Joanna Theresa** who was born on July 8, 1739 in Lapscheure, and who died in Lapscheureon October 25, 1801 when she was 62.
vi. **Theresia** (1741-1789)
vii. **N. N.** who was born on January 6, 1743 in Lapscheure. N. N. died in Lapscheure on the same day.
viii. **Joachim Joannes** (1744-1793)
ix. **Petrus Joannes** (1747-)
x. **Andreas** (1748-1815)
xi. **N. N.** who was born on September 22, 1752 in Lapscheure, and died in Lapscheure on the same day.
xii. **Judoca Francisca** who was born on 19 March 1754 in Lapscheure and died in Lapscheure on 13 December 1754 when she was less than 1 year old (burial with *Missa solemnis*).
xiii. **Livinus** who was born on December 18, 1755 in Lapscheure and died in Lapscheure on June 3, 1756 when he was less than 1 year old
xiv. **Brigitta Theresia** (1755-)

Joannes Anselmus De Zutter died in Lapscheure on January 23, 1769 when he was 58.

5. Fifth Generation: JOANNES FRANCISCUS DE ZUTTER was born on October 14, 1736 in Lapscheure. When he was 19 he married Joanna Cornelia Mabesone, on February 10, 1756 in Lapscheure. She was born ca. 1739 in Middelburg (Flandria). Joanna was the widow of Josephus Stul, who had died on 3 December 1755. They had the following children:

i. **Cornelius Lambertus** (1756-1802)
ii. **Mattheus Joannes** was born on November 25, 1758 in Lapscheure; he died in Lapscheure on April 7, 1790 when he was 31. On June 23, 1789 Mattheus Joannes married

Isabella Devriendt, in Lapscheure. She was born in 1744 in Hoeke. On June 30, 1790, Isabella re married with Joannes Franciscus Minnaert.

iii. **Regina** who was born on November 28, 1760 in Lapscheure. On April 29, 1783 when Regina was 22, she married Franciscus Watelle, in Lapscheure. He was born ca. 1759.

iv. **Petrus Joannes Sebastianus** who was born on January 20, 1764 in Lapscheure and died in Lapscheure on December 29, 1767 when he was 3.

v. **Emiliana** who was born on July 29, 1767 in Lapscheure and died in Lapscheure on August 5, 1767 when she was less than 1 year old.

vi. **Joannes Jacobus** who was born on March 3, 1769 in Lapscheure and died in Lapscheure on April 15, 1769 when he was less than 1 year old.

Joannes Franciscus died in Lapscheure on January 11, 1770 when he was 33. He was buried in the church choir with a first class service.

Sixth Generation: CORNELIUS LAMBERTUS DE ZUTTER was born on December 4, 1756 in Lapscheure. On June 14, 1784 when he was 27, he married *Isabella Paridaen,* in Lapscheure. She was born in 1766 in Hoeke. Isabella died in Lapscheure on January 11, 1847 when she was 81. They had the following children:

i. **Isabella Francisca** was born on May 25, 1786 in Lapscheure.

ii. **Josephus Bernardus** (1789-1856)

iii. **Maria Theresia** was born on February 7, 1792 in Lapscheure.

iv. **Regina Francisca** was born on August 2, 1794 in Lapscheure; she died in Lapscheure on November 9, 1794 when she was less than 1 year old.

v. **Cornelius Jacobus** was born on July 25, 1795 in Lapscheure.

vi. **Coletta** was born in 1799 in Lapscheure and died in Lapscheure on June 7, 1807 when she was 8.

vii. **Cornelius Joannes** was born on November 7, 1802 in Lapscheure.

viii. **Anna Maria** was born in 1797 and died in Lapscheure on May 11, 1855 when she was 58. Anna Maria married Petrus Henneman.

After the death of Cornelius, Isabella married Adrianus De Roeck. Cornelius Lambertus De Zutter died in Deinze on July 16, 1802 when he was 45.

Seventh Generation: JOSEPHUS BERNARDUS DE ZUTTER was born on January 8, 1789 in Lapscheure. When he was 27, he first married *Anna Maria Spelier,* on July 17, 1816 in Waterland Kerkje (Zeeland). She was born ca. 1795. Anna Maria died in Lapscheure on September 23, 1837 when she was 42. They had the following children:

i. **Antonia Serafina** was born on June 26, 1816 in Waterland Kerkje. She was legitimized at the wedding. On July 11, 1838 when Antonia Serafina was 22, she married Pieter De Valcke in Lapscheure, who was born on January 18, 1801 in Damme.

ii. **Leocadia** was born on February 17, 1821 in Lapscheure. On February 17, 1843 when Leocadia was 22, she married Joannes Franciscus Vercraye, in Lapscheure; he was born in Middelburg (Zeeland).

iii. **Angelina Christiana** was born on March 10, 1823 in Lapscheure. On June 21, 1848 when Angelina Christiana was 25, she married Bernardus D'Hondt in Lapscheure. He was born on March 8, 1809 in Lapscheure.

iv. **Eugenia Dorothea** was born on February 19, 1825 in Lapscheure. v. Josephus was born on April 24, 1829 in Lapscheure. He died in Lapscheure on July 31, 1834 when he was 5.

vi. **Rosalia** was born on August 30, 1831 in Lapscheure. She died in Lapscheure on September 2, 1831 when she was less than 1 year old.

vii. **Petrus** was born on May 11, 1833 in Lapscheure; he died in Lapscheure on September 7, 1834 when he was 1.

Josephus Bernardus married a second time, *Anna Maria Van Den Broecke* who was born in 1813 in Moerkerke. Anna Maria died in Lapscheure on December 8, 1887; she was 74. They had the following children:

i. **Amelia** who was born on July 10, 1840 in Lapscheure; she died in Brugge on July 29, 1912; she was 72. On July 23, 1869 when Amelia was 29, she married Pieter Joannes Deweerdt, in Lapscheure.

He was born on March 3, 1836 in Moerkerke. Pieter Joannes died in Moerkerke on July 2, 1897; he was 61. (Pieter was the widower of Sabina Ide who died on October 31, 1867)

ii. **Anna Maria** who was born on March 23, 1842 in Lapscheure. She died in Oudenaarde on August 11, 1910; she was 68. Anna Maria married Pieter Bernard Van Den Broeke who was born on November 12, 1832 in Deurne. Pieter Bernard died in Oudenburg on February 10, 1914; he was 81.

iii. Ludovicus Josephus who was born on January 7, 1844 in Lapscheure.

iv. **Leopold Marie** (1845-1914)

v. **Josephus Bernardus Leopoldus** who was born on July 12, 1848. Josephus Bernardus Leopoldus died on October 11, 1861; he was 13.

vi. **Barbara Theresia** who was born on April 17, 1851.

vii. **Leonie Barbara** who was born on April 17, 1852 in Lapscheure. She died in Menen on November 22, 1900; she was 48. Leonie Barbara married Bernard Jacobus Vlaminck who was born on June 8, 1837 in Moerkerke.

viii. **Pieter Bernardus** (1854-1922)

Josephus Bernardus De Zutter died in Lapscheure on January 1, 1856 when he was 66.

Eighth Generation: PIETER BERNARDUS DE ZUTTER was born on August 8, 1854. On October 16, 1878 when he was 24, he first married *Virginia Devisch,* in Lapscheure. She was born on October 31, 1846 in Lapscheure. Virginia died in Lapscheure on June 24, 1888; she was 41. They had the following children:

i. **Pieter Bernardus** (1878-1951)

ii. **Emilius Theophilus**, born on February 12, 1880 in Lapscheure; he died in Lapscheure on May 2, 1880; he was less than 1 year old.

iii. **Emiel** (1884-1964)

iv. **Sylvia Maria** who was born on June 6, 1888 in Blankenberge.

On October 28, 1891 when Pieter Bernardus was 37, he married a second time, *Valentina Troffaes,* in Blankenberge. Born on June 22, 1868 in Blankenberge, Valentina died in Blankenberge on September 15, 1937; she was 69. They had the following children:

i. **Alfons Frans** (1889-1955)

ii.	**Adelaide** who was born in 1892 in St Michiels. Adelaide died in Blankenberge on October 29, 1899; she was 7.
iii.	**Josef Pieter** (1894-1965)
iv.	**Jeroom Gustaaf** who was born on January 20, 1897 in Blankenberge. He died in Blankenberge on September 20, 1898; he was 1.
v.	**Brigitta Maria Louisa** who was born on October 8, 1899 in Blankenberge. She died on November 25, 1954; she was 55. Brigitta Maria Louisa married Albert Jan De Rycker who was born on February 25, 1897 in Blankenberge. Albert Jan died in Blankenberge on November 22, 1939; he was 42.
vi.	**Lodewijk Frans** who was born on February 13, 1902 in Blankenberge; he died in Blankenberge on May 14, 1954; he was 52.
vii.	**Arthur** (1903-)
viii.	**Frans Alfons** (1907-)

Pieter Bernardus died in Blankenberge on November 10, 1922; he was 68.

Ninth Generation: PIETER BERNARDUS DE ZUTTER was born on December 31, 1878 in Lapscheure. He married Irma Raes who was born on April 19, 1886 in Klemskerke. Irma died in Brugge on July 7, 1932; she was 46. They had the following children:

Figure 5.4 Pieter Bernard De Zutter, third from left, is shown as a coach driver who fetched tourists from the railway station to the hotel. (photo source: Elie Bilé: Blankenberge, 1971)

Figure 5.5 Pieter Bernardus De Zutter, great-grandfather of Hennie De Zutter.

i.   **Alida** (1906-1965)
ii. **Lodewijk** (1910-1980)
ii. **Emiel** (1912-1913)
iii. **Daniel** (1916-1990)

Pieter Bernardus died in Blankenberge on February 26, 1951; he was 72.

Tenth Generation
1. Alida DE ZUTTER was born on July 8, 1906 in Blankenberge. Alida died in Blankenberge on June 20, 1965; she was 58. Alida married Pierre Van Audenaerde who was born on October 2, 1910 in Uitkerke. Pierre died in Blankenberge on January 29, 1981; he was 70. They had the following children:

i.   **Raymond** (1936-)
ii. **Helene** was born on October 3, 1941 in Blankenberge; she died in Blankenberge on November 27, 1984; she was 43. Helene married Justin Vanwindekens.

Figure 5.6 Pieter-Bernardus De Zutter with Irma Raes and children, Alida, Lodewijk and Daniel.

2. Lodewijk DE ZUTTER was born on July 29, 1910 in Blankenberge; he died in Antwerpen on February 7, 1980; he was 69. Lodewijk married Francesca Van Dingelen who was born on November 8, 1911 in Oostham. They had the following children:

    i.   **Jean-Pierre** (1940-)
    ii.   **Daniel** (1942-)

3. Daniel DE ZUTTER who was born on October 15, 1916 in Blankenberge. Daniel died in Oostende on June 14, 1990; he was 73. Daniel married Irmgard Burkhardt who was born on March 1, 1923 in Braunichswalde in former East Germany. They had the following children:

    i.   **Hennie** (1946-)
    ii.   **Dirk** (1952-)

Eleventh Generation

1. Raymond VAN AUDENAERDE was born on February 15, 1936 in Blankenberge. Raymond married *Irma Pieters* who was born on April 14, 1935 in Blankenberge. They had the following children:

    i.   **Marcel** who was born on September 27, 1969 in Blankenberge.
    ii.   **Hennie** who was born on November 24, 1971 in Blankenberge.

2. Jean-Pierre DE ZUTTER who was born on October 27, 1940 in Kortrijk. On July 13, 1967 when Jean-Pierre was 26, he married *Anny Jacobs* who was born on October 26, 1947 in Tienen. They had the following children:

    i.   **Ingrid** who was born on January 20, 1969 in Blankenberge.
    ii.   **Annika** who was born on September 11, 1972 in Blankenberge.

3. Daniel DE ZUTTER who was born on June 7, 1942 in Kortrijk. Daniel married *Anita Pacquee* who was born on April 24, 1952. They had the following children:

    i.   **Velina** who was born on October 5, 1976 in Wilrijk.
    ii.   **Cathy** who was born on January 4, 1980 in Antwerpen.

4. Hennie DE ZUTTER who was born on August 29, 1946 in Blankenberge. On August 1969 when Hennie was 22, she married Guido Deboeck. They had three children (see Chapter 2).

5. Dirk DE ZUTTER who was born on November 3, 1952 in Nieuwpoort. Dirk married *Gratienne Louwye* who was born on August 21, 1954 in Nieuwpoort. They had the following children:

i.   **Hannes** who was born on January 4, 1982 in Oostende.
ii.   **Jana** who was born on September 26, 1984 in Oostende.

Irmgard Burkhardt

Irmgard Burkhardt (see Figure 5.7) was born on March 1, 1923 in Braunichswalde in former East Germany. Her father was Otto Burkhardt, who was born in Braunichswalde on September 18, 1889. He died in Werdau on March 24, 1979 when he was 89.

Otto was a farmer and worked his whole life at the Hemmans farm, one of the biggest farms in Braunichswalde.[19] Irmgard's mother was Klara Johanna Schumann who was born in Greiz-Pohlitz on September 19, 1890. She died in Braunichswalde on May 2, 1967. Klara Johanna was the second wife of Otto; his first wife died young and left him with two daughters (Lisbeth and Ilse).

Klara Johanna was a homemaker and worked at the Hemmans farm during harvest time. Both Otto and Klara Johanna were Lutherans *("Evangelish-Lutherisch")*. Irmgard's paternal grandfather was Johann Burkhardt married to Emma Zehmisch; her maternal grandmother was Sidonie August Seifert (see Figure 5.8).

Figure 5.7 Irmgard Burkhardt

---

19. Otto Burkhardt was shot in WWI (1914-18) and received a bullet in his upper leg. When he no longer could walk, this bullet was removed 25 years later; thereafter he was able to walk with a cane.

Figure 5.8 Johann Burkhardt and Emma Zehmisch; the young boy to the right is Otto Burkhardt, grandfather of Hennie De Zutter. (Photo ca. 1894-95)

Irmgard attended school until age 14. She first was a baby-sitter and later worked in the cigar factory in Braunichswalde. She belonged to the Hitlerjugend from 1933 till 1937. Until 1940 she had no interest in politics; during the war she became opposed to Hitler.[20]

Braunichswalde is a small farm village in Thüringen in east Sachsen (see Figure 5.10 and 5.11). In the late thirties it had some 600 inhabitants. Besides work on the farms there was a small cigar factory in which only women worked. Most people commuted by bicycle to neighboring villages where there were more employment opportunities in factories (e.g., the shoe factory of Weida). Some took the bus to Werdau, Ronneburg or Gera. Braunichswalde had a school building where classes were held that averaged eight to ten students per class.

Figure 5.9 Otto Burkhardt and Klara Johanna with Hennie and Dirk De Zutter, who were visiting their grandparents in Koksijde in 1953.

20. Hannes De Zutter, who is one of Irmgard's grandsons, interviewed her in 2001 about the circumstances before, during and just after the war in Braunichswalde. The transcript of that interview – which was a project he made for a history class at the University of Gent – is the basis for what follows.

Figure 5.10 Map of Germany showing location of Braunichswalde (arrow)

The village was governed by a mayor who was a veteran of WWI (1914-1918). The mayor was a standesbeamte, meaning he married people and he also ran a savings association. He was not a Hitler fan (nor were many others in the village)! After *Feldmarchall* von Hindenburg appointed Hitler as Chancellor for a new cabinet, there were elections, but the only name on the voting list was Adolph Hitler.[21]

The mayor was highly respected and helped a lot of people. During the war food was rationed and the only way to get food was through food stamps; Otto Burkhardt assisted the mayor on occasions for which he was paid.

When the war with France started in 1940 many in the village (who remembered WWI) were not happy. Even among the young there was opposition to the war. When Irmgard's brother Herbert[22] was called to arms he made every effort to be dismissed, including going through surgery to get disqualified. The political and military developments in those days were of little interest to the people; the main concern was to earn enough money to be able to buy food and to have some comfort in life.

Besides food rationings, the war also brought forced employment and contacts with prisoners of war (POWs). In 1941 Irmgard was forced to work in a sub-terrain factory located in the woods surrounding Mühlhausen. From the sky this factory could not be seen. At this factory war equipment was produced day and night. The work was monotonous.

After a while Irmgard was transferred to another factory in Werda that made textiles. In this factory a division made nets

---

21. Feldmarchall von Hindenburg was a German field marshal during World War I and second president of the Weimar Republic (1925–34). His presidential terms were wracked by political instability, economic depression, and the rise to power of Adolf Hitler, whom he appointed chancellor in 1933.

22. Presumably Irmgard's brother Herbert was called to arms early in the war. As a consequence of his surgery he was sent to Romania. During the invasion of Romania by the Russians he may have been killed. His wife received notice that he was missing after the war ended.

to prevent submarines from entering ports. In this factory many POWs were employed. Some were employed as carpenters, others as mechanics. Among these mechanics was Daniel De Zutter, who was responsible for the maintenance and repair of all machinery.

Daniel had been arrested on the thirteenth day of the war in Belgium and deported (just like René Deboeck, see Chapter 3) to Germany right after the capitulation of Belgium in May-June 1940.

It was in the factory in Weida that Irmgard encountered Daniel. She worked on a sewing machine to make nets. Her sewing machine broke down a lot because "she could not handle it properly" (she said). Daniel was called to repair her sewing machine; they got to know each other and after a while Irmgard helped Daniel by getting him to extra food.

In the factory in Weida POWs were well treated. Work was hard and long, ten to twelve hours a day, but POWs were paid with coupons that they could exchange. The main problem was getting food. To get more food POWs kept contact with German girls, who helped them to get access to the cellars where potatoes were stored.

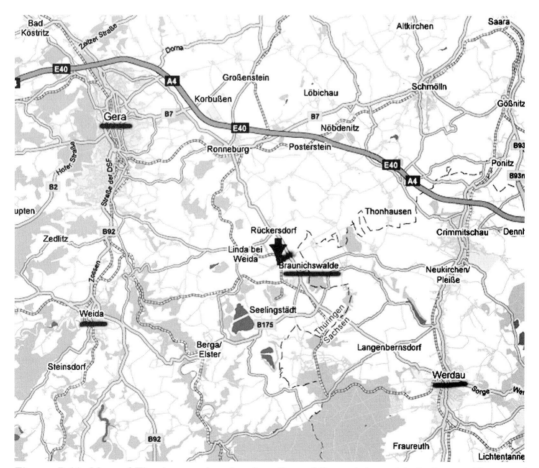

Figure 5.11: Map of Thuringen showing location of Braunichswalde between Gera and Werdau. Also shown in Weida. Mulhausen is to the west of Gera.

Every evening after work, the POWs were transported back to camp where they were locked up for the night. The cabin had steel bars in front of the windows. Daniel managed to pull wires through the steel window bars, so that they could easily be removed and put back without damage. This allowed Daniel and his friends to sneak out of camp at night to visit local cafes ("Biergarten") and to contact the German girls who helped them to get extra food.

One night when the prison guard became aware that Daniel and his friends had left camp, he searched for them in the village, and made them promise to get back to camp by a certain time, so that he, the guard, would not be punished...Sounds like straight out of the well-known TV series, Stalag 13, right?

Braunichtswalde and its surroundings were seldom bombarded. There were lots of planes that flew over, which caused frequent alarms as a result of which everyone had to evacuate to their basements or cellars. This caused depression and had a psychological impact on the villagers. Some alarms were caused by POWs to slow down the work in the factories. People were afraid and felt powerless to do anything about it.

One bombardment left a lasting impression; it was the bombing on February 13, 1945 of Dresden,[23] an old city with many gorgeous buildings. The whole sky was on fire and the burning city could be seen from far. Irmgard saw the burning city from a distance said: "it was an unbelievable event that was not necessary! Everyone already knew that the end of the war was near. After Stalingrad, Germany went downhill and could no longer win the war. Of course, we could not say this, as it would be considered treason." (She said in Flemish "mee heulen met de vijand.")

When the Americans came with their tanks, most villagers were home (because the railroad lines had been bombarded). It

---

23. One tactic used by the Royal Air Force and the United States Army Air Force was the creation of firestorms. This was achieved by dropping incendiary bombs, filled with highly combustible chemicals such as magnesium, phosphorus or petroleum jelly (napalm), in clusters over a specific target. After the area caught fire, the air above the bombed area became extremely hot and rose rapidly. Cold air then rushed in at ground level from the outside and people were sucked into the fire. In 1945, Arthur Harris (who was a Marshal of the Royal Air Force, commonly known as "bomber" Harris, was commander of RAF Bomber Command) decided to create a firestorm in the medieval city of Dresden. He considered it a good target as it had not been attacked during the war and was virtually undefended by anti-aircraft guns. The population of the city was now far greater than the normal 650,000 due to the large numbers of refugees fleeing from the advancing Red Army. On the 13th of February, 1945, 773 Avro Lancasters bombed Dresden. During the next two days the USAAF sent over 527 heavy bombers to follow up the RAF attack. Dresden was nearly totally destroyed. As a result of the firestorm it was afterwards impossible to count the number of victims. Recent research suggest that 35,000 were killed but some German sources have argued that it was over 100,000.

was quite a spectacle to see all those tanks and hear all the noise they made because no one had ever seen tanks in the village.

The Americans confiscated a few houses in the village. Irmgard and her family had to move out of her parents home. In the houses that the Americans occupied they made themselves quite comfortable, drank all the wine, slept with their boots in the beds. After a week most of the military moved out and only a few were left to keep the order.

Just before the liberation most POWs were transported to other German camps. A few POWs not knowing what would happen managed to hide and stayed behind. Among them was Daniel, who was freed by the Americans.

On June 2, 1945 Daniel de Zutter married Irmgard Burkhardt in Braunichswalde (see Figure 5.12). Irmgard said "on the night before the wedding they celebrated a lot, people broke a lot of plates and cups (which according to tradition brings luck)". They had a special permission to stay out beyond the curfew that had been imposed to keep the order.

After the takeover by the Allies there were

Figure 5.12 Marriage of Daniel De Zutter and Irmgard Burkhardt in Braunichswalde on June 2, 1945

no reprisals in the village. Many radical militant party members of the NSDAP (Nationalsozialistische Deutsche Arbeiterpartei, The National Socialist German Workers' Party or Nazi Party) were killed during the war. Nevertheless there remained some individuals who spied on other people, even after the war. Some who supported Hitler became communists and continued to spy on others.

Irmgard said: *"men zegt beter nooit te veel. Want men kan dat altijd tegen je gebruiken"* (One better never say too much, because whatever you say always can be used against you). For anyone who knows Irmgard, it must have been hard to keep silent because she loved to talk!

People in the village knew that after the Americans, the Russians would come and that Germany was going to be divided. However the speed with which things moved was surprising.

After they got married Daniel and Irmgard originally planned to stay in Braunichswalde; the takeover by the Russians changed those plans. All foreigners had to leave, including those married to foreigners. They had no other choice but to return to Belgium. Daniel arranged for transport permissions in Gera. On September nineteenth, 1945, he and Irmgard left Braunichswalde for Erfurt. Transport was free, but was in railway wagons for animals. From Erfurt the train went via Hoof[24] and Arlon to Brussels where they arrived on October 15, 1945.

On arrival in Brussels Irmgard was separated from Daniel. The immigrant police ordered Daniel to report back to his military unit in Blankenberge and return with an official transcript of his marriage license. Irmgard was transported in a police car ("'n dievenwagen") to the Justice Palace. Together with two other women they were brought to a large room where for the next three days they stayed with lots of other foreigners. They were fingerprinted, photographed, and had to fill out papers. Irmgard did not eat for three days…

When she was finally allowed to go, Daniel was waiting for her across the street from the Justice Palace. He was eating grapes, she recalled. Daniel managed, thanks to his brother Louis who was a "gendarme" (national security officer) and whom he ran into in Ypres, to get back from Blankenberge with the translation of his marriage license within the time limit imposed on foreigners

---

24. In Hoof at the border between East and West Germany the train stopped for a few moments. Imgard recalls there was a young girl on the platform who was lost. She tried to help her find her parents. Two Russian soldiers approached who wanted to take Imgard away "om rare dingen te doen" (to do strange things to her). Her husband who became anxious when she stayed away that long, came to search for her and hence nothing happened. Imgard recalls that Russians were known for such behavior. They would frequently stop women on their way to work or would enter houses to search for women. "Amerikanen deden zulke dingen niet, of althans, daar heb ik nooit iets van gehoord" (Americans did not do such things, or at least, I never heard about that).

locked up in Brussels. Those who did not meet the deadline were sent back to their country of origin.

After her release, Daniel and Irmgard traveled to Blankenberge. They were taken in by a cousin of Daniel. It was in the café near the railroad station in Blankenberge that Irmgard for the first time ate in Belgium (after being locked up); she had eggs and bacon, the best meal she ever had!

Daniel sold the coupons he had earned during the war and with that money paid rent for one year to Joseph Falleyn, a school friend who rented out rooms in Blankenberge (in the Sergeant De Bruynestraat number 33). During the war Daniel's family in Belgium spent all of his salary from his military service. While they were living in Blankenberge Hennie was born on August 29, in 1946. She was named after a famous skater, Sonya Hennie; her middle names were Irma (the name of her paternal grandmother) and Klara (the name of her maternal grandmother).

Irmgard recalls that in the hospital in Blankenberge (where she delivered Hennie) she was separated from other women. This was not because she was German, but because of her religion: she was Lutheran; the Catholic nuns of the hospital knew this. About four years after Hennie's was born, Irmgard converted to Catholicism. She was talked into it by Rev. Felix De Zutter, the fourth son of Alfons Frans De Zutter and Amanda Stephanie Vanhoutt, who joined CICM or the missionaries of Scheut and spent a lifetime in former Belgian Congo.

Irmgard got to know a lot of people in Blankenberge in those first couple of years, despite her original lack of knowledge of Dutch. She recalls that people were very friendly. When she went shopping, however, she kept conversations short and never revealed where she was originally from. When she took Hennie to the beach she preferred to sit in the dunes so that tourists, who mainly spoke French, another language she did not speak, would not bother her. She told her children and grandchildren that she preferred the dunes "because she knitted differently than the other women at the beach...."[25]

After the owners of the house in the Sergeant De Bruynestraat divorced, Daniel and Irmgard moved to one of the homes in the courtyard of Daniel's parents' home (in the Waterkasteelstraat number 9). They lived for free for five years before they moved to Koksijde on January 8, 1951. In Koksijde they lived (on the Koninlijkebaan number 13) in a villa called "Beau Soleil"; afterwards in the villa called "Pirabla" (on the Leopoldvoetpad number 4). It was in this period that on November 3, 1952 Dirk, Hennie's brother, was born in Nieuwpoort. Dirk married Gratienne Louwye; they had

---

25. During their first years in Koksijde, Daniel and Irmgard had sporadic contacts with the family in Blankenberge. After they bought a car in 1953 they made at least one ride per month to Blankenberge because Daniel as a fan of football would go with friends to support the Blankenberge football team.

two children: Hannes, born on January 4, 1982 and Jana, born on September 26, 1984, both born in Ostende.

On June 15, 1965 Daniel and Irmgard moved to Nieuwpoort where they stayed until September 30, 1966 (in the Deroolaan number 35). From Nieuwpoort they moved to Lombardsijde (now Westende) where they lived till September 11, 1976. Daniel and Irmgard lived in a military home in the Santhovenstraat 19.

In 1976 the De Zutter family bought a house in the same street (just across number 36). They lived there together till Daniel passed away on June 14, 1990. Irmgard continued to live in Westende till she moved in 2005 to "Ten Anker," a retirement home in Nieuwpoort.[26]

Daniel De Zutter

Daniel De Zutter was born on October 15, 1916. He was the son of Pieter Bernardus De Zutter, who was born in Lapscheure in 1878, and who married Irma Raes born in Klemskerke in 1886. Daniel's older sister was Alida born in 1906 and his older brother was Lodewijk (also called Louis or Pa Louis). Both his father and his brother were "gendarmes," i.e., made careers in national security. In contrast Daniel chose a military career.[27]

The "Fiche Matricularie/ Stamkaart" (military logbook) of Daniel De Zutter (that was retrieved from the military archives in Brussels) shows that he was selected to start military service in 1936. He became a Sergeant in 1937, a Guard Master in 1938. He was listed as POW from May 28, 1940 till May 31, 1945.

Figure 5.13: Pieter Bernardus De Zutter with his daughter Alida and two sons Lodewijk and Daniel (standing left to right).

26. The addresses of all the places where the De Zutter family are listed not because they have historical relevance, but because they indicate the degree of detailed record keeping that came from Imgard. Like her mother, Hennie excels in keeping detailed records of many things.

27. He told his children that he chose a military career because he lost his mother when he was 15; if his mother would have lived longer, she would have insisted that Daniel continued his studies.

Georges Tegethoff, who was 94 years old in 2006, wrote in his handwriting the following about the time Daniel and he (and several others) spent as POWs in Germany:[28]

> *In 1940 when the Germans invaded Belgium, the battle lasted just 18 days. Thereafter we were taken prisoners and sent via boat to Germany. We were (first) transported to the big camp in Nurenberg where as professional military we were sleeping in a tent for 20-22 men. It is there that I met Daniel, Nandt, Collant and Edward...*
>
> *Some time later we were transported to Stalag X C where we were lodged in a wooden cabin. Then came the announcement that everyone who wanted to work on a farm to help with the harvest, would later be released and could go home. Many of us took the risk and hence were put on a train to Bad Sulza for Stalag IX C. Each day in Stalag IX C we were called together to take the*

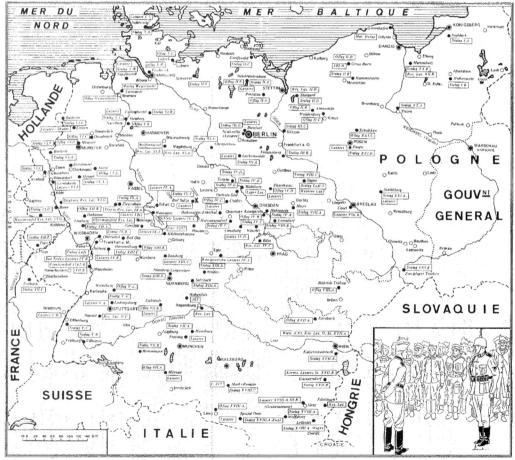

Figure 5.14 Map of Stalags in Germany during the war. Stalag IX C is shown with a cross, southwest of Berlin.

---

28. Translated from handwritten letters in Dutch received in 2006, 1995 and 1994.

train to Erfurt and from there to Bad Sulza.[29] *We worked in different places. We stayed together and were sent to a farm village Brandsdorf where we worked on different farms.*

In 1942 we were moved from Brandsdorf to Werda.[30] *Emiel Ferdinande (a friend of Georges and Daniel) was assigned as a carpenter; Daniel and Georges were the mechanics, responsible for repairs including repairs in the kitchen. Emiel made contact with Anneliese, who was the cook in the kitchen; she became friendly with Emiel.*

Anneliese knew the central phone operator. When in 1945 the telephone operator overheard that POWs would be evacuated, she passed this on to Anneliese who passed this on to Emiel. He warned his comrades and together they made a plan to hide. They found an old building, no longer in use, with an attic; this building was close to the kitchen and close to a storage place, where an electrician had found a radio. Guilaume, the electrician, listened at night to the BBC and told his friends about the latest news from the frontlines.

A few days after Anneliese had warned Emiel about the eminent relocation, all POWs were called to assemble. The five comrades (Emiel Jadot, Daniel De Zutter, Georges Labiau, Maurice - lastname not found back - and Georges Tegethoff) moved to their hiding place, making sure that there were no foot prints nor human odors left on their path. They literally climbed standing on wooden supports into the attic of the deserted building through a trap. Guards with dogs tried to find the missing POWs; but they never found them.

In a narrow, dusty, dark space all five men spent five days and nights together. The only one who knew where they were hiding was Anneliese. After a couple of days, Anneliese arranged for food in the kitchen and at night Emiel would climb out the hiding place and get the food in the kitchen. Emiel also went to get water from the storage room. This was very dangerous!

After five days the liberation came. Daniel took the train to Braunichswalde to see Irmgard. Anneliese helped Emiel to get a bicycle so that they could ride to her parents. Emiel and Anneliese got married with the help of the Americans and told Daniel about it. Daniel then married Irmgard on June 2, 1945.

---

29. In Wikipedia we find that "Stalag IX-C was a World War II German POW camp located near Bad Sulza, between Erfurt and Leipzig, in Thuringia. It was the base camp servicing a number of sub-camps and Arbeitskommandos spread over a wide area, particularly those holding prisoners working in the salt mines. A fairly large hospital, called "Reserve-Lazaret Obermassfeld," was operated by British, Canadian and New Zealand medical staff. It was located in the town of Obermassfeld, south-west of Erfurt, in a 3-story stone building that was previously a Hitlerjugend camp. Its staff was considerably augmented in October 1944 with the arrival of an entire ambulance team of the 101st Airborne Division, from Arnhem."

30. I was put to work in a laundry shop, until the liberation came. Bad Sulza near Jena can be compared to the headquarters of Stalag IX C. Stalag Scheiz Lazaret IX C was not a camp but a sort of clinic or hospital for the sick POWs. Daniel was never in this hospital; I myself spent a couple of days in that military hospital

They moved to Belgium and remained friends with Emiel and Anneliese (who changed her name to Annie) Ferdinande.

Figure 5.15 The work brigade 524-8 of Werda with German guards, showing standing fourth from the right, Daniel De Zutter. Photo taken in 1942 (made available by George Tegethoff).

On return to Belgium Daniel returned to his unit. On June 26, 1948 he took the oath of First Guard Master. One year later he transferred from the army to the air force and in 1950 became a military specialist. He was nominated First Sergeant Major Specialist on June 26, 1951, became Adjunct Specialist in September 1956 and was promoted to Adjunct Chef on March 26, 1965. He retired from the air force on January 1, 1977.

His service as POW was recognized in 1946 with a medal ("Herrineringsmedaille van de Oorlog 1940-1945") and a decoration in 1947 ("Militaire Ereteken van 2de Klasse", later upgraded to 1st class in 1951). In 1955 he received the *Gold Medal in the Order of Leopold II.* In April 1960 he received the *Golden Palm of the Crown Order.* Five years later he got the *Cross of Knight in the Order of Leopold II* ("Het Kruis van Ridder in de Orde van Leopold II") and then in 1970 got the *Cross of Knight in the Crown Order.* Finally on April 7, 1975, he received the *Cross of Knight in the Leopold Order.*

Daniel De Zutter spent a lifetime passing exams and learning new skills. At the end of his career he was responsible for the military installations in Lombardsijde. He was a hands-on-man, who could fix anything, highly skilled in wood as well as metal work, a good father and teacher and a proud Flemish military professional.

Figure 5.16: Daniel Alfonds Wilfried De Zutter (1916-1990)

Most of my initial exchanges with him were between 1966 and 1969 when I was a student in Leuven and was getting to know his daughter. On many occasions we drank a couple of beers, sometimes some whiskeys…Daniel loved beers and scotch. While he had a keen interest in many topics, his favorite topics were to discuss politics, the unfairness in the world and the advantages of the rich. He seldom talked about the war, which is why most of what was written here came from George, from Irmgard, from documents in military archives, and from the history of the war.[31]

31. According to the sons of "Pa Louis," i.e., Jean-Pierre and Daniel, sons of his brother, Daniel was an extrovert. Their uncle was sportive and was very conscious of duty and country. Daniel loved the four girls of Jean-Pierre and Daniel, as well as his grandchildren Hannes and Jana (children of Dirk and Gratienne), and Toni, Pascal and Nina whom he came to visit in the USA.

Daniel's hobbies included gardening, fishing and boat building. On the small lot behind the house in the Santhoven-straat, he maintained a small garden in which he grew potatoes, beans, tomatoes and other vegetables. He loved to fish on the pier in Nieuwpoort, on the canals and rivers surrounding Lombardsi-jde, and in the open North Sea. Fishing in the North Sea was for crevettes (small grey shrimp that are a specialty in Belgium). On many occasions Hennie helped her father to pull in the nets, sort the catch, and clean the fish.

In 1973 Daniel started building his own boat in his back-yard. He kept a detailed logbook of the construction of this boat, baptized it *Scarphout* and first let it in the water in April 1974. After several more tests he went regularly sailing. In 1976 on one of our home-leaves, he took his grandson, Toni (who was four years old at the time) sailing in Nieuwpoort harbor. Daniel sold his boat in 1989, a year before he died.

After building a full size boat Daniel went into model boat building. Between 1982 and 1989 he completed seven model boats, one for Hennie and Dirk and one for each of his grandchil-dren. These model boats have found their way to Texas, Indiana and Virginia.

Figure 5.17 The boat, called Scarphout, made by D. de Zutter (1974-1989). The Scar-phout was 17 by 6.2 feet (5.20 by 1.90 meters).

Figure 5.18 Model boats made by Daniel De Zutter for his daughter and grandchildren. From left to right, top to botten boat made for Toni, Hennie, Pascal, Jana, Nina and Hannes

On June 14, 1990, Daniel De Zutter died after a prolonged treatment for lung cancer. Throughout his life Daniel smoked hand-rolled cigarettes and drank a lot of coffee[32] which did not help the scars he retained on his lungs from being five years a POW in Germany.

Daniel's daughter, Hennie, celebrated her sixtieth birthday in 2006 (see Figure 5.19). For more than two decades she worked in Asia, Africa, Latin America and the Middle East as a project manager and financial analyst for the World Bank. During her many travels she encountered many women artisans and was struck by their creativity, their enthusiasm but also their poverty and economic position in life. Upon retirement from the World Bank, she decided to address these issues by establishing in January 2001 *e-maginativegifts,* a dynamic business creating markets for products made by women artisans from around the world.

Figure 5.19 Hennie Irma Klara Deboeck-De Zutter
(photo by GJD La Porte, TX, October 2006)

---

32. Coffee contains a considerable amount of caffeine. It affects the body mainly by stimulating the production of adrenalin. Caffeine is a strong diuretic and has a strong dehydrating effect. Coffee stimulates the secretion of HCl (Hydrochloric Acid) in the stomach causing increased acidity. It also causes serious decalcification and weakening of the bones. It is especially bad for women because in general they are at greater risk of osteoporosis.

e-maginativegifts buys high quality, hand made products directly from women, from women's cooperatives, as well as from suppliers that import from women cooperatives. The company also buys from physically impaired men and women. Among others, the company imports fashionable scarves, evening bags, cosmetic and lipstick cases and other quality women's accessories, smocked girls' dresses and children's sweaters, ties for men, picture frames, and other accessories for the home and office. The crafts come from all parts of the globe. Currently, *e-maginativegifts* sells goods from Bolivia, Cambodia, China, Ecuador, Guatemala, Honduras, Hungary, India, Madagascar, Mongolia, Pakistan, Philippines, Poland, Thailand, Ukraine and Vietnam. Some selected goods from women suppliers in the U. S. have also been added since 2006 so as to increase sales and channel proceeds from these sales to women in poor countries. In this way *e-maginativegifts* will be able to help even more women to better their lives.

e-maginativegifts combines a conventional approach of selling through crafts fairs and home shows with a modern marketing through e-stores, e-auctions at EBAY and through her website.

To visit e-maginativegifts go to

http://www.e-maginativegifts.com

Click on any of the products categories
(Women, Men, Baby, Children, Home Accessories…)
and browse the collections of products currently offered.

Chapter 6
Flemish Emigration to the USA

After 450 years in Flanders a descendant of the Deboeck family moved across the pond, as the English call the Atlantic Ocean, the fourteenth generation and subsequent descendants are Americans by birth. How did this come about? Spencer Wells wrote: "People move for three reasons: the lack of opportunities at home, the perception of better opportunities elsewhere, or forced relocation".[1]

The largest mass migration in human history took place between 1840 and 1920 when nearly 40 million people (more than double the U.S. population in 1840) moved from Europe to the United States. These immigrants included 4.5 million Irish, 5 million Italians, 2 million Jews, and a few hundred thousand Belgians. Flemish-speaking Belgians emigrated long before 1840 and not only to the USA, but the emphasis here is on emigration to the USA.

In this chapter I first discuss the early settlers in the seventeenth century; second, the massive immigration in the nineteenth and early twentieth centuries, and finally the recent emigration of professionals from Flanders to the USA. The underlying causes of past migrations and the reasons why Flemish are still leaving their country today will be revealed.

Flemish role in discovery of America

During the fifteenth and sixteenth centuries, there was an impressive economic and cultural boom in Flanders, as we saw from the historical sketches in previous chapters. There were also internal problems as a result of which many artists and craftsmen sought refuge elsewhere. Numerous highly talented people left Flanders for Holland to escape the Contra Reformation in the second half of the sixteenth century.

Flemish settlers introduced the first printing presses into Spain and Portugal. Flemish contributed to the exploitation and the population of the Azores islands, which for a long time were called the Flemish islands. Flemish missionaries such as Pieter van Gent in Mexico, Joos de Rijcke in Ecuador, Ferdinand Verbiest in China, Constant Lievens in India, and Damiaan de Veuster in Molokai, built a reputation in various countries; a reputation that continues even to this day. For example, in the gallery of the U.S. Congress in Washington there is a bust of Father Damiaan; he is the only Belgian honored with a bust in the U.S. Congress.

In the eighteenth and nineteenth century a combination of demographic explosion and inadequate economic growth resulted

---

1. Spencer Wells, Deep Ancestry: inside the Genographic Project, p 4.

in more emigration from Flanders. This emigration continued in the first half of the twentieth century.

Emigration from Flanders involved not only the so-called lower classes but also members of the better off classes who overseas built a future in teacher-training, engineering, or agriculture. For example, Louis Cruis, was a Flemish engineer who led expeditions to lay down the boundaries of Brazil and the city limits of the capital, Brasilia.

Some four hundred thousand Flemings settled in France where they often started in poor villages, stimulating new life into agriculture.

In the United States and Canada there are today more than one million Americans who have Flemish roots. How did they get there and how did Flemish and Walloons first come to America? In what follows the relatively unknown role of Flemish and Walloons in the discovery of America will briefly be reviewed.

It was Spain who led the European discovery of America in the 16th century. Spain took control of Florida, California and the southwest region of America. The Spanish explorer, *Ponce De Leon,* discovered Florida in 1513. Five years later, *Cabeza de Vaca,* explored parts of Texas, New Mexico and Arizona. Other Spanish adventurers included *Francisco Coronado,* who traveled up the Colorado River (1540), and *Hernando de Soto,* who explored the Mississippi River (1541).

About 200,000 Spaniards migrated to the new world and founded some 200 settlements in North America. Saint Augustine in Florida, founded by Pedro Merendez in 1565, was the first permanent settlement established by Europeans. Other important settlements established by the Spanish included Santa Fe, Albuquerque, El Paso, San Diego, San Francisco, Santa Barbara, San Jose, Monterey, and Los Angeles. The Spanish mined precious metals in Mexico and Peru and were able to ship back to Europe large quantities of gold and silver.

English explorers were sent to the New World in the sixteenth century to seek a passage to the Indies. Gradually the English government became interested in establishing overseas colonies to provide an outlet for surplus population,[2] to obtain a source of raw materials and a market for English manufactured goods.

---

2. In 1798 Thomas Malthus published his Essay on the Principles of Population. In his book, Malthus claimed the population of Britain was growing faster than food production. Malthus predicted that unless something was done about this, large numbers of people in Britain would starve. His book created panic and for the first time in history, the government agreed to count the number of people living in Britain. The 1801 census revealed that Britain had a population of 10,501,000. It was estimated that the population of Britain had doubled since 1750.

The move towards large-scale scientific farming greatly increased output but made many agricultural workers redundant. Some moved to the fast-growing industrial areas in search of work, whereas

In 1607 James I granted permission for a group of merchants to establish a permanent English settlement in America at Jamestown, Virginia. At first the venture attracted adventurers who hoped to make their fortunes in the colonies. The idea also appealed to people who were being persecuted for their political and religious beliefs.

The arrival of people from England grew steadily and by 1650 the population of Virginia reached 15,000. Settlements spread from the banks of the James River to the York and Rappahannock Rivers. Others decided to leave the coastal regions and move inland. In 1685 the population of Virginia had grown to 60,000.[3] Some three hundred years later the population of Virginia is 6.7 million, which is about the same as Flanders.

The early English arrivals in America were known as *colonists or settlers.* They traded with the Native Americans who were called *Indians.* The term *immigrant* was only used from 1787 onwards, because it was argued that there was a difference between the *colonists* who came to establish a new society, and those who arrived after the country's laws, customs and language were fixed. Woody Holton in his book *Forced Founders* describes the making of the American Revolution in Virginia. It was on the initiative of the convention delegates in the capitol of Virginia in Williamsburg that *"on May 15, 1776, an invitation was sent to Virginia's 12 sister colonies to join in a declaration of Independence".*[4] Thomas Jefferson of Virginia became the main author of the Declaration of Independence, signed on July 4, 1776, in Philadelphia.

The Dutch first arrived in America in 1609 when the Dutch East India Company vessel *De Halve Maen,* commanded by the English captain, *Henry Hudson,* laid anchor at Sandy Hook. At the time, the Netherlands was the richest nation on the globe. Their main source of supply was the East Indies. To render commerce more lucrative, it became desirable to seek a shorter passage to the Indies. The experienced and skillful English navigator Hudson was contracted to seek such a passage.

---

others decided to emigrate to Australia, New Zealand, Canada, South Africa and the United States.

After 1830 the numbers of people leaving Britain increased dramatically. This was particularly true of those farmers and laborers who had lived in counties that had been hardest hit by the agricultural depression such as Kent, Sussex, Hampshire, Dorset, Cornwall, Yorkshire, Derbyshire, Cheshire and Cumberland.

3. Another important English settlement was established in Massachusetts. In 1630 over 1,000 Puritans came to the Massachusetts Bay area and built homes in and around Boston. With harsh laws being passed in England against those criticizing the Anglican Church, a further 20,000 Puritans arrived over the next ten years.

4. Woody Holten: Forced Founders: Indians, Debtors, Slaves, the making of the American Revolution in Virginia, University of North Carolina Press, 1999, p 220.

Before Henry Hudson sailed up the river that now bears his name, *three Flemings played an important role*. The historian *Emanuel Van Meteren,* who was born in Antwerp in 1535 and became the Minister of the Netherlands at the Court of St. James induced Hudson to go and see some friends in Holland who desired to secure his services. *Petrus Plancius* (born near Ypers in Flanders), who had a thorough knowledge of maritime affairs, warmly welcomed Hudson in Amsterdam and supported the search for a northeastern passage to India. He provided Hudson with his maps and studies. Finally, there is *Jodcus Hondius* a skilled copper engraver, who acted as an interpreter, and advisor and friend of Hudson. Three Flemings, Van Meteren, Plancius and Hondius, made valuable contributions to the voyage of Henry Hudson, which opened the way to the first permanent settlements in New York.

The first Belgians in America

In 1614, Dutch merchants established a trading post at Fort Orange. Ten years later thirty families came from Holland to establish a settlement that became known as *New Netherland.*

The Dutch government gave exclusive trading rights to the Dutch West India Company and over the next few years other colonists arrived who established a large settlement on Manhattan Island. Inhabitants of the southern Netherlands (now Belgium) participated in the early settlement on Manhattan.

Henry C. Bayer, in his book *The Belgians, First Settlers in New York and in the Middle States,* wrote: *"The first settlers in New York were Belgians. They came to New York in 1623."* [5] Bayer discussed Belgian settlements at Wallabout, Long Island, and Staten Island, as well as in Hoboken, Jersey City, Pavonia, Communipaw, and Wallkill, New Jersey.

These place names are derived from both the Walloons who settled there, as well as from the Dutch version of words used to describe a locale.[6]

Pavonia, for example, got its name when Michael Pauw purchased land on the Jersey shore. Translating his own name, Pauw (which in Dutch means "peacock") into Latin, he got "Pavonia." Wallkill is the Dutch word for *Walloon's Stream.* Elsewhere, the Walloomsac River in Vermont derives its name from the Walloons who settled on the east branch of the Hoosac River in New York.[7]

---

5. Henry G. Bayer, *The Belgians, First Settlers in New York and in the Middle States,* page 40.

6. For example, Hoboken in the early years was called "Hoebuck", meaning "high bluff." Today it is called Castle Point. Lenni Lenape who camped seasonally on the island called the spot "Hopoghan Haskingh" or "Land of the Tobacco Pipe," for they used the green-colored serpentine rock abundant in the area to carve pipes for smoking tobacco.

7. Belgian settlements were also established during the seventeenth century in Connecticut, Delaware, and Pennsylvania.

Peter Minuit, who became governor of New Netherland, purchased the island of Manhattan from Native Americans in 1626 for $24 worth of trinkets, beads and knives. Many historians believe that Peter Minuit was of Belgian heritage. The chief port on Manhattan was renamed New Amsterdam.[8]

In 1658 Peter Stuyvesant, Dutch Governor of New Amsterdam, bought all the land between the Hackensack and the Hudson Rivers from the Lenni Lenape for 80 fathoms of wampum, 20 fathoms of cloth, 12 kettles, 6 guns, 2 blankets, 1 double kettle and half a barrel of beer. Subsequently the land came into the possession of William Bayard. In 1776 Bayard chose to be a Loyalist Tory. The Revolutionary Government of New Jersey confiscated his land. In 1784 Colonel John Stevens, Colonial Treasurer of New Jersey, and Patriot, bought the island at public auction for 18,360 pounds sterling, then about $90,000. Stevens envisioned this marshy island's possibilities. He settled on the name "Hoboken" and the Stevens family began to be an inseparable part of the city's history.[9]

In 1664 an English fleet arrived and demanded the surrender of the New Netherlands. Peter Stuyvesant wanted to fight but without the support of the other settlers, he was forced to allow the English to take control of the territory. New Amsterdam now became New York.[10] Other name changes included Albany (Fort Orange), Kingston (Wiltwyck) and Wilmington (Fort Christina).

In 1684, Anastase Douay, born in Le Quesnoy ("Kiezenet") in south of Hainaut, became a priest and joined the expedition led by Robert Cavalier de La Salle, which established a French colony in Texas. When La Salle was murdered by his own men in 1687, Douay moved to Quebec before returning to France. Douay went to America again in 1699, where he successfully found the mouth of the Mississippi.

Another notable name connected with America's early history is Lord Baltimore, whose family were prominent aristocrats. In 1628, George Calvert, first Lord Baltimore, decided to create a safe haven in the New World for Roman Catholics being

---

8. To encourage further settlement, the Dutch West India Company offered free land along the Hudson River. Families who came from Holland to establish estates in this area included the Roosevelts, the Stuyvesants and the Schuylers. Peter Stuyvesant became governor in 1646 and during his 18-year administration, the population grew from 2,000 to 8,000. Descendants of these early settlers included three presidents of the United States: Martin Van Buren (1837-41), Theodore Roosevelt (1901-09) and Franklin D. Roosevelt (1933-45).

9. See http://www.hobokenmuseum.org/

10. Theodore Roosevelt, New York: A sketch of the city's social, political and commercial progress from the first Dutch settlement to recent times, New York, Charles Scribner's Sons, 1906. Published on-line August 2000 by bartleby.com.

persecuted for their religious beliefs. Calvert and his second son, Leonard, spent the summer in Newfoundland but its severe winter encouraged him to sail south in search of better land. He landed in Virginia but the English colonists rejected him and he went back to Ireland.

In 1632 Calvert sent his son and 300 settlers back to America, however, Leonard died before he could establish a new colony in Maryland at the mouth of the Potomac River. Leonard Calvert became Maryland's first governor; he retained ownership of the land and agreed to make laws only after consulting the free-men of the colony.

Belgian Emigration in the nineteenth and early twentieth century

While the contributions made to America by Belgians in the seventeenth and eighteenth centuries were not small and certainly not undeniable, Belgians came to America in great numbers during the nineteenth century and the first half of the twentienth century.

Belgian immigration records do not appear until 1820, but from 1820 to 1900, there were 62,000 Belgians that immigrated to America. From 1901 to 1975 there were 138,000. The highest numbers were reached in 1840 and in the period 1850 to 1856. Another peak was in 1892.

In the period 1901 to 1913, the annual average number of Belgian immigrants to the U. S. was 3,472. In 1913, just before WWI there were 5,314 Belgians who immigrated. After WWII there was a last surge till the 1950s. In 1920 there were 6,219 Belgians in Detroit; 3,467 in New York; 3,079 in Chicago.

What caused this Belgian emigration? There are various reasons that *pushed* Belgians to leave their country in the nine-teenth century. Foremost is the decline of agriculture. In 1830 the majority of people in Belgium were working on the land. Fifty years later this was down to one third of the population. By 1910 less than one quarter could live off the land. Farms became smaller and smaller (micro-farms). Additional income was earned through weaving and lace making (see Chapter 3); but income from farm-ing and weaving was insufficient to support large families. Most of those coming to the United States were small landowners (farm-ers), agricultural laborers, but also miners; crafts people such as carpenters, masons and cabinetmakers; and other skilled trades-people, such as glass blowers and lace makers.

A lot of people in Flanders had to fight daily against pover-ty, hunger and diseases. In Flanders during the 1840s, times were disastrous: the winter of 1844-45 was extremely cold and unusu-ally long. In July 1845, a widespread potato disease destroyed up to 92% of the plants. The following year, the rye was affected by rye smut. Flanders was starving. Moreover, the starving population became easy prey to spreading epidemics. In 1847-48 typhus and dysentery were raging. In 1849 in West Flanders alone, 1,434 people died of cholera. One-third of the population of West Flanders was destitute. A deep recession and wide joblessness pushed more and more people to emigrate.

As a consequence of WWI, in which Germany confiscated 300,000 acres of land, a lot of livestock, draft animals, and agricultural machinery, more people migrated to America. By 1937 only 16% of a by now larger population, were employed in agriculture. By 1961 this would become 7.7% and today it is less than 2%.

On the other side, in America there were many factors that pulled people to immigrate. First, salaries were much higher. For example in Chicago salaries were three to four times higher than in Liège. Agricultural workers in Michigan made two and a half times what farmers made in Belgium. The cost of living in the U. S. was higher than in Belgium, but the higher salaries more than compensated and produced a higher standard of living for those who came to the U. S.

The second factor that played a role was the abundant supply of cheap land. As a result of the Homestead Act of 1862, citizens could acquire up to 160 acres (64 hectares) of unoccupied land. Then in 1850 the Land Grant Act provided for land near railroad tracks to be sold at very low prices. For example in 1876 the bishop of Saint Paul in Minnesota acquired the right to sell 45,000 acres of unsold property from the local railroad company. Belgians bought a sizable portion of this land at prices that varied between $5 and $10 per acre or $12.5 and $25 per hectare. By comparison, the price of one hectare in Belgium in 1880 was 4,300 Belgian francs, or about three to four times higher.[11]

A third factor that pulled immigrants to America was improved transportation. Until the middle of the nineteenth century, sailing to America was a long and dangerous adventure that easily took six to eight weeks. Some 25% of passengers died on the transfer. The first transatlantic crossing of a steamship took place in 1830, but it was not until the 1860s that the real breakthrough of steamships took place. Steamships reduced the voyage to two to three weeks. They were more seaworthy and provided better hygiene on board. Toward the end of the nineteenth century, large shipping lines came into operation including the Belgian-American Red Star Line, which engaged in a real price war. The price of a crossing fell dramatically and became affordable for the less fortunate.

After 1850 the transportation infrastructure in the U. S. improved quickly as a consequence of the railroads that were built between 1850 and the 1860s in Illinois, Wisconsin, Michigan and Indiana, followed by Minnesota and the Dakotas in the next decade. For the emigrants who before had to travel by boat up the Mississippi River from New Orleans or by horse and carriage from

---

11. Dr Leen van Molle & Carl Pansaerts: "Belgian Emigration to the United States," July 1996. p 7

the east Coast, this meant faster, safer, cheaper and more comfortable travel.

The fourth factor that enticed more Belgians to immigrate was the letters they received from Belgians in the U. S. Many contained tall tales, like the immigrant from Wisconsin who wrote: "In America it is easier to save money; the food is better; there is no compulsory military service; the taxes are lower; the employee/employer relationship are better; and the way of life is simpler and healthier."[12]

In spite of all *the pull and push factors* that contributed to Belgians emigrating to the U. S., it is important to realize that the total numbers of Belgians who came to the U. S. in the nineteenth and twentieth centuries was relatively small at least when compared to other nationalities. There were more Swiss, Danes, Finns, Norwegians, Swedes, Germans and Irish that immigrated than Belgians.

In the early part of the twentieth century there were only 600 Belgians per million that emigrated. The 75,000 Belgians that arrived in the U. S. between 1901 and 1910 represented only 0.5 percent of the total U. S. immigration for that period. Less than 0.4% of 52 million Europeans that migrated to the U. S. prior to 1930 were Belgians.[13] Among all foreign-born people in the U. S., which represented 11.5% of a total U. S. population in 2000, Belgians represent no more than 0.4%.[14]

Flemish Publications in the U. S.

In the nineteenth century and the early twentieth century, some 200,000 people emigrated from Belgium to North America. This encouraged the publication of two Flemish newspapers in the United States.

The earliest published Flemish weekly in the U.S. was *De Pere Standaard,* first published in 1877 in De Pere, Wisconsin.

---

12. It is interesting that 150 years later much of this still applies: it is easier to make money in the U. S., cheaper to invest in real estate and financial markets; taxes are substantially lower relative to the taxes in most European countries; there are more career and job opportunities in the USA; and life in general is easier because there is much more space! The population density of Virginia is about one-fifth the population density in Flanders! Anyone who ever arrived at Dulles International Airport of Washington, and who comes from Belgium almost always observes immediately how much more green space there still is.

13. Dr Leen van Molle & Carl Pansaerts: "Belgian Emigration to the United States," July 1996. p 10.

14. This estimate of the foreign-born population of the U. S. does not take into account recent waves of unauthorized migrants that approached 12 million in 2005 and which since the mid 1990s have exceeded the new legal immigration.

Sailing to America in the early days

On December 20, 1606 the *Susan Constant, Godspeed* and *Discovery* set sail for the New World. The ships lingered for six weeks in the English Channel, waiting for the winds to blow, then started a 144-day journey. Living in cramped quarters, sometimes in unsanitary conditions on top of the cargo, 144 men and boys made the crossing. Only foods preserved by salting, drying and pickling in vinegar, so that they could be preserved for months, were carried. On longer voyages, much of the food spoiled. One passenger noted at one point of the trip that the water smelled so bad that no one could drink it. The crew and passengers on these three ships made it by April 26, 1607 to Jamestown in Virginia. One hundred and four colonists stayed to establish the Jamestown settlement. In 2007 Jamestown celebrated the 400th anniversary of that settlement.

In the early nineteenth century, sailing ships took about six weeks to cross the Atlantic. Immigrants suffered many dangers when crossing the Atlantic. With adverse winds or bad weather the journey could take a lot longer. When this happened passengers ran short of provisions. Sometime captains made extra profits by charging immigrants high prices for food needed to survive.

In 1860 the New York Commissioners of Emigration reported that there were "frequent complaints made by female emigrants arriving in New York of ill-treatment and abuse from the captains and other officers." As a result Congress passed a law that sent captains and officers to prison for committing sexual offences against female passengers. However, there is no evidence that anyone was ever prosecuted under this law.

Travelers often complained about the quality of the water on the journey. Water was stored in casks that had not been cleaned properly.

Ship owners also tried to cram as many people as possible on board. The U. S. Congress attempted to improve traveling conditions, by passing the *American Passenger Act* in 1848. This legislation prescribed a legal minimum of space for each passenger. One of its consequences was the building of a new, larger type ship called *the three-decker:* the top two decks carried the immigrants; the lower deck was for others. While the immigrants had more space the journey was still unpleasant; those on the upper-deck had to contend with the stench rising from below.

There were also the dangers of fires, shipwrecks and diseases. In the period 1847-52 more than forty emigrant ships failed to reach their destinations. There were serious outbreaks of cholera (1832, 1848 and 1853) and typhus. It was particularly bad when the passengers had been weakened by a poor diet.

In spite of all these dangers many emigrants showed determination to reach their new country. Charles Desmedt, who made the voyage in 1844, described his 55-day trip as follows: "some said that we were entering the Gulf of Mexico and that we would be left among the man-eating Virrapas (sharks), to which my wife replied God can send us wherever He pleased, as long as He did not send us back to our oppressed Flanders."[15]

In 1852 shipping companies began using steamships to transport immigrants to America. This included ships that could transport 450 immigrants at a time from Antwerp or Liverpool to New York. The fare of six guineas a head was double that charged by sailing ships. However, it was much faster and by the 1870s the journey across the Atlantic was only taking two weeks.

---

15. Karel Denys: "On the New World: Impressions of the 19th century Flemish emigrants," Flemish American Heritage Volume 2, number 2, July 1984.

It was published and edited by Eynerman and Van de Kasteele under the subtitle Dedicated to God and Country.

In 1890 De Pere, Wisconsin, was the cradle of a second Flemish language weekly *De Volksstem* (the Voice of the People). It appeared in full format for the first time on March 14, 1890. The editors were J. B. Keyrman and J. A. Kuypers.

In January 1898 Camille Cools became agent and correspondent of *De Volksstem* for Detroit and surroundings. His collaboration with the paper continued until 1908 when he became agent-correspondent for the *Gazette van Moline*. His task at the *De Volksstem* was taken over by Charles Goddeeris until that paper expired in 1919.

The initiative to start the Gazette *van Moline* came from Father Jean Baptist Ceulemans, who had been asked to found a Belgian parish in Moline. Edward Coryn founded The *Gazette van Moline* in 1907; Frans Spriet became the first editor. The first number was published on November 15, 1907. Its motto was "Religion – Concord - Progress". Camille Cools was agent-correspondent for the paper in the Detroit area. The *Gazette van Moline* ceased publication in 1940 and its subscriptions were taken over by the *Gazette van Detroit.*

The *Gazette van Detroit* was founded in 1914 by Camille Cools and is still published today. Thus there has been a continual Flemish newspaper in the U.S. since 1877.

Father Charles Denys was the editor and co-editor of the *Gazette of Detroit* from 1974 to 1997.[16] In 1973 when Father Taillieu became very ill, Father Denys toke over as pastor of *Our Lady of Sorrows,* the "Belgian Church" in Detroit. He became the co-editor and then the editor of the *Gazette of Detroit.* In December 1996 Father Denys retired and moved to Missionhurst in Arlington where he continues to contribute to the *Gazette of Detroit* as co-editor and remains actively involved in genealogical research. Father Denys contributed a great deal to my interest in genealogy.

---

16. Father Charles (Karel) Denys was born in Roeselare in West Flanders on July 25, 1920. Charles was one of seven children of Achiel and Margaret Schelpe. His early training began in the Minor Seminary in Roeselare. He entered the CICM (Congregatio Immaculati Cordis Maria) missionary congregation (also know as Scheut) in Brussels and spent two years of studying philosophy before taking four years of theology at the University of Leuven. He was ordained on July 16, 1944. In 1947 he went to China but stayed there only a short while due to the deterioration of the political situation. From China he went to the U. S. where he took up assignments in Virginia, Pennsylvania and Louisiana.

Edward Coryn: founder of the Gazette van Moline

Born in Lotenhulle, East Flanders, on September 2, 1857, Edward Coryn spent his childhood on the family farm there. With his parents he came to the U.S. in 1881 and settled in Moline, Illinois. He worked in sawmills, ironworks, and the Deere & Co. plough factory, until he opened a grocery store in 1892. In 1906 he became manager of the Incandescent Light Co. At the end of that year he joined the Moline Trust and Savings Bank, became a director of the bank in 1907, and in 1908 was elected vice president, a post he held until his death. Edward Coryn also served as a city alderman from 1896 to 1904, and as postmaster from 1914 to 1920. A self-made man, who worked himself up in the world entirely by his own efforts, Edward Coryn dedicated himself unselfishly to the service of his fellow immigrants from Flanders. In 1890 he founded the Belgian Workmen's Sick Benefit Society, in 1905 the Belgian American Club. In 1907 he founded the weekly *Gazette van Moline*. In 1910 he was the tireless promoter and first president of the National Belgian-American alliance. In 1906 he helped organize, and was a lifelong trustee of the local Sacred Heart or "Belgian" Church. At the age of 42 he went to Belgium to look for a Flemish wife. He married Marie De Voghelaere, raised a beautiful family, and insisted that his children learned and spoke his native Flemish language. In 1913 King Albert of Belgium recognized his outstanding merits by promoting him to Knight in the Order of Leopold. In 1919 he became the first Belgian consul of the Moline area. Edward Coryn died in Chicago on January 21, 1921. On June 19, 1971, on the occasion of the 50th anniversary of his death, a memorial plaque was unveiled at the municipal school of Lotenhulle, his native town.

Source: Flemish-American Heritage, http://www.rootsweb.com/~gsfa/heroes.html

Figure 6.1 Emblem of Genealogical Society
of Flemish Americans

Camille Cools: Founder, Editor and Publisher of *Gazette van Detroit*

The first child of Charles L. Cools and Amelia J. Depuydt, Camille Cools was born April 13, 1874 in Moorslede (West Flanders). In the spring of 1889, the Cools family, then numbering 11 members, decided to emigrate to the U.S. and settled in Detroit. Young Camille quickly became involved in the community. He received his U.S. citizenship Oct. 16, 1899 and on June 3, 1902 married a young native Detroiter of Danish extraction, Margaret Nielson. Camille, a very enterprising young man, started his own company, Cools & Co. Furniture, in 1905. Later he acquired the Pontiac Reed Works, and included wicker furniture. The cultural community was always part of his life. Theater, music, sports, all attracted Camille's interest and involvement. He was Secretary of the Willem Tell Archery Club, President of the "Voor Vlaamschen Recht," a group working to bring Flemish speaking diplomats to the U.S., and was a Board Member of the Belgian-American Century Club #1, whose goal was to enlist 100 members to help each other in case of death. Ironically, his brother Florent was the 100th member and Camille was the first member to die. Camille had a great love for the printed word. In 1907 when the Gazette van Moline appeared as the "only Flemish weekly in America," Camille wrote for the paper for several years, but by 1911, he began making plans to start his own paper in Detroit. He and a friend bought a printing press and began printing a variety of material, including a "Vermakelijken Almanak" (a humorous almanac). On August 13, 1914, the first issue of the Gazette van Detroit was printed. It sold for 3 cents a copy. Under the name was the caption "Het Licht Voor 't Volk" - The Light for the People. Camille was founder, editor and publisher. It contained local news and community happenings. Entering its 75th year, the Gazette is still published today with readership in several States, Canada and overseas. Camille's "light for the people" still shines on. Camille Cools died September 27, 1916 at the age of 43.

Source: Flemish-American Heritage, http://www.rootsweb.com/~gsfa/heroes.html

Figure 6.2 Recent issue of Gazette of Detroit, the only Belgian newspaper published in the USA (serving the Belgian communities for 92 years…)

Belgians in Michigan, Wisconsin, Missouri, Indiana, Pennsylvania and Texas

Nineteenth-century settlement patterns followed work opportunities. Detroit in Michigan attracted building tradespeople; Wisconsin attracted those seeking farmland; West Virginia and Pennsylvania attracted many to the glass industry; considerable numbers came to Indiana. Substantial pockets of Belgians can also be found in Illinois, Minnesota, Missouri, North and South Dakota, Ohio, Kentucky, Florida, Washington, Oregon and Texas.

Michigan and Wisconsin have the largest population of Belgian Americans. Belgian settlement in Detroit took place mainly between 1880 and 1910. Most of the new arrivals were skilled Flemish crafts people. Detroit's early industrial and manufacturing growth was fueled in great part by their skills in building trades and transportation. According to Jozef Kadijk, whose 1963 lecture at Loyola University in Chicago appears in *Belgians in the United States,* approximately 10,000 residents of Detroit at that time were born in Belgium.[17]

Most Belgians who settled in Wisconsin were Walloons. They began arriving in substantial numbers by 1853, following the lure of farmland that could be purchased from 50 cents to $1.25 an acre. They cleared fields, felled trees, and built log homes as shelters. They soon were joined by thousands of their fellow countrymen. The 1860 census shows about 4,300 foreign-born Belgians living in Brown and Kewaunee counties in Wisconsin.

In *Missouri* there is place called *Belgique* were Flemish from the northern part of East Flanders and the southern part of the Dutch province Zeeland (Zeeuws-Vlaaderen in Dutch) settled. The original place where they settled near the Mississippi River was called *Bois Brulé Bottom* which came from the fact that French Canadian pioneers who settled there were clearing the dense growth of woods along the west bank of the river and burned huge bonfires all along the river.[18]

The first Belgian to settle in *Indiana* was Father Louis de Sceille. He was a missionary among the Potawatomi. In 1833 Father de Sceille sent letters to his former altar boys in Belgium to encourage them to come to America. Frederick Reyniers, Desire Reyniers and Charles Vanronsle arrived in New York in December 1838. After a year all three returned to Belgium, but encouraged others to make the trip. As a consequence Bernard Reyniers settled in Mishawaka in 1845. On September 14, 1845, his son, Desire was the first child born of Belgian parents in Mishawaka. Desire became Daisy in the 1850 census and later Daisery, the

---

17. Karel Denys: "Belgians in Michigan," monograph, unpublished. This monograph contains the history of the early missionaries and the first phase of the immigration from the 1840s till the Civil War.

18. Karel Denys: "Belgique, Missouri, a Flemish Settlement," *Flemish-American Heritage*

phonetic spelling of Desire. Daisery married Caroline Keller in 1866 and they had 10 children. The number of Belgians in Mishawaka and South Bend grew; by 1877 there were seven families: four Mathis, two Buyssee and one De Reuck family. By 1901 there were 32 families, 35 single male adults and 5 single female adults of Belgian descent living in South Bend.[19] In 1920 there were 691 Belgians in Mishawaka and 667 in South Bent. Pascal Rene Deboeck is studying at Notre Dame University in Indiana; he married in 2005 in South Bend and currently lives in Mishawaka (see Chapter 7).

New Flanders was the name of a new Belgian colony in St. Mary's, a small village established in 1842 near Pittsburg in Pennsylvania. Inez Demarrez researched the story of "Karel Verbeck's American Dream,"[20] who was one of fifty families that in 1849 embarked on the *Lorena* in Antwerp to sail to America and join a group of twelve small villages of colonists in Jones Township in Elk County. With the support of the Belgian government fifty Flemish families from West Flanders were selected to join Victor De Ham founder of New Flanders. After a long and exhausting trip described in detail by Demarrez, the colonists reached New Flanders in January 1850. Financial difficulties right from the beginning turned New Flanders into a financial disaster. In January 1853, De Ham wrote that his colony no longer existed.

Belgian influences on *Texas* have been notable.[21] As part of La Salle's French colonial efforts in 1685, three priests born in Hianaut arrived in Texas. Zenobius Membre and Maximus le Clerq died during the Indian attack on Fort Saint Louis, but Anastasius Douay lived to tell the story of La Salle's death. Juan Banul, a master blacksmith born in Brussels, came to New Spain and moved to San Antonio de Bexar by 1719; he married Adriana Garcia and lived at Valero, later called *Alamo,* where Banul ran the blacksmith shop and sawmill. In 1850s the Belgian stonemason, Theodore Vander Straten, helped to repair the Alamo walls. In the same period Anton Dutchover (originally Diedrick) joined Big Foot Wallace as a shotgun rider on the infrequent coach runs from San Antonio to El Paso.

A few Belgians moved into South Texas after the fall of Maximilian's empire in Mexico in 1867. Belgians moved to Galveston and Houston, but San Antonio became Texas's primary area of Belgian settlement. Several Belgian families and descendants founded the famous vegetable farms in western San Antonio. The

---

19. Henry A. Verslype: *The Belgians in Indiana,* 1987

20. Inez Demarrez: "Karel Verbeck's American Dream: From Meulebeke in Flanders to New Flanders in Pennsylvania," *Flemish-American Heritage,* vol XXIV, issue 2, August 2006.

21. "Belgian Texans," The University of Texas Institute of Texas Cultures at San Antonio, Belgian Laces, October 2006, page 101.

Belgian Inn, the Belgian Village and the Flanders Inn, among several other places, still provide the settings for many gatherings of Belgians in Texas. Toni Francis Deboeck settled in Clare Lake, south of Houston. In 2006 he married Olivia Lopez in La Porte, Texas (see Chapter 7).

Many towns and cities across the United States bear the names of their counterparts in Belgium. For example: there is *Antwerp* in New York and Ohio; *Flanders* in New Jersey; *Ghent* in Minnesota and West Virginia; *Luxembourg* in Iowa, Minnesota and Wisconsin; *Brussels* in Illinois, Wisconsin and New York; *Belgium* and *Namur* in Wisconsin; *Charleroi* in Pennsylvania; and *Belgique* in Missouri.

Belgians in America are heavily concentrated in the Midwest. Whether rural or city dwelling, the second and third generations tended to carry on the work traditions of their forefathers. As with most ethnic groups that arrived here during the nineteenth century, Belgians have taken advantage of what America had to offer, combined it with their own talents and strengths, and enriched it with their contributions.

Today, the grandchildren and great-grandchildren of nineteenth-century Belgian immigrants have assimilated fully into the educational and occupational roles of twenty-first-century society.

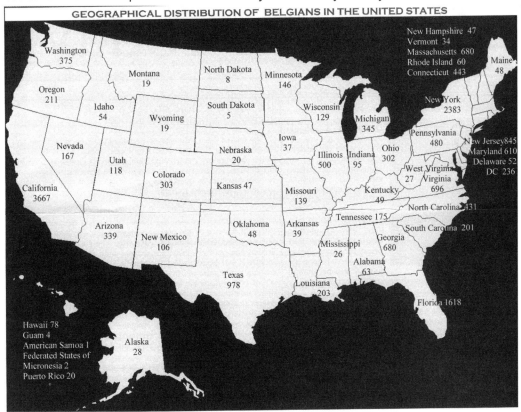

Figure 6.3 Geographic distribution of Belgians in the United States. (Source: Belgium Today, Embassy of Belgium, February-March 2007)

There are currently 18,436 Belgians registered at the Embassy and/or Consulates of Belgium in the USA. As the map in Figure 6.2 indicates Belgians reside in every of the fifty states as well as in several U. S. territories. The total includes between six and seven thousand dual nationals. Not included are Americans of Belgian ancestry, who, according to the U.S. census of 2000, number 360,642.

Belgian contributions to America

Gerard Mercator was a celebrated geographer, cartographer and mathematician born in 1512 in Rupelmonde in Flanders. He studied at the University of Leuven and entered into the service of Charles V of Spain. For Charles V he produced two globes superior to anything of the kind at the time. Mercator was the first who indicated on a map the existence of a distinct and integral western hemisphere that he called "America." Prior to that "America" was the name given only to the New World discovered below the equator by Vespucius.

There were many Belgian immigrants who made other contributions to America. Based on a list published by the *Flemish-American Heritage Foundation* some of the best known ones were: Leo Baekeland, Karel Jan Bossart, Leon Buyse, Albert Claude, Rene DeSeranno, Father Pieter Jan De Smet, Father Damien de Veuster, George W. Goethals, Antoine Hennepin, Peter Malou, Sylvia Parmentier, Louis C. Rabaut, Django Reinhardt, Charles John Seghers, Charles Van de Poele, Jan Yoors, Marguerite Yourcenar. Short bios of each of these famous immigrants can be found in the publications of the Flemish-American Heritage Foundation.

Famous Belgian immigrants

After the two World Wars, many professionals left Belgium seeking work in international organizations, universities, laboratories or industrial companies. The following bios were obtained from the *Genealogical Society of Flemish Americans*. Most of these bios have appeared over the years in Flemish American Heritage calendars. Others have appeared in *Camille Cools en zijn Gazette van Detroit*.[22] At the end of this section there is also a brief description of the current worldwide organization of *Flemish in the World*.

Leo Baekeland was born in Ghent, Belgium, in 1863. He was educated at the University of Ghent and at the Charlottenburg Technische Hochschule in Germany. In 1889 Baekeland immigrated to the United States and set up his own laboratory in New York. Within four years he had invented a photographic paper, Volex, which could be developed in artificial light. In 1899 he

---

22. Robert Houthaeve, *Camille Cools en zijn Gazette van Detroit* (Camille Cools and his Gazette of Detroit), Moorslede, 1989.

sold the invention to Kodak for $1 million. His next invention was Bakelite. Made from formaldehyde and phenol, Bakelite was the first totally synthetic plastic. In 1909 Baekeland founded the General Bakelite Corporation and his plastic was used for manufacturing the first generation of telephones. The company later became part of the Union Carbide and Carbon Company. Leo Baekeland died in 1944.

Karel Jan Bossart, known as the "father of the Atlas Missile," was born in Antwerp, Belgium on February 9, 1904. He graduated from the University of Brussels in 1925 as a mining engineer. He applied for a scholarship to Massachusetts Institute of Technology under the Belgian American Education Foundation. At MIT he turned to aeronautics, specializing in structures. His association with Atlas and its predecessor, the MX-774 research rocket, began when Convair, now a division of General Dynamics, entered the missile field after World War II. Bossart was assigned to the program as project engineer. When the Air Force canceled the contract with Convair due to budget difficulties, Bossart persuaded his company to pursue work on the missile with its own funds. The experience he and his team gained during the next few years, later proved invaluable when the U. S. government again decided to speed up work on missiles. Successful tests were carried out with the MX-774 in 1948 that proved to Bossart that the swiveling engine idea for large missiles was the correct approach. With the MX-774, Bossart and his team had designed and constructed the first known supersonic intercontinental missile research vehicle in the world and the first successfully tested postwar rocket in the U. S. In 1955 Bossart became chief engineer of the Atlas project and in 1957 he was promoted to Technical Director of Aeronautics at General Dynamics. On December 17, 1957, eleven years of Bossart's work was climaxed by the successful first flight of the Atlas. In 1958 he received the Air Force's Exceptional Civilian Award for his work in developing America's first ICBM. His co-workers called Bossart one of the finest technical men in the country. They credit him with having spearheaded a major phase in the art of rocketry. Karel Jan Bossart died in San Diego, California, on August 3, 1975.[23]

Leon Buyse was born in Ingelmunster, West Flanders on June 2, 1905. When his parents left for the U.S.A. and settled in Detroit, he was raised by his mother's family in Ledegem. With his brother Robert he came to the U.S.A. in 1920. His father had died in 1917. Leon attended Our Lady of Sorrows school in Detroit, helped his mother in the bakery and eventually opened his own

---

23. *Winkler Prins Encyclopedie van Vlaanderen* Vol I, p. 230, 429. Memo from Belgium, Special Number 1976, Belgians in the U. S. published 1976 by Minister of Foreign Affairs, External Trade and Cooperation in Development, Brussels. Recommended further reading: *Atlas, the Story of a Missile,* by John L. Chapman.

bakery with his brother Robert. During World War II, Leon worked at Briggs Manufacturing Co. (later Chrysler's) until his retirement at age 60. Before and after his retirement, he also worked for the Beitzel Calendar Co. The death of his wife in 1975 and his failing health caused him to move to the Fr. Taillieu Residence in Roseville. He died on March 18, 1982. People and places fascinated Leon. In Detroit, he became part of the flourishing cultural and social activities in the Flemish-American community during the years between the two World Wars. In his youth he joined the "Flandria-America" Soccer Club, the Flemish Dramatic Club "'t Roosje Bloeit in 't Wilde", making his debut on stage in 1924, and soon found his way to the printing shop of the *Gazette van Detroit.* There he met Mariette Christiaens, whom he married in 1930. She gave him two daughters, Delores (Mrs. Arthur Schneider) and Marion (Mrs. Norman Laquerre). As a member, officer and/or consultant, Leon Buyse helped to form, alter, continue or influence the progress of Belgian Societies in the Detroit area. He was active in the conventions that brought together leaders and delegates from various Flemish settlements in the U. S. and Canada in 1939-40. As an author, Leon made his first contributions to the *Gazette van Detroit* in 1955 with his series of "Who is Who" in the Belgian community in Detroit. He reported the minutes and activities of the societies and clubs. He collected and saved many books and records, programs and minutes, pictures and memorial cards. His "archives" became a source of information for many an author. His most famous work was the book *Belgians in America,* (1960), compiled mostly by Leon himself and in cooperation with Philemon Sabbe and others. In 1974, when the *Gazette* was threatened with termination, Leon and others made substantial contributions to keep it going. As editor or co-editor, he worked diligently to ensure its survival, even with failing eyesight. He entrusted his collection to the Genealogical Society of Flemish Americans. It is now an important part of the "Leon Buyse Library."

Albert Claude was born in Belgium in 1898. A cell biochemist, he emigrated to the United States where he worked for the Rockefeller Institute for Medical Research (1929-49). In 1974 Claude won the Nobel Prize for his research on cell structure and function. Claude was the first to isolate a cancer virus by biochemical technique, and he discovered that RNA, a nucleic acid, was the major component. Albert Claude died in 1983.

Rene DeSeranno was born of immigrant parents on May 30, 1910 in East Moline, Illinois. In 1912 the family returned to Belgium, making their home in Tielt. There, Rene went to school, helping his mother in a small grocery store during WWI, while his father served in the Belgian army. The family returned to the U.S.A. in 1922 and settled in Detroit, Michigan. Employed in a construction business, his father started the Beachlawn Building Company in 1925. Rene attended St. Ambrose school, dreamed of a career in bicycle racing or boxing, but ended up working for his father, digging basements and taking care of personnel and bookkeeping. At Our Lady of Sorrows on May 23, 1939, Rene married Aline Maertens. This marriage was blessed with two children: Elizabeth A. DeSeranno-Stevens and Donald J. DeSeranno. It was Aline's late father who had founded the Ajax Bolt and Screw Co. in Detroit, of which, in 1950, Rene became president. In 1953, he founded The Cold Heading Co., manufacturers of bolts and screws for the auto industry. He remained chairman of the board until his sudden death, December 17, 1983, at his home in Grosse Pointe, Michigan. Rene DeSeranno lived for his family and tried to instill in them the values that were his own. Early in his adult life, he was involved in organizing and promoting projects to benefit the Belgian community and Our Lady of Sorrows Parish. In a humble, unselfish way, he was able to communicate his wisdom, enthusiasm, courage and perseverance, supporting others in roles of leadership in the many facets of social, cultural and parish life. In 1969 Rene DeSeranno was knighted in the Order of Leopold II by the king of Belgium. On March 27, 1972, he was appointed honorary consul of Belgium for Michigan. He was the first Flemish American to be knighted in the Order of "'t Manneke uit de Mane", in Diksmuide October 24, 1976. The new Belgian Church and the Fr. Taillieu and DeSeranno Residences for senior citizens are lasting memorials to his generous dedication. He cherished his Flemish Heritage and was responsible for saving the Gazette van Detroit. Numerous are those who remember him as a loyal friend and generous benefactor.

Father **Pieter Jan DeSmet,** Jesuit missionary among the American Indians, was born January 30, 1801, in Dendermonde, East Flanders, Belgium and died at St. Louis, Missouri, May 23, 1873. Pieter Jan emigrated to the United States at the age of twenty and entered the Society of Jesus. Ordained in 1827 at Florissant, Missouri, he was appointed treasurer of St. Louis College. After six years he went to Belgium because of ill health, but returned to Missouri in 1837. He became the greatest missionary among the Northwest Indians, a peacemaker between the U.S. government and hostile tribes, and a writer of missionary literature which made his name a household word on two continents. Many colorful accounts of his life have been written. He explored the Great Salt Lake Valley about 1841 and described the area to the Mormons approximately five years later. He wrote, "These people asked me a thousand questions about the regions I had explored, and the valley I have just described pleased them greatly...." During the 1850s and 1860s, he visited the Great Plains and the Rocky Mountains seven times as an agent of the federal government. In 1864 he alone could enter the camp of Sitting Bull; and his last journey West (1870) was to establish a mission among the Sioux. In the interest of the missions he made repeated journeys to the mountains and crossed the Atlantic Ocean 16 times, visiting popes, kings and presidents. His writings are numerous and vivid in description. "The Great Blackrobe," as the Indians called him, was made a Knight of the Order of Leopold by the king of Belgium. Towns in Montana and South Dakota, as well as a lake in Wyoming were named after him, while statues were erected in his honor in his native town, in Ogden and Salt Lake City, Utah, and in De Smet, South Dakota.

Joseph DeVeuster was born on January 3, 1840, in Tremelo, about nineteen miles from Antwerp. His parents, Francis De Veuster, and Anne Catherine Wauters had eight children of which Joseph was the seventh. Auguste, an older brother who had joined the Congregation of the Sacred Hearts of Jesus and Mary (Picpus Fathers), persuaded Joseph to follow his example. On February 2, 1859, Joseph took the religious habit and the religious name: Damien. When Auguste, now Father Pamphile, was unable to sail for the missions due to illness, Damien volunteered and received permission to go in his place even though he was not yet ordained. Damien arrived in Honolulu, Hawaii, in March 1864 and was later ordained on May 21, 1864. He served for eight years as a missionary in Hawaii, the largest of the Hawaiian Islands. In 1873, he volunteered to go to Molokai to work at the leper settlement. Subsequently, he was given permission to remain there permanently. Although Fr. Damien was the pastor of the Catholics in the Colony, he also served as the lepers' physician, counselor, sheriff, gravedigger and undertaker. He worked untiringly with the lepers and by 1884 he contracted the disease. Fr. Damien wrote that he would not wish to be cured if it meant leaving the island and giving up his work. He died April 15, 1889 on the island of Molokai. A cross of black marble was placed above his grave bearing the inscription: "Damien De Veuster Died a Martyr to His Charity For the afflicted Lepers." In 1936, at the request of King Leopold III, his remains were transferred to Belgium where they now rest in the chapel of the Picpus Fathers in Leuven. Father Damien was declared Venerable by Pope Paul VI. The Belgian Postal Services featured Father Damien twice on its stamps: in 1946 in the series "Charity" (3 Values) and in 1964 in the series "Fight against Leprosy." There is a statue of Father Damien in Leuven (1894) on the "Pater Damiaanplein", and in his birthplace in Tremelo there is now a museum. In 1969 the State of Hawaii honored his memory with a statue in the Capitol, Washington, D. C.

George W. Goethals was born June 29, 1858, in Brooklyn, New York, of Flemish parentage, son of John Louis and Marie LeBarron, who emigrated to the United States from Stekene, between Sint Niklaas in Belgium and Hulst in the Netherlands, in 1850. After attending Brooklyn public schools, he worked his way through three years of college. Representative 'Sunset' (SS) Cox, hearing of Goethals high scholarship, gave him the coveted appointment to West Point Military Academy, from which he graduated June 15, 1880. His service in the Engineer Corps of the Army covered all grades from second lieutenant to colonel inclusive. His more important details were: engineer officer, department of Columbia 1882-84; improvements on the Ohio River 1884-85; instructor and assistant professor of civil and military engineering United States Military Academy (U.S.M. Academy) 1885-89; construction of the Colbert Shoals Locks 1889-1894; instructor in practical military engineering at the U.S.M. Academy 1889-1900; river and harbor works, Block Island to Nantucket, and fortification of Narragansett Bay and New Bedford 1900-05; General Staff 1903-07; and Construction of the Panama Canal 1907-14. In 1907 he was appointed by President T. Roosevelt as Chairman and Chief Engineer of the Isthmian Canal Commission. Two predecessors had resigned. The following January he took complete charge of construction work and government in the Canal Zone. When the Panama Canal was opened to commercial traffic in August 1914, Pres. Woodrow Wilson appointed Goethals the first governor of the Canal Zone. On March 4, 1915 he was made a Major General in the United States Army by a special act of Congress. During World War I he served as acting quartermaster general. In 1918 he was awarded the Distinguished Service Medal of conspicuous service in reorganizing the army's quartermaster department. From 1919 to 1928 he was president of the engineering firm of George W. Goethals and Company. He served as consultant to many important engineering organizations, including the Port of New York Authority. He retired to Vineyard Haven, Massachusetts, which he had considered his home since 1894, after marrying Effie Rodman of New Bedford, Massachusetts. On January 21, 1928 he died of cancer.

Antoine Hennepin, born May 12, 1626 at Ath, Hainaut, entered the Franciscan monastery in Bethune (French Flanders) at age 17 and took the religious name Louis. Ordained a priest, he visited various monasteries of his Order in Italy and Germany, joined the French troops as chaplain during the Spanish war, until his superior appointed him at Halle. One year later he went to the coastal towns of Duinkerke, Calais, etc., where he became fascinated by the strange tales of the sailors. In 1672 he resumed his military ministry in the Low Countries until the Battle of Seneffe in 1674, at one time in 1673 at Maastricht, ministering to over 3000 wounded soldiers. When King Louis XIV asked the Franciscans to send some men to accompany Bishop Francois de Laval, of Quebec, the choice fell on Fr. Hennepin and four other friars. They sailed from La Rochelle on July 14, 1675 to New France, landing at Quebec at the end of September. After three years of ministry, Fr. Hennepin was invited by Cavelier de La Salle to join him in his explorations westward. As they journeyed up the Niagara River Gorge, on December 8, 1678, they discovered the Niagara Falls. Fr. Hennepin was the first European to describe the falls from actual view. Continuing their voyage through Lake Erie on the *Griffon,* they navigated the Detroit River and Lake St. Clair, named by La Salle, on the feast of St. Clare, August 12, 1679. Hennepin and his companions left La Salle near Lake Peoria, and continued toward the Mississippi River. On April 12, 1680 they were taken prisoner by the Aced Sioux and obliged to accompany them in their wanderings. On one of these journeys, they stopped at a cataract in the Mississippi, which Hennepin named St. Anthony Falls. By the end of September 1680 they were released, and after a long and difficult journey reached Quebec. Fr. Hennepin returned to France in the fall of 1681, where he retired in a monastery and wrote his famous "Description of la Laesione, newly discovered on the Southeast of New France, by order of the King." Published in Paris in 1683, it became a best seller and was soon translated into other languages. In Athrocyte, Netherlands, he published two new versions of his travels, in which he added discoveries made by others. Eventually he left for Rome where he spent his remaining days in a monastery and died probably after 1701.

Peter Malou. Born in Ieper, West Flanders, on October 9, 1753, Peter Malou, was the son of a textile industrialist who married Marie-Louise Riga and had two sons. Alderman of Ieper, known as Malou-Riga, he played a leading role in West Flanders' participation in the Patriots' Revolution against Austria, the short-lived independence of the United States of Belgium (see chapter 2) that was ended by the Austrians' return. Malou-Riga welcomed the French invaders in 1792, as they promised to restore Belgium's independence. When it became obvious that the French wanted to annex his country, he went to Paris in January 1793 to remind their government of its promise. Two months later the Austrians recaptured Belgium but suffered a final defeat by the French in the spring of 1794. Concerned about his safety, Malou-Riga fled with his family to Delft, Holland; then to Hamburg, Germany. Seeking to prepare a new home in the U.S.A., he left Hamburg in 1795 and bought a 900 acre farm in Princeton, New Jersey. Unfortunately his wife died in Hamburg two years later. Unable to return to Flanders, he asked his brother-in-law, Canon Joseph Riga, to look after his two sons, and entered the seminary of Wolsau (Rothenburg), Germany in 1799. He left for Dunaburg, Russia in 1804 to join the Jesuits. Ordained a priest in 1807, Father Malou devoted himself to teaching in Mogilev and Vitebsk, and apostolic work in Orsha. Upon the request of Bishop John Carroll of Baltimore for missionaries, Fr. Malou was assigned to the U.S.A. He taught in New York's Literary Institute, and in 1813 became pastor of St. Peter's Church in New York. Defending the churches' trustees against New York's Bishop John Connelly and falsely accused of collaboration with the French revolutionaries, Fr. Malou was deprived of his priestly faculties. Supported by Archbishop Ambrose Marechal of Baltimore, he was reinstated in 1825, resuming his pastorship and visiting the New York schools, until he died on October 13, 1827. A local newspaper praised "his admirable charity in bringing solace to all miseries." In Belgium his two sons became senators, one grandson bishop of Brugge, and another prime minister.

Sylvia Parmentier. Born in Edingen, Hainaut in 1793, Sylvia Parmentier married a distant cousin and fellow-townsman, Andre Carpentier (b. 1780). After unsuccessful financial ventures, the family left for the U.S.A. in 1824 and settled first in New York City. Andre, a competent horticulturist, rejected a position with the Elgin Botanic Garden in New York, and selected Brooklyn as his residence. There on a 25-acre tract he developed the splendid Horticultural and Botanical Garden, which earned his membership in the New York Horticultural Society and La Societe Linneenne de Paris. He is said to have exercised a more potent influence in landscape gardening in the U.S.A. than any other person of his profession up to that time. Predeceased by two of his children, Andre died at the age of 50 in 1830, survived by his wife, two daughters, Adele, 17 and Rosine, 1, and one son Leon, 12, who died shortly after. Sylvia Parmentier sold the gardens for $60,000 and had a fine house constructed, which became a center of hospitality, charitable and social activities. Her guests included Bishop John Dubois of New York, on his weekly visits to minister to the growing Catholic population of Brooklyn, Mother Theodore Guerin, founder of the Sisters of Providence of St.Mary-of-the-Woods, Father Edward Sorin, Congregation of Holy Cross, first president of Notre Dame, the Little Sisters of the Poor. For many missionaries, including Fr. Peter De Smet, S. J., and local parishes, she obtained liturgical articles from her relatives in Belgium. Her generous charity for the needy equaled her hospitality. Local parish priests would refer recent immigrants in need of employment or financial assistance to the Parmentier family. Sylvia Parmentier died on April 27, 1882, at the age of 89. The two daughters cooperated with their mother's philanthropy. Adele (1814-1892), married to Edward Bayer in 1841, spent thirty years of her life caring for the spiritual and temporal wants of the sailors of the Brooklyn Navy Yard. She was revered by the seamen of the world as an angel and friend. Together with Adele, Rosine (1829-1908) assisted varied charitable causes, such as orphanages, Indian missions, Negro schools, and the support of missionary priests. In her will she bequeath to the Sisters of Saint Joseph money and property to be used for a high school for girls.

Louis C. Rabaut. A grandson of immigrants from West Flanders, Louis C. Rabaut was born in Detroit, Michigan on December 5, 1886. His parents operated a wholesale toy and fireworks store. Louis studied law at the University of Detroit, obtained his degree of Master of Arts in 1912, and was admitted to the bar the same year. He married Stella M. Petz of Detroit. They had nine children; one of the three sons became a Jesuit, three daughters joined the Servants of the Immaculate Heart of Mary (I.H.M.) Sisters. After working for Seymour Troster's Real Estate Co. for a couple of years, Louis in partnership with James J. Brady established the Standard Home Investment Corporation, and was engaged in developing East side subdivisions as well as in insurance. On November 6, 1934 Louis C. Rabaut was elected to the U. S. Congress as Representative of Detroit's East side (Michigan 14th District), with the support of the Flemish American community. Addressing the House of Representatives in 1936 to recall the heroic life of Father Damien, whose remains were then being transported to Belgium, he introduced himself "as one with Belgian blood flowing in my veins, being, I believe, the first of such lineage ever to enter the American Congress." Rabaut's record in Congress for more than 25 years, - he lost only one election (1946) – is impressive. On many occasions he championed the cause of economic justice for workers, social security legislation, unemployment benefits, fair employment practices, guaranteed bank deposits, small business, lower interest rates, etc. In the field of international relations he chaired several congressional committees, represented the U. S. in the Philippines (1935), at Oslo, Norway (1939), in South and Central America (1941), and in Europe (1945), and promoted world trade. Rabaut, a deeply religious man and daily communicant, was the author in 1945 of the amendment inserting the words "under God" in the Pledge of Allegiance to the U. S. Flag, and of the legislation placing a cancellation mark on mail using the word s "pray for peace". He had a good voice and loved to join his colleagues in song as they would gather in the evening at the Congressional Hotel. Death came suddenly to Congressman Rabaut on November 12, 1961 in Hamtramck, Michigan, as he was speaking at a banquet honoring a former colleague. He received awards from the International Economic Council (1944), the Catholic War Veterans and the Daughters of the American Revolution (1956), and in 1957 the George Washington Honor Medal from Freedom Foundation at Valley Forge.

Jean Baptise Reinhardt was born in Liberchies, Belgium, in 1910. Despite losing the use of two fingers on his left hand in a caravan fire, he developed a distinctive style of guitar playing. Now known as Django Reinhardt, he moved to France where he joined up with jazz violinist, Stephane Grappelli.

Reinhardt moved to the USA in 1946 where he joined the Duke Ellington Orchestra. Reinhardt played both acoustic and electric guitar and influenced a generation of musicians. Django Reinhardt died in 1953.

Charles John Seghers, the Apostle of Alaska, was born at Ghent on December 26, 1839. Ordained May 31, 1863, he was assigned to Vancouver Island. Fr. Seghers made up for his frail health with an apostolic zeal that knew no bounds. Made curate of the Cathedral at Victoria and temporary administrator of the diocese by Bishop Demers, Fr. Seghers was theologian to the aging prelate during Vatican Council I. Bishop Demers died shortly after their return from Rome and Fr. Seghers's own health grew worse. Catholicism desperately needed an apostle in the Northwest, and after a seemingly miraculous recovery, Charles John Seghers was consecrated Bishop of Vancouver Island on June 29, 1873. Bishop Seghers spent over sixteen months in the undeveloped frontiers, personally leading expeditions along the coast, among the Hesquiat and Cauichan Indians. In 1878 he was recalled from Vancouver to become coadjutor to the Archbishop of Oregon City. He was elevated to Archbishop on December 12, 1880. The high and deserved ecclesiastical honors were the first ever bestowed on a son of the American College at Leuven. Under his administration a new era dawned for the Faith in the Northwest. But his heart was still in the missions. In 1885 while attending and ecclesiastical council, he humbly begged to be sent back to Alaska. His wish was granted. Accompanied by Jesuits Tosi and Robout, and a servant, Francis Fuller, he set out for Alaska in July 1886. Leaving the two priests to care for settlements along the coast, the beloved prelate and Fuller journeyed into the almost unknown interior. After months in light canoes on swollen rivers, and arduous mountain climbing, they reached their destination. Totally committing himself to the work of civilizing the unfriendly Indians, Bishop Seghers soon became aware of another danger. Fuller, spent and worn from the journey had become deranged and turned against him. On November 28, 1886, while resting in a deserted cabin in the Alaskan foothills, Bishop Seghers was shot through the heart. His body was borne back to a grief-stricken people and his remains rest under the high altar in the Cathedral at Victoria.

Charles Van Depoele was born in Lichtervelde, Belgium, in 1846. He emigrated to the United States in 1869 and eventually became a successful manufacturer of church furniture. This provided him with the money to pursue his interest in electricity. He developed an electric generator in 1880 and three years later took out a patent for an electric railway. In 1888 Van Depoele sold his electric railway patents to Thomson-Houston Electric Company of Lynn, Massachusetts.

Other patents by Van Depoele included an alternating-current electric reciprocating engine (1889), a telpher system for a car suspended from cables (1890), a coal-mining machine (1891) and a gearless electric locomotive (1894). Charles Van Depoele died in 1892.

Jan Yoors. Born in Antwerp on April 12, 1922, Jan Yoors, son of artist Eugeen Yoors, left home at the age of twelve to join a kumpania, or tribe of gypsies roaming through Western Europe and the Balkans. In 1940, because of the Nazi persecution of gypsies, he became a liaison operative between Allied intelligence units and gypsies behind the German lines. Arrested by the Gestapo in 1943 and condemned to death after six months of solitary confinement and torture, he escaped and resumed his activities.

A year later he went to London, where he studied at London University and the School of Oriental Studies. Inspired by an exhibition of medieval tapestries, he took up the art. In 1950 he came to New York City and continued his hand-woven art. The first museum showing of his tapestries was in 1956 at the "Twentieth Century Tapestries" exhibition of the Montclair, New Jersey Art Museum. Dominating the gallery were 14 of Jan Yoors's dramatic works ranging from 8 to 90 feet square. They portrayed simple objects in stark and sharp outlines, using brilliant solid-color contrasts of men and animals. Art in America magazine called him "a new talent in the U.S.A." In 1962 and 1965 he represented the U. S. at the International Biennale of Contemporary Tapestries in Lausanne, Switzerland. Fifty of his tapestries were exhibited in 1974 in St. Peter's Abbey at Ghent in a celebration marking the 1,000th anniversary of the founding of this Flemish city. In 1976, 50 of his tapestries were exhibited in Chicago.

In 1963 Jan Yoors made a feature-length documentary film, "Only One New York," and in 1965 Simon & Schuster published a photo album on the same subject. In 1966 and 1967 he travelled in the Amazon territory, much of the Far East and Russia, taking photographs. He wrote The Gypsies, a nonfiction account of six of the years he lived among nomads in Europe before WWII, in 1967, followed by a sequel, Crossing, an autobiographical journal, in 1971.

Jan Yoors died at the age of 55, after suffering a heart attack, on November 27, 1977 at New York City.

Marguerite Yourcenar. Born in Brussels, June 8, 1903, Marguerite Yourcenar was only a week old when her mother died. Her father Michel Cleenewerck de Crayencour returned with her to French Flanders. It was on the "Zwarteberg" that Marguerite, as a small child, discovered the beauty of nature. Marguerite was educated by her father. He taught her Greek, Latin and history. Her father had a book of her poems printed privately when she was sixteen, and they devised her almost anagrammatic penname. She spent her formative years traveling with her father, until he died, leaving her, at the age of 24, financially independent. At the beginning of WWII Marguerite moved to the U. S. By that time she had published four books. At her home in Northeast Harbor, on Mount Desert Island off the coast of Maine, she devoted her time to translating Negro Spirituals in French, giving conferences and teaching comparative literature at Sarah Lawrence College. Now she could return to her research for her historical masterwork, *Memoirs of Hadrian.* It was published in 1951, an English translation in 1954. Fascinated with her Flemish roots, which she could trace to 1600, she wrote *Work in Black* (1968, transl. 1976), a novel of the late Renaissance, with Brugge as its main scene of action. In 1974 she published her *Souvenirs Pieux* and in 1977 her *Archives du Nord.* Besides many awards, both in the U. S. and in France, she was the first woman to be admitted to the Academie Francaise, in 1981. Marguerite Yourcenar died in Bar Harbor, Maine on December 17-18, 1987.

Flemish in the World

Flemish in the World is a worldwide organization that originated during WWII in the former Belgian Congo. Isolated individuals of Belgian descent looked for friendship and communication through a magazine called *De Band.* After the independence of Congo in 1960 a group of people organized a socio-cultural workgroup to provide material and psychological support to old colonials. Based on this experience one quickly came to the realization that this action could be extended to other parts of the world for those who migrated to foreign countries. This resulted in the establishment of *Belgians in the World* in 1963. In 1967 this organization split into two autonomous organizations according to languages, and the Flemish section (België in de Wereld) was quickly rebaptised as *Flemish in the World* (Vlamingen in de Wereld, VIW).

In 1991 *Flemish in the World* was recognized by a Royal decree as an institution of public good with headquarters in Mechelen. Besides a Board of Directors, an international secretariat and local offices in five provinces, VIW is well organized abroad. On each continent there are clubs which are led by local VIW representatives.

In the USA there are clubs in Detroit, Chicago, San Francisco, New York and Washington. The VIW-Washington started its activities in the 1980's. Jef Goethals of Baltimore was the first promotor. After a short interruption, Tom Verheyer restarted VIW-WFC in June 1994. In May 1996 MIne Peeters took over for two years, to pass the baton to Patrick Hinderdael who represented VIW-Washington Flemish Club (VIW-WFC) from May 1998 till August 2006. Marc Quintyn has been the VIW-WFC President since August 2006. He can be reached via VIW-Washington, 6862 Williamsburg Pond Court, Falls Church, VA 22043.

VIW- WFC is a non-political organization. Its goal is to bring together a diverse group of people with an interest in or ties to Flanders, to exchange information and to periodically organize activities around a cultural or social event.

Source: Mieke Ghesquiere, an active contributor to VIW- WFC.

Chapter 7
Deboeck family branches out to the USA (1964-present)

In the second half of the twentieth century reasons for migration shifted dramatically. The USA became a gravity pole for higher education. In the late sixties there were few university programs that offered Masters degrees in Europe. In various fields there were doctoral programs in Europe but those were less structured than programs abroad and required at least twice as long to complete. In the U. S. there were a vast number of colleges and universities that offered Masters and Doctoral programs requiring two to four years of graduate education beyond the Masters.[1]

Most important of all: there was more money to fund graduate education. Through fellowships and research grants American universities attracted foreign students because they wanted to obtain a more diversified student population (hence expose American students to foreign cultures). This "pull" to graduate work in the States was quite substantial.

For many professors in Belgium (and in Europe in general), it was quite prestigious to see graduates go overseas. Many professors had studied abroad and considered the foreign education a good way to round off an academic education. Professors in Europe "pushed" students to study abroad; they helped with contacts, letters of recommendation and encouragement. There was no discussion about brain drain in the 60s, because no one was willing to address the issue of lack of job opportunities for graduates in the home country. The welfare state that had emerged was perfectly happy with the notion that graduates go abroad for further study.

This chapter contains a personal retrospective on how I ended up undertaking graduate studies in the U. S., which led to a career path in international organizations. The first phase of my career involved work for World Health Organization in Geneva; the second phase involved work for the World Bank in Washington. Each of these phases brought about a lot of overseas travel. This had vast consequences for the next generation who underwent undergraduate and graduate studies in the U. S., and now work in various new frontiers. All of this started with a voyage in the late 60s, that sowed the seed for graduate studies in the States.

---

1. A greater variety of possible specializations was offered at American colleges. For example, health economics, which in Belgium was quite new, my license thesis being one of the first in that field, was taught at the graduate level at various universities in the USA in the late 1960s.

A voyage that sowed the seeds

On July 15, 1966, I boarded motor ship M.V. *Seven Seas* in Rotterdam for my first crossing of the Atlantic.[2] The trip was organized by the United States National Student Association which was a non-profit organization serving the American student community. The price tag of this 25-day tour of the U. S. was $446 (US$ 2,780 in today's dollars), including the roundtrip transatlantic transportation, the inland travel, all accommodations, orientation sessions and even accident and health insurance.

The voyage from Rotterdam via Le Havre to New York took ten days. The living conditions on the ship were a hundred times better than what the first emigrants experienced.

The motor ship M.V. *Seven Seas* was packed with students. It had cabins with bunk beds for 10-12 students. Three times a day meals were served; lectures and entertainment were provided. My cabin was on lower level C, cabin 503 in the mid ship area, close to the machine room (which was noisy and prevented a lot of sleep). In spite of all this ten days on the ocean can turn out to be boring. It is hard to image how the first emigrants must have felt who did not have all these amenities.

On July 25 around 5 am, our German steward, Charly (most likely Karel in German), came shouting: *"Alle aussteigen, New York!"* The first sight of America was the Verrazano Bridge, which has a span of 4,205 feet. Then came the island of Manhattan. The morning fog did not make it easy to take good pictures. The Statue of Liberty was on the left. Years later I learned that a poem on the Statue of Liberty's base reads: *"Give me your tired, your poor. Your huddled masses yearning to breathe free…."* Our ship moved slowly to Pier 40. Twelve hours after Charly had shouted that we should get off, we finally made it off the ship.

Figure 7.1 Guido Deboeck with parents on July 25, 1966, boarding the M.V. Seven Seas in Rotterdam for a ten-day voyage to New York.

In the three weeks that followed, we traveled with a motor coach in a group of 12 from New York to Pittsburgh, Indianapolis, St. Louis, Memphis, Knoxville, Richmond, Washington and back

---

2. The M.V. *Seven Seas* was built in Chester, Pa., in 1940. It was rebuilt as the escort aircraft carrier, U.S.S. *Long Island;* rebuilt again in 1949, 1953 and 1955. The voyage it made in 1966 was the last it would make. The ship which had served as a student ship for years would, after its last trip to New York, return to Rotterdam where it would become a hostel for students.

to New York. In each city the emphasis of our visit was different. For example: Pittsburgh was all about agriculture and industry; in St. Louis it was about American education with visit to a large campus of the Midwest; in Memphis we got Southern hospitality by staying with an American family and made a visit to the Cotton Exchange; in Knoxville we learned about the Tennessee Valley Authority and nuclear power plants; Richmond and Washington were all about American history, including the Civil War, the Capitol, the memorials and lots of museums. It was on one of those days in Washington in the summer of 1966 that "I had a dream" (sorry, Martin…): to come back to America and live in this wonderful capitol.

After returning to New York, we boarded on August 18, 1966 the M/S *Aurelia,* an Italian ship, newer than the *Seven Seas,* in which we made the westbound voyage. After 10 days on the sea we arrived back in Le Havre on August 27, 1966.

In the academic year that started in October 1966 at the University of Leuven I decided that I was going to continue graduate studies in the States. Thus, three years before I graduated I knew that I would apply to an American university to study economics. The voyage I undertook in 1966 produced the seeds for that decision.[3]

Studying in Leuven and the student rebellion of 1968

After three years at Our Blessed Mary School in Vilvoorde, – the school mentioned in Chapter 3 – and three more years of high school[4] in Sint Pieter's College in Jette, a suburb of Brussels, I was anxious to start university.[5] Already in high school my inclination was to study economics. My initial interest in economics was obtained from a high school teacher who explained economics in plain layman's terms and who was systematic. Ironically, eight years later I made a dissertation on economic education that underscored the importance of teaching in a systematic and organized way.

Initially, I wanted to study economics at the Catholic Economic High School of Tilburg in the Netherlands, but after a brief visit to Tilberg, I came to the realization that spending seven years for an undergraduate degree (which is how long it took in the

3. Personal Journal of G. Deboeck of a trip to the United States, July-August, 1966

4. On June 28, 1963 I graduated from the *Institutum Santi Petri* in Jette with first prizes in History, Chemistry and Physics; the year before I obtained first prizes in Economics, History and Physics.

5. Secondary education in Belgium took place in a "college" whereas tertiary education was at either a "high school" or university, the opposite terminology from the USA.

Netherlands) in crammed student accommodations, would be a high price to pay. As a consequence I enrolled instead in 1963 in Sint-Ignatius High School for Commerce in Antwerp.

The first year of my university life at Sint-Ignatius, I commuted by train from Vilvoorde to Antwerp, which required daily walks of 15 minutes to the train station in Vilvoorde, half-an-hour train to Antwerp, and another 15 minutes to the school. I lost every day about two hours in commute time and had virtually no student life! Why go to college if you cannot participate in student life?

At Sint Ignatius the main specialization areas were confined to maritime economics (in which I was not interested), consular studies (in which I was marginally interested) and commerce. Without taking the first year exams I decided in the spring of 1964 to enroll at the Catholic University of Leuven.

From 1964 to 1969 I studied in Leuven, first commerce ("kandidatuur handelswetenschappen") then after the second year economics ("licentie ekonomie"). My main interests were development economics and international trade. During the course of my two license years, a third optional year was created, for a degree called *license-doctorandus;* so I completed all three years.[6]

The early years in Leuven were marked by a lot of upheaval; students around the world were rebelling against the political structures. In Leuven the student rebellion was focused on the university itself. It was the student rebellion of 1968 that eventually led in 1979 to all courses being offered in Dutch in Leuven and all courses offered in French being given at a new Université Catholique de Louvain located in Louvain-la-Neuve. A brief history of the University can be found in a box.

Catholic University of Louvain (K.U. Leuven)

At the end of the fourteenth century Leuven was the capital of Brabant and the residence of the Dukes of Burgundy. Anton of Burgundy wanted to increase his prestige by establishing a university in his domain. On the council of Englebrecht I, Earl of Nassau (1380-1442), Duke Jan IV (1403-1427), son of Anton and nephew of Phillip the Good, addressed a request to Pope Martinus V to establish in Leuven a university. Martinus V, who already had approved two other universities, did not hesitate.

---

6. Several Professors exerted a major influence during my undergraduate education: I got intrigued, fascinated and enriched by the classes of Professor Gaston Eyskens, former Prime Minister of Belgium, who taught public finance; Professor Albert Coppé, former Commissioner of the European Coal and Steel Union (the precursor of the European Union), who taught statistics; Professor Robert Vanes, who taught international trade; Professor Mertens de Wilmar who taught international finance; and especially by Professors Karel Tavenier, who taught macro economics, Mark Eyskens, who taught micro-economics and Louis Baeck who taught economic development, demographics and economic sociology. Someone whose classes were challenging, but that I now wish I could take again, was Professor Herman Van der Wee, who taught economic history.

In the papal bul of December 9, 1425, the Pope granted to Jan IV and the city the privilege to establish a university in Leuven. Originally this was only for arts, law and medicine. On September 6, 1426 the first academic year was inaugurated with 12 professors. In 1432 Pope Eugenius V, successor of Martinus V, granted the rights for a faculty in theology.

The university was originally modeled after the Universities of Paris, Cologne and Vienna. In a short time, it grew into one of the largest and most renowned universities in Europe. Its academic fame attracted numerous scholars who made valuable contributions to European culture. In the sixteenth century the humanist Desiderius Erasmus lectured in Leuven, where he founded the Collegium Trilingue in 1517 for the study of Hebrew, Latin, and Greek; the first of its kind. The tutor of the young emperor Charles V, Adriaan Cardinal Florensz of Utrecht, was a professor before being elected in 1522 as the last non-Italian Pope before Pope John Paul II. The philologist, legal scholar, and historian Justus Lipsius taught in Leuven for many years.

The mathematician Gemma Frisius helped to lay the foundations of modern science and tutored many famous scientists, including the cartographer Gerard Mercator, whose map projection is still in use, the botanist Rembert Dodoens, and the father of modern anatomy, Andreas Vesalius. In a later period, the theses of the Leuven theologian Cornelius Jansenius provoked a large and heated controversy both inside and outside the Church.

In the seventeenth and eighteenth centuries, the university was an important training centre for Roman Catholic intellectuals from Protestant countries. At the end of the Age of Enlightenment, in 1783, the chemist Pieter Jan Minckelers discovered the suitability of coal gas for lighting. In the nineteenth century, at the instigation of Pope Leo XIII, the university became an important centre of Thomist philosophy.

The forces of the French Revolution suppressed the university in 1797, but in 1834 the Belgian episcopate reestablished it as a French-language, Roman Catholic university.

The university's famous library was burned during the German invasion in 1914, and 300,000 books were reduced to ashes. A new library was built between 1921 and 1928 with American funds and books donated by many nations. The library was again destroyed by fire during the German invasion in 1940 (only 15,000 out of 900,000 volumes were saved) but was subsequently restored.

In the 1930s Louvain began to teach some courses in Dutch. Although the Belgian government had previously forbidden the use of Dutch in universities, it changed its policy in 1932 in response to growing pressure from Belgium's sizable Dutch-speaking population.

In 1968, after student riots, ethnic protests, and government upheavals, the Catholic University of Louvain was reorganized into separate Dutch- and French-language divisions. Each of the two divisions was given separate legal status in 1970, and the first faculties were installed in Louvain-la-Neuve in 1972 at the Université Catholique de Louvain. Louvain-la-Neuve ("New Louvain") is 15 miles (24 km) south-southwest of old Leuven and within the French speaking part of Belgium.

At present, K.U. Leuven caters to more than 31,000 students; around 12% are international students from more than 120 nations. In terms of its personnel, there are 5,287 members in the academic staff, 2,730 in the administrative /technical staff, and 8,172 university hospital staff. With regard to its physical facilities, the university occupies a total area of 1,058,445 square meters and it has a total of 26,606 rooms. On the academic side, the university is composed of 14 faculties, 50 departments, and about 240 sub-departments. Further, its network of 30 auxiliary libraries now houses a total of 4.3 million volumes, 14,500 magazines and journals, and 7,492 full text electronic magazines. The medical facilities of the University of Leuven support 5 hospitals and 3 affiliated hospitals, with a total of 2,057 hospital beds for the acutely ill.

Sources: Dr V. Denis: *Katholieke Universiteit te Leuven* 1425-1958, Leuven 1958; 550 *Jaar Universiteit Leuven,* Stedelijk Museum, January 31-April 25, 1976; "Louvain, Catholic University of," *Encyclopædia Britannica,* 2006; website of KUL Leuven.

After the second year I went in search of a topic for a thesis. I chose to work on health economics, which at the time was a rather new field requiring inter-disciplinary work with the Department of Public Health. Under the sponsorship of Professor Mark Eyskens (former Minister of Finance in Belgium) and with the support of Professor Dr. Jan Blanpain (Chairman of the Department of Public Health; and many others) I completed in July 1969 a thesis on *Health Planning: macro-economic analysis of Public Health.* Little did I know that three years later this thesis would contribute to my selection for a job in the World Health Organization (WHO).

In retrospect, the most important development during my studies in Leuven was not the development of my scientific interests in economics, but the encounter in the second half of the first academic year of a young lady, who five years later would become my wife (see Chapter 5).

To this date it is hard to determine whether we went to classes to listen to the professors or to sit next to each other and "flirt." Every professor guessed that we were "dating," although we ourselves may not have thought of it that way. We exchanged course notes, helped each other through difficult exam periods, and enjoyed many *"tea dansants"* or dance evenings. We enjoyed even more the beer drinking at club evenings in *den Bruegel.* In my fifth year in Leuven I was nominated President of the Economists, which was part of Economica, a student association for students of both economics and business administration.

In between academic years I traveled to many different places. In the summer of 1962, before enrolling for Sint Ignatius in Antwerp, I went to Southhampton in the United Kingdom to take English language classes and live for a month with an English family. In 1963 I went to Bayreuth in Germany to take German language classes and spent a month with a German family.[7] In 1964 I attended classes at the Studio School of English in Cambridge (U.K.) and then at the Université Catholique Notre Dame in Paris. In 1965 I attended classes at the University of Vienna—the Wiener Internationale Hochschulkurse—and thereafter at the Centro de Estudios de Español in Barcelona.

In each of these places I made friends who usually spoke another language than where we were. Hence, I learned more English from Americans in Paris, more French from Parisians in Germany, more German on the beach in Spain, than I learned in those various classes. The best way of learning a language remains making friends, living abroad and indulging in a foreign culture!

In 1966 I traveled for the first time to the States. This trip left a lasting impression especially the openness, friendliness, and generosity that I encountered in all places that were visited.

---

7. In Bayreuth I attended the Richard Wagner Festival where during the long intermezzos I met Ms Sylviane Delaby, a young charming Parisian, with whom I corresponded for more than a year.

After my return from the USA I worked for a month in the Kibbutz Lahavot Haviva in Israel. After picking apples for a month I made a tour of Israel involving visits to Haifa, Nazareth, Tel Aviv, Jerusalem, Beersheba, and Eliat. Also this trip left indelible impressions.[8]

In 1967 I traveled to Japan[9] to study economic growth. Japan was in the 60s one of the fast growing economies in the world. My interest was to learn how Japan could grow so fast and what lessons could be learned for other developing countries. The trip to Japan was prepared through interviews with Rev. Spae (CICM), specialist in Japanese culture and long-term resident of the country.

The trip to Japan was quite an adventure. My journey to Japan involved a flight from Paris to Moscow, a weekend in Moscow, a long flight in a Russian plane to Khabarovsk; then the Trans-Siberian express train to Vladivosstock, followed by a boat trip to Yokohama and finally a train to Tokyo. In Japan I traveled mainly by bullet trains.

On return from Japan I wrote a monograph under the title *Kontakt van Beschavingen: een tragisch dilemma?* (Contact of civilizations: a tragic dilemma?). This monograph was about the exceptional economic growth of Japan but also about the integration of old Japanese customs and Western culture.[10]

In early 1968 I proposed to Hennie De Zutter (see Chapter 5). We got engaged in June of 1968 and got married a year later in Leuven. Since I was applying for graduate studies at American universities and needed a visa to enter the USA, we decided to marry first in the City Hall (so that all our papers immediately could be filed as a couple).

On May 14, 1969 we married in the City Hall of Leuven. It was a brief event with our parents and a couple of witnesses.

---

8. Especially the contrasts between the achievements of the Jewish people who turned a desert into fertile land, and the Palestinians and Arabs living in villages like Nazareth, who stagnated, lived in poverty, and had yet to accept that greater Palestine was history. My kibbutz experience, where people were on guard day and night, left lasting impressions. The right to live without fear in a free and democratic society is often not appreciated; this right should not be taken lightly. It ought to be a right to anyone who desires it and an objective for those who do not have it.

9. The trip to Japan started off by a flight from Paris to Moscow, an overnight stay in Moscow follow by an inland flight from Moscow to Khabarovsk; then a train ride to Vladivostok and finally the crossing by boat of the sea of Japan to Yokohama. The tour in Japan from August 3 till August 23, 1967, and took us from Tokyo to Hakone, Nagoya, Kyoto, Osaka, Hiroshima, Miyajima, Nagasaki, Unzen, Beppu, Kobe, and back to Tokyo.

10. This monograph was published in the bulletin of UCOD (the University Clearing Office for Development), the periodical of a student organization for which I was Chief Editor from 1967 to 1968.

On the way out of the City Hall, my colleagues and friends from the Economics Department surprised us by a standing guard of honor, not with swords as is customary with military weddings, but with books of John Maynard Keynes who at the time was our most favored author. The book they held up was *The General Theory of Employment, Interest and Money,* first written in February 1936.

Three months later, on August 14, 1969 we married in the Chapel of the Castle of Heverlee in Leuven. As this chapel is small, participants were mainly our parents, our witnesses and a few family members. A large reception was held in Restaurant George in Leuven where many colleagues, professors and family came to wish us luck, followed by a dinner only for the immediate family.[11]

Late in the afternoon on our wedding day we departed via high-speed train to Paris where we spent our honeymoon. A week later we returned to Brussels to pack for our trip to the United States.

In May 1969 I received word from Clark University—one of twenty plus schools

Figure 7.2 City Hall of Leuven

11. Since two of our kids are by now married and have each organized their weddings being very budget conscious, it may be of interest to point out that our civil wedding cost 4,775 BF and our church wedding, including a reception for about 100 people and dinner for 11, amounted to BF 21,667. The grand sum total of these wedding expenses translated into US dollars amounted in 1969 to US$ 528 (which is the equivalent of $2,908 in 2006 US dollars). Our honeymoon week in Paris added $280 in 1969 dollars or $1,540 in 2006 dollars.

Figure 7.3 Civil marriage of Hennie De Zutter and Guido Deboeck on May 14, 1969 in the City Hall of Leuven

to which I had applied—that the Economics Department had granted me a fellowship to undertake graduate studies for a Master's in economics. The fellowship entailed free tuition plus a stipend of $600 (US$ 3,900 in today's dollars) for the year. On Labor Day of 1969 we arrived in Worcester, Massachusetts, where in the next three years I would become a *quantitative economist.*

Graduate studies at Clark University

Clark University is a private, coeducational institution of higher learning in Worcester, Massachusetts. Jonas Gilman Clark, a Worcester native and successful merchant, and G. Stanley Hall, a psychologist, established Clark University in 1887. Clark was the first independent, all-graduate university in the United States; it began undergraduate instruction in 1902.[12] Total enrollment

12. Clark's first president was G. Stanley Hall, founder of the American Psychological Association, who at Harvard earned the first Ph.D. in psychology in this country. Clark has played a prominent role in the development of psychology as a distinguished discipline in the United States. In 1909, Clark was the location for Sigmund Freud's famous "Clark Lectures," which introduced psychoanalysis to this country. Clark also has played an important role in the development of geography as a discipline. Clark has granted more Ph.D.s in this environmentally related area than any other school in the nation. The George Perkins Marsh Institute was the first research center created to study the human dimensions of global environmental change. Researchers who have held Clark appointments include A. A. Michelson, the first U.S. Nobel Prize winner in the sciences and Robert Goddard, the father of the space age and the inventor of rocket technology.

at Clark University was and still is approximately 2,600.[13] This relatively small size implied that classes were small especially in the Economics Department in which I was enrolled from 1969 to 1972.[14] Professor Roger Van Tassel was the Chairman of the Department of Economics in 1969. He hired the husband-wife team of Dr. David Ott and Dr. Attiat Ott to the department, as well as Dr. Puffer and Dr. D. Weiss, both econometricians. He also broad Dr. Peter Sloan to the department.

In my first academic year I took the basic requirements for a Master's degree including macro- and micro economic theory, mathematics for economists and introduction to econometrics. Under the guidance of Professor David Ott I wrote a Master's thesis on *The applications of decision models and macro economic models to the health care sector.* This study was later published as an article in *Tijdschrift voor Ekonomie* (Journal of Economics) in Leuven.

After completing a Master's degree in one year, and some hand-wringing about funding of my stay at Clark, I obtained a teaching fellowship for one semester, followed by a research fellowship that allowed me to enroll in the Clark Ph.D program in Economics.

I chose public finance, money and banking and economic education as fields of specialization. Those were the fields taught by professors who had the most research money (call it Flemish pragmatism). Attiat Ott taught public finance; David Ott taught money and banking; Peter Sloan taught economic education. It was under the guidance of Peter Sloan that I completed in 1972 a Ph.D dissertation on *Factor-analytic study of the teaching-learning process of introductory economics.* Commencement was May 28, 1972.

Already in 1971 I had undertaken course evaluations that provided feedback to the faculty about student attitudes towards course content and methods of teaching. The local student newspaper *The Scarlet,* reported on March 5, 1971 about my initial findings of applying two tests to courses taught in the Economics Department. My dissertation was an extension of these initial evaluations and involved testing students in five colleges in the Worcester area, with a battery of economic and psychological tests, both at the beginning and at the end of a semester. The data

---

13. See http://www.clarku.edu/academiccatalog/introduction/aboutclark. cfm and "Clark University." Encyclopædia Britannica. 2006.

14. Noteworthy facilities on campus include the Heinz Werner Institute for Developmental Analysis, Jacob Hiatt Center for Urban Education, and the George F. and Sybil H. Fuller Foundation Center for Music. Among its research centers are the George Perkins Marsh Institute devoted to interdisciplinary study of the relationship between humanity and the changing environment; and the Center for Holocaust Studies, which initiated a doctoral degree program in 1998 and maintains an extensive collection of books and materials.

Figure 7.4 Commencement May 28, 1972.

that was collected was processed on a mainframe computer at Worcester Polytechnic Institute (WPI). Since this was long before any micro or personal computers became accessible, the time for processing the data was mainly at night (because mainframes were used during the day time for more important tasks than research...), which required long shifts of night work to obtain the results for my dissertation. This experience had a profound impact on my eagerness to pioneer and adopt microcomputer technology in later years. It also accounts for my computer literacy, since I learned to program all the software for my dissertation instead of contracting it out to computer programmers. This provided years later a considerable advantage in catching the microcomputer revolution in the early days (not to mention the impact it had on the computer literacy of our children and hence their career choices).

Twelve days after receiving my doctorate, our first son, Toni Francis was born. A week earlier I received a telegram from Geneva offering me a job as health systems analyst in WHO Between May 28 and June 13, a lot of changes occurred in our lives.

The cost of university education then and now

It is worth pausing to reflect on the cost of higher education then and now. Detailed records about the expenditures made for my studying in Leuven in the period 1964-1969 were kept. From these records the following can be extracted. The annual tution for my studies in Leuven went from Bfr. 4,000 to Bfr 6,600 between 1963 and 1968. Tuition for five years was Bfr. 33,600, i.e., US$ 3,696 in 2006 dollars. My annual expenses on books was about Bfr 1,000 to Bfr. 2,000 or in total Bfr 10,000 for five years, i.e., US$ 1,100 in 2006 dollars. The rent of a student room ("kot") went from Bfr 10,979 in the first three years to Bfr 15,315 in the last three; total for five years amounted to Bfr 66,274, i.e., US$ 7,287 in 2006 dollars. Then there were minor costs such as printing of a thesis that amounted to about Bfr 5,400, i.e., US$ 594 in 2006 dollars. The biggest expenses were my extracurricular activities, which involved all the travels in between academic years that amounted to Bfr 80,025, i.e. US$ 8,800 in 2006 dollars.[15]

In sum, Bfr 115,274 or US$ 12,677 in 2006 dollars was spent between 1964 and 1969 for five years of undergraduate education in Belgium. In addition US$ 8,800 was spent on courses taken abroad. The sum of these totals converted in current dollars is US$ 21,477.

This was a huge sum, a significant investment. My parents made a lot of sacrifices for this. Additionally, in Belgium my parents paid high income taxes (much higher than in the USA), from which the Belgian government subsidized the bulk of university costs.

The above total paid for five years of undergraduate studies is about the cost of one year at an in-state university at present. It is substantially less than the cost of one year at an Ivy League school (which can be about one third more).

Four years traveling for WHO (like a sailor)

While at Clark University I applied to an announcement in *The Economist* that was advertising for a position as health systems analyst at the World Health Organization. I traveled from Worcester to Washington, D.C., in the spring of 1972 to be interviewed. Dr Gutierrez at the Pan American Health Organization interviewed me; he mailed a favorable report about my interest in health economics to Geneva. On August 1, 1972, I joined the World Health Organization, a specialized UN agency established in 1948 to strive for the attainment of the highest possible level of health[16] for all the people on the globe.

---

15. What is not accounted for here is food, which with or without higher education would be consumed anyway. All conversions into US dollars were made at the prevailing exchange rate of Bfr. to US dollars at the time; and adjusted for inflation between 1964/69 and 2006.

16. Health is defined in WHO's Constitution as a state of complete physical, mental and social wellbeing and not merely the absence of disease or infirmity. WHO is governed by its 190+ Member States through the World Health Assembly; it is managed by a Managing Director selected by the World Health Assembly on recommendations of the Board of Directors.

More specifically I joined Project Systems Analysis (PSA), a project led by Dr. Maurice Piot, a Swiss medical doctor whose early career in WHO had been made as epidemiologist fighting malaria and tuberculosis in India. PSA was a small inter-disciplinary team in WHO composed of medical doctors, public health, and management specialists; at least that was until I arrived because after my arrival there was also one health economist. PSA's mission was to help Ministries of Health to design projects and country health programs that provided health services to the most needy in rural areas. In consequence, the PSA team traveled a lot to many different countries to undertake project formulation and country health programming exercises in collaboration with local counterparts. Almost all exercises involved two months' stay in a country. To save travel costs some exercises were scheduled back-to-back, e.g., projects in Thailand and Malaysia (see below).

In the period from August 1972 till December 1975 I participated with PSA in the following exercises:
-        **Thailand,** October-November 1972, project formulation for health services development and establishment of Provincial health planning system in Chonburi Province. This project formulation took place in Ban San.
-        **Indonesia,** January-February 1973, project formulation for rural water supply system development in West Java. This project formulation took place in Bandung.
-        **Bangladesh,** August-September 1973, country health programming for integrated rural health and family planning services. This exercise took place in Dakka.
-        **Kenya,** September 1974, project on national improvement of rural health services and training.
-        **Afghanistan,** October 1974, country health programming for comprehensive health planning (as a result of which I was able to visit Kabul before the Russian invasion).
-        **Pakistan,** January-February 1975, country health programming for basic health services, which involved visits to all four provincial capitals of Pakistan.
-        **Congo,** April 1975, country health programming for district water supply and training of health auxiliaries, which was undertaken in Brazzaville, the capital of the People's Republic of Congo.
-        **In Brazzaville** I also was involved in a Regional Workshop for Africa on Country Health Programming.

This heavy travel schedule and especially the back-to-back exercises eventually caused enough dissatisfaction to seek alternative employment. In the summer of 1975 I came across an ad in *The Economist* about a research position in the Economics Department of the World Bank. I applied and got invited to Washington for interviews.

Meanwhile the PSA project of WHO had come to an end. An expert panel evaluated the project in December 1975. Subse-

quently all staff of the project were reassigned by the Managing
Director of WHO—at that time Dr. H. Mahler—to various regional
offices to continue the transfer of project formulation and country
health programming. I was supposed to move to Congo (Brazzaville) to work in the Regional Office of WHO in Africa; instead I
accepted an offer from the World Bank in Washington, D.C.

Twenty-two years, four months and 15 days

The offer to join the World Bank did not come easy! I
was interviewed in October 1975 for a research position on human resources in the Economics Department.[17] My interest was
however to work in rural development, in continuation of the work
done in WHO, and because of the work done by Monty Yudelman,
who contributed to the 1972 Nairobi speech of Mr. R. McNamara,
President of the World Bank. In his speech McNamara for the first
time focused the bank on reducing absolute and relative poverty
in the world.

Three months after the interviews in Washington I still had
not heard from the bank. I called the bank from Geneva and was
immediately told that the position for which I was interviewed had
been allocated. When I inquired about the extra interviews in rural
development I was told by a personnel officer that there was an
opening…that may be available. Minutes later I received a call
from Leif Christofferson, the assistant to M. Yudelman. He offered
me a position on Monitoring and Evaluation (M&E) of Rural Development projects. I accepted an offer that was about 1/3 less in
salary than I earned at that time; and agreed to be in Washington
by April 1, 1976.

I had no idea why the bank wanted me for the M&E position, but maybe neither did they…. Years later I realized that maybe the work that I did on evaluation of graduate courses at Clark
University stimulated one manager who interviewed me, to think
that the same could be applied to rural development projects. Was
this a huge leap in thinking or was it confidence?

From 1976 to 1979 I was involved in M&E of the poverty
orientation of the bank's projects. My work was mainly to review
bank project reports and to extract what part of the targeted population were below the absolute or relative poverty levels, both of
which had been defined with mathematical precision.

The other part of my work was developing a methodology
for monitoring and evaluating of rural development projects in the
countries. This was far more interesting, although few knew how
to design a systematic approach to check if projects reached their
objectives. After some research, a methodology was created that
involved distinguishing between outputs, effects and impacts and
to measure the attainment of objectives at three different levels,
going from the measurement of outputs, to the estimation of impacts,

17. After two days of interviews in Washington I insisted on extra interviews with managers in the Rural Development Department.

and eventually to the guessing of impacts. It was all rather logical, hence called the logical framework, but the practical applications of this new methodology required quite a bit of work. What is most surprising is that thirty years later this approach is still being applied; the design of M&E systems is now part of every project the bank approves.

What I enjoyed the most in those first couple of years at the bank was the organization of Regional Workshops in Nairobi and Kuala Lumpur. These workshops were intended to bring local people together to share experiences in executing M&E. Bill Kinsey and Ronald Ng collaborated with me in organizing and conducting these workshops. After they took place it was with their support that the lessons learned from M&E in various countries were documented in two Staff Working Papers that to this date are listed on amazon.com but have been long out of print.[18]

In those first years at the bank I worked on M&E systems for rural development projects in Indonesia, Philippines, Kenya, Brazil and a few others. The emphasis in each of these projects was different. For example, in Indonesia it was the difficult problem of transmigration involving moving people from over-populated Java to other islands; in Brazil it was on improving nutrition through education, agriculture, and raising standards of food production. However, something was wrong. The projects that were designed in those days were so complex that they required levels of management, organization and coordination that were way beyond the capacity of countries to implement. For example, the first nutrition project of the bank in Brazil contained 16 components and required coordination between dozens of agencies.

In 1980 I transferred from rural development to planning and budgeting in the bank where I became instrumental in introducing new technology. A year earlier I joined the microcomputer revolution, built my own microcomputer, and offered courses about *personal computers.* At that time the bank had one centralized mainframe computer. I established a personal computer club in the bank and gave lunch hour lectures. This rapidly led to a transfer that pulled me in the direction of where computers were already in heavy use. Planning and budgeting in the bank served the President's office. McNamara had a unique way of managing that was entirely based on a limited set of tables of targets and budgeted versus actual expenses, an approach that he used at Ford and also as Secretary of Defense during the Vietnam War period.

From 1980 to 1987 I worked in various capacities in the administration side, mainly on developing, organizing and maintaining institutional databases and on introducing computer tech-

---

18. "Managing information for rural development: Lessons from Eastern Africa," WB Staff Working Paper no 379 (based on a workshop held in Nairobi in May 1979), Washington, March 1980; and "Monitoring Rural Development in Asia," WB Staff Working Paper no 439, (based on a workshop held in Kuala Lumpur in December 1979) Washington, October 1980.

nology,[19] After a few years I became an *intrapreneur*. This was a term coined for "a person within a large corporation who takes responsibility for turning an idea into a profitable finished product through assertive risk-taking and innovation".[20]

After introducing microcomputers, spreadsheets, Power-Point presentations and networks of small computers, I got interested in rule-based or so-called expert systems. These are software programs that can store rules and through which knowledge bases can be developed. In- or less experienced staff could use well-designed knowledge bases to rapidly gain experience or solve problems.

In April 1980 I organized the first workshop on artificial intelligence (A.I.) and expert systems in the bank (again using lunch breaks…). This workshop was well attended by both managers and staff. Its effect was that I was transferred to the Investment Department of the bank. The bank chose to apply A.I. to its moneymaking apparatus![21]

From 1987 to 1994 I was employed first as a facilities manager responsible for all the technology in the Investment Department and later as a researcher for developing machine-based trading models. In the role of facilities manager I quickly accumulated a dozen highly technical staff that took care of various technologies in the Department and in the trading room.

This was an interesting time because there were big challenges and there was great team spirit among a dozen people that reported to me. At the time I had a Japanese Director, who gave me a lot of leeway.[22] What was interesting was that the group

---

19. The managers in rural development had dismissed my idea that microcomputers should be used in the countries for monitoring project work. Did I need to be reminded of the experience in Belgian Congo? Rural development should be labor and employment-intensive, not capital intensive (as if microcomputers were expensive). Their viewpoint changed quickly when in 1979 a few Nigerians flew to Washington, bought some Apple II Plus computers and implemented project administration on laptops in the field in Nigeria.

20. Gifford Pinchot III and Elizabeth S. Pinchot first wrote about "Intra-Corporate Entrepreneurship" in 1978, but it was Norman Macrae who in *The Economist* of April 17, 1982 popularized it in an article under the title "Intrapreneurial Now." In 1985 Gifford Pinchot wrote a book entitled *Intrapreneuring*. His book became my guiding rod.

21. The Investment Department is responsible for investing all liquid assets the bank so as to maintain and guarantee the continuation of its core operations, which is still making loans for development to poor countries. To make loan commitments the bank still needs to remain a bank, capable of raising vast amounts of money in the financial markets and maintaining a high credit rating.

22. Maybe my trip to Japan in the late sixties and my study of the contact of civilizations had not been in vain after all. The payoff on that trip came in the late eighties.

reporting to me included ten different nationalities and contained Christians, Muslims, Jews, a Buddhist and a Hindu. All worked harmoniously together.

The biggest challenge in that period was the renovation of the trading room. With colleagues I visited trading rooms in London, Hong-Kong and Tokyo, before working with an architectural firm specialized in the redesign of trading floors.

As a result of renovating the trading room, which took months of effort and especially weekend work (because the existing trading floor had to remain operational), I was called upon to advise on trading floors for the Asian Development Bank in Manila as well as the Central Bank of China of the People's Republic of China. Setting up a trading floor for investments of the Central Bank in China was a big challenge. These were interesting assignments and they were rewarding by teamwork and sharing of knowledge between my team and our foreign counterparts.

After the completion of the renovation in early 1990 I organized another workshop on technologies (this time not over lunch) that I had observed in Japan. This involved machine-learning techniques including neural networks, genetic algorithms and related analytical techniques. These techniques were based on software algorithms that learned from patterns in the data and created mathematical formulas that could translate inputs into outputs.

The Treasurer of the bank decided that research in this area was a must. He allocated funds for undertaking research; I was assigned and established a *Trading Analytics Lab* with consultants and a couple of graduate students and together we built trading models. A year later when those models were operational they blew the minds of the traders and in particular the Chief Trader. Nightly these models would make recommendations to buy or sell Treasury securities; those recommendations would then be executed late in the evening in Tokyo. The success of these models was however overshadowed by the eagerness of the traders to outperform the models. In short, the psychology of working with machine-based systems, robots if you like, became a stumbling block.[23] Against all evidence that these trading models were profitable the bank decided in 1994 to eliminate this research effort. The integration of machine- and human-based trading continued in Japan and was later also adopted in Wall Street.[24]

---

23. The same problem was encountered when autopilots were first introduced in planes and still is a subject of great concern in the design of modern airplanes like the Airbus planes. How much automation can make flying overly boring for experienced pilots?

24. It is not difficult to understand why the models worked: these models worked based on machine learning that is hard to match by the slow pace at which our own brains learn. It took on average three to four years before someone with advanced degree(s) in economics, finance, math, or engineering, could become an "experienced trader." In contrast, machine-based learning algorithms could train overnight on the patterns that

My four years of research on model-based trading was assembled in a book. With others, who had developed similar models in other banks, I edited *Trading on the Edge: neural networks, genetic algorithms and fuzzy logic for chaotic financial markets* that was released in April 1994 by John Wiley and Sons in New York. As a result of publishing this book I got invited to speak at conferences in New York, London, Paris, Frankfurt, Tokyo, Singapore, and Seoul. More than a dozen years later this first book is still in demand.

Four years after publishing my first book, I wrote a second book[25] under the title *Visual Explorations in Finance using Self-Organizing Maps.* This book was a sequel to the first in the sense that it covered un-supervised neural networks as opposed to the supervised neural networks demonstrated in the first book. This second book was the result of virtual teamwork with Professor Teuvo Kohonen (and his team at the University of Helsinki), Dr Gerhard Kranner (CEO of Eudaptics Inc. and his team of software engineers in Vienna, Austria), and I in Arlington (Virginia). This book was released in 1998 by Springer-Verlag in London, right on the day of my retirement from the bank. Two years later a Japanese translation of this work appeared in Tokyo and in 2001 a Russian translation was released in Moscow.

Large international organizations are like huge cruise ships that can turn only over a large distance. It takes years in large organizations to adopt even the most elementary ideas of change. Innovation and interpreneurship are not encouraged in those places. What a difference with investment firms in Wall Street, where the people who contribute the most to the bottom-line are annually handed out the highest bonuses!

From day trading to investment management

Just about the time I left the bank in 1998 day trading became popular. Day trading is an active style of trading that uses

---

are embedded in market data and based on those patterns make recommendations to buy or sell securities. Models could be retrained any time and be tuned to make minimal losses. They produced profits because they were not affected by feelings of fear or greed. Humans when making substantial profits fear that they can lose them and hence tend to jump too quickly to realize gains. On the flip side, when losses are made there is a tendency to believe that the markets will turn around and hence, humans tend to wait too long to realize losses.

Neither is it difficult to understand why these models became a threat to traders: models that crunch numbers at night and trade more profitably than humans leave little to do for human traders.

25. These books, written while I was still on the bank's payroll, were never cleared, edited, or even subsidized by the bank. They competed with other financial books in the marketplace; and have over time through their sales proven their mettle. What better reward could I have imagined than receiving regular small royalty payments?

timing the market as a core principle. This is in sharp contrast to the belief that timing the market is impossible. Day traders try to make profit on any move in stock prices no matter how small, hence use intraday price movements. In 1998 and 1999 lots of books described the advantages of day trading.

Day trading was made possible by significant changes in technology. In less than a decade the trading technology that was used in big investment firms as well as at the bank, had evolved to the point where private individuals could afford a trading workstation at home. Prices of computers came down; the cost of monitors dropped; real-time data services became affordable. Vast amounts of financial information became available for free on the Internet. On-line brokerage services became popular. The cost of transacting in the markets decreased to the point where they no longer were a significant factor in influencing turnover.

The end of the nineties was also a bonanza year in the U. S. stock markets. A friend said: "almost anything you threw money at would make money even in a short time frame."

After leaving the bank in August 1998 I got into day trading! I established an inexpensive trading workstation at home and started in the spring of 1999 to learn about active day trading. Based on a dozen books I became familiar with trading tactics and the intricacies of NASDAQ Level II screens, the newly established electronic exchanges and the new investment world. This however did not last long.

In March 2000, just about a year after my home-based trading operations became operational, the financial markets around the world collapsed. They started a depression that was one of the most severe market depressions since the big one in 1929; this stock market depression lasted until October 2002.

While in 1999 the good strategy for investing was to jump in and out of the market, from the spring of 2000 till the end of 2002 the most rewarding strategy was to stay out of the markets. This was not easy, because no one anticipated that the market collapse was going to be so severe. However after a while it became clear that a sound investment approach was to stay in cash. The lessons learned in 1998-1999 were invaluable to minimize losses in 2000-2002.[27]

By March 2003 the markets turned around. Despite all the political developments (terrorist attack of the World Trade center

---

26. Many friends at my retirement party will remember that I tried to explain un-supervised neural networks with a box of nails and screws...

27. From 2000 till October 2002, the stock markets in the USA (and around the world) lost about half of their value. The S&P 500 dropped by 45%, the NASDAQ lost 78% of its value. From March 2003 till October 2006 (time of this writing) the markets recovered some of their losses. The S&P 500 went from 848 in March 2003 to 1368 in October 2006, an increase of 61%; the NASDAQ recovered from 1341 to 2342, a gain of 74%.

in 2001, the war in Afghanistan, the war in Iraq) and climatologi-cal disasters (Katrina in 2005), the U. S. economy recovered and sprinted ahead, achieving the fastest growth rate in over three decades. The stock markets recovered a substantial part of the losses sustained in 2000-2002; they provided ample opportunities for making money.

In retrospect, it was a blessing to leave the bank in August 1998, since it provided the time to set up a home-based trad-ing operation and learn crucial lessons that helped to survive the deep market depression that followed.

The next generation

The Deboeck family that branched out to the U. S. is blessed with three children all born in the USA: Toni, Pascal and Nina (see Chapter 2). The education and interests of this next generation are totally different from that of their grandparents or even their parents. In Chapter 3 I demonstrated how their grand-parents were entrepreneurs in lace making and artisans in beer brewing. Above I described how I became an intrepreneur in a large international organization. In what follows I briefly describe the education and interests of the next generation.

1. The engineer

Toni Francis was born in 1972 in Worcester, Massachusetts. He obtained his Bachelor of Sci-ence in mechanical engineering in May 1994 and his Masters of En-gineering in May 1995 from Cor-nell University. He then spent two years in the Department of Aero-nautics and Astronautics at Purdue University in graduate studies.

After leaving Purdue, Toni worked as an Orbit Analyst at Irid-ium Satellite Operations in Lees-burg, Virginia. Iridium launched the first global telephone system using a network of sixty-six satel-lites. As one of the *Orbit Analysts* for the Iridium constellation, Toni was responsible for performing or-bit determination on the satellites, maintaining the onboard state (position and velocity), and plan-ning maneuvers to correct the on-board state.

Figure 7.5 Olivia and Toni Francis Deboeck, on their wedding day, October 7, 2006 (Photo GJD,

Since November 1999, Toni has worked for United Space Alliance in Houston, Texas in support of Space Shuttle mission operations. Toni's two primary roles are that of a *Navigation Flight Controller* and a *Navigation Mission Engineer.* Navigation Flight Controllers support Space Shuttle missions in the Mission Control Center (MCC) at the Johnson Space Center in Houston, Texas. These controllers are responsible for performing orbit determination on the Space Shuttle and the International Space Station (ISS), maintaining accurate state vectors on the ground and on-board the vehicle, and assisting the Flight Dynamics Officer in planning the trajectory of the vehicle. The process of preparing for a Space Shuttle flight, executing the flight, and performing post-mission work involves a myriad of details. The Navigation Mission Engineer oversees all the work associated with Navigation for a particular flight. As of September 2006, Toni was selected as the *Mission Engineer Lead,* overseeing the efforts of all Mission Engineers in the Department.

On August 28, 2005 Toni received the *Silver Snoopy Award.* The Silver Snoopy is the most prestigious award given by the members of NASA's astronaut corps. The award is a sterling silver Snoopy lapel pin that has flown on a Space Shuttle mission, plus a certificate of appreciation and commendation letter. The award was presented by Astronaut Barbara Morgan and read as follows:

"Toni Deboeck is a member of the flight control team in the Navigation and Flight Design Integration (NAV & FDI) department, United Space Alliance (USA). He has demonstrated superior performance as a Space Shuttle flight controller from the moment he became part of the department, through his real-time console operations and analysis support. Toni's trademark is his attention to detail and commitment to quality, reliability, safety, efficiency and performance.

Toni's consistent high level of support is an asset to the Navigation department, the NASA customer, and the national space program. His relentless efforts have truly made a difference to the mission control team and are most deserving of the Silver Snoopy award."

Besides being a certified pilot and certified SCUBA diver, Toni has interests in youth ministry. On October 7, 2006 Toni Francis married Olivia Lopez of La Porte, Texas. The announcement published in the *Washington Post* of October 14, 2006 provides further details.

2. The quantitative psychologist

Pascal Rene Deboeck was born in Fairfax, Virginia, on April 15, 1980. He graduated from the University of Virginia in May 2002 with a Bachelor of Arts in Psychology and Physics. He obtained a Masters in Psychology in 2005 from the University of Notre Dame du Lac in Indiana. In August 2007 he obtained from the same university a Ph.D. in quantitative psychology based on a dissertation on *Smoothing-independent estimation of a linear differential equation model.* In addition to conferences and presentations, he has contributed to several papers [28].

On October 1, 2005 Pascal married Lynn Mary Duesterhaus. The announcement published in the Washington Post of October 5, 2005 provides further details.

Pascal is a certified diver, avid cook and enjoys carpentry. He has participated in several construction projects for repairs of homes for the needy.

3. Youth Ministry.

Nina Maria Deboeck was born in Fairfax, Virginia, on April 8, 1983. She is a graduate of the University of Mary Washington. She double majored in English and Religion. As part of her four years of undergraduate education she attended the advanced studies program in England where she participated in the Study Abroad Program at the University of Bath.

Figure 7.6 Lynn and Pascal Rene Deboeck on their wedding day, October 1, 2005
(Photo GJD Mishawaka)

While at the University of Mary Washington, she was very involved with her campus ministry serving as retreat chair, president, and communications chair. She was also part of the University of Mary Washington Equestrian Team in 2004-2005.

After her graduation in 2005 she spent a full year providing services for the Vincentian Volunteers in Liverpool in the UK. Prior to her work in the UK, she worked for four summers at Sandy Hill Camp in North East, Maryland.

Nina is currently working at Saint Luke Catholic Church in McLean, Virginia, as a Coordinator of Youth Ministry. She has been involved in fund raising, construction and restoration of homes for the needy, hospice work for AIDS patients and elderly homeless. She is an accomplished horse rider, plays the piano and multiple other instruments and enjoys juggling and swing dancing.

---

28 P. R. Deboeck & S. M. Boker, (under review). "Estimation of Individual Damped Linear Oscillator Models." Multivariate Behavioral Research; S. M. Boker, E. S. Covey, S. S. Tiberio, & P. R. Deboeck, "Synchronization in Dancing is Not Winner-Takes-All: Ambiguity Persists in Spatiotemporal Symmetry Between Dancers." 2005 Proceedings of the North American Association for Computational, Social, and Organizational Science, (2005). A complete list of P. R. Deboeck's papers and contributions can be found at http://www.nd.edu/~pdeboeck/papers_conferences.html

Washington Post, October 5, 2005
Lynn Duesterhaus is Bride of Pascal Deboeck

Lynn Mary Duesterhaus, daughter of Judie and Richard Duesterhaus of Vienna, Virginia was married on October 1, 2005 to Pascal Rene Deboeck, a son of Hennie I. Deboeck-De Zutter and Guido J. Deboeck of Arlington, Virginia. The Rev. Andre Leveille and Rev Neil Ryan of Little Flower Catholic Church, Rev. Michael Duesterhaus, brother of the bride, and Rev. Paul E. Staes, CICM, Roman Catholic priests, officiated at Little Flower Catholic Church in South Bend, Indiana. The matron of honor was Katherine Murphy, the bride's sister; the best man was Toni Deboeck, the groom's brother.

The bride received her B.A. in Theater from James Madison University. She is employed at the Madison Center in South Bend, Indiana. The bride's mother is a retired RN who used her profession to raise eight children and is now also the grandmother of seven boys and seven girls. The bride's father also shares in the joy of these children and is a conservationist employed by the National Association of Conservation Districts in Washington D.C.

The groom received his B.A. in Psychology and Physics from the University of Virginia. In 2005 he received his Master's degree in Psychology from the University of Notre Dame in Indiana. Pascal Deboeck is a PhD candidate in Quantitative Psychology at the same university.

The couple met at Bishop O'Connell High School in Arlington; they plan to make their home in Mishawaka, Indiana.

Washington Post, October 14, 2006
Olivia Lopez is Bride of Toni F. Deboeck

Olivia Yvonne Lopez, daughter of John F. Lopez and Minnie Lopez of La Porte, Texas was married on October 7, 2006 to Toni Francis Deboeck, a son of Hennie I. Deboeck-De Zutter and Guido J. Deboeck of Arlington, Virginia. Rev. Tom Rafferty, Catholic priest, officiated at St Mary of the Immaculate Conception Catholic Church in La Porte, Texas. The matron of honor was Irene Lopez Larucci, the bride's sister; the best man was Pascal Deboeck, the groom"s brother. In accordance with the Spanish tradition, other attendants were Michael Mader and Sonia Lopez Mader, Lazo (religious bond they will share), John Dunkel and Belinda Lopez Dunkel, Arras (riches they will share), Nina Deboeck, Bible (the Catholic religion that binds them) and Rosario Oandasan, Rosary (prayers they will share). Flower girl was Maria Theresa Larucci, niece of the bride and ring bearer was Patrick Blaze Dunkel, nephew and godson of the bride.

The bride received her B.A. in communications from the Southwestern University of Georgetown, Texas. She is employed at Dansby and Miller Architects in Houston. The bride's mother is retired from banking and a former tax consultant. The bride's father was retired from St. Mary's Catholic Church before his demise in 1998.

The groom, who is the 14th generation descendant of Gillis De Bock born ca 1530 in Sint-Amands in Flanders, received his Bachelor of Science and Masters in aeronautical engineering from Cornell University. He is currently employed as a flight controller and navigation engineer for United Space Alliance in Houston. The couple met at a fireworks display party for Catholic young adults in Clear Lake City, Texas. They plan to make their home in Clear Lake City, near Houston, Texas.

The career paths chosen by the fourteenth generation descendants of the Deboeck family (see Figure 7.7) are totally different from those of previous generations. In the first part of their lives they already have accomplished more in terms of education, skill acquisition and work experiences than any of their predecessors. It will be interesting to read in fifty years what will be the addendum to this chapter. An addendum to this chapter could potentially be written by Anastasia Gabriella Deboeck, the firstborn daughter of Lynn and Pascal Deboeck who was born on November 14, (at 12:33 am) 2006, in Mishawaka, Indiana (see Figure 7.8).

Figure 7.7: The Deboeck children: Toni Francis (middle), Pascal René (left) and Nina Maria (Photo GJD, October 7, 2006)

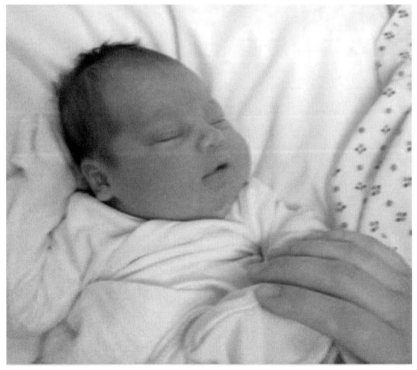

Figure 7.8: Anastasia Gabriella Deboeck, born on November 14, 2006 in Mishawaka, Indiana.

236   *Flemish DNA & Ancestry*

Chapter 8
The genetic inheritance of the Deboeck children

Until I started in genealogy, I seldom thought about my ancestors. Brian Sykes wrote about his ancestors that they were "an amorphous collection of dead people with no solid connection to me or the modern world, and certainly no real relevance to either." My feelings about my ancestors were not so different until I discovered what genetic genealogy could contribute to our understanding of our ancestors. Quickly thereafter I realized how through genetics it was possible to "touch" the past and feel connected to the future. In short, genetic genealogy drastically changed my views and feelings about my ancestors.

Sykes wrote, "DNA is the messenger, which illuminates that connection, handed down from generation to generation, carried, literally, in the bodies of [our] ancestors."[1] Via genetic genealogy and finding out about DNA it is possible to trace a journey through time and space, a journey made by the long lines that spring from our ancestral mothers and fathers.

The family histories I described in the previous chapters were assembled based on research undertaken in Belgium as well as in Virginia and Maryland (in particular via the use of microfilms at the Family History Centers). This research on three Flemish families may appear overly detailed (on occasions even too specific...) but in each case only a small portion or narrow branches of the family trees was discovered. More branches of each family remained undiscovered or unconnected. For example, I found at least ten more family trees with the surname Deboeck not linked to the clan of the 'de Bock' family that I described in Chapter 2. I described a few descendants of the Girardin family, but there are many more with that family name in Belgium, France, Canada, and even in the USA. There are a lot of people in Belgium whose family name is De Zutter, hence the De Zutter family is much larger than the family from Blankenberge described in Chapter 5.

Despite all the research already covered and all the sources that were consulted, there still is a lot of missing data. Some documents were unreadable, especially those from the sixteenth century. Some documents contained incorrect information. Some relationships were never recorded; for example, who was the father of Franciscus Alexius Girardin?

By exploring the history of my ancestors, I discovered another journey, one that led to my venture into genetic genealogy

---

1. Bryan Sykes: *The Seven Daughters of Eve: the science that reveals our genetic ancestry*, p.288.

(hereafter abbreviated as GG). This venture was started in 2004 when I first read about DNA testing, but the earliest results were not obtained until the summer of 2005 when I received my own DNA test results.

I have already introduced the basic concepts of genetic genealogy in Chapter 1. In this chapter I build on those concepts and provide a more in-depth framework for understanding genetic genealogy. I outline the most common DNA tests currently offered by half a dozen DNA testing companies around the globe as well as suggest how to select among them. I also describe how to take a DNA test. In the second part of this chapter I show how to read and interpret DNA results including my own Y-chromosome and mtDNA test results. Based on this I show how to define our genetic inheritances. In the next chapter I provide more illustrations and show how DNA tests can be used to enhance genealogical research.

Genetic genealogy is moving to become mainstream

In an article that was published in *Flemish-American Heritage* in February 2006[2] I asked: Has Genetic Genealogy (GG) become mainstream? "If it is not yet, it will be very soon..." said Bennett Greenspan, CEO of Family Tree DNA (FTDNA) Inc, at the 2nd International Conference on GG held in Washington, D.C. on November 4 and 5, 2005.

A year later at the 3rd International Conference on GG, the evidence of genetic genealogy becoming mainstream was even more convincing.

Max Blankfeld, the VP of Operations and Marketing of FTDNA provided the following statistics: as of November 2006 FTDNA had processed 220,000 DNA kits. The company started in 2000 with the analysis of some 300 DNA samples. The rate of growth is now about 4,000 new DNA samples per month, or approximately 50,000 per year. As of the April of 2007 FTDNA had 4,000 surname projects with 61,000 unique surnames on its website. The company maintains a database of 94,000 Y-DNA and 46,000 mtDNA records.

Genetic genealogy is clearly moving to become mainstream, meaning more and more people are getting interested in getting their DNA signature(s).

Beyond the basics

The *human genome* contains about 3.2 billion chemical bases or *nucleotides*. These chemicals define each human being and provide a blueprint for life. These chemicals are adenine, guanine, cytosine, and thymine, commonly abbreviated as A, G, C, T. These chemicals always combine in a certain way: C always pairs with G, and A always pairs with T. Pairs of AT or CG are arranged in a long spiral, a coiled thread structure, like a double stranded helix. DNA is the sequence of these combinations of chemicals. Simply put this spiral coil looks like a ladder that is twisted.

---

2. *Flemish American Heritage* is a publication of The Genealogical Society of Flemish Americans (GSFA), which helps people trace their Flemish and Belgian heritage. It publishes a newsletter and magazine of pictures, stories, queries, and genealogy information; and has a large library of genealogy and Belgian heritage material at the Fr. Tallieu Residence near Detroit, Michigan, USA

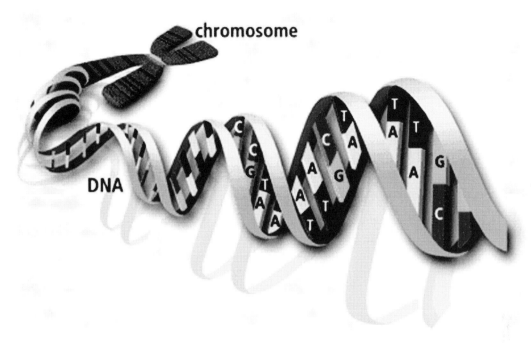

chromosome

DNA

Figure 8.1: Double-stranded helix of human DNA

A *gene* is a specific section of this long double-stranded helix of DNA. Thousands of genes make up a chromosome: 46 of them are arranged in 23 pairs of which only one pair defines the gender. It is the 23rd pair of chromosomes that contains the sex chromosomes. The 46 chromosomes contain approximately 30,000 genes.

Each human cell that contains DNA has a *cell nucleus* and a *membrane.* Between the genes on all the chromosomes there are many areas that do not code for proteins. These areas are odd bits and pieces that are not proper coding parts. Outside the nucleus but still within the cell membrane (in the cytoplasm) is the *mitochondrial DNA (mtDNA).*

Each human cell has several hundred to thousands of *mitochondria.* These mitochondria are the providers of energy for the cell. Muscle or brain cells have more mitochondria than the liver or lung cells.

In each mitochondrion, there are between two and ten copies of mtDNA. A mature egg when fertilized contains about 100,000 mitochondria, each containing its usual number of copies of mtDNA (usually one to ten). When fertilized the sperm will contribute about 50 mitochondria, which provide energy for the sperm tail to the egg. A sperm has about 50 mitochondria, mostly to be found in the tail, but on fertilization the tail falls off and no male mitochondria enters the egg, at least not under normal circumstances. Hence only the mtDNA from a mother is passed to her offspring. Thus mtDNA is handed down by every mother to all of her children.

The small amount of non-nuclear DNA found in each mito-chondrion, is a circular piece of genome with about 16,569 nucle-otides. Hence the DNA outside the nucleus of each human cell is quite different from the DNA in the nucleus that contains 3.2 billion pairs of chemicals and is arranged in a long spiral coil or double stranded helix.

The ring of non-nuclear mitochondrial DNA is divided in regions. There are two hyper-variable regions labeled HVR-1 and HVR-2 (plus to be complete:13 genes coding for proteins, 2 genes to produce ribosomal proteins, and 22 transfer RNA genes, each relating to a specific amino acid). The HVR-1 region goes from position 16024 to 16383 and contains 359 base pairs (bps); the HVR-2 region goes from position 00057 to 00372 and contains 315 bps. The entire spectrum is called the *D-loop or Control Region* and contains 917 bps. All the rest of this circular genome is a coding region. Figure 8.2 provides a graphic representation of the structure of mtDNA.

A typically basic mtDNA test yields a standardized result of 400 base pairs (out of 917 bps) that are compared to a DNA standard (which will be described in the next section). The result of a typical mtDNA test that includes the HVR-1 and HVR-2 regions can yield a few base pairs that differ from this standard. The more differences there are with the standard the farther back in time the tested mtDNA would have split from the base of the genetic tree. The maternal haplogroup is determined from this basic mtDNA test.

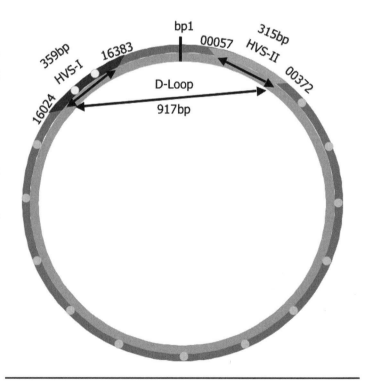

Figure 8.2 Structure of mtDNA containing about 16,569 base pairs. In this figure two regions are labeled HVS-I and HVS-II; these correspond with the HVR-1 and HVR-2 referred to in the text (Source: Doron M. Behar, 3rd International Conference on GG, November 2006.)

The non-nuclear DNA present in the mitochondria has nothing to do with the X-chromosome of females. An egg from a woman contains 22 autosomal chromosomes and one X-chromosome. All children receive an X-chromosome from their mother; additionally, daughters receive an X-chromosome from their father. Hence, sons receive a Y-chromosome from their father and an X-chromosome from their mother (YX). The Y chromosome can be used to trace the exclusively male line of a family. Daughters receive an X-chromosome from each of their parents (XX).

When a cell divides, all of the DNA in it replicates. Occasionally a mutation occurs during the replication process, so that the DNA copy is slightly different from the original. There are two types of mutations: point mutations and short tandem repeats.

Point mutations are one-letter changes in DNA segments. For example, if CTTCAGGGTC...is a segment of DNA and if one mutation occurs so that it becomes CTTCAGGGCC...(notice the change in the next to last letter), then this is called a **Single Nucleotide Polymorphism or SNP** (pronounced "snip"). Y chromosome SNPs have a slow mutation rate and produce low resolution haplogroups. Mitrochondrial SNPs have a fast mutation rate and produce high resolution haplotypes. SNPs are used to plot the phylogenetic tree[3] that shows the relationship of all current human haplogroups to the original ancestor who walked out of Africa.[4] Each mutation creates another sub branch of the tree of the phylogenetic tree.

Short tandem repeats are the repeating segments in a DNA segment. For example, when Y-chromosome DNA test looks at a small number of markers it may find

CTTCTAGATAGATAGATAGATAGATAGATAGATAG-
ATAGATAGATAGATCCTAG

---

3. A phylogenetic tree is a graphical representation of the evolutionary relationship between taxonomic groups. The term phylogeny refers to the evolution or historical development of a human tribe or similar group. Taxonomy is the system of classifying tribes by grouping them into categories according to their similarities. A phylogenetic tree is a specific type of cladogram where the branch lengths are proportional to the predicted or hypothetical evolutionary time between organisms or sequences. Cladograms are branched diagrams, similar in appearance to family trees, that illustrate patterns of relatedness where the branch lengths are not necessarily proportional to the evolutionary time between related organisms or sequences. Bioinformaticians produce cladograms representing relationships between sequences, either DNA sequences or amino acid sequences. For more information see Susan Cates, http://cnx.org/content/m11052/latest/

4. For a Y-chromosome phylogenetic tree example see: "http://www.familytreedna.com/haplotree.html." For a Y-chromosome phylogenetic tree examples see: "http://www.familytreedna.com/haplotree.html" and "http://www.isogg.org/tree/index.html."

where starting from the fifth letter there are 12 repeats of TAGA, before hitting TCCTAG. The repeating patterns that occur in DNA are **Short Tandem Repeats** (STRs). Hence since this DNA string shows 12 repeats of TAGA, *the allele value* that would be recorded for the specific marker for this DNA sample string would be 12. The same process of counting repeating patterns is applied to other markers.

At any single STR location, it is estimated that a mutation will occur only once every 500 "transmission-events" – or roughly 0.2% per generation. Basically, a transmission event is the birth of a baby boy, but it is also an event where a mutation can occur and be passed on. The rate of this genetic clock is still under debate – some STR's will change more rapidly than others and more research needs to be done in that area, but overall 0.2% per generation is a good working estimate.

In the past, DNA testing for the Y chromosome focused on only 12 markers; more details can be obtained from testing more markers, e.g., 25, 37 or 67 markers. It is however wise to start off with testing for just 12 markers; if 10 or more markers match then upgrading to 25 or 37 markers may be desirable.

STRs have the fastest mutation rates, are characterized by multi-state characters and produce high resolution haplotypes. With the increase in the number of markers tested, the observed number of mutations will go up accordingly. Using 37 markers, one can expect to see a mutation once every 13 transmission events. (i.e. 500 / 37 markers = ~13)

Common DNA Tests

There are several DNA tests that can be employed to investigate relationships. The two most common are the Y-chromosome and the mtDNA test. Each of these common DNA tests will be discussed separately. I will also touch briefly on the SNP test.

1. The Y-Chromosome DNA Test (Y-DNA)

The Y-chromosome or Y-DNA test yields a series of numbers that represent the allele values or number of repeats on various markers. The number of markers tested can vary from 12 to 67.

From a genealogical perspective, useful markers are those that can change but do not change too often. By selecting a mix of markers that change slowly, hence are relatively stable, as well as those that are more rapidly changing,[5] the best selection

---

5. The fast moving markers are
DYS 385a,b
DYS 439
DYS 458
DYS 449
DYS 464a,b,c,d
DYS 456
DYS 576
DYS 570
CDYa,b

is provided for genealogical purposes. For markers to have value for genealogical purposes they must be stable but not so stable that they cannot differentiate lineage, and also change, but not change so quickly that closely related persons don't match.

In this marker mix the multi-copy markers are very important. A multi-copy marker is one where several copies of the marker exist on the Y chromosome. The name of multi-copy markers include small letters, such as a or b following the marker DYS label. For example, DYS 464 is a rapidly changing Y chromosome marker with multiple copies. It most often has four copies labeled DYS464a, DYS464b, DYS464c, DYS464d.[6] Since multi-copy markers change more rapidly, these markers are an excellent tool to identify branches or identify persons who are not related in a genealogical timeframe.

By comparing two series of DNA test results one can find out about paternal relationships. The Y-chromosome of every male is virtually identical to that of his father, his paternal grandfather, his paternal great-grandfather and so on. It also is similar to that of any male cousin of any degree of relationship of the same male ancestor. A test of the Y-chromosome provides a clear set of genetic marker results, known as a *haplotype.*

A haplotype—derived from the contraction of "haploid genotype"—is a set of alleles (or repeating patterns) for specific genetic markers inherited as a unit. The term is commonly used in genetic genealogy for the series of Y-STR numbers derived from a Y-chromosome test of various DYSs or markers. Haplotype is also used to describe a set of alphanumeric results from a mtDNA test.

By comparing the haplotypes from two or more males, one can determine the degree of genetic relationship between their respective lines. Combined with other information, such as whether they have the same or similar surname, one can determine if their lines are closely related within a timeframe of genealogical interest (usually considered to be 500 to 600 years or the advent of surnames).

A group of similar patterned or related descendant haplotypes, that share a common ancestor sometimes hundreds or thousands of years ago, is called a *haplogroup.* These haplogroups are assigned alphanumeric designators by geneticists. These alphanumeric haplogroup names are diagrammed in a tree format on a chart to link groups of human beings together to form a Phylogenetic Tree. There is a *Phylogenetic Tree* for the male

---

6. When testing a random sample of 679 males for DYS464, scientists have found that the result 15,15,17,17 occurred in 10.6% of those tested, 15,15,16,17 occurred in 7.5% of the samples, and all the other results occurred less than 5% of the time, with over half these results only occurring once. This illustrates that marker DYS464 is valuable in differentiating unrelated persons. Source: *Facts and Genes,* volume 6, no. 2, April 17, 2007, FTDNA.

lines of descent and one for the female lines of descent.[7] Illustrations of part of these trees will be provided later.

2. The Mitochondria DNA Test (mtDNA)

mtDNA is passed on by every mother to all of her children. The mtDNA test looks at the DNA of the mitochondria and thus the 917 basis pairs that are inherited down the female line. mtDNA is generally used to study long-term population developments and human migrations.

The results of mtDNA sequencing are compared to a standard reference, namely the mitochondrion of a woman sequenced in 1981. This standard is called the Cambridge Reference Sequence (CRS).[8] Any place in the mtDNA where there is a difference from the CRS, is characterized as a mutation. If there are no mutations at all, it means that the tested mtDNA matches the CRS. A mutation happens when a/ a base replaces another base, for example a C (Cytosine) replaces an A (Adenine); and/or b/ a base is no longer in that position, for example if a T or A are missing; and/or c/ a new base is inserted between the other bases without replacing any other, for example if an extra C is inserted in a particular location.

The mtDNA test reveals details about the distant origins and deep ancestry of our maternal ancestors and can be used to link individuals via the female line. The mtDNA test also deter-

---

7. An example of phylogenetic tree for the male line can be found at http://www.familytreedna.com/haplotree.html.

8. A reanalysis of the Cambridge reference sequence by resequencing the original placental mtDNA sample, done in 1999, produced the revised CRS. See
http://www.mitomap.org/CambridgeReanalysis.htm and http://www.mitomap.org/mitoseq.html

9. Professor Bruce Walsh of the University of Arizona has estimated that a full sequence mtDNA would give about the same resolution as the 37-marker Y-DNA test. There is, however, as far as I know, no scientific consensus yet. Professor R. DeCorte of the KUL wrote, "The reliability of using mtDNA to determine the MRCA is based on one paper – http://www.cs.edu.unc.edu/~plaisted/ce/mitochondria.html --about the mtDNA mutation rate in families. This has already been solved: if you look at families then you have a higher chance to identify mutations at positions that show a high mutation rate. These mutations will be less observed in phylogenetic studies where you want to calculate the MRCA of two lineages. As explained in the referenced paper there is still some debate about how to deal with these different mutation rates. It could be that for family studies you need to use the faster mutations rate as there is a higher probability to observe mutations for two members maternally related a few generations ago. Maybe in the future it will be possible to incorporate knowledge about fast mutating sites in mtDNA into models for calculating the MRCA." (private correspondence, January 23, 2007).

mines the maternal haplogroup from which one can derive the area of the world where our female ancestors may have come from or may have lived.

Even if tested with the enhanced/refined mtDNA test—called the mtDNA Plus test by FTDNA—mtDNA does not have the same resolving power as the male Y-DNA test in providing the time to Most Recent Common Ancestor (MRCA).[9] In consequence, the mtDNA test is generally not as useful for genealogical purposes as the Y-DNA test,[10] however mtDNA has been extensively studied for over 20 years and is used quite extensively for anthropological studies. Interesting migration maps have been created to show the spread of different female lines throughout the world.

3. "SNIP" Test

In addition to the Y-DNA and mtDNA tests there is also a SNP or "snip" test that defines the haplogroups. Based on Y-DNA testing a haplogroup can be predicted for a male haplotype; the "snip" test can confirm this prediction about the deep and ancient ancestry haplogroup affiliation. This test checks for known variations in the nucleotide allele at an exact specified nucleotide position in the human DNA genome. These single letter changes in our DNA sequence occurred over time many thousands of years ago and are indicative of the major groups of human populations called haplogroups. In other words, the earlier test may provide a classification in a particular haplogroup, based on similarity between patterns discovered in the DNA and the one known to be most common for each haplogroup. Only the SNIP test provides an actual confirmation of the haplogroups by testing specific variations at exact positions in the DNA, known to have created the variations between haplogroups.

The singular nucleotide allele variations in the human genome DNA sequence occur at a frequency of about one in every 1,000 bases in the genome. When a change, i.e., mutation is observed at a nucleotide position it is called a polymorphism, which literally means many forms. But in the case of the nucleotides looked at with SNP tests there are usually only two forms, the original base letter and the more recent mutated base letter such as the A at that location becomes a T. These single nucleotide variations are used to determine very deep ancestry inheritance in groups and subgroups or clades of people over long periods of time and in the evolution of the human genome over time.

In sum, SNIP or "snip" testing provides confirmation of the best estimate classification in haplogroups that is obtained via Y-chromosome. All mtDNA testing is basically SNP testing, even though it is not always called as such.

---

10. It can however be used to confirm scientifically that two people share a common maternal ancestor if one is suspected via traditional genealogical research.

Taking a DNA test

Taking a DNA test is straightforward. Today there are about a dozen companies that offer commercial DNA testing services. You can order a testing kit from any of them either on-line, by phone or via mail (see the footnote for details).11

The three main companies that specialize in genetic genealogy are *Family Tree DNA, Relative Genetics and DNA Heritage.* The products offered by these three companies vary a little but in essence, Family Tree DNA provides the widest choice of tests. Other companies that specialize in DNA testing for genealogy include *Oxford Ancestry* (founded by Dr Bryan Sykes, author of *The Seven Daughters of Eve),* and African Ancestry (specialized in testing African-Americans).

There is an entire chapter on DNA Test Checklist and how to select a DNA testing Company in *DNA and Family History: How genetic testing can advance your genealogical research,* by Chris Pomery. C. Fitzpatrick and A. Yeiser's DNA and Genealogy provides another source of information on the difference in services offered by various companies. The basic choice between DNA tests were discussed in the previous section: only males can take the Y-DNA test, which traces their father's fathers's paternal line. Both males and females can take the mtDNA test, which traces their mother's, mother's maternal line. For males only there is also a combination test which analyzes Y-NDA and mtDNA.

After you order a test kit and receive it in the mail, you take the test following the instructions included in the kit. The typical DNA specimen collection test kit comes in a small envelope and usually consists of two swabs that look like toothbrushes. No needles or blood samples are used.

A DNA test takes less than a minute and requires nothing more than scraping your inner cheek for 30 seconds to gather cells for DNA testing. It is simple and totally painless. Upon completion of the test you mail the kit back to the testing company, who a couple of weeks later will mail you the results.

Your DNA results can then be uploaded to one or more public databases (see below). This can be done while maintaining absolute privacy because uploads are done by kit number. Surname projects allow comparisons with people with the same (or similar) surname (see in Chapter 9). Geographic projects allow comparisons with people from the same geographic origin e.g. Flanders-Flemish DNA project (see in Chapter 10).

---

11. Prices of DNA tests by FTDNA run from about $149 for a Y-DNA 12 marker analysis, to $259 for a Y-DNA 37 marker analysis, to $389 for a combined Y-DNA 37 marker with mtDNA Plus test. Group discounts for surname study projects are available from most test labs. Prices are dropping every year as more and more people are taking a DNA test and economies of scale are achieved by testing labs. Updated prices of various tests can be found on http://www.familytreeDNA.com/products.html. A comparison chart on Y-DNA testing can be found at http://www.isogg.org/ydnachart.htm

How do you read Y-DNA and mtDNA results?

To illustrate the DNA tests reviewed above I discuss in this section the DNA results from my own Y-chromosome and mtDNA tests that were taken in the summer of 2005, results which were received in October 2005, as well as the mtDNA test taken by my wife in 2006.

1. The Y-Chromosome DNA Test (Y-DNA)

My own Y-chromosome 12 marker test results are {13, 24, 14, 11, 11, 15, 13, 12, 11, 13, 13, 30} which represent the allele values obtained at the following markers DYS393, DYS390, DYS019, DYS391, DYS385a, DYS385b, DYS426, DYS388, DYS439, DYS389a, DYS392, DYS389b.

This set of numbers is easier to read in a simple table as shown in Table 8.1, in which the first column provides the marker number, the second column the marker identification or location, and the third column the allele values at each marker.

This series of numbers represents my haplotype, or simply put, this is my DNA signature. This signature is very close or identical to the one of my father, my paternal grandfather, my paternal great grandfathers including my oldest known ancestor, Gilles de Bock, born circa 1530 in Sint-Amands in Little Brabant. Hence I share this DNA signature (or something very close) with all my paternal ancestors.

By getting my Y-chromosome DNA tested, I discovered something I have in common with all male descendants of Gilles de Bock. This string of DNA has been passed on from generation to generation and it made it from Sint-Amands to Vilvoorde and was then brought to Arlington in Virginia.

On the basis of this Y-DNA series of numbers a haplogroup can be predicted or estimated which with greater than 99% accuracy may very well be the haplogroup that can reliably be determined with a SNP test.

Table 8.1
Low resolution DNA signature:
Y-DNA 12-marker results
of the author

	Y-DNA 12 markers	
Number	DYS#	Value
1	393	13
2	390	24
3	19 *	14
4	391	11
5	385a	11
6	385b	15
7	426	13
8	388	12
9	439	11
10	389I	13
11	392	13
12	389II	30

* also known as DYS 394

The first 12 numbers of my haplotype indicate that I belong to the large haplogroup named **R1b** that is of Euroasian origin. This haplogroup originated about 40,000 years ago (in the Paleolithic era) and was introduced into Europe by the early settlers.

The high frequency of R1b in Europe has its origin in the population expansion that took place after the Ice Age when there was a repopulation of the northern parts of Europe by a refugee population in the South. I will discuss this in more detail in the last section of this chapter.

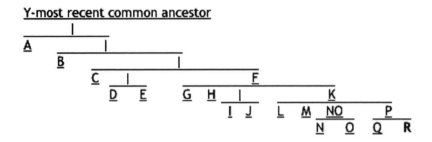

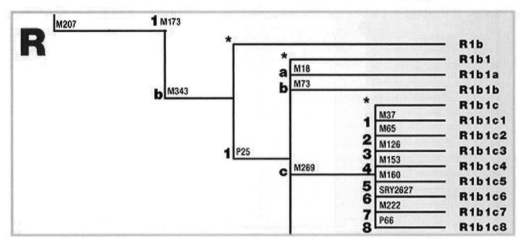

Figure 8.3 Y-most recent common ancestor and placement of R1b haplogroup on the Phylogenetic Tree. Source: Family Tree DNA, http://www.familytreedna.com/haplotree.html

Figure 8.3 shows a portion of the 2005 Phylogenetic Tree of human species. The complete tree can be viewed at http://www.ftdna.com/haplotree.html. The portion shown in Figure 8.3 provides the breakdown of the R1b haplogroup.

My 12-marker haplotype indicates that I am likely related to other male lines that go back to a time frame prior to the adoption of surnames, i.e., from 500 to 600 years or more ago. Other haplotypes may or may not share (or nearly share) the 12 markers identified as *the Western Atlantic Modal Haplotype* (WAMH) that is the most common Y-DNA signature of Europe's most common haplogroup R1b.

This most common haplogroup exists in high or very high frequencies in all Western Europe from Spain in the south to the British Islands and western Scandinavia in the north. It appears that approximately 1.1% of Western European males share this striking common genetic 12-marker signature. R1b's Western Atlantic Modal Haplotype has contributed more than its fair share in populating Western Europe.

How different is my haplotype from this most common Y-DNA signature of Western European males? Table 8.2 provides

Table 8.2: Super Western Atlantic Modal Haplotype (SWAMH)

1			2			3			4		
DYS-393			**DYS-390**			**DYS-019**			**DYS-391**		
N=1418			N=1427			N=1417			N=1425		
Repeats	Count	Freq.	Repeats	Count	Freq.	Repeats	Count	Freq.	Repeats	Count	Freq.
			21	1	.1%						
12	30	2%	22	14	1%	13	7	.5%	9	5	.3%
13	1352	95%	23	405	28%	14	1320	93%	10	454	32%
14	36	3%	24	787	55%	15	82	6%	11	896	63%
			25	209	15%	16	6	.4%	12	69	5%
			26	10	1%	17	2	.1%	13	1	.1%
			27	1	.1%						

5			6			7			8		
DYS-385a			**DYS-385b**			**DYS-426**			**DYS-388**		
N=1421			N=1434			N=1416			N=1416		
Repeats	Count	Freq.	Repeats	Count	Freq.	Repeats	Count	Freq.	Repeats	Count	Freq.
9	2	.1%	11	23							
10	40	3%	12	24	2%	10	2	.1%	11	4	.3%
11	1275	90%	13	125	8%	11	7	.5%	12	1393	98%
12	83	6%	14	992	52%	12	1388	98%	13	16	1%
13	7	.5%	15	236	20%	13	14	1%	14	3	.2%
14	9	.6%	16	32	1%	14	5	.3%			
15	4	.3%	17	2	.1%						

9			10			11			12		
DYS-439			**DYS-389a***			**DYS-392**			**DYS-389b***		
N=1428			N=1426			N=1416			N=1431		
Repeats	Count	Freq.	Repeats	Count	Freq.	Repeats	Count	Freq.	Repeats	Count	Freq.
10	5	.3%	10	1	.1%				13	2	.1%
11	208	15%	11	6	.4%	12	8	.6%	14	0	0%
12	1058	74%	12	52	4%	13	1277	90%	15	72	5%
13	136	10%	13	1223	86%	14	125	9%	16	1134	79%
14	18	1%	14	140	10%	15	6	.4%	17	197	14%
15	1	.1%	15	4	.3%				18	23	2%
16	1	.1%							19	13	1%

* DYS-389a = DYS-389i; DYS-389b = (DYS-389ii − DYS-389i)

Source Whit Athey, http://www.worldfamilies.net/SWAMH.html

the *Super Western Atlantic Modal Haplotype* (SWAMH), a composite derived from analysis of 1400+ haplotypes from Western Europe, against which my haplotype is then compared in Table 8.3.

In comparing the allele values between two haplotypes we detect differences, which can be translated in frequencies. For example, in the SWAMH the frequency of getting a 13 on DYS393 is 95%, meaning 95% of the samples tested for SWAMH yielded

Table 8.3
STR allele frequencies for haplogroups R1b
(analysis based on data assembled by Whit Athey) [12]

Marker	Sample Size	SWAMH value at each marker /frequency	My allele value at each marker /frequency
393	1418	13 (95%)	13 (95%)
390	1427	24 (55%)	24 (55%)
019	1417	14 (93%)	14 (93%)
391	1425	11 (63%)	11 (63%)
385a	1421	11 (90%)	11 (90%)
385b	1434	14 (52%)	**15 (20%)**
426	1436	12 (98%)	**13 (1%)**
388	1416	12 (98%)	12 (98%)
439	1428	12 (74%)	**11 (15%)**
389a	1426	13 (86%)	13 (86%)
392	1416	13 (90%)	13 (90%)
389b	1431	16 (79%)	**17 (14%)**

Source:
http://www.worldfamilies.net/Super%20Western%20Atlantic%20Modal%20Haplotype.htm

a 13 on that marker. Table 8.2 shows that although my haplotype belongs to R1b haplogroup, there are some differences in at least three markers. For DYS426 the SWAMH value is 12, which occurs in 98% of 1436 Western Europeans, while I have a 13, which is found in only 1% of the sample of Western European haplotypes. There are three other markers where the values differ from those of the SWAMH (DYS385b, DYS439, DYS389b).

The low resolution of my DNA signature can be improved by checking more markers. This low resolution Y-chromosome test can be augmented to a medium resolution by adding a second panel of 13 more markers so as to obtain a 25-marker haplotype. With this I obtained more precision, in other words it narrows down where my family belongs in the human population of the world. A higher resolution of my DNA signature is shown in Table 8.4. A certificate of this 25-marker test is shown in Figure 8.4

---

12. http://www.worldfamilies.net/Super%20Western%20Atlantic%20Mod al%20Haplotype.htm

Table 8.4
Medium resolution DNA signature:
Y-DNA 25-marker results of the author

	Y-DNA 12 markers			Y-DNA 25 markers	
Number	DYS#	Value	Number	DYS#	Value
1	393	13	13	458	17
2	390	24	14	459a	9
3	19 *	14	15	459b	10
4	391	11	16	455	11
5	385a	11	17	454	11
6	385b	15	18	447	25
7	426	13	19	437	15
8	388	12	20	448	19
9	439	11	21	449	29
10	389I	13	22	464a	14
11	392	13	23	464b	15
12	389II	30	24	464c	18
			25	464d	10
* also known as DYS 394					

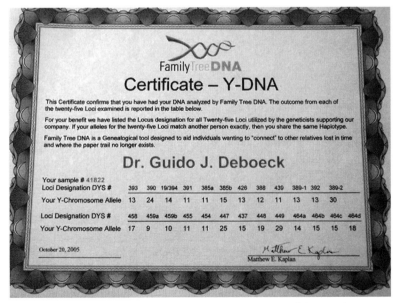

Figure 8.4 Certificate of Y-DNA 25-marker test of the author obtained on October 20, 2005.

These 25-marker results narrow down the pool of other male lines who could possibly be related but probably still have many, many matches with people of different surnames. In a macro sense, the exact or near matches to my 25-marker haplotype are more likely to be related to me than the pool of matches (or near matches) segregated out of the whole population using only 12 markers.

Again the 25-marker DNA results can be augmented to 37 markers by testing for 12 more markers. The results are shown in the third column of Table 8.4. If 37 markers of two men match exactly or if there is only one (or at most four markers are) off by a count of one step, then these two men are closely related in a timeframe of genealogical interest. They most probably have a Most Recent Common (male) Ancestor (MRCA). If based on 37 markers the DNA of two men match exactly 37/37 and if they share the same (or similar surname) then they probably share a common ancestor within the last 5 generations.

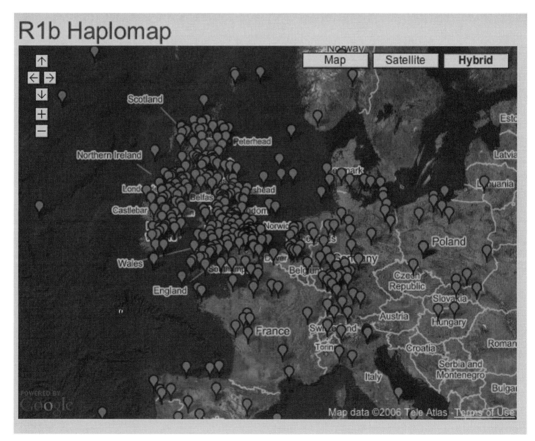

Figure 8.5 Frequency of R1b haplogroups in Western Europe based on Y-chromosome tests uploaded to Y-search. This map shows "sample bias" since a larger proportion of people who uploaded their Y-DNA to Y-search are of British ancestry.

Table 8.5
Highest resolution Y-DNA of the author 67-marker results

Number	DYS#	Value	Number	DYS#	Value
1	393	13	38	531	11
2	390	24	39	578	9
3	19 *	14	40	395S1a	15
4	391	11	41	395S1b	16
5	385a	11	42	590	8
6	385b	15	43	537	10
7	426	13	44	641	10
8	388	12	45	472	8
9	439	11	46	406S1	10
10	389I	13	47	511	10
11	392	13	48	425	12
12	389II	30	49	413a	23
13	458	17	50	413b	23
14	459a	9	51	557	16
15	459b	10	52	594	10
16	455	11	53	436	12
17	454	11	54	490	12
18	447	25	55	534	16
19	437	15	56	450	8
20	448	19	57	444	12
21	449	29	58	481	22
22	464a	14	59	520	20
23	464b	15	60	446	14
24	464c	18	61	617	12
25	464d	10	62	568	11
26	460	10	63	487	13
27	GATA H4	11	64	572	10
28	YCAIIa	19	65	640	11
29	YCAIIb	23	66	492	12
30	456	16	67	565	12
31	607	15			
32	576	19			
33	570	17			
34	CDYa	36			
35	CDYb	36			
36	442	11			
37	438	12			

* also known as DYS394

The more mismatches that are found, the further back in time the MRCA is likely to be.[13]

Finally, the highest resolution Y-DNA test that can be obtained today from Family Tree DNA is the 67-marker test. The results of upgrading the earlier test to this level are shown in Table 8.5. As few people have so far opted for taking the 67-marker test it is less relevant for comparisons than it may become in the future.

Charles Kerchner suggested that the Y-chromosome DNA test can help to determine:

a.   whether two or more males share a common male ancestor;

b.   whether that ancestor lived in a time frame of genealogical interest;

c.   Whether two or more men with the same or similar surnames are directly related through a common male ancestor.

d.   how many common male ancestors any given group or clan shares;

e.   who is not related although having the same surname;

f.   to which broad pre-history, deep ancestry haplogroup each individual haplotype belongs.

g.   the degree of separation between individual males in terms of number of generations since the separation occurred based on an analysis of the mutations in the Y-chromosome. Most Recent Common Ancestor (MRCA) is another way of expressing this separation.[14]

In sum, by taking DNA tests one can learn about the DNA signature or the genetic code that was passed on from generation to generation. In my case I detected the genetic code that most likely is close or similar to the genetic code that was passed on for 12 generations or over 500 years from Gilles de Bock to me.

---

13. To get the best estimate as to the timeframe the shared common ancestor lived, test as many markers as you can afford. I recommend at a minimum of 37. Here is why: http://www.kerchner.com/zip+4-analogy.htm See this website for an example of using Y-DNA for genealogy: http://www.kerchner.com/kerchdna.htm or http://www.kerchner.com/success.htm

14. There is currently a debate over the "natural" rate of mutation over time. A mutation can occur at any time. Natural mutations have been postulated to be occurring on average about once per 500 generations per marker. But some family surname Y-DNA studies are observing average mutation rates of about twice that rate, i.e., once per 250 generations per marker. See this website for more information on Y-DNA Y-STR mutation rates: http://www.kerchner.com/dnamutationrates.htm . It is now acknowledged that some Y-DNA DYS markers mutate at a higher average rate than other Y-DNA DYS markers. Professor R. DeCorte wrote "Population geneticists consider a mutation as a polymorphism when it has at least a 5% frequency in the population."

It is also the genetic code I passed on to my sons who are the 14th generation descendants of Gilles de Bock and all of their future male offspring, the 15th generation and beyond. Given this, there is no need for any male descendants of this family to undertake another Y-chromosome DNA test unless more advanced tests become available in the future that could further improve on the resolution of this DNA signature and hence better locate our family on the phylogenetic tree of the human species.

The Y-DNA signature defined above is one part of the genetic inheritance to the Deboeck family.

2. The Mitochondria DNA Test (mtDNA)

After discussing Y-DNA results I turn to mtDNA test results. A concrete example of my mtDNA test results follows. Before I get to that point let me review what conventional genealogy revealed about my maternal lineage.

My mother (see Chapter 2) was Marie-Louise Girardin, born in 1918 in Sint-Ulriks-Kapelle. Marie-Louise was one of two daughters of Josephine De Maseneer (1893-1945) also born in Sint-Ulriks-Kapelle (see Chapter 4). Josephine De Maseneer was the daughter of Maria Ludovica Verbruggen born in 1866. Maria Ludovica Verbruggen was the daughter of Rosalia Catharina Kerremans (1836-1903). Rosalia Catharina Kerremans was the daughter of Anne Maria De Greve (sometimes spelled De Greef) born in Asse in 1792. She was the daughter of Anna Catherina De Coster born in 1762 in Asse. Finally, Anna Catherina De Coster was the daughter of Johanna Maria Hoemans married to Petrus De Coster. Hence, *my great, great, great, great, great-grandmother was Johanna Maria Hoemans, probably born in the early part of the eighteenth century.*

Testing my mtDNA, which I inherited from my mother, and hence from my maternal gr gr gr gr gr grandmother, I can trace back further, actually all the way to my ancestral "Eve."

My mtDNA test results are shown in Table 8.6. The first part shows that my maternal haplogroup is **H***. Mitochondrial haplogroup H is a predominantly European haplogroup that arrived in Europe about 30,000 years ago, and participated in a population expansion beginning approximately 20,000 years ago. Today, about 40% of all mitochondrial lineages in Europe are classified as haplogroup H.[15] This haplogroup, which is rather uniformly

---

15. Specific mitochondrial haplogroups are typically found in different regions of the world, and this is due to unique population histories. In the process of spreading around the world, many populations—with their special mitochondrial haplogroups—became isolated, and specific haplogroups concentrated in geographic regions. Certain haplogroups have been identified that originated in Africa, Europe, Asia, the islands of the Pacific, the Americas, and even particular ethnic groups. Of course, haplogroups that are specific to one region are sometimes found in another, but this is due to recent migration.

distributed throughout Europe played a major role in the population of Europe. Descendant lineages of the original haplogroup H appears in the Near East as a result of migration.

My HVR1 haplogroup H is shown with an "asterisk" (or star), meaning that my mtDNA could not be classified in any of the sub-clades of the H haplogroups. H* is not a true sub-clade but a group that can be described as "known to belong to the H clade but lacking the coding region mutations for the (so far) accepted sub-clades." The wait is for science to find new sub-clades. H* is spread throughout Europe and the ancestors of H* haplogroups can be traced from Finland to Italy and from Britain to Romania.

My HVR1 also indicates that compared to CRS, my mtDNA contains a C in position 16,519. This is quite common. My HVR2 sequencing of my mtDNA shows three differences with CRS, namely 131C, 263G and 315.1C (the latter implies an insertion of a C at position 315). The 263G and 315.1C are mutations that are quite common. However, so far the mutation 131C appears to be quite rare. This finding is very common for mtDNA analyses: about one in 2 samples tested gives a mtDNA profile that is not published yet or has not yet been observed in a population. So far in public databases I have found only 13 records that contain the combination of 131C, 263G and 315.1C.

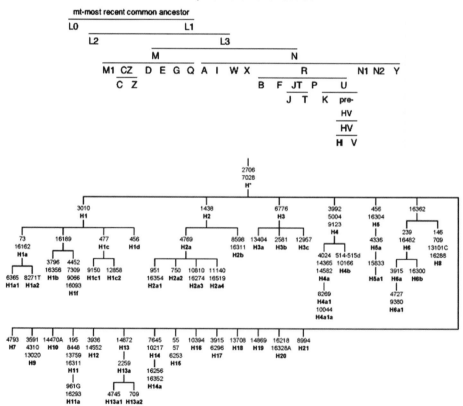

Figure 8.6 Haplogroup H and its sub-clades of haplogroups H. A detailed chart showing all sub-clades can be found at http://www.familytreedna.com/hclade2.html

Ian Logan of The Brooking Society wrote me: "So you are an H*! From the list you can expect to have the following mutations:
A750G - 12S-rRNA
315.C - HVR2
A4769G - ND2
A1438G - 12S-rRNA
A15326G - CytB
A8860G - ATP6
A263G - HVR2 and
indeed you have the HVR 1 and 2 mutations at 315 and 263.

Your other mutations form a branch off the 'CRS to Eve' line, (or 'Eve to CRS' if you prefer, see below). You have 131C - which is very uncommon[16] indeed and 16519C -

Table 8.6

mtDNA results of the author compared to CRS

HVR1 Haplogroup	H*
HVR1 differences	16519C
from CRS	
HVR2 differences	131C
from CRS	263G
	315.1C

which is very common. The place of 16519C is interesting if one puts it in the 'CRS to Eve' line, then one has to quickly put a 16519T in. Are you the only H* with 131C   - is this unique to your family? With complete sequencing you can find out in the future

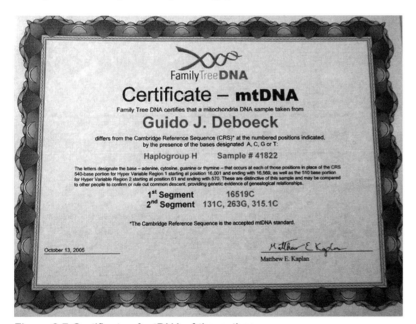

Figure 8.7 Certificate of mtDNA of the author

---

16. Ian Logan wrote: You asked about 131C, are you familiar with: http://www.genpat.uu.se/mtDB/ go to polymorphic sites, then 1-1000, and down to 131. It says there are just 13 131C's, and 1748 131T's. Now click on the '13', and the list appears showing 11 are Japanese, 1 is Chinese, and the last is Siberian. So, none are Haplogroup H - you are unique ! There is no published haplogroup H sequence with 131C - which makes it all the more worthwhile having your complete sequence done. (private mail November 10, 2005)

as science progresses whether you have your own H sub group? Haplogroup 'H-Deboeck' looks good![17]

Professor Ronny DeCorte of the KUL wrote however: "I do not think that complete mtDNA sequencing gives you additional information. Apparently the profile with 131C has not been described before. You need to treat a mtDNA profile as a haplotype just as for the Y-chromosome. You cannot look at independent positions in the sequence. So for the moment I do not recommend complete mtDNA sequencing as this will not give you any new information. This could change over time so that the same mtDNA profile is reported with other individuals. Then it might be necessary to go for complete mtDNA sequencing to further delineate the profile.[18]

Yet another example of mtDNA test results are those of my wife. Conventional genealogy revealed that Hennie De Zutter is the daughter of Irmgard Burkhardt born in Braunichswalde (former East Germany) in 1923. She was the daughter of Klara Johanna Schumann born in Greiz-Pohlitz in 1890. Klara Johanna Schumann was the daughter of Sidonie Augusta Seifert. The mtDNA of Hennie De Zutter and hence of Irmgard, Klara Johanna, and Sidonie Augusta Seifert are shown in Table 8.7.

The results in Table 8.6 show that all the women mentioned above belong to the haplogroup H and within H to the sub-clade **H6**. This can be derived from the work of Eva-Luis Loogväli, et. al.[19] She wrote, "the overall pattern of human maternal lineages in Europe is largely uniform because of insufficient depth and width of the phylogenetic analysis." With her collaborators at the Institute of Molecular and Cell Biology at the University of Tartu in Estonia she made use of the coding sequence information from 267 mtDNA haplogroup H sequences, and analyzed 830 mtDNA genomes, from 11 European, Near and Middle Eastern, Central Asian and Altaian populations. Her team defined fifteen novel sub-clades of H present in the existing human populations

Table 8.7
mtDNA results of the author's wife compared to CRS

HVR1 Haplogroup	H6
HVR1 differences	16362C
from CRS	16482G
HVR2 differences	239C
from CRS	263G
	309.1C
	315.1C

---

17. Private mail, November 9, 2006. See also Doron M. Behar, "The Complete mtDNA Sequence: a must or an overkill?" 3rd International Conference on Genetic Genealogy, Houston, November 2006.

18. R Decorte private e-mail of November 14, 2006.

19. Eva-Luis Loogväli et. al.: "Disuniting Uniformity: A Pied Cladistic Canvas of mtDNA Haplogroup H in Eurasia," *Molecular Biology and Evolution,* July 14, 2004

H6

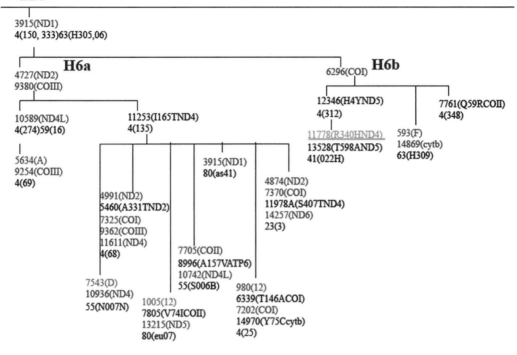

Figure 8.8 Breakdown of H6 sub-clade of Haplogroup H.
Source: mtDNA Haplogroup H Project, Laura Hayden Co-Admin, mtDNA Haplogroup H Project, e-mail:hmtdna@gmail.com

of western Eurasia (see Figure 8.7) in addition to the seven previously specified sub-haplogroups.[20]

As shown in Figure 8.6, H6 is a sub-clade that branches off at 16,362 and 16,482. H6 is an older branch of haplogroup H. Its age is estimated at around 40,000 years. Studies suggest that this haplogroup is Middle Eastern or Central Asian in origin. It is also found at very low frequencies in Europe. A breakdown of the H6 sub-clade of haplogroup H is shown in Figure 8.8. Further re-

---

20. This refinement of the phylogenetic resolution has allowed to resolve a large number of homoplasies in phylogenetic trees of haplogroup H based on the first hypervariable region of mtDNA. As many as 50 out of 125 polymorphic positions in HVR-I were found to be mutated in more than one sub-cluster of H. The phylogeographic analysis revealed that sub-haplogroups H1*, H1b, H1f, H2a, H3, H6a, H6b and H8 demonstrate distinct phylogeographic patterns. The monophyletic sub-haplogroups of haplogroup H provide means for further progress in the understanding of the pre-historic movements of women in Eurasia and for the understanding of the present-day genetic diversity of western Eurasians in general.

search may resolve the distribution and historical characteristics of these haplogroups.

The HVR2 mutations of the women mentioned earlier are 239C, 263G, 309.1C and 315.1C.

The mtDNA presented in Table 8.7 is the one of Hennie De Zutter that she inherited from her mother and hence from her maternal grandmother. While further enhancements are possible by full sequencing, it should be clear that this is also the mtDNA passed on to all the Deboeck children with little or no change.

More importantly, it is the mtDNA of Nina Maria and any children she may give birth to. It is the mtDNA that will be passed on by her daughter(s) to all grandchildren she (or they) may potentially have. This is the other part of the inheritance of the Deboeck family.

3. "SNIP" Test

You recall that a SNIP test defines the haplogroup. Based on Y-DNA testing a haplogroup can be "predicted" for a male haplotype, but until a SNIP test is done there can be no hundred percent certainty about the predicted haplogroup. Only the SNIP test can confirm this prediction about the deep and ancient ancestry haplogroup affiliation.

The results of a SNIP test that I obtained in May 2007 based on my Y-DNA test taken in the Fall of 2005, confirmed the following

1/ positives for the following SNPs: M173+, M207+, M269+, M343+ P25+; and

2/ negatives for the following SNPs: M126- M153- M18-, M222-, M37-, M65-, M73-, P66-, SRY2627-.

According to the current classification this assigns me to **Haplogroup R1b1c**

A certificate to this effect is shown in Figure 8.9

Figure 8.9 Certificate of Haplogroup of Guido Deboeck

What does all this tell us about deep ancestry?

Through both the Y-DNA and mtDNA tests, information can be gathered about our deep ancestry. In this section I bring together everything that can be derived from the haplogroups that have been identified through my Y-DNA and mtDNA testing and the mtDNA testing of my wife about our deep ancestry. I start with male ancestry followed by female ancestry.

1. DNA testing and male ancestry.

Based on my Y-DNA it was inferred with high confidence that my haplogroup is R1b; my SNIP test confirmed with complete certainty that I belong to haplogroups R1b1c.

Within the R1b haplogroup there are modal haplotypes. One of the best characterized of these haplotypes is the West European Atlantic Modal Haplotype (WAMH).[21] This haplotype reaches the highest frequency in the Iberian peninsula and in the British Isles. In the Iberian peninsula it reaches 33% in Portugal.[22]

Within the R1b haplogroup, my haplotype belongs to the subclade called R1b1c. Specifically this narrows me to Western Europeans who have a mutation called SNP M269 that share my haplotype exactly. Nearly all present-day Europeans with M269 also have M343 and P5 markers. These markers define the R1b1c subclade.[23]

---

21. There also exists a haplotype of R1b with the DYS393=12 which is known in the literature as Haplotype 35, or ht35, as opposed to the AMH which is known as haplotype 15. The members of this haplotype are thought to be descended from early R1b's who found shelter in Anatolia during the Last Glacial Maximum instead of in Iberia. They can be found in high numbers in Anatolia and Armenia with smaller numbers throughout the Middle East, in Jewish populations, in Southeastern Europe, and in the Caucasus Mountains. There is also a sizable pocket of ht35 in Uyghur populations in western China, which is thought to be a remnant of the Tocharians, an Indo-European speaking people that inhabited the Tarim Basin in Central Asia until they were later absorbed by various Turkic peoples. Ht35 is also present in Britain in areas that were found to have a high concentration of Haplogroup J, suggesting they arrived together, perhaps through Roman soldiers.

22. Based on the work of Luigi Luca Cavalli-Sforza (1994). *The History and Geography of Human Genes.* Princeton University Press.; Semino et al (2000): "The Genetic Legacy of Paleolithic Homo sapiens sapiens in Extant Europeans," Science, Vol 290; Wells et al (2001), "The Eurasian Heartland: A continental perspective on Y-chromosome diversity," PNAS, Vol 98; C. Cinnioglu et al. (2004), "Excavating Y-chromosome haplotype strata in Anatolia," *Human Genetics* 114(2):127-48.

23. Note that in earlier literature the M269 marker, rather than M343, was used to define the R1b haplogroup. Then, for a time (from 2003 to 2005) what is now R1b1c was designated R1b3. This shows how nomenclature can evolve as new markers are discovered and then investigated.

This subgroup probably originated in Central Asia/South Central Siberia and appears to have entered prehistoric Europe mainly from the area of modern Iran or Central Asia (Kazakhstan) via the coasts of the Black Sea and the Baltic Sea. It is believed by some to have been widespread in Europe before the last Ice Age, and associated with the Aurignacian culture (32,000-21,000 BC) of the Cro-Magnon people, the first modern humans to enter Europe.

The Cro-Magnons were the first documented human artists, making sophisticated cave paintings. Famous sites include Lascaux in France, Cueva de las Monedas in Spain and Valley of Foz Côa in Portugal (the largest open-air site in Europe).

When the Ice Age intensified and the continent became increasingly uninhabitable, the genetic diversity narrowed through *founder effects* and *population bottlenecks,* as the population became limited to a few coastal refugia in Southern Europe and Asia Minor.

The present-day R1b population is believed to be descended from a refuge in the Iberian peninsula (Spain and Portugal), where the R1b1c haplogroup may have achieved genetic homogeneity. As conditions of the Ice Age eased in about 12,000 before the present (bp), descendants of this group migrated and eventually re-colonized all of Western Europe, leading to the dominant position of R1b in variant degrees from Iberia to Scandinavia, so evident in haplogroup maps.

An alternative belief is that R1b represents the Western or centum-speaking branch of the Proto-Indo-Europeans, although this too remains uncertain.

A second R1b1c population, reflected in a somewhat different distribution of haplotypes of the more rapidly varying Y-STR markers, appears to have survived alongside other haplogroups in Asia Minor, from where they spread out to repopulate Eastern Europe. However, they do not have the same dominance that R1b has in Western Europe. Instead the most common haplogroup in Eastern Europe is haplogroup R1a1, often thought to be associated with a subsequent migration of Indo-Europeans (or perhaps their ancestors) from the East.

The haplogroup R1b and haplogroup R1a first existed at very different times. The mutations that characterize haplogroup R1b occurred ~30,000 years bp, whereas the mutations that characterize haplogroup R1a occurred ~10,000 years bp.

In his book *Deep Ancestry: Inside the Genographic Project,* Spencer Wells provides the origin of this R1b male line of descent. The Y-chromosome mutations on the male line of descent all point to Africa, but the male common ancestor, hereafter called ancestral Adam, lived only about 60,000 years ago. The trace back of R1b to ancestral Adam is according to Spencer Wells as follows (shown here as a series of mutations that occurred):

"ancestral Adam" -> M168 -> M89 -> M9 -> M207 -> M173 -> M343.

Wells suggested that around 30,000 years ago, a descendant of the clan making its way into Europe gave rise to a marker M343, the defining marker of the haplogroups R1b. These travelers are direct descendants of the people who dominated the human expansion into Europe, the Cro-Magnon.[24]

Fossil Hominids: Cro-Magnon Man

In Les Eyzies in France workmen discovered in 1868 at Cro-Magnon 5 skeletons (3 adult males, an adult female, and a child) which had been buried there, along with stone tools, carved reindeer antlers, ivory pendants, and shells approximately 30,000 years ago.

The Cro-Magnons lived in Europe between 35,000 and 10,000 years ago. They are virtually identical to modern man, being tall and muscular and slightly more robust on average than most modern humans. They were skilled hunters, toolmakers and artists famous for the cave art at places such as Lascaux, Chauvet, and Altamira.

The skull of one Cro-Magnon shows a male with a brain size of 1600 cc, some 200 cc larger than the average modern human.

The term "Cro-Magnon" has no formal taxonomic status,[25] since it refers neither to a species or subspecies nor to an archaeological phase or culture. The name is not commonly encountered in modern professional literature in English, since authors prefer to talk more generally of anatomically modern humans. They thus avoid a certain ambiguity in the label "Cro-Magnon," which is sometimes used to refer to all early moderns in Europe (as opposed to the preceding Neanderthals), and sometimes to refer to a specific human group that can be distinguished from other Upper Paleolithic humans in the region. Nevertheless, the term "Cro-Magnon" is still very commonly used in popular texts because it makes an obvious distinction with the Neanderthals, and also refers directly to people rather than to the complicated succession of archaeological phases that make up the Upper Paleolithic.

This evident practical value has prevented archaeologists and human paleontologists—especially in continental Europe—from dispensing entirely with the idea of Cro-Magnons.

Source: Abstracted from Fossil Hominids FAQ
http://www.talkorigins.org/faqs/homs/cromagnon.html

More than 95% of European men alive today apparently are, according to Wells, descended from 10 ancient groups of forefathers; 80% of European men inherited their Y-chromosomes from primitive hunter-gatherers who lived up to 40,000 years ago. The remaining 20% of male ancestors are likely to have been migrants who arrived in Europe from the Near East about 10,000 years ago, bringing with them farming technology.

Professor Bryan Sykes from Oxford University has a slightly different theory. He believes that only 15-20% of modern Europeans can be linked to Middle Eastern populations; many farmers left the Middle East to resettle in Europe; and Europeans copied their way of life.

---

24. Spencer Wells, Deep Ancestry, pp 226.

25. The Oxford Companion to Archaeology suggests that Cro-magnons are, in informal usage, a group among the late Ice Age peoples of Europe. The Cro-Magnons are identified with Homo sapiens sapiens of modern form, in the time range ca. 35,000-10000 b.p.

2. DNA testing and female ancestry.

You recall that based in mtDNA test both my wife and I belong to haplogroups H. In Deep Ancestry Spencer Wells also provides how the H haplogroup can be traced back to our *ancestral Eve* as follows (again shown here as a series of mutations):

"ancestral Eve" -> L1/L0 -> L2 -> L3 -> N -> R -> pre-HV -> HV -> H.

Ian Logan provided the following more specific trace:

"ancestral Eve"-> L0 -> L1 -> L5 -> L2 -> L6 -> L4 -> L3 -> N -> R -> pre HV -> H & V -> H -> H2 (or any other sub-clade).

Based on this, the full sequence of mutations from our ancestral Eve to haplogroup H can be derived. This full sequence is provided at the end of this chapter. By adding one mutation to that table one can also trace the path of my wife's ancestral Eve to her H6 haplogroup.

It may be of interest to point out that while the current common practice is to compare mtDNA results with CRS, a woman whose mtDNA was sequenced in 1981, there is no longer a scientific obstacle or good reason not to compare any mtDNA results with the full sequence of mutations going back to an ancestral Eve.

Coming back to our haplogroups H* and H6: As members of the haplogroup H my wife and I have reached a destination of a genetic journey that began some 150,000 years ago with an ancient mtDNA haplogroup L3.

Our ancestral Eve, the common ancestor of all living humans, was born in Africa some 150,000 years ago. All existing mtDNA diversity began with her. A single person of the L3 lineage gave[26] rise to the M and N haplogroups some 80,000 years ago. All Euro-Asian mtDNA lineages are subsequently descended from these two groups.

About 50,000 years ago a period of warmer temperatures and moist climate made parts of the arid Sahara habitable. This climatic shift out of the African Ice Age, likely spurred hunter-gatherer migrations into the Sahara and beyond. This Saharan gateway led humans out of Africa to the Middle East. When the climate again turned arid, expanding Saharan sands slammed the Saharan gateway shut—the desert became at its driest between 20,000 and 40,000 years ago—which isolated the Middle East migrants from Africa. From their new Middle East location, they would go on and populate much of the world.

The N and M haplogroups that descended from the African L3, spawned sub-lineages in the eastern Mediterranean and

---

26. This haplogroup L3 occurred only in Africa and L3's sub-clades are most prevalent in East Africa.

Near East region. They likely coexisted for a time with pre-modern hominids such as the Neanderthals.[27]

Haplogroup R descended from N and has since dispersed across much of the globe. Subgroups pre HV, U, Y, and J are found in Europe and the Near East.

Haplogroup H is a large lineage that first appeared on the R line of descent. Spencer Wells suggested that "today haplogroups H comprises 40 to 60 percent of the gene pool of most European populations. Moving eastwards the frequency of H gradually decreases, illustrating the migratory path the settlers followed as they left the Iberian Peninsula after the ice sheets had receded."[28]

While haplogroup H is considered the western European lineage due to its frequency there, it is also found much further east. Today it comprises around 20% of southwest Asian lineages, about 15% of people living in central Asia, and around 5 percent in northern Asia.

The age of haplogroup H lineages differs quite substantially. In Europe its age is estimated at 10,000 to 15,000 years old. H made it into Europe substantially earlier—30,000 years ago—but reduced population sizes resulting from the ice age significantly reduced its diversity compared to its estimated age. In Central and East Asia, however, its age is estimated at around 30,000 years old, meaning the lineage made it into those areas during some of the earlier migrations out of the Near East. A map showing the migration path of the L3 lineage to the Middle East and then to Europe is shown in Figure 8.10.

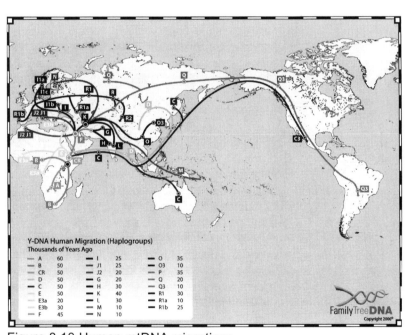

Figure 8.10 Human mtDNA migrations
Source: www.mitomap.org

27. Excavations in Israel's Kebara cave (Mount Carmel) have unearthed Neanderthal skeletons at least as recent as 60,000 years ago.

28. Spencer Wells: *Deep Ancestry: Inside the Genographic Project,* pp. 197-198

This chapter demonstrated how genetic genealogy complements conventional genealogy, which relies on documents. The findings summarized in chapters 2 to 5 have taken years to assemble. Digging into the records has been time-consuming and expensive. A professional genealogist was recruited to research the records in Belgium and to help out deciphering documents written in old Flemish.

In contrast to conventional genealogy, DNA testing is quick, easy, painless and does not cost a lot. Prices of a Y-chromosome or mtDNA test continue to come down and have become affordable, hence the increasing popularity of DNA testing.

Through DNA testing, I found the genetic code that I inherited and has been passed on over many generations. Through Y-chromosome DNA testing I found my haplotype or my DNA signature. Through my haplotype it was possible to predict with high confidence my haplogroup. Based on my Y-DNA test I learned that I belong (to the R1b haplogroup or to be more specific to the R1b1c subgroup in R1b). Based on my mtDNA test I learned that I belong to the H* haplogroup that was passed on from my gr gr gr gr gr grandmother. The mtDNA of my wife showed that she belonged to the H6 haplogroup, and that her DNA was passed on through several women from former East Germany.

Thus both our mtDNAs belonged to the H haplogroup that can be traced back to the L3 lineage out of Africa. The complete listing of mutations provided at the end of this chapter shows how this L3 lineage that started from our ancestral Eve found its way to Western Europe. These mutations defined the migration paths that were followed starting some 30,000 years ago. They provided the link between the DNA that was tested and our ancestral Eve.

In sum, a few DNA tests have revealed more about our ancestors than years of document research. In fact, anyone who has yet to start with genealogy may find it more productive to start with genetic genealogy than with conventional genealogy, simply because the former provides a better guidance to what to research. Of course, if the interest is merely in documenting two to three generations of ancestors, conventional genealogy still remains the best approach. Conventional and genetic genealogy complement each other and contribute to a more in-depth study of our ancestors.

Note that Y-DNA and mtDNA provide information only on two of our ancestors (our paternal and maternal line) in the "n-th" generation. When you go back "n" generations you have 2 to the power n-1 ancestors per generation. Thus, looking back 12 generations, I really should be concerned with 2 to the power 11 or 2048 ancestors. In consequence, someone who wants to study genetic inheritance of more than his or her paternal or maternal line, will probably want to test also a number of genetic cousins!

This chapter demonstrates the value of DNA testing for both retrospective and prospective analyses. Through DNA testing we document our identity, we learn about where that identity came from and we define the identity that will be passed on to future generations!

Full sequence of mutations from H to "ancestral Eve"

A750G - 12S-rRNA* Mutation used to define Haplogroup H2a
315.C - HVR2 Mutation within Haplogroup H2
A4769G - ND2 (Met > Met) Mutation within Haplogroup H2
A1438G - 12S-rRNA* Mutation defines Haplogroup H2
A15326G - CytB (Thr>Ala) Mutation within Haplogroup H2
A8860G - ATP6 (Thr > Ala) * Mutation within Haplogroup H2
A263G - HVR2 Mutation within Haplogroup H
C7028T - COX1 (Ala >Ala) Mutation used to define Haplogroup H
A2706G - 16S-rRNA Mutation used to define Haplogroup H
C14766T - CytB (Ile>Thr) * Mutation used to define Haplogroups H & V
G11719A - ND4 (Gly > Gly) Mutation used to define Haplogroup pre*HV
A73G - HVR2 Mutation used to define Haplogroup pre*HV
C16223T - HVR1 Between the N and R points
C12705T - ND5 (Ile > Ile) Between the N and R points
G15301A - CytB (Leu > Leu) Between 'L' haplogroups and N point
T10873C - ND4 (Pro > Pro) Between 'L' haplogroups and N point
A10398G - ND4 (Thr > Ala) * Between 'L' haplogroups and N point
T9540C - COX2 (Leu > Leu) Between 'L' haplogroups and N point
A8701G - ATP6 (Thr > Ala) * Between 'L' haplogroups and N point

And this is my tentative list going back further:
G1018A - 12S-rRNA Between Haplogroup L4 and the 'L3 series'
G769A - 12S-rRNA Between Haplogroup L4 and the 'L3 series'

C16278T - HVR1 Between Haplogroup L6 and Haplogroup L4
C13650T - ND5 (Pro > Pro) Between Haplogroup L6 and Haplogroup L4
C7256T - COX1 (Asn>Asn) Between Haplogroup L6 and Haplogroup L4
C3594T - ND1 (Val > Val) Between Haplogroup L6 and Haplogroup L4
T152C - HVR2 Between Haplogroup L6 and Haplogroup L4

G7521A - tRNA Asp Between Haplogroup L2 and Haplogroup L6
A4104G - ND1 (Leu > Leu) Between Haplogroup L2 and Haplogroup L6

T16519C - HVR1 Between Haplogroup L5 and Haplogroup L2
T16311C - HVR1 Between Haplogroup L5 and Haplogroup L2
T16189C - HVR1 Between Haplogroup L5 and Haplogroup L2
C16187T - HVR1 Between Haplogroup L5 and Haplogroup L2
A15301G - CytB (Leu > Leu) (CRS value) Between Haplogroup L5
  and Haplogroup L2
C13506T - ND5 (Tyr > Tyr) Between Haplogroup L5 and Haplogroup L2
A13105G - ND5 (Ile > Val) Between Haplogroup L5 and Haplogroup L2
T10810C - ND4 (Leu > Leu) Between Haplogroup L5 and Haplogroup L2
G10688A - ND4 (Val > Val) Between Haplogroup L5 and Haplogroup L2
C8655T - ATP6 (Ile > Ile) Between Haplogroup L5 and Haplogroup L2
T825A - 12S-rRNA Between Haplogroup L5 and Haplogroup L2
G247A - HVR2 Between Haplogroup L5 and Haplogroup L2

C8468T - ATP8 (Leu > Leu) Between Haplogroup L1 and Haplogroup L5
A7146G - COX1 (Thr > Ala) Between Haplogroup L1 and Haplogroup L5
T2885C - 16S-rRNA Between Haplogroup L1 and Haplogroup L5
G2758A - 16S-rRNA Between Haplogroup L1 and Haplogroup L5

A16230G - HVR1 Present in Haplogroup L0 & the Chimp
G12007A - ND4 (Trp > Trp) Present in Haplogroup L0 & the Chimp)
G11914A - ND4 (Thr > Thr) Present in Haplogroup L0 & the Chimp
G9755A - COX2 (Glu > Glu) Present in Haplogroup L0 & the Chimp
T6185C - COX1 (Phe > Phe) Present in Haplogroup L0 & the Chimp
C4312T - tRNA Ile Present in Haplogroup L0 & the Chimp
C1048T - 12S-rRNA Present in Haplogroup L0 & the Chimp

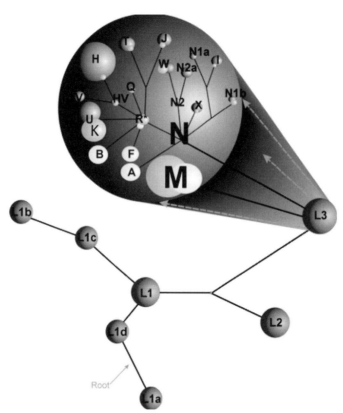

Figure 8.11 Network of mtDNA lineages
Source: Ian Logan, private mail, November 2006.

Chapter 9
Applications of Genetic Genealogy

Documenting genetic inheritance is only one possible application of genetic genealogy. There is much more that can be done with DNA results. In this chapter I will illustrate some of the most common applications.

DNA results can be used to answer simple questions such as, "Are we related?" "Do we have a common ancestor?" "How long ago did our common ancestor live?" DNA results can also be used to solve family puzzles, brick walls or non-paternity events (such as the one raised in Chapter 4).

DNA results can be uploaded to a *Surname Project* that researches individuals that have the same surname or a variant. Joining a Surname Project can be helpful to verify relationships with individuals who share a similar surname. There are over 4,000 surname projects at FTDNA that cover over 61,000 unique surnames.

DNA results can be used in a *Geographic Project* that studies ancestors from a particular country, region, or even a small area in the world. A Geographic Project connects individuals who believe their direct line comes from a specific location. For example, at the FTDNA website you can find geographic projects for British Islands, Scotland, Essex or even Lancaster. Similarly, there are geographic projects for the Benelux[1] as well as for Flanders.[2] These projects group haplotypes by markers tested and by haplogroups.

DNA results can also be contributed to the *Genographic Project* established in April 2005 by the National Geographic Society and IBM to study human migration patterns across the globe.

There are a wide variety of public databases to which DNA results can be uploaded to find matches or study uniqueness. Each of these applications will be discussed in some detail in what follows.

---

1. The Benelux yDNA Geographical Project is for any male's FTDNA test result who shares a family origin in the Benelux region of Europe. Benelux consists of the area presently composed of the countries of Belgium, the Netherlands and Luxembourg, in other words, the lowlands. You can join this Geographic project if you have been tested by FamilyTreeDNA and have solid roots in this region. See http://www.ftdna.com/surname_join.aspx?code=C84735&special=True&projecttype=G

2. http://www.familytreedna.com/public/Flanders/

Are we related? The Deboeck Surname project

The simplest question that can be addressed by DNA testing is: are we related? Comparing the haplotypes of two individuals with the same surname—or slightly different surnames—can resolve the issue of whether these individuals are related. It can also provide information concerning the Most Recent Common Ancestor (MRCA) of two individuals as well as how far back this MRCA may have lived.

This application can be illustrated with a simple test. In Chapter 2 I showed that Guillaume and Victor were brothers, as they are the sons of Everard Deboeck. Guillaume is my grandfather, who died some 21 years before I was born. Robert Deboeck is a grandson of Victor.

In August 2005 on a trip to Belgium I asked Robert to take a DNA test and he accepted. Prior to leaving for Belgium I took my own DNA test, the results of which were discussed in Chapter 8.

The results of the 37-marker Y-DNA tests of Robert and me are compared in Table 9.1. The first column shows the location number; the second column identifies the actual DYS marker; columns three and four show the DNA results of kit #41822, my own, and kit #41823, that of Robert.

How do we derive from this that we are related? By measuring the differences between the allele values of each marker and adding these differences it is possible to determine whether two individuals are related.

The differences between our two kits are shown in the fifth column of Table 9.1. If in a test of 37 markers only one marker out of 37 shows a difference, then one can safely assert that two individuals are related.

FTDNA provides the following table for 37-marker test to assess the chances that two individuals are related:

Zero Differences: Very Closely Related

37/37 Your perfect match means you share a common male ancestor with a person who shares your surname (or variant). Your relatedness is extremely close with the common ancestor predicted, 50% of the time, in 5 generations or less and with a 90% probability within 16 generations. Very few people achieve this close level of a match. All confidence levels are well within the timeframe that surnames were adopted in Western Europe.

One Difference: Closely Related

36/37 You share the same surname (or a variant) with another male and you mismatch by only one "point" at only one marker—a 36/37 match. It's most likely that you matched 24/25 or 25/25 on a previous Y-DNA test and your mismatch will be found within DYS 576, 570, CDYa or CDYb. Very few people achieve this close level of a match. Your mismatch is within the range of the most well established, surname lineages in Western Europe.

Two Differences: Related

35/37 You share the same surname (or a variant) with another male and you mismatch by only two "points" —a 35/37 match. It's most likely that you matched 24/25 or 25/25 on previous Y-DNA tests and your mismatch will be found within DYS 439 or DYS 385 A, 385 B, 389-1 and 389-2, from our first panel of 12 markers, or from within the second panel at DYS 458, 459a, 459b, 449, or within 464a-d. If you matched exactly on previous tests you probably have a mismatch at DYS 576, 570, CDYa or CDYb in our newest panel of markers. Your mismatch is likely within the range of most established surname lineages in Western Europe.

Three Differences: Related

34/37 You share the same surname (or a variant) with another male and you mismatch by three "points" —a 34/37 match. Because of the volatility within some of the markers this is slightly tighter than being 11/12 or 23/25 and it's most likely that you matched 24/25 or 25/25 on previous Y-DNA tests. Your mismatch will most often be found within DYS 439 or DYS 385a, 385b ,389-1 and 389-2 from our first panel of 12 markers, or within the second panel: DYS 458, 459a, 459b, 449, or within 464 a-d. If you matched exactly on previous tests you probably have a mismatch at DYS 576, 570, CDYa or CDYb in our newest panel of markers. Your mismatch is likely within the range of most established surname lineages in Western Europe.

Four Differences: Probably Related

33/37 You share the same surname (or a variant) with another male and you mismatch by four "points" —a 33/37 match. Because of the volatility within some of the markers this is about the same as being 11/12 and it's most likely that you matched 23/25 or 24/25 on previous Y-DNA tests. If you matched exactly on previous tests you probably have a mismatch at DYS 576, 570, CDYa or CDYb in our newest panel of markers. If several or many generations have passed it is likely that these two lines are related through other family members. That would require that each line had passed a mutation and one person would have experienced at least 2 mutations. The only way to confirm this is to test additional family lines and find where the mutations took place. Only by testing additional family members can you find the person in between each of you...without this "in between-er" the possibility of a match exists, but further evidence must be pursued. If you test additional individuals, you will most likely find that DNA results fall in-between the persons who are four apart, demonstrating relatedness within this family cluster.

Five Differences: Only Possibly Related

32/37 You share the same surname (or a variant) with another male and you mismatch by five "points" —a 32/37 match. It is most likely that you did not 12/12 or 24/25 or 25/25 in previous Y-DNA tests. If several or many generations have passed it is possible that these two group members are related through other family members. That would require that each line had experienced separate mutations and one person would have experienced at least two mutations. The only way to confirm or deny is to test additional family lines and find where the mutation took place. Only by testing additional family members can you find the person in between each of you…this "in between-er" becomes essential for you to find, and without him only the possibility of a match exists, further evidence should be pursued. If you test additional individuals, you must find the person whose DNA results falls in-between the persons that are five apart, demonstrating relatedness within this family cluster.

Six Differences: Not Related

31/37 is too far off to be considered related, unless you can find an "in-between-er" for determining "Only Possibly Related," above. It is important to determine what set of results most typifies the largest number of members of the group you are "close" to matching. You may be 31/37 with an individual, but 34/37 with the center of the group, and your potential relatedness to him is through the center of the group.

More than six Differences: Not Related

30/37 You are not related and the odds greatly favor that you have not shared a common male ancestor with this person within thousands of years. You are probably even in different haplogroups on the Phylogenetic tree of *Homo Sapiens*.[3]

Table 9.1 shows that between kit #41822 and kit #41823 there is a difference in allele value only on marker DYS464d; the difference at that marker is 3 "points." This counts as either three mutations in the *stepwise mutation model* or as one mutation in the *infinite allele model* (see box for more details). Hence the comparison of these two DNA kits demonstrates that Robert and I have a common ancestor. We both inherited our Y-chromosome from Everard Deboeck who inherited his from Gillis de Bock, born three hundred years earlier.

More on measuring genetic distances can be found in the box on Stepwise Mutation Model.[4]

---

3. A similar table for assessing differences between two DNA signatures tested for 67 markers can be found at http://www.familytreedna.com/gdrules_67.html

4. And also on the following web sites: http://nitro.biosci.arizona.edu/ftDNA/Distance.html
http://www.familytreedna.com/GDRules_12.html
http://nitro.biosci.arizona.edu/ftdna/models.html

Table 9.1
Comparison of two Y-DNA kits
from the Deboeck Surname Project

Location	DYS#	Allele Values kit #41822	Allele Values kit #41823	Difference In allele values	Count of Mutations*
1	393	13	13	0	0
2	390	24	24	0	0
3	19 *	14	14	0	0
4	391	11	11	0	0
5	**385a**	11	11	0	0
6	**385b**	15	15	0	0
7	426	13	13	0	0
8	388	12	12	0	0
9	439	11	11	0	0
10	**389I**	19	19	0	0
11	392	13	13	0	0
12	**389II**	29	29	0	0
13	458	13	13	0	0
14	**459a**	30	30	0	0
15	**459b**	17	17	0	0
16	455	9	9	0	0
17	454	10	10	0	0
18	447	11	11	0	0
19	437	11	11	0	0
20	448	25	25	0	0
21	449	15	15	0	0
22	**464a**	14	14	0	0
23	**464b**	15	15	0	0
24	**464c**	15	15	0	0
25	**464d**	15	18	3	1

* based on infinite allele mutation model

The Stepwise versus the Infinite Allele Mutation Model

The general accepted mutation model for STRs is the *Stepwise Mutation Model.* Most mutations (85-90%) are a one-step deletion or insertion. In each generation there is a possibility of observing a mutation. The frequency of these mutations is between .002 and .004.

When analyzing multiple markers on the Y chromosome, the frequency of observing one mutation increases with the number of markers tested: for a 12 Y-STR set this will be between .024 and .048, for a 25 Y-STR this will be between .05 and 0.10, and so on.

The difference in allele values on a particular marker is not automatically one mutation. It could be one, two or more depending on the differences between the alleles. If there are zero differences there still can be several mutations depending on the genealogic distance or the number of generations between two individuals. For example, you can have an insertion in one generation and 10 generations later a deletion at the same marker that as a result will give the same allele as before the insertion.

It becomes more complicated when several markers on the Y chromosome have been duplicated during human evolution or from one generation to another. Therefore a mutation can have been duplicated which will result in 2 differences instead of one. DYS389-2 is a region that includes also DYS389-1. If a difference in DYS389-1 can also be observed in DYS389-2, the correct way of counting differences is then more complicated.[5]

In contrast to the stepwise mutation model, the *Infinite Allele Model* assumes that with each mutation each new mutant is different (i.e. there are an infinite number of states that an allele can mutate to, hence each mutation is assumed to be unique.) If each new mutant is different, then we do not have to correct for mutations that we did not see and hence did not score, and we can simply look at the differences between marker loci and count the actual number of mutations that have occurred.

The stepwise model describes more accurately the mutation process for (tandem) repeat markers such as those used on the Y chromosome. Another property of the stepwise mutation model is that not all mutations will lead to a new allele that is the basic assumption of the infinite allele model.

Source: More on the differences between these models can be found at http://nitro.biosci. arizona.edu/ftDNA/Distance.html
http://www.familytreedna.com/GDRules_12.html
http://nitro.biosci.arizona.edu/ftdna/models.html

While the comparison of two DNA signatures of individuals with a common surname provides a simple case of verification of genealogical data, this approach can be extended to any two or more individuals with similar surnames or variant thereof. For example, are Robert and I related to Jean De Boeck of Meise? Are the Deboecks of Sint-Amands related to those of Halle, Steenhuffel, Sint-Martens Bodegem or any others mentioned in Annex 1? In consequence, it is not necessary to find paper records to determine whether individuals with similar surnames are related

---

5. To count the differences at the combo set 389: first subtract each kits 389-1 values from each other; second for each, subtract the 389-1 value from the 389-2 value, then subtract these from each other; and third add the two results together and that provides the difference. Adrian Williams's presentation at 3rd International GG Conference, Houston, 2006

or not. Through DNA testing it is possible to find if descendants from each of the family trees discussed in Annex 1 are related, assuming one or more living descendants from each branch is willing to take a DNA test. Through DNA testing it is possible to find the MRCA and when approximately this MRCA lived.

The Surname Project Deboeck—Soundex Code D120—that I started in November of 2005 on the FTDNA website provides the means to find answers to these questions. Its purpose is to collect Y-chromosome DNA test results from any male descendant with the surname Deboeck or its variants. Way back in 2005 I wrote:

> *The purpose of the DEBOECK/de BOECK/ de BOCK Surname Project is to share knowledge about our family ancestors. Through Y-DNA we attempt to facilitate finding various DEBOECK ancestral lines and how they are related to each other. This project facilitates the ordering of Y-DNA test kits for all those with DEBOECK surname who like to participate. If you are interested in ordering a Y-DNA test kit, fill out the form and click on Join. I recommend you go for the 37-marker test. If you have any questions about ordering or using the test kit, please contact the Group Administrator link before you order the kit.*
>
> Surnames in the project are Bocx, Boecx, de Bock, De bocq, de boec, de Boeck, de boecq, De Bouche, De Bouck, de Boucq, De Boucque, de Buck, Deboeck, Du Bouck, sboeckxs

The project objectives are to establish which of the Deboeck clans have a common ancestor; whether any of them are related, and how long ago our common ancestor has lived. When enough people with the surname Deboeck participate in this project the questions raised earlier will be answered.

If your name is not Deboeck but you would like to find out if there already is a Surname Project that covers your surname visit http://www.familytreedna.com/surname.asp and choose one of the letters under Y-DNA surname. If a project already exists, all you need to do is take a DNA test and join that project to find out if you are related.

At the 2nd International Conference on Genetic Genealogy, held in Washington in November 2005, Terry Barton showed how through DNA analysis he and his partners have been able to identify most Barton families in the USA (151 men in the project); how they have tied US Bartons to Bartons living in England in 1100s; and have identified 14 Barton genetic lineages. Terry Barton has achieved impressive results through four years of pioneering work and DNA research.

Solving the Girardin family puzzles.

In Chapter 4 we ran into a brick wall because the birth certificate of Franciscus-Alexius Girardin did not contain the name of his father. Who was the father of Franciscus-Alexius Girardin?

Public belief, plenty of circumstantial evidence and even distinct patterns in the data supported the assertion that Leopold I, first King of Belgians, was the father of Franciscus-Alexius. The historical background for this assertion is assembled in Appendix 5.

There are no written documents that confirme or contradict this assertion.[6] The absence of any documents, however, is not proof that there was no relationship.

After years of conventional genealogical research I turned to genetic genealogy and DNA testing. The well-known historian H. Claessens, who wrote a book about Leopold's love life, put me in contact with the daughter of Prinz Andreas von Sachsen-Coburg and Gotha, the current head of the Sachsen-Coburg dynasty, who lives with his family in Coburg. It is his daughter who handles all correspondence to the Prinz.

On September 2005 I wrote to Prinz Andreas to inquire about his interest in DNA testing. I explained what he could get out of it in terms of his own family history. Neue Presse in Coburg had just published a remarkable book by Harald Sandner about *Das Haus Sachsen-Coburg und Gotha* (the House of Saxen-Coburg and Gotha) at the occasion of the 175th anniversary of the dynasty. After corresponding with Harald Sandner I wrote to Prinz Andreas, who had been brought up in the States and who has two sons and one daughter about the same age as my children. My letter to him clearly demonstrated the advantages of taking a DNA test in order to learn about deep ancestry of the Sachsen-Coburg family.

My letter was either intercepted, was lost or never reached Prinz Andreas because a response was never received. I found this quite surprising, because even if Prinz Andreas were not interested in providing a DNA test, a simple courtesy reply could have indicated that he would take my suggestion under consideration.

After Henriette Claessens passed away in early 2006, her husband Rick found in her files a contact she knew from her days of doing research on Leopold's life. Her husband provided me this contact information and thanks to him I was able to find a great-grandson of Leopold I. Through a letter and several phone calls, I was able to convince him to take a DNA test. In mid 2006 I obtained the DNA of a great-grandson of Leopold. Prior to this

---

6. All attempts that were made to find any evidence that Augustine Girardin may have worked at the Royal Palace in Brussels, as was claimed in newspaper articles published in 1996, yielded no results. The Archivist of the Royal Palace has refused to provide information in response to several letters and numerous e-mail inquiries. Even after meeting with him in person, access to the relevant employee records of the Royal Palace has been denied, although the Royal archives are a public source of information concerning the Royal family in Belgium.

Table 9.2
Comparison of two Y-DNA kits for solving a family puzzle

		Y-DNA 37 markers			
		Value	Value	Diff.	Count
		kit 41828	kit 41824		
Location	DYS#				
1	393	13	13	0	
2	390	24	24	0	
3	19 *	14	14	0	
4	391	11	11	0	
5	**385a**	11	11	0	
6	**385b**	14	14	0	
7	426	12	12	0	
8	388	12	12	0	
9	439	11	11	0	
10	**389I**	12	13	1	
11	392	13	13	0	
12	**389II**	28	29	1	1
13	458	17	18	1	1
14	**459a**	9	9	0	
15	**459b**	9	9	0	
16	455	11	11	0	
17	454	11	11	0	
18	447	25	25	0	
19	437	14	15	1	1
20	448	19	19	0	
21	449	30	29	1	1
22	**464a**	15	15	0	
23	**464b**	16	16	0	
24	**464c**	17	16	1	
25	**464d**	17	16	1	
26	460	11	10	1	1
27	GATA H4	11	11	0	
28	**YCAIIa**	21	19	2	1
29	**YCAIIb**	23	23	0	
30	456	15	18	3	1
31	607	15	14	1	1
32	576	18	18	0	
33	570	16	17	1	1
34	**CDYa**	36	35	1	
35	**CDYb**	37	38	1	1
36	442	13	12	1	1
37	438	12	12	0	

in the summer of 2005 I collected in Belgium, the DNA of a great-great-grandson of Franciscus-Alexius Girardin. Both DNA swabs were analyzed in the same lab at the University of Arizona.

Table 9.2 shows the results of these two DNA tests under the kit labels #41828 and #41824. The hypothesis that I am interested to test is: was Leopold I the father of Franciscus-Alexius Girardin?

The DNA test results shown in Table 9.2 are quite different from each other. In addition to DYS464, there are 4 other markers among the first 25 that show a difference and the number of transmissions does not give a sufficient answer to simply accept or reject our hypothesis.[7]

Based on an analysis of *the first 25 markers* it appears that the individuals tested here do not have a common ancestor. On the basis of only 25 markers there nevertheless remains uncertainty. As a result I requested analysis of 12 more markers. The results of the upgraded test, can also be found in Table 9.2.

Prof. R. DeCorte of the KUL was consulted to interpret these results. He wrote: "As expected when you extend the number of markers additional differences were found. In this case seven more differences were found. Notice that based on 37 markers there are at least 12 differences which means that at least 12 mutations have occurred in the past if these two individuals are paternally related. It could be even more according to the stepwise mutation model but we do not have evidence for it: the other markers are identical. Because of these 12 mutations, it is excluded that the individuals that have been tested have a common paternal relationship in the past 200 years."[8] He added the following: "It could be that in the following generations there is another 'father' involved that will lead to a difference in Y chromosome. This is similar to the study published several years ago concerning the illegitimate sons of Thomas Jefferson. You have to test several lineages in order to find out if the Y chromosome information collected are representative for each lineage".

---

7. Prof. De Corte wrote: The way the results are presented for DYS464 (a, b, c and d) are confusing. In fact, this marker shows 4 copies on the Y chromosome and they are simultaneously analyzed by the same test. However, it is not possible to assign the number of repeats to each marker as it is represented in these results. International nomenclature for this marker is as follows: the identified alleles are represented by a genotype (combination of different alleles) and they are ranked in ascending order; the results should be read as 15-16-17 for kit #41828 and 15-16 for kit #41824. Based on this it is impossible to say which DYS464 marker shows a difference: at least two of them show 15, 16 or 17, and you cannot tell which one; DYS464a, DYS464b, DYS464c or DYS464d. It has been reported that the mutation rate is 10 times higher than for the other tested markers on the Y chromosome: therefore, you have a higher chance of observing mismatches at DYS464.

8. Private mail of October 18th, 2006

Only two individuals were tested. Based on the results received it appears that they did not have a common ancestor in the past 200 years.[8] However *it is not possible to claim that the DNA samples were representative; that the samples were correctly analyzed or that no errors occurred in the process.*

"Determination of the exact value of the alleles is straightforward with current technology, but one cannot exclude poor sampling (e.g., a contaminated swab), errors made in the lab, or human error in transcription of the results", according to Prof. DeCorte.

In sum, to properly test the hypothesis under investigation one would need to test several more lineages to confirm that the preliminary findings are correct, meaning that Leopold I was not the father of Franciscus-Alexius, in other words my hypothesis should be rejected.

Confirmation of this finding would mean that public beliefs about Franciscus-Alexius have been wrong; that all the circumstantial evidence and other patterns in the data, as outlined in Annex 5, are incorrect.

If, however, follow up tests were to show that these preliminary findings were caused by contaminated swabs, incorrect analyses, or other potential errors, then the hypothesis would stand and popular beliefs would be confirmed.

The value of the result so far is therefore mainly to demonstrate an approach that can be followed for more thorough investigations of this or other hypotheses using DNA testing.

The above case illustrates that genetic genealogy does not always confirm beliefs, circumstantial evidence or other patterns in the data. Both conventional genealogy and DNA testing complement each other in producing more complete genealogical findings.

What does this suggest for future research? To confirm the findings from these two DNA tests, it would be essential to obtain other swabs, specifically to assure that the swab obtained from a great grandson of Leopold I, really represents the DNA of Leopold. This could be done by obtaining the DNA of several other male descendants—including possibly the sons of the current head of the Sachsen-Coburg family. To assure that the only swab obtained from a great great-grandson of Franciscus-Alexius truly represents the DNA of Franciscus-Alexius other DNA swabs should be collected e.g., from the two living great-grandsons of Franciscus-Alexius. Only through testing of multiple lineages will it be possible over time to confirm (or contradict) the findings presented in this section.

Public Databases of DNA

The increase in popularity of DNA testing has promoted the establishment of online public databases that allow comparison with thousands of records uploaded to these databases. These databases, which are sponsored by major DNA testing companies, are accessible, mostly for free to everyone. The most popular databases are:[9]

1.   **Y-SEARCH.org:** This database, provided by Family Tree DNA, accepts Y-STR results from all other testing laboratories for comparison with its database.[10] To access this database, a user must create a free account by submitting his Y-STR results and providing information on his most distant known ancestor along the male line. The user can select the number of markers and mismatches to search.

2.   **Y-BASE.org:** This database, sponsored by DNA Heritage, provides a way of comparing haplotypes. There is a search engine based on both haplotype and surname that provides the contact information of contributors. The site also provides a "haplomatic" for predicting the haplogroups from a STR profile, along with statistics on the allele values and haplogroups composition of the database.

3.   **MITOSEARCH.org:** This database, provided by Family Tree DNA, provides for matching of mtDNA results. Use of the database requires the creation of a free account through the submission of mtDNA results. Searches can be performed on the basis of mtDNA SNP results or on haplogroups.[11]

4.   **SMGF.org:** This database, sponsored by the Sorenson Molecular Genealogy Foundation, correlates genetic and genealogical information. The site provides a drop-down menu where you can enter a haplotype for easy comparison with the database. Closely related haplotypes are returned with a table indicating the status of the match for each marker, but without giving the actual value of any of the markers. The table is linked to the pedigrees of each matching haplotype and to an estimate of the most recent common ancestor for each match. To add a haplotype to the SMGF database you have to request a free test kit and return the sample to the Sorenson laboratory. No personal results are returned. All results are added to the publicly accessible database but personal information on haplotype composition and vital statistics are not provided with the match information. Sorenson actively recruits

---

9. Based on C. Fitzpatrick and A. Yeiser, DNA and Genealogy, p. 81-86

10. It also accepts family trees in GEDCOM format, a standard file format for transfer of family pedigrees from one computer to another.

11. FTDNA recommends that customers with full mtDNA sequence compare their results to other records using the BLAST search engine on NCBI (National Center for Biotechnology Information) website. http://www.ncbi.nlm.nih.gov/BLAST/. The site also accepts family trees in GEDCOM format.

individuals with extensive genealogies, family surname groups, and members of specific populations.

In addition to the public databases provided above, there are some public databases that serve more special interests. There is the YHRD.org, a database, created by the Forensic Y-User Group, called the Y Chromosome Haplotype Reference Database, a successor to the www.ystr.org database. The website provides haplotype frequency estimates for both forensic and genealogical use, and also for wider studies of population composition. The site only accepts submissions from laboratories that pass a quality control. A list of contributing laboratories with contact information is provided on the site.

There is also CSTL.NIST.GOV. Created by John M. Butler and Dennis L. Reeder of the National Institute of Standards and Technology (NIST) this database contains a repository of information related to the use of STRs in human identity testing. The site covers many more markers than those in the core and extended STR sets. It has an excellent library of information on STRs more suited to the experienced researcher, including the information on the properties of the markers and the population data.[12]

To illustrate the application of the public databases mentioned above I uploaded my Y-DNA results to Y-Search and Y-base and my mtDNA to the Mitosearch database. I also searched the Sorenson database for matches with my Y-DNA. Note that all these records are uploaded based on a user ID and password and that in these database records are identified by a user ID number, not by the name of the person who submitted the DNA.

Y-Search Database Results

After uploading my Y-DNA to the Y-Search database I was able to search for all records that tested for at least 25 markers, that belonged to the R1b haplogroups, and that were less than three distances from my Y-DNA (to fall within the realm of relatedness). The result of this search showed that (so far) only two records out of 891 that are R1b in this database, matched with my Y-DNA. The results are shown in Table 9.3. Note that there are differences on DYS#385b DYS#426 and the combo DYS#464.

If the search criteria are relaxed and we look for any matches of records that contain at least eight markers, belong to the R1b group and have 3 or less mismatches then the number of records increases dramatically but also reveals that there are few records in the Y-search database that so far contain more than 12 markers.

---

12. MitoAnalyzer. National Institute of Standards and Technology, Gaithersburg, MD, USA.
http://www.cstl.nist.gov/biotech/strbase/mitoanalyzer.html

Table 9.3
Y Search Results

No	DYS#	user ID / Last Name / Origin: UBXAG / Warner / S. Carolina	XBXER / Chandler / n/a	38JPN / Deboeck / Belgium
1	393	13	13	13
2	390	24	24	24
3	19	14	14	14
4	391	11	11	11
5	385a	11	11	11
6	385b	**15**	**14**	**15**
7	426	**13**	**12**	**13**
8	388	12	12	12
9	439	**12**	**11**	**11**
10	389-1	13	13	13
11	392	13	13	13
12	389-2	30	30	30
13	458	17	17	17
14	459a	9	9	9
15	459b	10	10	10
16	455	11	11	11
17	454	11	11	11
18	447	25	25	25
19	437	15	15	15
20	448	19	19	19
21	449	29	29	29
22	464a	**14**	**15**	**14**
23	464b	15	15	15
24	464c	**15**	**17**	**15**
25	464d	18	18	18

Y-Base Database Results

The Y-Base database contains some 9,200 haplotypes and 9,150 unique surnames. Sixty-eight percent of the records belong to the R1b haplogroups. After uploading my Y-DNA I found no matches both on surname basis as well as on the basis of my haplotype. The most common haplotypes in this database for a few haplotypes are shown in Table 9.4. Another interesting feature is the frequency distributions that are provided for each marker. (see http://www.ybase.org/statistics.asp#haplocommon)

Table 9.4 Common Haplotyes within predicted haplogroup entries within Ybase.

Marker/Haplogroup	E3b	I	R1a	R1b
DYS 19	13	15	15	14
DYS 385a	16	14	11	11
DYS 385b	17	15	14	14
DYS 388	12	14	12	12
DYS 389i	13	13	13	13
DYS 389ii	30	29	30	29
DYS 390	24	23	25	24
DYS 391	10	10	10	11
DYS 392	11	11	11	13
DYS 393	13	14	13	13
DYS 425		12	12	12
DYS 426	11	11	12	12
DYS 437	14	16	14	15
DYS 438		10	11	12
DYS 439	12	11	10	12
DYS 447	25	24	24	25
DYS 448	20	20	20	19
DYS 449	31	28	32	29
DYS 454	11	11	11	11
DYS 455	11	9	11	11
DYS 458	16	15	15	17
DYS 459a	9	8	9	9
DYS 459b	9	9	10	10
DYS 460		10	12	11
DYS 461		12	11	12
DYS 462		12	11	11
DYS 464a	14	12	13	15
DYS 464b	16	14	14	15
DYS 464c	16	15	15	17
DYS 464d	17	15	16	17
YCAII a		20	19	19
YCAII b		21	23	23
GATA A10		13	13	13
GATA C4/DYS635		22	23	23
TAGA H4		11	13	12
GGAAT1B07		11	9	10

Mitosearch Database Results

Another public database provided by FTDNA contains mtDNA records. This database can be searched for matches of mtDNA. After uploading my mtDNA to this database I found 1063 records matched my HVR-1 where the only difference with CRS was a C in position 16519 (see Table 8.5).

When searching all records that have both HVR-1 and HVR-2 tested, I found 96 records that matched my HVR-1 and HVR-2 results. Among these there were only 11 that had been classified as H*. None of these eleven records had however 131C which was discussed in Chapter 8. When the same procedure was followed for the mtDNA shown in table 8.6 I found 50 records that matched; among these 50 there were 19 that had been classified in the H6 haplogroup.

The Genographic Project

An unprecedented effort to map humanity's genetic journey through the ages was launched in April 2005 by National Geographic Society, IBM, the Waitt Family Foundation and geneticist Spencer Wells.

The objectives of the Genographic Project are to collect and analyze DNA samples from over 100,000 indigenous and traditional people around the globe. This is the world's largest study of its kind in the field of anthropological genetics. Most of what is known about anthropological genetics is based on DNA samples donated by approximately 10,000 indigenous and traditional people from around the world. While this has given a broad view of the patterns of human migration, it represents but a small sample of humanity's genetic diversity.

Over the next five years the Genographic Project will map world migratory patterns dating back 150,000 years and will fill in the huge gaps in our knowledge of humankind's migratory history. This data will eventually comprise the largest database of its kind.

In his recently released book, *Deep Ancestry,* Spencer Wells wrote: "The Genographic Project is a purely anthropological, non-medical, nonpolitical, nonprofit international research project involving scientists from both the developed and developing world. Our goal is to enable indigenous communities rather than to take from them".

The Genographic Project has established ten research laboratories around the globe. Scientists are visiting Earth's remote regions in an effort to complete the planet's genetic atlas.

While this effort of collecting DNA samples from indigenous people is ongoing, anyone can participate in this project. You can take part in the project by purchasing a Genographic Project Public Participation Kit (for only $100) and submit your cheek swab sample. Personal DNA results are stored anonymously to protect the privacy of participants.

National Geographic will regularly update the public and the scientific community on project findings, through the website and through National Geographic's many other media platforms worldwide.

If you already have taken a DNA test with one of the DNA testing companies, you can request your testing company to make the results available to the Genographic Project or use the facilities provided on the web to join the project.

Why is it important to participate in this project? By participating in the Genographic Project, we all can be part of a real-time research effort, have an opportunity to learn more about our deep ancestry as well as learn about the migratory journey that our ancestors followed. By participating in this project we contribute financially to the project since the net proceeds from the sales of the Genographic Project Public Participation Kits will support the field research, the education programs and the preservation efforts of indigenous and traditional cultures.

**For more information on
The Genegraphic Project visit**

https://www3.nationalgeographic.com/genographic/index.html

To participate in the Genegraphic Project visit

https://www3.nationalgeographic.com/genographic/participate.html

Risks and rewards of DNA testing

Given the illustrations provided above the rewards from DNA testing are obvious to any genealogist. They can either confirm or refute an hypothesis that two people are related through a common ancestor. The value in this can be immense given the amount of time and expense that most genealogical enthusiasts spend on time-consuming research based on documents.

While the rewards can be great, the risks can be daunting as well. In practically every genealogical project an example of a "surprise negative" can become visible. These unexpected events arise when two known relatives show up as not matching, sometimes even to the point of being in different haplogroups or with no likelihood of a common ancestor for thousands of years back in time.

Charles F. Kerchner[13] suggested that some reasons for these sometimes embarrassing surprises are":

1.   Prior research error. The prior historical genealogical research of earlier family members, county histories, or lineage societies, etc., is simply wrong.

2.   Unannounced and hidden adoptions. Many times in the past a calamity has take place: a neighboring youth would be raised by the family; a couple was childless and someone arranged an "adoption" but no one was told about it nor was it written down. A child may have been given the surname of the adoptive family as he/she was raised as one of his own.

3.   False paternity event or non-paternity event. The biological father was different from the historically known father and/or

---

13. Charles F Kerchner Jr: "Genetics & Genealogy: An introduction with some DNA Case Study Examples," http://www.kerchner.com/anonftp/pub/introg&g.htm

the legally recorded father and no one until now knew (or if they knew they were not talking about it).

4. Family name change. An ancestor decided to change their name and adopt the surname of another family in their original area of residence and then moved away. This could have been done because they didn't like their real surname or maybe because they liked the other surname and decided to use that name to start a new life. This is sometimes seen in history with people adopting the names of famous or rich deceased people and then pretending to be a descendant and heir to that family line.

Population geneticists estimate that the incidence of some of these situations over the generations is estimated to average between 2-5% per generation.[14]

In spite of these risks, there is great value in adopting genetic genealogy as an extension of conventional genealogy. In my opinion the first priority in the use of genetic genealogy is to document the genetic inheritance that is handed over from generation to generation and from us to our children. Next priority is to solve issues that may have emerged from conventional genealogy. Then there is also the question as to whom else are we related. And finally, genetic genealogy can be used to contribute to a variety of projects that are focused on a surname, a geographic area, or the study of world migrations.

---

14. When results come back and a surprise negative is found, it can be a very delicate situation for a family to deal with. If a re-construction project is underway within the family, after a re-test of the individual(s) is completed to double confirm the surprise negative, this is the time for the "Family Coordinator" to sit down and have a polite but open, frank discussion with the person who is surprised by the results and talk about how they would like these facts treated. Every situation is different and different people will react to such information in very different ways. Therefore, great care must be taken in presenting such information when doing a family re-construction project.

Chapter 10
Flanders-Flemish DNA Project

The last chapter of this book focuses on one geographic project, the Flanders-Flemish DNA project. After attending the 2nd International Conference on Genetic Genealogy I created the Flanders-Flemish DNA project (hereafter abbreviated as FF-DNA or Flemish DNA). This project, currently located on the Family Tree DNA website, establishes *a single place on the web where DNA can be uploaded of people who were born in Flanders or belief to have Flemish roots.* The objectives, participation, preliminary results and future directions of this project are discussed in this chapter.

Objectives of Flanders-Flemish DNA Project

Surname Projects focus on a surname and/or its variants. Different areas of the world have, however, adopted surnames at different periods in time. They were coming into regular use first by the nobility, then by the gentry, by the time of the Middle Ages. After the fall of the Roman Empire, Ireland was one of the first countries to adopt hereditary surnames, and Irish surnames are found as early as the tenth century.

Surnames are generally derived from one of four sources (as discussed in Chapter 1). More than half the English surnames in use today derive from geographic descriptions. Various suffixes are common to indicate a topographical feature. As a result, people with different surnames may have a common ancestor because their ancestor lived in the same village. Therefore geographical based projects that focus on DNA from people from the same area can contribute to genealogical research.

The *Flanders-Flemish DNA project* was established in 2005 to bring together on the web the DNA from people who believe they have Flemish roots. This project is not limited to those living or who were born in Flanders. It aims to collect DNA from all those who have Flemish ancestors no matter where you live, or were born.

In sum, this project can help Flemish-Americans and -Canadians who want to find out about their ancestors in Flanders. This Flanders-Flemish DNA project can also be of interest to descendants of Flemish ancestors living anywhere in the world.

This project accepts the DNA of people who are first, second, or third generation descendants of ancestors born in Flanders. Anyone who thinks they have Flemish roots can join and find out if they actually do have Flemish roots.

This project brings together both Y-DNA (male) and mtDNA (female), as well as genealogical information of Flemish people. It gathers the DNA of most typical surnames; DNA of the most common haplogroups; and studies the deep ancestry of Flemish people.

Participation in this project is free. If you already had your DNA tested you can go to your personal page on Family Tree DNA and click on the "Join" button and select the Flanders-Flemish DNA project listed under the Dual DNA projects list. If you had your DNA tested with another company you can request that your result be converted and uploaded to this project.

To participate in the Flanders-Flemish DNA project visit http://www.familytreedna.com/public/Flanders/.

When you click on Join this Project, you are provided an option to order a test if you do not yet have your DNA tested.

Results can be viewed by clicking on the tab Y-DNA or mtDNA.

If you live in Europe you may be interested in the following:

As of November 2006 Family Tree DNA started distributing its kits in Europe, through an arrangement with iGenea in Switzerland. The kits can be ordered and paid in local European currencies from http://europe.familytreedna.com and the web site, including the results pages can be seen in the following languages: English, French, German, Italian and Spanish. The Swiss office of FTDNA also provides customer services for European customers.

If you have any questions, contact the Flanders-Flemish Project Group Administrator email: guido@dokus.com

Current Participation

Since November 2005 the project has accumulated 45 Y-DNA and 15 mtDNA records. Among the Y-DNA records there are 24 (53%) that were uploaded with 12 markers, 9 (20%) with 25 markers, 8 (18%) with 37 markers, and 4 (9%) with 67 markers.

The complete Y-DNA data collected as of March 2007 can be found on the above website. After downloading the data in a spreadsheet the records were grouped by the number of markers tested. An abbreviated version showing only 12 markers is shown in Table 10.1.

Likewise, the complete mtDNA collected via the Flanders-Flemish DNA project can also be found in the above website. An abbreviated version is shown in Table 10.2. It is interesting to observe that six out of 15 records show H haplogroup, two records each are J, K haplogroup, and there are single records of L1c2, T1, U5a1a, V and X haplogroups.

Table 10.1 Y-DNA data in Flanders-Flemish DNA Project as of March 15, 2007

Haplo	Kit Num	393	390	19	391	385a	385b	426	388	439	389-1	392	389-2	458	459a	459b	455	454	447	437	448	449	464a	464b	464c	464d
R1b1c	N30664	14	23	14	11	11	14	12	12	12	13	13	29													
R1b1	N30325	12	24	14	10	10	14	12	12	12	14	13	30													
R1b1	N34019	13	23	14	11	11	14	12	12	13	13	13	29													
R1b1	N5667	13	23	14	11	11	14	12	12	12	13	13	30													
R1b1	82492	13	23	15	11	11	14	12	12	12	13	13	29													
R1b1	N15184	13	24	13	10	12	14	12	12	12	13	13	30													
R1b1	75763	13	24	14	10	12	16	12	12	12	12	13	28													
R1b1	N42945	13	24	14	11	11	11	12	12	12	13	13	29													
R1b1	N35655	13	24	14	11	12	15	12	12	13	14	13	30													
R1b	74557	13	24	14	11	11	14	12	12	12	13	13	29													
R1b	N44862	13	24	14	11	11	14	12	12	12	13	13	29													
R1b	N41200	13	25	14	11	11	14	12	12	11	14	14	30													
R1a	N33536	13	25	15	10	11	14	12	12	11	13	11	29													
R1a	N31586	13	25	17	9	12	15	12	12	10	13	11	30													
R1a	N29118	14	25	15	10	11	14	12	12	10	13	11	30													
I1b	N36752	13	23	15	11	12	15	11	16	12	14	11	30													
I1a	N40315	13	23	14	10	14	14	11	14	11	12	11	28													
	N31282	13	22	14	10	13	14	11	14	12	12	11	28													
	N45319	13	22	14	10	13	14	11	14	11	12	11	28													
	N32140	14	22	14	11	13	13	11	14	11	12	12	28													
	N37055	14	23	15	10	14	16	11	13	11	14	12	32													
E3b	N41597	13	24	13	10	16	18	11	12	13	13	11	30													
-	N37115	13	24	14	11	11	15	12	12	12	12	13	31													
-	N14597	13	24	15	11	11	14	12	10	12	13	13	29													
R1b1c	57099	12	26	14	11	11	14	12	12	12	14	13	30	17	9	10	11	11	25	14	20	30	15	15	15	15
R1b1	18055	13	23	15	10	11	15	12	12	13	13	13	29	17	9	10	11	11	25	15	20	30	14	15	16	17
R1b1	66666	13	24	14	11	11	14	12	12	12	12	14	28	16	9	10	11	11	25	15	19	32	15	16	17	18
R1b1	41823	13	24	14	11	11	15	13	12	12	13	13	30	17	9	10	11	11	25	15	19	29	15	15	15	15
R1b1	10821	13	24	15	10	11	15	12	12	13	13	13	29	15	9	10	11	11	25	15	20	30	14	15	16	17
R1b1	15522	13	24	15	11	11	15	12	12	14	13	14	29	17	9	10	11	11	26	15	20	30	14	15	16	18
	41827	13	23	17	10	15	16	11	11	10	13	12	28	16	8	9	8	11	23	14	20	28	13	15	16	17
-	N42224	13	22	15	10	13	14	11	14	11	13	11	29	14	8	9	9	11	22	16	20	26	12	14	15	15
E3b	54961	13	24	13	11	11	16	11	12	12	13	13	30	15	9	9	12	11	26	14	20	32	14	15	15	17
R1b1	64602	13	23	14	11	11	15	12	12	12	13	13	29	17	9	9	11	11	25	14	19	30	15	16	17	17
R1b1	41828	13	24	14	11	11	14	12	12	11	12	13	28	17	9	9	11	11	25	14	19	30	15	16	17	17
R1b1	41824	13	24	14	11	11	14	12	12	11	13	13	29	18	9	9	11	11	25	15	19	29	15	16	16	16
R1b1	66665	13	24	14	10	11	14	12	12	12	13	14	28	15	9	10	11	11	26	15	19	32	15	16	17	18
R1b1	11279	13	24	15	11	11	15	12	12	13	13	13	29	17	9	10	11	11	26	15	20	30	14	15	16	17
I1c	47348	13	23	17	10	15	16	11	13	10	13	12	29	15	8	8	8	11	23	15	20	28	11	13	13	15
I1a	N6262	13	22	14	10	13	14	11	14	11	13	11	28	16	8	9	8	11	23	14	20	28	12	12	14	15
G	N9779	13	22	15	10	14	14	11	13	12	12	11	29	16	9	9	9	11	23	16	21	30	12	13	13	14
R1b1c	41822	13	24	14	11	11	15	13	12	11	13	13	30	17	9	10	11	11	25	15	19	29	14	15	15	18
I1a	66527	13	22	14	10	13	14	11	14	11	11	11	28	16	8	9	8	12	23	16	20	31	12	14	13	16
G	31992	15	22	15	10	14	14	11	13	11	12	11	29	16	9	9	9	11	23	16	21	32	12	13	13	14
G2	N32937	15	22	15	10	14	15	11	12	11	12	11	29	17	9	9	11	11	22	16	21	28	12	13	13	14

Table 10.2
Modal of Flanders-Flemish DNA
N= 45 Records
(as of March 2007

No	DYS#	Allele Value	No	DYS#	Allele Value
1	393	13	39	578	8
2	390	24	40	395S1a	15
3	19	14	41	395S1b	16
4	391	11	42	590	8
5	385a	11	43	537	11
6	385b	14	44	641	10
7	426	12	45	472	8
8	388	12	46	406S1	12
9	439	12	47	511	9
10	389-1	13	48	425	14
11	392	13	49	413a	23
12	389-2	29	50	413b	23
13	458	17	51	557	15
14	459a	9	52	594	10
15	459b	9	53	436	12
16	455	11	54	490	12
17	454	11	55	534	17
18	447	25	56	450	8
19	437	15	57	444	13
20	448	20	58	481	22
21	449	30	59	520	22
22	464a	14	60	446	18
23	464b	15	61	617	13
24	464c	15	62	568	11
25	464d	17	63	487	13
26	460	10	64	572	11
27	GATA H4	11	65	640	11
28	YCA II a	19	66	492	12
29	YCA II b	23	67	565	12
30	456	16			
31	607	15			
32	576	17			
33	570	17			
34	CDY a	35			
35	CDY b	37			
36	442	12			
37	438	12			
38	531	11			

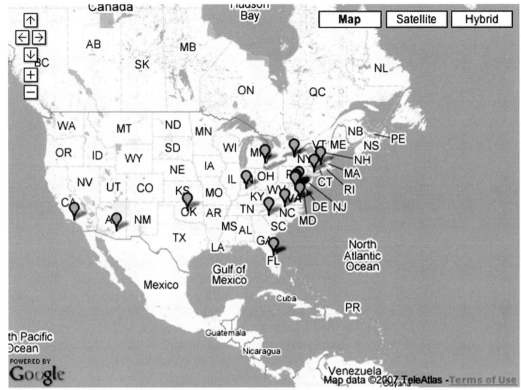
Figure 10.1 Members of the Flanders-Flemish DNA project

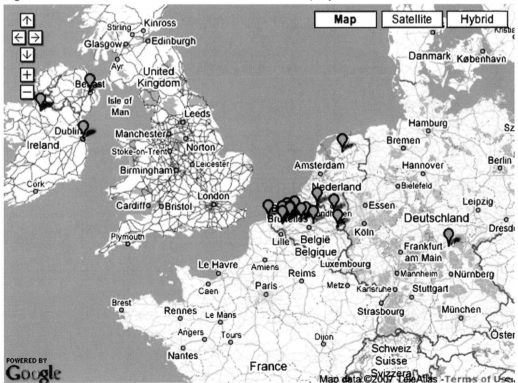
Figure 10.2 Location of the Y-DNA most common ancestor

The map in Figure 10.1 shows the location of current members of the Flanders-Flemish DNA project. It is interesting to note that the majority of the current participants in this project are people who live in the USA who have traced their ancestors to Flanders. Figure 10.2 provides the location of the Y-DNA most common ancestor from those who have uploaded Y-DNA results. The location of the Y-DNA contributed to this project is from all over Belgium. You will also notice that some locations are in Ireland, Netherlands or Germany. Figure 10.3 provides the location of the most common ancestor of those who have uploaded mtDNA to the project. The most common ancestors of the mtDNA results that have been contributed are from a few specific places in Belgium.

Figure 10.3 Location of the mtDNA most common ancestor

Some Preliminary Results

A comparison of Y-DNA records collected via the Flanders-Flemish DNA project can be made through web-based utilities. Some preliminary results are provided in this section.

The first result obtained by entering all 45 Y-DNA records in the Y-DNA Comparison Utility[1] is the modal of all DNA records of this project. The modal provides the most common allele values for each DYS-marker. Table 10.3 shows the modal values for 67+ markers based on 45 DNA records collected through the FF-DNA project as of March 2007.

See http://www.mymcgee.com/tools/yutility.html?mode=ftdna_mode

Table 10.3

Modal values for 12 markers Y-DNA

Flanders Project vs Leuven sample

(as off March 2007)

No	DYS#	Flanders DNA N=45 Allele Value	Leuven DNA N=112 Allele Value
1	393	13	13
2	390	24	24
3	19	14	14
4	391	11	10
5	385a	11	11
6	385b	14	14
7	426	12	
8	388	12	
9	439	12	
10	389-1	13	13
11	392	13	13
12	389-2	29	29
13	458	17	
14	459a	9	
15	459b	9	
16	455	11	
17	454	11	
18	447	25	
19	437	15	15
20	448	20	
21	449	30	
22	464a	14	
23	464b	15	
24	464c	15	
25	464d	17	
26	460	10	
27	GATA H4	11	
28	YCA II a	19	
29	YCA II b	23	
30	456	16	
31	607	15	
32	576	17	
33	570	17	
34	CDY a	35	
35	CDY b	37	
36	442	12	
37	438	12	12

Note that for the first 12 markers, this modal is based on all 45 records; however for the other makers, the modal is based on a much smaller subset since few DNA records uploaded were tested for 25, 37 or 67 markers.

Some 54% of the Flanders Flemish DNA records have R1b1 as predicted or confirmed haplogroups. The distribution of haplogroups among the collected data is shown in Figure 10.4

Distribution of Haplogroups Flemish DNA Project

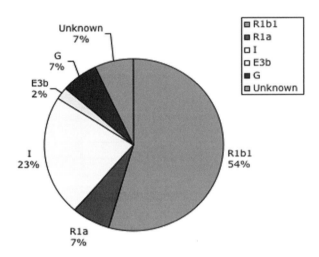

Figure 10.4 Distribution of Haplogroups in F-F DNA project

The F-F DNA modal is not that different from the modal of the R1b1 haplogroup. Among the first 25 markers, we observed the following differences between the modal of Flemish DNA and the modal of R1b1:

- modal value of DYS#459b is 9 in F-F DNA project instead of 10 in R1b1 modal
- modal value of DYS#448 is 20 in F-F DNA project instead of 19 in R1b1 modal
- modal value of DYS#449 is 30 in F-F DNA project instead of 29 in R1b1 modal
- modal value of DYS#464a is 14 in F-F DNA project instead of 15 in R1b1 modal
- modal value of DYS#464c is 15 in F-F DNA project instead of 17 in R1b1 modal

Since most of the participants in the project are people living in the USA who traced their roots to Flanders, another question can be raised as to how representative these modal values are for people who are from Flanders.

Through the support of Professor DeCorte of the KUL I obtained 113 DNA records extracted from blood samples from people mostly from Leuven in Belgium. The modal of 12 markers of these 113 Y-DNA samples corresponds exactly with the

Table 10.4 Frequencies of allele values in Flemish DNA records obtained by merging Flanders-Flemish and Leuven DNA Sample

DYS# >>>	393	390	19	391	385a	385b	426	388	439	389-1	392	389-2	458	459a	459b	455	454	447	437	448	449	464a	464b	464c	464d
Allele Values																									
8				1%										24%		14%									
9				4%	1%				1%					76%	57%	5%									
10	1%			48%	4%			2%	8%						43%										
11				46%	53%	1%	36%		32%	1%	36%					76%	95%					5%			
12	9%			1%	8%	1%	60%	69%	47%	26%	5%					5%	5%					29%	5%		
13	80%		7%		18%	3%	4%	11%	11%	59%	54%					5%						5%	19%	14%	
14	8%		65%		9%	59%		16%	1%	15%	4%		5%						32%			33%	10%	5%	14%
15	3%		22%		3%	20%					1%		14%						52%			29%	52%	33%	24%
16			3%		3%	9%		2%					29%						16%				14%	29%	10%
17			4%		2%	3%							48%											19%	38%
18						2%							5%												14%
19						1%														33%					
20						1%														52%					
21						1%														14%					
22		16%																10%							
23		23%																24%							
24		47%																							
25		12%										1%						48%			5%				
26		1%																19%							
27												1%													
28												19%									19%				
29												51%									14%				
30												20%									38%				
31												4%									5%				
32												4%									19%				
33																									

modal values obtained through the 45 records collected on the web. There was only one exception: DYS 391's modal value is a 10 in the FF-DNA project but 11 in the Leuven sample. Table 10.4 shows these results.

After a modal has been defined it is possible to compute the frequencies of different allele values for each marker. Table 10.5 shows the frequencies of different allele values for 37 markers based on 158 Y-DNA records that were obtained by merging the Flanders-Flemish data set with the Leuven sample. Note that for 12 markers this data is based on 158 records while for the other markers it is based on the FF-DNA data only.

For example, the most common allele values for DYS 393 is 13, for DYS 390 is 14, for DYS 19 is 10 or 11, for DYS 385a it is 11 and for DYS 385b it is 14.

The Y-DNA Comparison Utility that was mentioned above also provides the genetic distances between records in a database. The full genetic distance table for the current data collected through Flemish DNA project produces a 45x45 table in which there are only a few records that show close matches. This kind of analysis will become more meaningful when much larger data sets are assembled.

Future Directions

Where do we go from here? The first priority of the Flanders-Flemish DNA project remains providing a location on the web where Flemish DNA can be uploaded and compared.

The addition of more Flemish DNA records will in the future allow us to enhance the analyses provided above. For this more active promotion of the website and more active participation of people from Flanders and Flemish around the world would be desirable. When a larger data set becomes available, attempts can be made to follow the example of the British and German geographic projects, which already classify records by county or province.

Over time more data should also allow to identify the subclades that are most typical for Flemish DNA. Finally, it should become possible to more clearly distinguish Flemish DNA in the main haplogroup R1b1.

In the future additional web pages will show more refined analyses along the lines provided above. These web pages will be linked to main page at http://www.familytreeDNA.com/pulbic /Flanders.

If you do not have Flemish roots but are interested in joining another geographic project go to http://www.familytreedna.com/surname.asp

Select under either Y-DNA, mtDNA or dual geographic projects the country or area of the world you are from.

Epilogue:
A Fantastic Voyage

Any genealogist who traveled back through time to discover family history from documents already knows what a great voyage our ancestors have made. The stories of the three families highlighted in this book provide further evidence of this.

From the early sixteenth century, the De Bock family made it after three hundred-plus years of farming in Sint-Amands to Vilvoorde, an urban, industrial town six miles from Brussels. In the late nineteenth century, my grandfather met my grandmother in a lace factory. Some time after they got married in 1896 my grandfather became an *entrepreneur*. He started a factory for unwinding of thread on bobbins that later grew into a mechanical embroidery and lace making business. After my grandfather died in 1925, the factory remained in business thanks to my grandmother, who at the same time raised four children.

The family struggled through the First World War. The enterprise grew from six employees to twenty by 1935. In 1940 another World War broke out. Belgium capitulated three weeks after the invasion of the Germans, who occupied the country for the next four years. My father and my father-in-law became prisoners of war (POWs) and were transported to Germany. Unique in the history of warfare, Flemish POWs were released in 1940, months after Belgium was invaded. My father returned from Germany via Berlin to Vilvoorde in August 1940.

In January 1941, five months after my father's release, the enterprise started by my grandfather was formally established under the name *Deboeck Brothers PVBA* (or Ltd. in English law). It continued to operate during the war and survived difficult times even after the Second World War.

In the early fifties, revenues and profits rose and business expanded. Almost half of the production was exported to other countries in Europe. Employment grew to about 60. Then in the late sixties darker times came about: social security charges reached over thirty percent of the salaries; they became a significant burden. Increasing foreign competition, especially from France and Eastern Europe and delay in getting a work permit, culminated in problems that were summed up in a report made by my father in 1966. Disagreements among the shareholders on the gravity of the situation and means to overcome the problems, led to the liquidation of the company on June 5, 1967. The disinterest of older shareholders led first to the decline and later to the complete closure of Deboeck Brothers Ltd. in 1973.

Meanwhile, in 1969 I finished five years of university education in Leuven, got married, and moved to the USA. Upon completion of my graduate studies in 1972, my wife and I returned to

Europe, where I worked as a *health systems analyst* for the World Health Organization on projects for improving rural health services in countries all over the world. In 1976 my wife and I returned to the USA where for the next twenty-plus years we both worked for the World Bank in Washington, D.C.

The entrepreneurship of my grandfather and the management skills of my father must have been passed into my genes: I became an *interpreneur* introducing new technology and systems first for rural development and later for improving the bank's investments. As an interpreneur I took big risks to make things work; in the process I made lots of mistakes, which accelerated my learning.

Twenty-two years, four months and fifteen days after entering the bank, I retired in August 14, 1998. My wife who worked a similar period of time on a variety of assignments, retired two years later after commuting several years, several times a year, to China.

The history of the other two families discussed in this book is no less impressive. From the seventeenth century in France, the Girardin family made it to Brussels where for the past 125 years they have concentrated on making the unique artisan beers of Pajottenland. Lambic, gueuze, cherry and framboise beers are still made, based on traditions that are over 400 years old.

The De Zutter family from Moerkerke and Lapscheure, moved to Blankenberge and made it from there to Nieuwpoort. The public service that Daniel De Zutter, his brother and their father provided in the army, the air force, and the national security guard, taught us is a lot about their love for country.

All three families followed different paths but managed to survive in a world that was dangerous—through two world wars—and a world that became more competitive, more global and more free.

As a result of our work experiences, our children had the opportunity to travel a lot. They grew up accumulating a lot of knowledge and experiences while observing two professional careers: Dad was either going to the office in DC or was off to a conference in London, Frankfurt, Seoul or Tokyo; Mom was either fighting the bureaucracy in Washington or in Beijing.

All this globetrotting would not have been possible without Rosario Oandasan (a.k.a Charing) who joined us in January 1981 and has for the past 25 years taken care of our home, our kids, and all the other chores that needed attention. Our extended family managed to grow three kids into young adults who finished high school, college, and two out of three (so far) obtained graduate degrees. All three are today professionals exploring new frontiers into space, psychology and youth ministry.

While change for our ancestors came slowly and required years of effort, *for our children change is a given*. Maurice Piot, whom I first met in Geneva in 1972, now well into his eighties, recalls the dramatic changes in his lifetime. As a young medical doctor he joined WHO to fight tuberculosis in South Asia, and later was in charge of a project that advocated rural health services for the poor around the world. He wrote me recently:

> As a child of the 'crazy years' that followed WW1, I grew up in an environment without a telephone (something most people can no longer imagine), when the sound of human voices came directly from people, and when music instruments were the necessary mediators between composers and audiences; when images, unless hand drawn, were stills, sepia or on glass plates.
> At that time, when radio was just opening the mass communications era, my father, who had been one of the first speakers on the local station, acquired an awesome contraption with bulbs glowing on top of a gothic box, surmounted by a horn like a tuba. Besides emitting the most mysterious sounds when searching for a station, it opened the wonderful world of music.
> As a teenager during the WW2 years, I built my first, hand-operated gramophone/phonograph to enjoy breakable 72 rpm records. Soon thereafter I got a "pick-up," electrically driven, that plugged into his first amplifier, built by my uncle. When the 33rpm vinyl records came in "after" the war, I waited to be convinced by the stereo recordings to begin upgrading his sound recording equipment. I even had a bout of experimentation with steel-wire magnetic recording equipment, before the tapes came. The cathode tube, digital recording and laser decrypting, which soon followed allowed not only music, but also images to be omnipresent.
> I wonder how can humans adapt to absorb so many changes and of such quantitative impact on their most delicate sensitive organs? It is not only sound and images that changed drastically, everything else did and often so more: the ecology, the demography, the economy, the sociology etc. Nothing is the same, not even the future! The only constant is change.

Piot's story can easily be extended with anecdotes we observed over the past fifty years. Remember the snow filled, black and white TV programs of the early fifties? Remember the first jet planes in the sixties? Remember the first calculators followed by *the personal computer revolution* in the late seventies? In the early seventies I bought a HP45 calculator, just before joining WHO. This calculator provided me with a huge technological advantage over my colleagues, who at the time still used four function calculators. In the late seventies I built a personal computer from a kit, a Heath Kit. Years later my oldest son built a robot also from a Heath Kit; his "Hero" would years later get him into machine learning, neural nets and genetic algorithms.

Fast forward to the first days of the Internet; the first browser was Netscape in the early nineties. Seven years ago the Internet was merely a large encyclopedia. It was difficult to imagine at that time how the Internet could be used for on-line shopping (which is what Amazon started by selling books), on-line auctions (which is what eBay launched), e-businesses (through websites like, e-maginativegifts.com), or for fundraising, available to entrepreneurs everywhere on earth via KIVA.org. And then came Google, a search engine that turned into a verb! Today the younger generation can hardly remember what it was like to search for information before Google…

Only ten years ago work on the International Space Station was started by the launch of a control module, Zarya. In December 1998 space shuttle mission STS-88 delivered the Unity module. In 1999 a logistics delivery was made. Zvesda, a service module was added in July 2000. ISS received its first permanent residents, a crew of three, starting in October 31, 2000. Twelve shuttle missions followed before the *Columbia* accident of February 2003, which reduced the permanent ISS crew to two. NASA recovered from this setback with the launch of *Discovery* (STS-114) on July 26, 2005. A year later STS-121 brought another crew into space; *Atlantis* STS-115 followed in September; then *Discovery* was launched in December 2006 (STS-116).

In the short time span of about 10 years, mankind achieved permanent residence in space. Michael Griffin, the head of NASA, recently said: "humanity is setting out on an interplanetary quest not dissimilar to what the Vikings began some 1000 years ago."[1] Viking sailors as you recall became Europe's first great maritime explorers.

Griffin and NASA have big plans for the future. The concrete proposals are contained in the *Vision for Exploration* that President Bush announced in 2004, a program to return Americans to the moon before 2020 and plan for travel onward to Mars. Some nineteen more space shuttle missions are planned between the fall of 2007 and the middle of 2010.

In a few short decades, a very significant part of the Earth's economy has become a global economy instead of a patchwork of national economies. The next challenge is to turn this global economy into a space-economy. *"In the long run, we know that Earth and its resources are finite,"* says Griffin, *"there are resources in space – solar power, particular materials, precious metals, or even water and fuel, which in the context of a space-based economy can be very valuable. As we learn and develop the art and science of spaceflight, we will want to make use of those resources rather than bringing them up from Earth."*

Figure E.1 International Space Station when completed in 2010.

1. "NASA Looks to the Future; Eye on the Past," *Washington Post,* December 4, 2006

Stephen Hawking, the celebrated British astrophysicist, author of *A Brief History of Time,* recently on a space flight simulating zero gravity, added that *"Life on Earth is at the ever-increasing risk of being wiped out by a disaster, such as sudden global warming, nuclear war, a genetically engineered virus, or other dangers. I think the human race has no future if it does not go into space. I therefore want to encourage public interest in space."*[2]

While traveling in space, going to the Moon or even Mars is mind boggling, it was only seven years ago that the most *"wondrous map ever produced by humankind"* was completed by the first complete sequence of the human genome. Thanks to the pioneering work of Francis Collins and Craig Venter and the commercial services for DNA testing introduced in the USA by Bennett Greenspan, I was able to extend my research from conventional into genetic genealogy.

In the past two years I collected DNA from several people discussed in this book. Based on those DNA tests it was possible to quantify what was inherited from past generations and what was passed on to the next generation (with possibly minor changes.) While conventional genealogy obtained through years of research provided information about our ancestors who lived 450 years ago, through DNA tests we learned about our deep ancestors who lived 10,000 to 30,000 years ago.

New advances in genetics are made everyday; DNA testing becomes faster, cheaper and more accurate.[3] The most important developments will, however, come from discoveries about ways to extend life. In 2004 Ray Kurzweil and Terry Grossman, M.D., published a book called, *Fantastic Voyage: Live long enough to live forever.: The Science behind Radical Life Extension.* Chapter 11 in their book talks about the *Promise of Genomics* or the medical applications of DNA testing.

Genomics is a new field of medicine that enables us to discover our entire genome. *In contrast to what was discussed in this book, genomics is not focused on the single pair of sex chromosomes but on the entire genome.*[4] Genomics appeared first in the 1980s, but took off in the 1990s with the initiation of genome

---

2. P. Whoriskey, "A Long-awaited taste of outer space: Stephen Hawking takes a buoyant ride on a zero-gravity flight", Washington Post, April 17, 2007.

3. In the short time span since I first started with DNA testing, the available tests have grown. Twelve-marker tests were replaced by 37-marker tests; 37-marker tests can, since mid 2006, be upgraded to 67-marker tests. mtDNA tests went from sequencing HVR-1 to sequencing HVR-1 and HVR-2; and full sequencing is now becoming more and more affordable. In the future there may be Y-DNA tests that, at more affordable prices, can document the entire genome.

4. Investigation of single genes, their functions and roles is something very common in today's medical and biological research, and cannot be said to be genomics but rather the most typical feature of molecular biology.

projects. The study of the full set of proteins in a cell or tissue, as well as the changes during various conditions is called *proteomics*. This will lead to individualized therapies rather than the one-size-fits-all type of medicine that physicians have practiced so far.

Genomic testing is already in full swing. Almost all of the most common, disabling, and deadly degenerative diseases of our time, including cardiovascular disease, cancer, diabetes, and Alzheimer's disease, are the results of interaction between genetic and environmental factors. Through genomic testing a deeper understanding of disease processes can be gained to develop more specific and effective interventions. Thus, genetic testing is changing medicine. Only a few years after scientists announced they had sequenced the human genome, new knowledge about how genes affect health is transforming the way diseases are understood, diagnosed, treated and even predicted. Today gene tests are available for more than 1300 diseases.[5]

DNA testing discussed in this book entails limited risks. DNA data is stored by kit number, uploading of DNA results to public databases can be done without violation of privacy concerns. However, *DNA testing of the entire genome may reveal medical implications.* Ian Logan warned, *"before agreeing to (full) mtDNA sequencing, it is important to consider just how one might be affected by the results. About 5 to 10% of people (tested) can expect results that show significant mutations associated with medical conditions."*[6]

Genomic testing can produce information about medical conditions that may have been inherited. Thomas H. Shawker wrote *Unlocking your Genetic History: a step-by-step guide to discovering your family's medical and genetic heritage.* His book emphasizes the importance of assembling medical family histories.[7]

Little attention was paid to the medical histories of the families in this book, because little information is so far available. *In the future much more attention should be paid to recording medical family histories. Where there is cause to believe that certain conditions are inherited, genomic testing may be called for.*

Kurzweil and Grossman wrote, *"Today you have the ability to both know and modify the expression of the genes you were born with through diet, nutrition, and lifestyle choices. These tech-*

---

5. Kalb Claudia, "Peering into the Future: genetic Testing – Health for Life." MSNBC.com, Newsweek, December 11, 2006. Two companies that provide genomic testing include Genovations: Predictive Genomics for Personalized Medicine,
http://www.genovations.com/home/overview.html;
and DNA Direct, http://genesanddrugs.dnadirect.com/.

6. Ian Logan, "The Medical Implications of Complete Mitochondrial DNA Sequencing," http://www.jogg.info/12/Logan.htm, November 2005.

7. Thomas H Shawker, Unlocking your Genetic History

niques will soon be joined by more powerful biochemical strategies to alter the expression of your genes. Not too long after that, you should be able to change your genes entirely and choose the ones you want."[8]

The next generation will face enormous challenges, vastly greater than those experienced by their ancestors. These challenges can only be met if one realizes what changes have preceded, how they were met. Those challenges will be a continuation of *a long process of human discovery and evolution.* Three Chinese idioms (quoted in my first book)[9] can help to meet these challenges.

One Chinese idiom, *zhòng Yòng* suggests that *change has an absolute limit,* which produces two modes, yin and yang, that produce four forms, eight trigrams determining fortune and misfortune. To dwell too much on any misfortune is a waste of time. *No matter what happens, life demands always starting over, getting up again.* Do the best you can and do not worry about what other people think, my mother wisely advised.

The second Chinese idiom, *shui di shi chuan* means that *constant dripping wears away any stone,* in other words *even an infinitesimal force can accomplish a seemingly impossible feat with persistence.* The sky is the limit; nothing is impossible! And as Glynn Lunney, the flight director of Apollo 13 pointed out after an accident happened that left three astronauts stranded between the Moon and Earth: *Failure is not an option!*

The last Chinese idiom, *sui ji fing bian,* means, nothing is more important than adapting to changing conditions. Whether at work, in the job market or in the financial markets, adapting to changing conditions is essential, especially as the world is changing rapidly.

I hope that the journey we took back in time, into the history of three Flemish families over five centuries using conventional as well as genetic genealogy, has shown how much can be found via conventional sources; what can be discovered via DNA testing as well as what genetic genealogy can contribute to genealogy. I hope that our travel back in time has shown how much still needs to be done to connect other branches of the families covered in this book. I also hope I convinced you about the value of researching our ancestors and our deep ancestry. Better understanding of our ancestors and where they came from is essential to know where we are heading. A young medical doctor told me thirty-five years ago, *"if you do not know where you come from, do not know where you are, or don't know where you are heading, you will end up somewhere, and not know where you are."*

---

8. Ibid, page 159

9. Deboeck G., *Trading at the Edge: neural, Genetic and Fuzzy systems for Chaotic financial markets,* John Wiley & Sons, New York, 1994.

Annexes

Annex 1
Branches of the Deboeck Family Tree

In the sixteenth and seventeenth centuries many members of the *de bock* family lived on farms in small villages like Sint Amands, Lippelo, Opdorp, Malderen, Londerzeel, Grimbergen. Chapter 2 provided evidence that many of my ancestors were farmers. My oldest known ancestor, Gillis de Bock owned about 5 hectares of land. The de bock family moved from agriculture to industry and produced several entrepreneurs. Chapter 3 showed that Guillaume and Victor Deboeck started up separate businesses in the beginning of the 1900s, one in lace and the other in lemonade making. These businesses flourished under the management of their descendants for more than five decades or till about the third quarter of the twentieth century.

The de boeck family also produced artists, brewers, priests, and missionaries. In this annex I highlight some of them. You may recall that these other branches of the family are so far not connected, meaning no documented evidence has been found that they are (but neither did I invest time and money to find out). I do not know at this stage if all these branches on the de boeck family tree have a single common ancestor. If we go back far enough, we all of course have a common ancestor... So, in a way all the people mentioned below can be considered *family,* at least in the sense that we share a common surname.

Famous Flemish Artists

The 8th descendant of *Huybrecht de Bock* is *Julianus Maria August de Boeck* (see figure 1.1). He was a Belgian composer, organist and music pedagogue.

August de Boeck was born in Merchtem on May 9, 1865 and died there on October 9, 1937. From 1880 he studied organ at the Royal Conservatory in Brussels under Alphonse Mailly, to whom he became an assistant until 1902. In 1889 he met the young Paul Gilson who became his close friend, and, despite the fact that they had the same age, his teacher for orchestration and his motivator for composition. He became an organist at various churches in Belgian villages (1892-1894 in Merchtem, 1894-1920 in Elsene). His academic career continued in 1907 as harmony professor at the conservatory of Antwerp (1909-1920) and the conservatory of Brussels, and as director of the conservatory of Mechelen (1921-1930). In 1930 August de Boeck retired to his birthplace. His style was together with that of Paul Gilson influenced by the Russian Five, (especially Rimsky-Korsakov). They introduced *musical impressionism* into Belgium.

Ancestors of August De Boeck

Henrick DE BOECK
bp. Malderen

- Huybrecht DE BOECK
  d. 19 May 1628, Malderen
  & Ursula VAN DER STAPPEN
  d. 15 Jul 1650, Malderen

  - Jan DE BOECK
    d. 1 Jun 1671, Steenhuffel
    & Anna LEMMENS
    d. 11 Sep 1650, Steenhuffel

    - Robrecht DE BOECK
      b. ± 1631, Steenhuffel
      d. 6 Mar 1725
      & Magdalena MEERTE
      d. 23 Apr 1722
      m. 15 Oct 1662

      - Andries DE BOECK
        b. 30 Sep 1678, Rossem
        d. ± 1750
        & Maria MERTENS
        b. ± 1678
        d. 28 Nov 1763, Rossem
        mp. Londerzeel

        - Robrecht DE BOECK
          b. 19 Jan 1707, Impde
          d. 8 Apr 1782, Wolvertem
          & Maria VAN SCHELLE
          d. 9 Jul 1784, Wolvertem
          m. 22 Apr 1727, Wolvertem

          - Jacobus DE BOECK
            b. 29 Jun 1746, Londerzeel
            d. 26 Apr 1807, Humbeek
            & Joanna VAN SEGHBROECK
            b. 9 Sep 1753, Humbeek
            d. 21 Dec 1816, Humbeek
            m. 12 Sep 1775, Humbeek

            - Cornelius DE BOECK
              b. 20 Sep 1793, Humbeek
              d. 5 Dec 1878, Humbeek
              & Joanna Barbara MATTON
              b. 30 Nov 1794, Brussel
              d. 31 Jan 1882, Humbeek
              m. 16 Apr 1817, Humbeek

              - Florentinus DE BOECK
                b. 18 Nov 1826, Humbeek
                d. 26 Feb 1892, Merchtem
                & Petronella Amelia BRIERS
                b. 30 Apr 1821, Merchtem
                d. 25 Oct 1895, Merchtem
                m. 9 May 1857, Merchtem

                - Julianus Maria August DE BOECK
                  b. 9 May 1865, Merchtem
                  d. 9 Oct 1937, Merchtem

Figure 1.1 Pedigree chart of Julianus Maria August De Boeck 1865-1937.

Another famous Flemish artist is Felix De Boeck who was born on January 12, 1898 and died January 18, 1995 in Drogenbos. *Felix* was the great-great-grandson of Judocus De Boeck who was born December 30, 1754 (see chart).

Felix De Boeck is often called the *Picasso of the North*. He decided in 1916 to become an artist and started with pen and charcoal to draw figures and portraits. He was a farmer who devoted Sundays to art. In 1916 he painted landscapes with animals. In 1918 Vincent Van Gogh became his idol. He painted his first self-portrait in 1918. After a short futuristic period, his shapes became simpler and simpler and evolved to non-figurative paintings. Felix De Boeck is one of the founders of abstract art in Belgium. He became the painter of light. In 1996 a museum on Felix De Boeck opened in Drogenbos. Many of his paintings were reproduced by Raoul Maria de Puydt in his book, *Felix De Boeck,* published by Stichting Kunstboek in 2004.

Ancestors of Felix De Boeck

Judocus DE BOECK
b. 30 Dec 1754, Sint-Kwintens-Lennik
d. 8 Jul 1841, Sint-Kwintens-Lennik
& Isabella Livina EVENS
b. 23 Sep 1764, Neigem
d. 4 Nov 1808, Sint-Kwintens-Lennik
m. 25 Feb 1794, Neigem

  Pierre DE BOECK
  b. 13 Aug 1801, Sint-Kwintens-Lennik
  d. 2 Sep 1855, Sint-Kwintens-Lennik
  & Marie Thérèse SCHOUKENS
  b. 16 Jul 1808, Gooik
  d. 7 Sep 1863, Sint-Kwintens-Lennik
  m. 1838, Gooik

    Maria Constantia DE BOECK
    b. 11 Nov 1842, Gooik
    d. 21 Apr 1914, Drogenbos

      Joannes DE BOECK
      b. 5 Aug 1869, Sint-Kwintens-Lennik
      d. 2 Apr 1925, Drogenbos
      & Maria Ludovica VAN BREETWATER
      b. 8 Apr 1854, Drogenbos
      d. 21 Feb 1925, Drogenbos
      m. 21 Apr 1894, Brussel

        Felix Henricus Constantius DE BOECK
        b. 12 Jan 1898, Drogenbos
        d. 18 Jan 1995, Drogenbos

Figure 1.2 Ancestors of Felix Henricus Constantius De Boeck (1898-1995)

Brewers

In *Bier en Brouwerijen te Brussel van de Middeleeuwen tot vandaag* (Beer and Breweries in Brussels from the Middle Ages to the present),[1] I found references to several De Boecks who were brewers in Brussels. The story that follows provides the history of the well known brewery, Belle-Vue now part of Interbrew, the largest privately owned brewery in the world (at least in volume).

The history of Belle-Vue can be traced via the evolution of mergers and acquisitions of many smaller breweries in Brussels. Pierre and Andre De Boeck were at the source of this incredible evolution. It again underscores the entrepreneurial spirit of some De Boeck ancestors.

Some time between 1866 and 1873, Pierre De Boeck started a brewery called *Almanach du Commerce,* located in the Vlaamsesteenweg in Brussels. He was already a brewer, bought the Guden Dog (Gulden Hond or Chien d'or) from Jean Henry Briard, and started brewing in the Vlaamsesteenweg. His brother Andre De Boeck was also a brewer on the same street, but both continued to brew beer separately until 1877.

In 1878 the De Boeck brothers created one big brewery called *Brasserie De Boeck Frères,* (Vlaamsesteenweg, 187-188). They brewed lambic, faro and table beer, both light and dark beers, but their specialty was gueuze (see Chapter 5).

In 1878 the De Boeck brothers acquired a storage room in Koekelberg. Between 1878 and 1885 they built in Koekelberg a new facility to make malt. Later they also added a brewery. They continued brewing in the Vlaamsesteenweg till 1897-1899; thereafter they moved to Koekelberg where they remained active until the 1960s.

After WWI, Brewery De Boeck merged with Brewery Goossens. The name changed to *Les Brasseries Unies De Boeck-Goossens.* This new brewery bought the remaining smaller breweries in Brussels including in 1950-60 the Brewery *De Kroon* of Vanderborght; the Brewery Espagne of Toussaint and after 1963 the brewery *De Coster-Heymans* of Van Kerkhoven.

After this period of growth the De Boeck brothers sold in 1969 their brewery to *Belle-Vue-Vanden Stock.*

Belle-Vue had in the 1950s merged with *De Coster* in Groot-Bijgaarden and *Timmermans* in Sint-Pieters-Leeuw. The Brewery De Coster was located along the canal in Molenbeek (Henegouwkaai); it became the new headquaters of the Brewery Belle-Vue-Vanden Stock.

In 1970 more breweries were taken over: Brewery *De Keersmaker* in Wolvertem, Brewery *Vanderperre* in Schaarbeek and Brewery *La Becasse-Brabaux* in Anderlecht.

Brewery Belle-Vue and all her branches employed more

---

1. *Archief en Museum van het Vlaams Leven te Brusel,* Brussels 1996, 247 pp.

than 500 people and concentrated on export, especially to France and other European countries. In 1981 Belle-Vue received an award for its export.

Brewery Stella Artois, the best known Belgian beer in the world, acquired on July 4, 1991 a majority participation in now industrial production of gueuze by brewery Belle-Vue.

In 1992 the buildings along the canal were opened for the public. The brewery became an active brewery museum.

In August 2005 without being aware of the history of the Brewery Belle-Vue or its buildings, I visited with Anne-Marie Deboeck, the Belle-Vue brewery museum in Brussels.

While the brewers mentioned in this section may not be related a rather interesting development occurred in 1996. A Christmas present from my son that year included a basic home brewers kit. Ever since then I have been brewing Belgian-style beers in Arlington, Virginia. All my brewing is for home consumption or private parties; none is for commercial purposes. In 2004 I built a mini microbrewery as an annex to my home office; each year my brew design has been improved. I now regularly brew five gallons of beer in a few hours through a fairly automated micro home brewing process; my favorites are to brew Triples, Dubbels, strong ales, imperial stouts and barley wines. *Maybe there is a genetic link after all with the brewers described in this section?*

Religious

Among the religious who carried the name de Bock there was a beguine by the name of *Joanna Francisca de Bock,* born in Sint-Amands on October 10, 1814. As early as the commencement of the twelfth century, there were women in the Netherlands who lived alone, and without taking vows, and devoted themselves to prayer and good works. At first there were not many of them, but their numbers increased. It was the age of the Crusades, and the land teemed with desolate women—the raw material for a host of neophytes. These solitaries made their homes not in the forest, where the true hermit loves to dwell, but on the fringe of the town, where they attended to the poor.

About the beginning of the thirteenth century, some of them grouped their cabins together, and the community thus formed was the first Beguinage. These Roman Catholic religious communities that were active in the thirteenth and fourteenth centuries, were living in a loose semi-monastic community but without formal vows. They were influenced by Albigensian teachings and by the pantheism of a mystical sect, the Brethren of the Free Spirit, which flourished in and near Cologne around the same time but was condemned as heretical.

Joanna Francisca de Bock was the daughter of Tobias (1776-1831), a beer brewer in Sint Amands.[2] She became a beguine in 1858 and became the Head of the Beguinage ("Grootjuffrouw") of Dendermonde in 1874. There were also priests and missionaries with the name De Boeck. They included

- **Bishop D. Egied De Boeck** born in Oppuurs (1875-1944), Rev. Achiel De Boeck born in Sint-Amands (1882-1938), Juul De Boeck (1891-1981) and Rev. Louis De Boeck born in Vilvoorde (1914-1966) who all four served in Congo;

- **Rev. Evarist De Boeck** born in Hofstade (1858-1913), Rev. Frans De Boeck born in Buggenhout (1863-1917), Rev. Piet De Boeck born in Wolver tem (1852-1938) who all three served in Inner Mongolia;

- **Rev. Louis De Boeck** (1905-1987) and his brother Gerard De Boeck (1916-2004) both born in Steen huffel who served in the Philippines.

- **Brother Pieter-Jan De Boeck**, born in Steenhuffel in 1911 who departed for the Philippines in 1946 and died in Baguio, Philippines in 2004.[3]

Other De Boecks

In addition to all the people mentioned so far, there are other branches on the De Boeck family tree. Some of these branches are well documented; others rely on information that has not been entirely verified. Hence, only the verified ones will be reproduced here. Others will just be referenced.

One branch of the family can be traced back to *Philippus Arnoldus De Boeck* who married Elisabeth Kiekens, raised ten children and lived in Sint-Martens-Bodegem. Phillippus Arnoldus De Boeck died in 1809.

Another branch can be traced back to *Petrus de Boeck* who was born in 1831 in Steenhuffel, married Johanna De Mesmaeker and raised 13 children. Petrus is possibly a descendant of *Jan de Boeck* who is a descendant of *Huybrecht de Bock,* one of the ancestors of *August De Boeck,* that I discussed earlier.

A carefully documented branch of the family is the one from Halle that was quoted in the beginning of Chapter 2 and was based on the work of H. J. Vandenweghe. The oldest known ancestor of this family is *Pieter de Boucq* going back six centuries. The following figure shows 10 generations of descendants of Pieter de Boucq of Halle.

---

2. The life of Joanna Francisca de Bock has been documented and beautifully illustrated by Stanny Van Grassdorf and can be found at http://www.stanny-van-grasdorff.be/begijnen.htm

3. This information provided by Rev. Karel Denys and Rev. Paul E, Staes came from Elenchus Sodalium Defunctorum, CICM, 1977, 1994 and 2002.

Figure 1.3 Descendants of Pieter de.Boucq

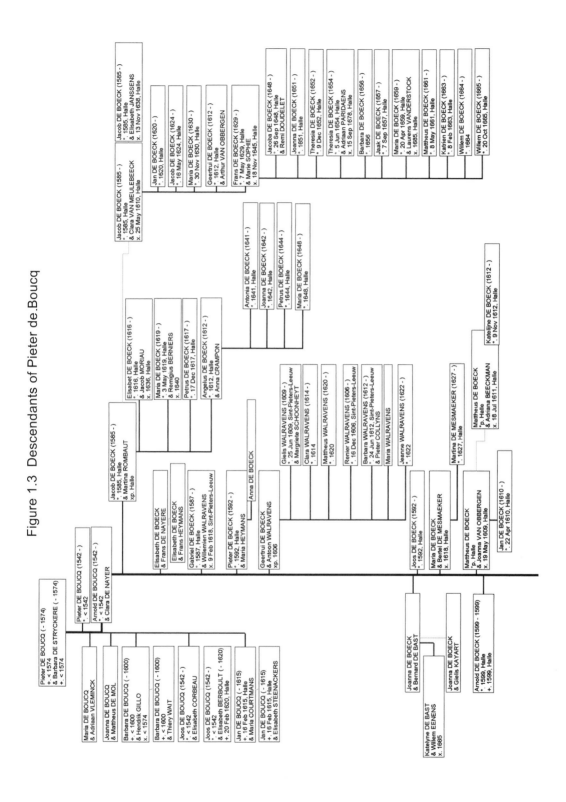

Figure 1.3 Descendants of Pieter de Boucq, continued

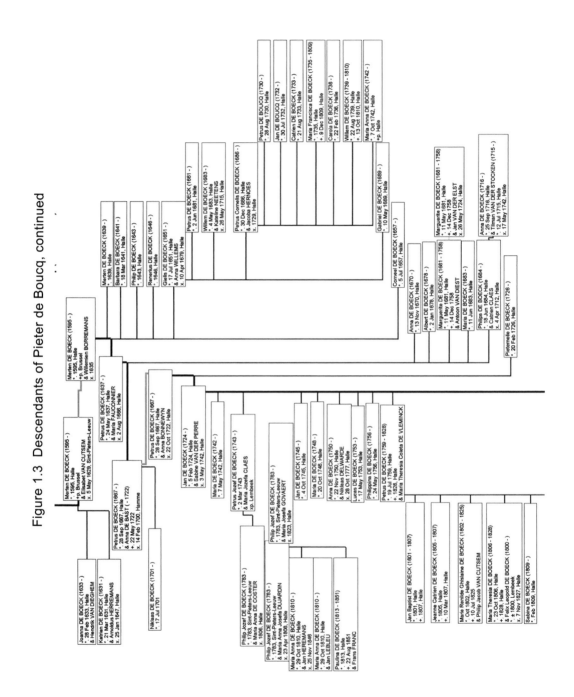

Figure 1.3 Descendants of Pieter de Boucq, continued

Sabina VAN LIER (1795 -)
* 7 May 1772, Halle
+ 4 Oct 1795, Halle

Pauline VAN LIER (1801 -)
x. 1 Aug 1801, Halle

Catrien DE BOECK (1772 - 1805)
* 7 May 1772, Halle
+ 1805
& Leopold VAN LIER
x. 10 Feb 1795, Halle

Philippina DE BOECK (1764 -)
* 27 Sep 1764, Halle

Albert DE BOECK (1767 -)
* 5 Mar 1767, Halle

Jacob Jan DE BOECK (1762 -)
* 2 Feb 1762, Halle
& Joanna VAN DEN BERGHE
x. 16 Nov 1789, Halle

Sabina DE BOECK (1790 -)
* 24 Mar 1790, Halle

Jeanne Marie DE BOECK (1807 - 1807)
* 1807, Lembeek
+ 23 Sep 1807

Jan Jacob DE BOECK (- 1882)
+ 1882

Jeanne Marie DE BOECK (1792 -)
* 14 Apr 1792, Lembeek
& Andreas Jozef DU ROUSSAUX

Felix Leopold DE BOECK (1800 -)
* ± 1800, Lembeek
& Maria Theresia DE BOECK (1806 - 1828)
+ 1828, Halle
x. 7 Nov 1827, Halle

Felix Leopold DE BOECK (1800 -)
* ± 1800, Lembeek
& Philippina NERINCKX

Felix Philip DE BOECK (1831 - 1838)
* 1831
+ 1838

Rosalia Petronille DE BOECK (1833 -)
* 17 Jan 1833

Sabina Leontina Albertina DE BOECK (1833 -)
* 28 Dec 1833
& Ferdinand Jozef LACOURT
x. 1859

Louis Leopold DE BOECK (1839 -)
* 1839
& Philomena COUSINNE
x. 1879

Jan Jozef Isidoor DE BOECK (1844 -)
* 1844
& Maria Coleta DELACROIX

Adela DE BOECK

Maria Melanie DE BOECK (1835 -)
* 1835
& Gustaaf Leopold Albert DE BOECK (1837 -)
x. 14 Apr 1837

Maria Elisabet Leopoldina DE BOECK (1858 -)
* 1858, Halle

Rosalia Leonia Albert DE BOECK (1860 -)
* 1860, Halle
& Fr. L. Victor BOTTEMANNE
x. 26 Nov 1886, Halle

Maria Louisa Helena DE BOECK (1861 -)
* 1861, Halle

Maria Helena Victor DE BOECK (1862 -)
* 23 Apr 1862, Halle
& Hendrik Adolf CORNELIS
x. 14 Dec 1886

Jeanne Anna DE BOECK (1868 -)
* 27 Jan 1868, Halle

Maria Jozef DE BOECK (1871 -)
* 16 Jan 1871, Halle

Leon Ph. Leopold DE BOECK (1874 -)
* 3 Dec 1874, Halle
& Maria FAESTENAEKELS

Leopold Jozef DE BOECK (1846 -)
* 2 Feb 1846
& Anna Maria DE BOECK (1845 -)
x. 26 Mar 1845, Halle
x. 13 Sep 1871, Halle

Maria Melanie DE BOECK (1875 -)
* 1875, Halle

Maria Emilie DE BOECK

Gustaaf Joris Georges DE BOECK (1876 -)
* 20 Aug 1876, Halle

Elisabeth Ghislaine Laure DE BOECK (1878 -)
* 13 Jul 1878, Halle

Emile Frans Armand DE BOECK (1881 -)
* 27 Jan 1881, Halle

Maurits Jozef Paul DE BOECK (1883 -)
* 3 Oct 1883, Halle
& Esther LEPOUTRE

Maria Mathilde Julia DE BOECK (1885 -)
* 8 May 1885, Halle
& Emile DE GROEVE

Marguerite Marie DE BOECK (1888 -)
* 1 Feb 1888, Halle
& Paul TONDREAU

Catrien Jozefa Justina DE BOECK

Philip Jacob DE BOECK

Victor Guillaume DE BOECK (1843 -)
* 20 Jan 1843

Maria Eleonora DE BOECK (1847 -)
* 22 May 1847
& DEWÉE

Maria Louis Oscar DE BOECK (1872 -)
* 17 Sep 1872, Halle
& Rosalia Anna KENNIS

Josefina Anna Maria DE BOECK (1874 - 1874)
* 21 Mar 1874, Halle
+ 29 Mar 1874, Halle

Albert Leopold DE BOECK (1812 -)
* 22 Oct 1812
& Maria Theresia MERCIER

Jan Jaak DE BOECK (1843 - 1843)
* 1843, Halle
+ 1843, Halle

Anna Maria DE BOECK (1845 -)
* 26 Mar 1845, Halle
& Leopold Jozef DE BOECK (1846 -)
* 2 Feb 1846
x. 13 Sep 1871, Halle

Leopold Jozef DE BOECK (1811 -)
* 1811, Halle

Albert Leopold DE BOECK (1812 -)
* 22 Oct 1812
& Rosalia VAN HEMELRIJCK (1812 -)
* 1812, Halle

Gustaaf Leopold Albert DE BOECK (1837 -)
* 14 Apr 1837
& Maria Melanie DE BOECK (1835 -)
* 1835

Maria Elisabet Leopoldina DE BOECK (1858 -)
* 1858, Halle

Rosalia Leonia Albert DE BOECK (1860 -)
* 1860, Halle
& Fr. L. Victor BOTTEMANNE
x. 26 Nov 1886, Halle

Maria Louisa Helena DE BOECK (1861 -)
* 1861, Halle

Maria Helena Victor DE BOECK (1862 -)
* 23 Apr 1862, Halle
& Hendrik Adolf CORNELIS
x. 14 Dec 1886

Jeanne Anna DE BOECK (1868 -)
* 27 Jan 1868, Halle

Maria Jozef DE BOECK (1871 -)
* 16 Jan 1871, Halle

Leon Ph. Leopold DE BOECK (1874 -)
* 3 Dec 1874, Halle
& Maria FAESTENAEKELS

Maria Louis Oscar DE BOECK (1872 -)
* 17 Sep 1872, Halle
& Rosalia Anna KENNIS

Josefina Anna Maria DE BOECK (1874 - 1874)
* 21 Mar 1874, Halle
+ 29 Mar 1874, Halle

Maria Melanie DE BOECK (1875 -)
* 1875, Halle

Maria Emilie DE BOECK

Gustaaf Joris Georges DE BOECK (1876 -)
* 20 Aug 1876, Halle

Elisabeth Ghislaine Laure DE BOECK (1878 -)
* 13 Jul 1878, Halle

Emile Frans Armand DE BOECK (1881 -)
* 27 Jan 1881, Halle

Maurits Jozef Paul DE BOECK (1883 -)
* 3 Oct 1883, Halle
& Esther LEPOUTRE

Maria Mathilde Julia DE BOECK (1885 -)
* 8 May 1885, Halle
& Emile DE GROEVE

Marguerite Marie DE BOECK (1888 -)
* 1 Feb 1888, Halle
& Paul TONDREAU

Descendants of Pieter de Boucq (continued)

Source: M.J. Vandenweghe, The Family De Boeck, Hallensia III, Oud Series No III, 1935, p.73-75

Annex 2
Distance, Land Measurements and Land Prices

From the sixteenth to eighteenth century, common distance and land measurements were the *rod, roede* and *rood.* Some of these were derived from old English measurements. The *Dictionary of Units of Measurement* by Russ Rowlett describes these and other measurements.[4]

A *rod* was a traditional unit of distance equal to 5.5 yards (i.e., 16 feet 6 inches or 5.0292 meters). The rod was the basic distance unit used in England. *Rod* is a Saxon word for straight stick. The Normans preferred to call it a *pole or a perch* (because a pole was used to control a team of 8 oxen). When the modern *foot* became established in the twelfth century, the Royal government did not want to change the length of the rod because it was used as the basis for land measurements, land records, and taxes. The rod was re-defined to equal 16.5 of *new feet.* This length was called the "king's perch." Although *rods and perches* of other lengths were used, the king's perch prevailed. The Parliamentary statute of 1592 defined the statute mile to be 320 rods or 1760 yards, thus forcing the rod to equal exactly 5.5 yards or 16.5 feet.

The *roede* was a traditional Dutch unit of distance reinterpreted in 1820 as a metric unit equal to exactly 10 meters (i.e., 32.8084 feet). *The roede* has also been used as a unit for the measurement of area equal to one square (linear) roede; this is equal to 100 square meters or one *are.*

A *rood* was an old unit of distance. *Rood* is an old Dutch word for a rod or pole; so a *rood* is in some cases another name for a rod. In old England and Scotland a *rood* was often longer than a "modern" *rod* of 16.5 feet; sometimes it was 20 feet, 21 feet, or even 24 feet.

A *rood* was also a traditional unit for the measurement of land. A *rood* is the area of a narrow strip of land one *furlong* (40 rods, or 660 feet) long and one rod (16.5 feet) wide. Thus a *rood* is equal to 40 square rods (or perches), which equals 1210 square yards, or 10,890 square feet, or exactly 1/4 acre. This is the area of a lot 22 yards wide and 55 yards deep, about the size of many suburban lots. One rood is approximately 1011.714 square meters or one tenth of a *hectare.*

Prices of rents and land in Flanders from the sixteenth to eighteenth century (that were used to estimate the wealth of my oldest known ancestor Gillis de Bock (see Chapter 2) are shown in the following table. The currency units used in this table are explained in Chapter 1 and further elaborated in the following annex.

---

4. Russ is a mathematics educator at the University of North Carolina at Chapel Hill, serving as Director of the Center for Mathematics and Science Education. His "Dictionary of Units of Measurement" can be found at http://www.unc.edu/~rowlett/units/

Table 2.1 Prices of Land and Rents in Flanders: 1550-1800

	selling price arable land			rents			selling price arable land
	ponden groten Vlaams. per hectare	index 1610=100	10-year moving av.	ponden groten Vlaams per hectare	rent index 1610=100	10-year moving av.	in pounds groats of Brabant per hectare
1550	32	62		0.73	32		48
1570	47	92	100	1.43	62	77	71
1580	54	106	89	2.38	103	84	81
1590	14	27	34	0.71	31	46	21
1600	40	78	74	1.67	72	67	60
1610	51	100	95	2.32	100	92	77
1620	75	148	162	3.55	144	126	113
1630	137	269	264	2.73	117	178	206
1640	188	368	330	5.61	241	250	282
1650	170	334	306	5.6	241	244	255
1660	150	294	303	5.73	246	255	225
1670	124	243	257	6.97	299	238	186
1680	193	202	193	4.85	208	197	290
1690	76	150	154	3.85	165	163	114
1700	99	194	169	3.82	164	161	149
1710	108	211	222	3.58	154	173	162
1720	128	250	248	5	215	202	192
1730	130	255	260	5.15	221	206	195
1740	129	253	275	4.55	196	208	194
1750	151	296	289	5.12	220	210	227
1760	162	317	313	5.29	227	216	243
1770	234	459	422	5.23	225	219	351
1780	287	562	501	6.64	286	240	431
1790	314	616	597	6.96	299	296	471
1795	318	624		6.13	263		477

Sources: E. De Wever, "Rents and Selling Prices of Land at Zele," in H. van der Wee and E. van Cauwenberghe, eds., *Productivity of Land and Agricultural Innovation in the Low Countries (1250-1800)*,
(Leuven: Leuven University Press, 1978), 55-63;
and tranposition of prices in pounds Flemish groats into prices in pounds of groats of Brabant.

Annex 3
Evolution of prices, wages and the value of money in Belgium over the past six centuries.
by Paul Duran[5]

This note presents a brief survey of the evolution of prices, real wages, and the purchasing power of money in Belgium since 1400. Available studies for the period 1400–1700 follow in the footsteps of leading work in this area undertaken by E. H. Phelps Brown and S. Hopkins on southern England. It was, therefore, considered of interest to provide comparisons between Belgium and the UK.

Data on the evolution of prices, the purchasing power of money, and real wages are contained in the tables of this annex. Information on the evolution of the value of money makes it possible to express historic prices of items from the past in terms of current (2006) Euros (EUR) and derive changes in prices in real terms of equivalent items over time. Regarding wages, data provide a broad indication of trends in the purchasing power of wage earnings and the pace of increases spanning more than six centuries.

The validity of the results depends on the extent to which data on prices and wages are representative of real living conditions for the period under investigation. As indicated below, the price indices have been constructed on the basis of multiple budgets reflecting actual expenditures during the period concerned. The basis for the wage data is narrower, because, for the period prior to 1945 for England, and prior to 1840 for Antwerp, they represent wages in one particular sector, namely construction. However, in general, these data can be considered to be sufficiently representative of general wage trends in the overall economy.

1. Evolution of prices and the value of the currency in Antwerp/Belgium compared to southern England/UK

There was a very substantial loss in the real value of money in both countries over the past six centuries. In 1400, the purchasing power of currency, equivalent to one EUR/Belgian Franc (BF), was equal to the value of 4,098 EUR/BF of 2006, while that of one pound sterling (LS) was equal to 870 LS of 2006. This reflects the different pace of inflation experienced in the two countries.

---

5. Paul Duran is a good friend and experienced econmist that I first met when I was studying in Leuven, some 40 years ago. The annex presented here is a slightly shorter version of a longer paper that Paul prepared on my request for help on how to translate money values of long ago into today's values. This annex is based on data from many sources and computations of indices that have never been published before. Questions on this annex can be send to pjduran@msn.com

The factors that contributed to the inflation in both countries during the period from the fifteenth to the eighteenth century were coinage debasement, and the Price Revolution of ca. 1520–1650, which was initiated by the South German–Central European silver mining boom.[6] The resulting quintupling of Europe's silver supplies between the 1460s and 1540 had a monetary impact across Europe, leading to a global acceleration of inflation. Subsequently, especially from the 1560s, monetary growth was fueled by an even greater influx of silver from Spanish America.[7]

Following a decline in prices during the 'General crisis' era, 1640–1740, during the period 1750–1825 there was renewed inflation with sharp fluctuations of prices, especially in England, aided by a stepped up output of the silver mines in Mexico and Peru, following a decline in the second half of the seventeenth century,[8] and the effects of political upheaval and warfare.[9]

During the era 1825–1914, very modest rates of inflation were recorded since monetary growth was limited to accommodating economic growth, which was higher than in previous centuries. This was achieved by a rise in the share of bank (paper) money in the total money supply, which through flexible monetary management allowed smoothing out the widely fluctuating

---

6. John Munro, "Real Wages and the 'Malthusian Problem' in Antwerp and South-Eastern England, 1400 – 1700: A regional comparison of levels and trends in real wages for building craftsmen," Department of Economics and Institute for Policy Analysis, University of Toronto, *Working Paper No. 27,* April 2006, pp. 16-17. This paper was presented at the Second Dutch-Flemish Conference on *The Economy and Society of the Low Countries in the Pre-Industrial Period,* at the University of Antwerp, on April 20, 2006.

7. John Munro, "Money and Monetary Movements in Early-Modern Europe: ca. 1500 –ca. 1750," Lecture Topic No. 15, *Economics 210Y1,* January 2007, p.2 (http://www.economics.utoronto.ca/munro5).

8. John Munro, "Review of David Hackett Fisher. The Great Wave: Price Revolutions and the Rhythm of History, H-Net Reviews in the Humanities and Social Sciences, February 1999, p.8; John Munro, "Builders' Wages in Southern England and the Southern Low Countries, 1346 – 1500: A Comparative Study of Trends in and Levels of Real Incomes," Department of Economics and Institute for Policy Analysis, University of Toronto, *Working Paper No. 21,* July 2004, p. 42; and John Munro, "South German Silver, European Textiles, and Venetian Trade with the Levant and Ottoman Empire, c. 1370 to c. 1720: A Non-mercantilist Approach to the Balance of Payments Problem," Department of Economics and Institute for Policy Analysis, University of Toronto, *Working Paper No. 26,* April 2006, p. 33. The influx of silver from Spanish America generally exceeded the outflow to trading partners in the Baltic area, the Levant, and Southeast Asia.

9. In the Antwerp region, while prices declined by 21 percent between 1800 and 1835, the average price level in 1801 – 35 exceeded that of 1726 – 50 by 34 percent.

increases in silver and gold stocks during this period, while preserving exchange rate and gold price stability.[10]

Apart from the impact of two World Wars and their aftermath, the emergence of fiat paper money after 1914 (as the sole legal tender), the phasing-out of domestic convertibility into metallic currencies, the abandoning of exchange rate stability, and large budget deficits[11] played a significant role in the sharpest acceleration in inflation recorded over the past six centuries.

The higher inflation in Belgium compared with the UK occurred in the period prior to 1950, reflecting the much higher debasement of the currency between 1400 and 1750, as well as the much higher increase in prices during the two World Wars (owing to foreign occupation of Belgium). Between 1950 and 2006 the pace of inflation was much faster in the UK, which registered a 24-fold increase in prices compared with only 7 in Belgium.

For the UK, the price index data for the period prior to 1850 were taken from the path breaking studies undertaken in the 1950s by E. H. Phelps Brown and S. Hopkins, who constructed an index of the prices of consumables and real wages in the building sector in southern England for the period from 1264 to 1954 (PHB index).[12, 13] For the years after 1850, data presented in Research Paper 03/82 of the UK House of Commons Library, and updated through 2006, have been used.[14]

Based on these data, there was a 769-fold increase in prices between 1401-1425 and 2001-2006 in England/UK. In absolute terms, some 94 percent of the increase occurred over the

---

10. R. Triffin, "The Myth and Realities of the So-called Gold Standard," in R. N. Cooper, ed., *International Finance* (Middlesex, England; Baltimore, MD, USA: Penguin Books, Inc., 1969), pp. 49-60.

11. In Belgium, after a suspension in August 1914, convertibility of the currency was restored in 1926, from then on into gold bullion. Except for an interruption in 1935-36, convertibility remained in effect until May 1940, when it was again suspended, never to be restored.

12. E.H. Phelps Brown, and Sheila V. Hopkins, "Seven Centuries of the Prices of Consumables, Compared with Builders' Wage-Rates," *Economica,* Vol. 23 (Nov. 1956), pp. 296-314.

13. The basket in the PBH index includes six groups of essential consumer goods selected on the basis of historical budget information, while the reference for prices are the averages of the period 1451-75. Four of the subgroups comprise food and drink products, while one includes heating and lighting goods, and another textiles. The overall price index is a weighted average of the indices of the six groups, while the components of the groups are adjusted over time to reflect shifting habits of consumption and the entry of new products.

14. Grahame Allen, "Inflation: the value of the pound 1750-2002," House of Commons Library Research Paper 03/82 (November 2003).

last 50 years, corresponding to an average annual rate of inflation of some 6 percent between 1951-60 and 2001-05. This 6 percent inflation is much higher than the average rate of less than 1 percent per year over the preceding five centuries.

As a result, the pound sterling has undergone a steady and considerable erosion of its purchasing power.[15] To purchase what was one pound during the first quarter of the fifteenth century, some 833 pounds with purchasing power of 2006 would be needed. The amount of pounds of 2006 required to purchase one-pound's value amounts to 24 in 1950, and 85 in 1900.

The evolution of prices and the value of the currency in Belgium is provided in Table 3.1 at the end of this annex.

For the period 1400-1700 (column (a)), data are taken from Herman Van der Wee's seminal article on prices and wages in the western part of the duchy of Brabant and southern England, published in 1975.[16] The price index for the Antwerp/Brussels region tracks the cost of a basket of 10 essential consumer goods, selected on the basis of various expenditure budgets, spread over the fifteenth, sixteenth, and the seventeenth centuries, and prices prevailing in Antwerp, Lier, Mechelen, and Brussels, and with the averages of the stable years of 1451-1475 used as reference.

In constructing his price index, Van der Wee was guided by the method embodied in the PBH index, except that the basket does not have separate groups of commodities and was unchanged for the entire period (in view of the very small differences between the 1275 and 1500 budgets in the PBH index.)

Data for the period 1700-1835 (column (b)) are based on a study by Robert Allen comparing differences in price and wage developments among various European cities (including Antwerp) from the fourteenth century through 1913.[17] The Allen price index covers a basket of 12 goods with the weights established in accordance with many consumer budgets, with a base period of

---

15. Since its introduction by the Normans, the pound sterling has remained the only money of account and exchange money in England, and later the United Kingdom. Its subdivision was changed with the adoption of the decimal system on February 15, 1971, when one new penny became equal to 2.4 old pence and the shilling was abandoned.

16. Herman van der Wee, "Prijzen en lonen als ontwikkelingsvariabelen: Een vergelijkend onderzoek tussen Engeland en de Zuidelijke Nederlanden, 1400-1700," in *Album aangeboden aan Charles Verlinden ter gelegenheid van zijn dertig jaar professoraat* (Wetteren: Universum, 1975), pp.413-47; reissued without the tables as "Prices and Wages as Development Variables: A Comparison between England and the Southern Netherlands, 1400-1700," *Acta Historiae Neerlandicae,* X (1978), pp. 58-78.

17. Robert C. Allen, "The Great Divergence in European Wages and Prices from the Middle Ages to the First World War," *Explorations in Economic History,* 38:4 (October 2001), pp. 411-447.

1745-54.[18] The Allen index for Antwerp uses prices in the Antwerp/ Brussels area, with many taken from the Van der Wee study and its sources. The Allen index shows changes in prices expressed in silver equivalents; however, as the silver weight of the money of account is assumed to remain unchanged during the period 1700–1835, the price index in terms of the moneys of account provided the same results as the index based on silver equivalents.[19]

For the years 1835-1914 (column (c)), data are used from Peter Scholliers's study on real industrial wages in Belgium in 1840-1939.[20] The Scholliers index is based on price data in the Ghent region for 14 consumer goods, including 11 basic food-stuffs, and rents, which represent 85 percent of total spending in working class budgets, using two sets, 1835-80 and 1880-1914.

Starting with 1920 (column (c)), data are taken from the official price index compiled by the National Institute of Statistics (NIS) of the Ministry of Economic Affairs of Belgium.[21] The latter index is updated regularly to reflect changes in private sector expenditure over time. Column (d) presents a combined price index covering the whole period with 1950 as base. Column (e) contains annual price changes compounded over the given periods.

Between 1400 and 2006, prices in Belgium rose about 3350-fold. The pace of the increase varied much over this long time period, spanning six centuries.

During the first three centuries, from the first quarter of the fifteenth century through the last quarter of the seventeenth century, the increase was 10-fold, followed by a most significant slowing in the following centuries, when prices rose by only slightly more than 10 percent through the middle of the nineteenth century, and 40 percent through the eve of the First World War. The next 40 years, dominated by the effects of the two World Wars with foreign occupation, and their aftermath, witnessed a spectacular acceleration of inflation, with prices rising 27-fold. After a significant stabilization in the nineteen fifties, inflation accelerated again, resulting in increases in prices between 1970 and 1990 of some 80 percent per decade, reflecting in part the effects of the oil shocks and large budget deficits during that period. In the years 1991-2006, this rate was reduced to some 22 percent per decade.

---

18. While the Van der Wee and PBH indices include grain prices, the Allen index includes bread prices.

19. In fact, during this period the silver content of the Brabant guilder was reduced from 10.33 grams to 8.22 grams.

20. Peter Scholliers, "A century of real industrial wages in Belgium, 1840-1939," in Peter Scholliers and Vera Zamagni, eds., *Labour's Reward* (Aldershot, England; Brookfield, VT, USA: Edward Elgar, 1995) pp. 106-37.

21. Ministerie van Economische Zaken, Nationaal Instituut van de Statistiek, *Historiek Indexcijfer der consumptieprijzen (vanaf 1920)* (http:// economie.fgov.be/informations/indexes/history_indexes.xls).

Given these price developments, the decline in the internal value or purchasing power of the currency in the Antwerp region/Belgium between 1400 and 2005 could be established. During this period four moneys of account are distinguished: the EUR, the BF, the Brabant guilders, and the Brabant groat.[22]

For 1400-1600, the money of account selected as currency in Table 3.1 is the *Brabant groat,* which was predominant during that era. For the period 1601-1835, the money of account chosen is the *Brabant guilder,* which became increasingly used following its introduction during the fifteenth century. It was the official money of account during the periods of Austrian, French and Dutch rule, and in newly independent Belgium until the end of 1832.[23] After 1600, the Brabant groat continued to be used, although it tended to become displaced by the *stuiver.* Because of the fixed relationship between the groat, stuiver, and guilder, the results in Table 3.1 can easily be converted into the other moneys of account.[24]

The evolution of the value of the currency over time in terms of the purchasing power of the EUR or BF[25] in 2006 in Belgium is presented in three columns. Column (f) shows for the indicated years or periods (for which an average is given) the amount of EUR or BF of 2006 required to make a purchase worth an amount of Brabant guilders or Brabant groats equivalent to one EUR/BF in the years or periods under consideration.

The amount of 2006 EUR/BF required for obtaining the purchasing power of currency equivalent to one EUR/BF in 1401-25, which amounts to 1334.24/33.075 Brabant groats, is equal to 3132, and of currency equivalent to one EUR/BEF in 1601-25, which amounts to 22.24/0.55125 Brabant guilder, is equal to 304.

In column (g) are indicated the amounts of EUR with purchasing power of 2006 in Belgium needed to make a purchase worth one unit of the money of account used in the year or period under consideration. Thus, the value of one Brabant groat in

---

22. Valery Janssens, *Le Franc belge: Un siecle et demi d'histoire monetaire* (Brussels, 1976), pp. 23-35; Herman van der Wee, *The Growth of the Antwerp Market and the European Economy, 14th-16th Centuries,* 3 vols. (The Hague, 1963), Volume I, pp.107-114; and Ch. Verlinden, J. Craeybeckx, E. Scholliers and others, Dokumenten voor de geschiedenis van prijzen en lonen in Vlaanderen en Brabant (XVe-XVIIIe eeuw) (4 volumes, Bruges, 1959-73), Volume I, 1959, pp. 16-29, and Volume II.A, 1965, pp. XXXII-XXXIX.

23. The Belgian Franc was introduced at the beginning of 1833 at a rate of one BF per 0.55125 Brabant guilder.

24. One Brabant guilder is equal to 20 stuivers, and one stuiver is equal to 3 groats, so that one Brabant guilder is equal to 60 Brabant groats. See Ch. Verlinden and others, *Dokumenten,* Volume I, pp. XXXII-XXXIII.

25. The exchange rate BF/EUR is 40.3399.

1401-25 was equal to 2.4 EUR of 2006, and that of the Brabant guilder in 1601-1625 to 15.5 EUR of 2006.[26]

Regarding price developments during the period between 1400 and 1700, data show that price increases escalated over time, although interrupted by near stability in the third quarter of the fifteenth century and the second quarter of both the sixteenth and seventeenth centuries. Whereas over the period 1400-1550 quarter century average prices rose by 142 percent, during the following one hundred years they more than quintupled. A limited reversal occurred during the second half of the seventeenth century, when prices fell by some 16 percent. An important factor contributing to the increase in prices in the fifteenth century was the steady depreciation of the Brabant groat between 1400 and 1435 from 1.02 grams of silver to 0.54 gram, and the rapid devaluations under Maximilian of Austria between 1480 and 1489, when the silver value of the groat was cut from 0.35 gram to 0.16 gram.[27] A reversal of the latter debasement later in 1489 was gradually eroded subsequently.

The inflation during the sixteenth and first half of the seventeenth centuries was part of the Price Revolution in Europe (ca.1520–ca.1650), which was closely linked to a sharp increase in the money supply as a result of the silver mining boom in Central Europe, and later the influx of silver from Spanish America. Another source of increases in the money supply was financial innovation, in particular the development of new credit instruments.[28] In addition, the Revolt in the Netherlands and the Eighty Years' War contributed to the high inflation in the Antwerp region during that era.[29]

2. Developments of real wages in southern England/ UK and Antwerp/Belgium

A common feature of developments between 1400 and 1700 in Southern England and the Antwerp region was the stickiness of wages during prolonged periods of time, with the effect

---

26. Column (h) provides data on the value of one unit of the money of account in terms of a notional BF of 2005 or 0.024789 (1/40.3399) EUR, which are obtained by multiplying the amounts of ccolumn (g) by the BF/ EUR conversion rate.

27. Van der Wee, "Prijzen en lonen" pp. 425-26; and Munro, "Real Wages and the 'Malthusian Problem'" p. 18.

28. Munro, "Real Wages and the 'Malthusian Problem'" pp. 16-17, and John Munro, "Wage-Stickiness, Monetary Changes, and Real Incomes in Late – Medieval England and the Low Countries, 1300 – 1450:Did Money Really Matter?" Department of Economics and Institute for Policy Analysis, University of Toronto, Working Paper No. 3, November 2000, pp.56-58.

29. Van der Wee, "Prijzen en lonen" p. 434.

that developments in real wages during these periods reflected only changes in prices.[30]

Over the whole period 1400-2006, real wages rose more than twice as fast in Belgium compared with the UK, a result fully on account of developments between 1875 and 1980. In both countries, real wages in the second quarter of the seventeenth century were significantly lower than in the first quarter of the sixteenth century, and it took until the third quarter of the nineteenth century before the level of 1400 and the highest level previously obtained were recovered.

Reflecting Antwerp's early transition to a modern economy with a higher degree of industrialization and orientation toward exports, at 24 percent the drop in real wages in Antwerp was well below that of the UK, where it amounted to 52 percent. As a result, the real wage level in Antwerp, which was lower than in England during most of the fifteenth century, exceeded the English level during the sixteenth and seventeenth centuries.[31] Subsequently the English level regained its comparative higher level during the eighteenth century, owing to its lead in the Industrial Revolution.[32]

Between 1900 and 2006, there was another reversal of the comparative lead of the two economies, as Belgium achieved a six-fold increase in real wages compared with a three-fold in the UK. However, over the last twenty-five years, the average annual increase in real wages in the UK at 1.7 percent has been more than five times the rate obtained in Belgium.

Data on the evolution of real wages in Belgium are presented in Table 3.2. Sources for the data covering the period 1400-1700 (column a) include Herman van der Wee's 1975 study on prices and wages cited above, his 1963 book on the growth of

---

30. Munro, "Real Wages and the 'Malthusian Problem'" pp. 14-15. This was particularly the case in Antwerp in 1442-1485 and in 1595-1668, and in southern England in 1412-1535, 1579-1625, and 1657-1697, all periods with no changes in nominal wage levels. This resulted into a significant increase in real wages in the Antwerp region between the last quarter of the sixteenth and first quarter of the seventeenth century, followed by a severe drop during the second quarter of the seventeenth century, and, in England, significant declines in real wages during the first half and last quarter of the sixteenth century and large increases during the second half of the seventeenth century.

31. Munro, "Real wages and the 'Malthusian Problem'" pp. 11-12.

32. Based on official exchange rates industrial wages in Belgium amounted to 36 percent of those in Great Britain in 1850, 52 percent in 1896 and 64 percent in 1905. On the basis of purchasing power parities, in 1905, Belgian industrial wages represented 67-70 percent of those in Great Britain. See V. Zamagni, "An International Comparison of Real Industrial Wages, 1890 – 1913: Methodological Issues and Results," in Peter Scholliers, ed., *Real Wages in the 19th and 20th Century Europe, Historical and Comparative Perspectives* (Berg: New York, 1989) p.117.

the Antwerp market[33] and several of John Munro's articles on the evolution of prices and wages in the Southern Netherlands and England in 1400-1700.[34] The annual wage index data are based on the daily wage of a master mason in Antwerp with 1451-75 as reference period.[35]

The source of the data for 1700-1850 (column (b)) is Robert Allen's study mentioned above. The source of the data for the period 1840-1939 is the above-mentioned study by Peter Scholliers (column (c)). His index is based on yearly wages of men and women in eight to 13 industries with variable weights for the periods 1840-60, 1851-80, and 1875-1913, covering the whole of Belgium.[36] The Scholliers study provided the data for 1840-1913, while for 1920-39, the Scholliers index numbers on nominal wages have been deflated by the official price index as published by the NIS. Data used for the years since 1940 (column (d)) are those of the index of hourly earnings contained in IFS,[37] as reported by the national authorities, deflated by the NIS price index. A combined real wage index is presented in column (e) and the annual compound rate of change is shown in column (f).

Overall, between the first quarter of the fifteenth century and 2001-2006, real wages rose more than tenfold. However, until the middle of the nineteenth century, there was no clear trend, and movements consisted of upward and downward fluctuations around a level representing less than 10 percent of that prevailing in 2006, with a low of 6 percent. Fluctuations could be quite significant: during six quarter-centuries they exceeded 20 percent of the level of the preceding quarter century.

During the period 1401-25 to 1601-25, the average real wage level was some 10 percent higher than during the subsequent two and a quarter centuries ending in 1850. However, there were fluctuations during the earlier period.

---

33. Van der Wee, *The Growth of the Antwerp Market,* Vol. I: History of prices and wages in Brabant, Part II. Statistical data, pp.457-468.

34. Real wages are measured by the purchasing power of nominal wages in terms of baskets of essential consumables used for the price index in Antwerp and southern England; these baskets can be considered to be largely equivalent. Munro, "Real Wages and the 'Malthusian Problem'" pp. 14-15 and John Munro, "Price Movements in Early-Modern Europe during the eras of the 'Price Revolution' and the 'General Crisis of the 17th Century," Lecture Topic No. 16, *Economics 301Y1,* January 2006.

35. During the sixteenth century, in addition to a higher real wage level, higher employment and higher complements to money wages for craftsmen from the sale of supplies and piece-wages contributed to higher real incomes in Antwerp than in southern England.

36. For 1914-39, annual data collected from the industrial injuries' insurance sector were used.

37. International Monetary Fund, *IFS,* various issues, 1948-2007.

The decline in real wages during the last quarter of the fifteenth century resulted from the large rise in prices linked to currency debasements. The recovery of real wages and their maintenance at a high level in the sixteenth century during the Price Revolution was the result of very substantial nominal wage increases (nearly six fold between 1500 and 1600), reflecting successful action by wage earners, support from the guild structure, and growing exports. These increases were obtained notwithstanding strong population growth in Antwerp and were made possible by rising economic productivity and further specialization.[38]

Changes in population played an important role in the evolution of real wages during the first half of the seventeenth century.[39] The rise in real wages in 1601-25 was strongly influenced by the decline in population related to war and emigration, while a demographic revival contributed significantly to the large drop in real wages during the second quarter of the seventeenth century. A subsequent demographic stagnation helped to reverse the trend of declining real wages.

Other factors in the weakening of the economy of the Antwerp region and pressure on real wages in the seventeenth century were the growing mercantilist policies of several nation states and the slowing of technological innovations in the Antwerp region, owing in part to the rigidity of the artisanal structure of specialized industries, both with an adverse impact on Antwerp's exports.[40]

The fall of real wages in the second half of the eighteenth century and beginning of the nineteenth century reflects in general a stagnation of nominal wages, and a steady rise in prices, especially at the beginning of the nineteenth century, related to political upheaval and foreign wars. The recovery of real wages was delayed until the upward adjustment of nominal wages in 1820-35.

Between 1841-1850 and 1901-1913, real wages rose at an average annual rate of about 1 percent, followed by a similar increase in the period 1914-39. The increase in the first period reflects the industrial recovery from the economic crisis in the 1840s, which was accompanied by declining real wages, and increasing productivity.[41] There were some fluctuations: periods of rapid increases, 1853-1870 and 1905-13, alternated with a slowdown in 1870-95, owing to a slackening in productivity and industrial stagnation, and a decline in 1895-1905, when resumed growth in industrial activity was met by an enlarged labor supply.[42]

---

38. Van der Wee, "Prijzen en lonen" p. 432-33.

39. Van der Wee, "Prijzen en lonen" p. 432-33.

40. Van der Wee, "Prijzen en lonen" pp. 434-35.

41. Scholliers, 'A century of real industrial wages' p. 128.

42. Scholliers, 'A century of real industrial wages' p. 128.

The increase in real wages during 1913-39 was well below the estimated increase in productivity of close to 2 percent, as a large part of the gains was absorbed by a reduction in working hours.[43]

During the second half of last century, real wages, measured by hourly earnings, more than tripled. The growth was particularly rapid during the sixties and seventies, amounting to 160 percent between 1951-60 and 1971-80, before slowing steadily over the last 25 years, to reach only 26 percent between 1971-80 and 2001-06. Data for 1950–2006 are not fully comparable with those for the period 1840-1913, which track annual family income, as annual income growth is lower than that of hourly earnings as the number of working hours decline, and total family income increases less rapidly than hourly industrial wage earnings.

Table 3.1 Price Developments and Value of the Currency in Belgium, 1400-2006

	Antwerp Consumables price index	Antwerp Consumer price index	Ghent Consumer price index	Combined price index	Annual change in prices compounded	Value of Euro/BF equivalent in Brabant/Belgium in terms of Euro/BF of 2006 in Belgium	Value of money of account in Brabant/Belgium in terms of Euro of 2006 in Belgium	Value of money of account in Brabant/Belgium in terms of BF of 2006 in Belgium
	(1451-75 = 100) (a)	(1745-54 = 100) (b)	(1913/14 = 100) (c)	(1950 = 100) (d)	(in percent) (e)	(f)	(g)	(h)
							Brabant groat	Brabant groat
1400	66.1			0.21		3356.2	2.5	101.5
1401-1425	78.1			0.25	1.40	3131.6	2.4	94.7
1426-1450	106.7			0.34	-0.12	2110.8	1.6	63.8
1451-1475	100.0			0.32	0.33	2237.2	1.7	67.6
1476-1500	139.3			0.45	0.44	1674.1	1.3	50.6
1500	110.1			0.36		2013.7	1.5	60.9
1501-1525	147.0			0.47	0.81	1545.5	1.2	46.7
1526-1550	189.2			0.61	1.06	1186.8	0.9	35.9
1551-1575	323.4			1.04	2.59	709.5	0.5	21.5
1576-1600	667.8			2.16	2.57	356.8	0.3	10.8
1600	762.9			2.46		290.6	0.2	8.8
							Brabant guilder	Brabant guilder
1601-1625	661.4			2.14	1.13	343.5	15.5	623.2
1626-1650	959.6			3.10	0.42	232.6	10.5	421.9
1651-1675	839.4			2.71	-0.57	269.1	12.1	488.2
1676-1700	807.8	107.0		2.61	-1.20	270.7	12.2	491.2
1700	720.7	111.3		2.33		307.6	13.8	558.0
1701-1725		105.5		2.57	-0.22	279.8	12.6	507.5
1726-1750		99.3		2.42	-0.16	298.3	13.3	537.5
1751-1775		101.6		2.48	0.22	289.4	13.0	525.0
1776-1800		115.1		2.81	0.98	257.6	11.6	467.3
1800		136.7		3.33		214.9	9.7	389.8
1801-1835		133.5		3.26	-0.69	229.1	10.3	415.5
							Belgian franc	Belgian franc
1836-1850		120.1	80.3	2.93	0.45	246.3	6.11	246.3
1851-1875			90.6	3.30	0.71	219.0	5.43	219.0
1876-1900			97.6	3.56	0.04	202.3	5.01	202.3
1900			93.0	3.39		211.2	5.24	211.2
1901-1914			99.9	3.64	0.56	193.7	4.80	193.7
1914-1920					28.74			
1920-1930			604.3	22.02	6.74	35.8	0.89	35.8
1931-1940			735.1	26.79	-0.22	26.8	0.67	26.8
1940-1947					16.52			
1947-1950			2716.8	99.00	12.37	7.2	0.18	7.2
1951-1960			3143.5	114.55	1.92	6.3	0.16	6.3
1961-1970			3875.0	141.20	3.02	5.1	0.13	5.1
1971-1980			6834.1	249.03	7.36	3.0	0.08	3.0
1981-1990			12408.7	452.17	4.51	1.6	0.04	1.6
1991-2000			16084.7	586.12	2.09	1.2	0.03	1.2
2000			17379.4	633.30		1.1	0.03	1.1
							Euro in Belgium	Belgian franc
2001-2006			18669.4	680.30	2.06	1.1	1.05	1.1
2006			19643.3	715.79		1.0	1.00	1.0

Sources: Herman van der Wee, "Prijzen en lonen als ontwikkelingsvariabelen. Een vergelijkend onderzoek tussen Engeland en de Zuidelijke Nederlanden, 1400-1700," in *Album aangeboden aan Charles Verlinden ter gelegenheid van zijn dertig jaar professoraat* (Wetteren:Universum, 1965); 436-47.
Robert C. Allen, 'The Great Divergence in European Wages and Prices from the Middle Ages to the First World War,' *Explorations in Economic History*, 38 (2001), 411-447; Peter Scholliers, "A century of real industrial wages in Belgium, 1840 - 1939," in Peter Scholliers and Vera Zamagni, eds., *Labour's Reward* (Aldershot, England; Brookfield, VT, USA: Edward Elgar, 1995), 106-37; FOD Economie, Algemene Direktie Statistiek, *Historiek Indexcijfers der consumptieprijzen (vanaf 1920)*.

43. Scholliers, 'A century of real industrial wages' p. 129.

Table 3.2 Read Wage Developments in Belgium, 1400-2006

	Antwerp region	Antwerp region	Belgium	Belgium		
	Real wages index	Real wages index	Real wages index	Real wages index	Combined real wage index	Annual change in real wages compounded
	(1451-75 = 100) (a)	(1745-54 = 100) (b)	(1913 = 100) (c)	(2006 = 100) (d)	(1950 = 100) (e)	(in percent) (f)
1400	94.6				38.2	
1401-1425	87.9				35.5	-1.1
1426-1450	78.3				31.3	1.8
1451-1475	100.0				40.4	-0.3
1476-1500	73.2				29.5	-0.3
1500	93.9				37.8	
1501-1525	81.0				32.5	-0.5
1526-1550	80.1				32.1	5.0
1551-1575	82.6				33.2	-2.5
1576-1600	78.8				31.7	-2.5
1600	78.6				31.6	
1601-1625	90.7				36.6	-1.1
1626-1650	62.5				25.3	-0.4
1651-1675	73.0				29.5	0.9
1676-1700	78.8	93.7			31.7	1.1
1700	86.7				34.9	
1701-1725		94.8			32.1	0.2
1726-1750		100.7			34.0	0.2
1751-1775		98.4			33.2	-0.2
1776-1800		86.9			29.5	-1.0
1800		73.2			24.8	
1801-1820		67.9			23.0	0.1
1821-1840		105.1			35.5	1.1
1841-1850		94.9	49.6		32.1	0.4
1851-1875			63.8		41.2	5.4
1876-1900			79.5		51.4	1.0
1900			97.0		62.7	
1901-1913			90.0		58.1	0.3
1920-1930			105.8		68.3	4.8
1931-1939			134.0		86.8	0.1
1946-1950				24.5	92.9	2.7
1951-1960				30.3	115.2	2.9
1961-1970				45.1	171.0	5.0
1971-1980				78.8	299.0	5.0
1981-1990				90.3	342.5	-0.1
1991-2000				95.9	363.5	0.7
2000				98.3	372.7	
2001-2006				99.5	377.5	0.3
2006				100.0	379.2	

Sources: John Munro," Real Wages and the 'Malthusian Problem' in Antwerp and South-Eastern England, 1400-1700:
A regional comparison of levels and trends in real wages for building cradfsmen," Department of Ecconomics and Institute
for Policy Analysis, University of Toronto, *Working Paper No. 27* , April 2006, pp.31-66; Herman van der Wee, *The Growth of the*
of the Antwerp Market and the European Economy, 14th-16th Centuries , 3 vols. (The Hague, 1963), Vol. I: Statistics, pp. 457-75;
pp. 457-75; Robert C. Allen, "The Great Divergence in European Wages and Prices from the Middle Ages ot the First World War,"
Explorations in Economic History , 38:4 (October 2001), and tables on website; Peter Scholliers, "A century of real industrial
wages in Belgium, 1840-1939," in Peter Scholliers and Vera Zamagni, eds., *Labour's Reward* (Aldershot, England; Brookfield, VT,
USA: Edward Elgar, 1995), pp.106-37; IMF. IFS, various issues, 1948-2007; and FOD Economie, Algemene Direktie Statistiek,
Historiek der consumptieprijzen (vanaf 1920).

Annex 4
Value of investments in Belgium in US dollars
by Paul Duran

In Chapter 3 this book discussed capital investments made in the early part of the twentieth century by the Deboeck family as well as investments made in Belgian stock and bond markets between 1950 and 1980 by René Deboeck. This note shows how to convert the amounts cited to current values in US dollars. Table 4.I in this annex contains the value in 2006 dollars of 1 Belgian franc investments made in the periods 1935-1980 and 1937-1980. Table 4.2 provides the yields on long-term government bonds both in Belgium and in the U. S.

There are two ways to calculate the present values in 2006 dollars of investments made in Belgian francs 20 to 80 years ago.

The first approach is to convert the historic Belgian franc cost of an asset into US dollars at the exchange rate at the time and then calculate the 2006 US dollar value by applying the loss of purchasing power of the US dollar from the original year of investment to 2006. This loss of purchasing power is based on the rise of the cost of living in the US. The second approach consists of taking the value of the investment in Belgian francs, computing its value in current Belgian francs (by applying the loss of purchasing power of the Belgian franc), and then converting the latter value into dollars based on the exchange rate in 2006.[44]

Using the figures in Table 1 the first approach can be illustrated as follows. An investment made in 1979 of BF 1,000 is equal to $20 using the exchange rate of 1970 of the US$/BF (see the first column in Table 1). This $20 in 1970 had a purchasing power of US$ 104 in 2006 (using the second column 5.195 times 20).

Alternatively, a 1000 BF investment made in 1970 can be converted to 4,395 BF in 2006 (using Table 1, fourth column) an amount that is equivalent to US$ 136 in 2006 US dollars (4,395/32.12 where 32.12 was obtained by dividing the fixed conversion rate of 40.3399 BF to the Euro with the 2006 EUR/US$ exchange rate, 1.2556) The results of the calculations under both approaches are quite different for most years (only for seven years is the difference less than 10 percent).[45] The difference between the values under the two calculation methods is equal to *the real appreciation or depreciation of the Belgian franc against the dollar* or the change in the external purchasing power of the Belgian franc relative to the domestic purchasing power. The latter results from a difference between the nominal appreciation/depreciation of the Belgian franc against the dollar and the inflation/deflation in the U. S. relative to Belgium.

---

44. The corresponding Euro value is obtained by dividing the 2006 Belgian franc value by the fixed conversion ratio of 40.3399. Similarly the $/EURO exchange rate is obtained by multiplying the $/BF rate by 40.3399.

45. 1945-46, 1972-74 and 1976.

In the period 1935-2006, the nominal exchange rate of the Belgian franc was subjected to devaluations in 1935, 1944 and 1949. There was stability during 1950-70 under the Bretton Woods par value system followed by the appreciation of the main European currencies under a system of floating currencies. As there was a nominal depreciation after 1980, for the period through 2006 the Belgian franc underwent a nominal depreciation against the dollar in the years 1978-80.

Inflation was much higher in Belgium than in the U. S. during the period 1940-45, reflecting the much stronger impact of WWII in Belgium. In 1940-45 the annual price increase amounted to 24.5 percent in Belgium compared with 5.2 percent in the U. S. This evolution was reversed after 1945, with annual increases declined to 3.4 percent in Belgium and 4.0 percent in the U. S. Despite the higher inflation in Belgium in 1940-45, the change in the cost of living in the U. S. relative to Belgium for the period ending in 2006 rose from 37 percent in 1940 to 46 percent in 1945.

A nominal depreciation of the Belgian franc that falls short of the deflation in the U. S. (relative to Belgium), results in *a real appreciation.* This was the case between 1935–40 and in 2006. Similarly, a nominal appreciation exceeding the inflation in the U. S. (relative to Belgium) results in a real appreciation of the Belgian franc against the dollar. This was the case for the evolution between 1946–1972 and 2006. For the years 1973-77, the nominal appreciation with respect to 2006 was smaller than the higher inflation in the U. S. (relative to Belgium), thus resulting in a *real depreciation* of the Belgian franc. As the nominal depreciation between the years 1978-80 and 2006 was accompanied by a higher inflation in the U. S. than in Belgium, there was a substantial real depreciation of the Belgian franc.

Table 4.1 Value in 2006 dollars of 1 Belgian franc in 1935-80

| | US dollar per Belgian franc | 2006 dollar per historic dollar | 2006 dollar per historic Belgian franc | 2006 Belgian Fr per historic Belgian franc | 2006 dollar per historic Belgian franc | For period ending in 2006 | | |
						Nominal appreciation/ depreciation (-) of BF	Change in relative cost of living US/Belgium (in percent)	Real appreciation/ depreciation (-) of BF
1935	0.0364	14.712	0.535	30.011	0.934	-14.5	-51.0	74.5
1936	0.0339	14.500	0.492	28.663	0.892	-8.2	-49.4	81.5
1937	0.0339	13.997	0.474	26.731	0.832	-8.2	-47.6	75.4
1938	0.0339	14.294	0.485	25.809	0.803	-8.2	-44.6	65.8
1939	0.0339	14.500	0.492	25.515	0.794	-8.2	-43.2	61.6
1940 1/	0.0339	14.396	0.488	22.966	0.715	-8.2	-37.3	46.5
1944	0.0227	11.452	0.261	--	--	--	--	--
1945	0.0227	11.197	0.255	7.669	0.239	36.8	46.0	-6.3
1946	0.0227	10.336	0.235	8.060	0.251	36.8	28.2	6.7
1947	0.0227	9.038	0.206	7.877	0.245	36.8	14.7	19.2
1948	0.0227	8.363	0.190	6.865	0.214	36.8	21.8	12.3
1949	0.0207	8.468	0.175	7.097	0.221	50.3	19.3	26.0
1950	0.0200	8.363	0.167	7.158	0.223	55.6	16.8	33.2
1951	0.0200	7.752	0.155	6.546	0.204	55.6	18.4	31.4
1952	0.0200	7.606	0.152	6.488	0.202	55.6	17.2	32.7
1953	0.0200	7.549	0.151	6.506	0.203	55.6	16.0	34.1
1954	0.0200	7.493	0.150	6.393	0.199	55.6	17.2	32.8
1955	0.0200	7.521	0.150	6.425	0.200	55.6	17.0	33.0
1956	0.0200	7.410	0.148	6.277	0.195	55.6	18.0	31.8
1957	0.0200	7.173	0.143	6.085	0.189	55.6	17.9	32.0
1958	0.0200	6.974	0.139	6.007	0.187	55.6	16.1	34.1
1959	0.0200	6.926	0.139	5.934	0.185	55.6	16.7	33.3
1960	0.0200	6.809	0.136	5.917	0.184	55.6	15.1	35.2
1961	0.0200	6.741	0.135	5.861	0.182	55.6	15.0	35.3
1962	0.0200	6.674	0.133	5.777	0.180	55.6	15.5	34.7
1963	0.0200	6.587	0.132	5.656	0.176	55.6	16.5	33.6
1964	0.0200	6.502	0.130	5.429	0.169	55.6	19.8	30.0
1965	0.0200	6.398	0.128	5.217	0.162	55.6	22.6	26.9
1966	0.0200	6.221	0.124	5.008	0.156	55.6	24.2	25.3
1967	0.0200	6.034	0.121	4.869	0.152	55.6	23.9	25.6
1968	0.0200	5.792	0.116	4.738	0.147	55.6	22.2	27.3
1969	0.0200	5.492	0.110	4.567	0.142	55.6	20.2	29.4
1970	0.0200	5.195	0.104	4.395	0.137	55.6	18.2	31.7
1971	0.0206	4.977	0.103	4.212	0.131	51.1	18.1	27.9
1972	0.0227	4.822	0.110	3.995	0.124	37.0	20.7	13.5
1973	0.0257	4.539	0.116	3.735	0.116	21.3	21.5	-0.2
1974	0.0257	4.088	0.105	3.315	0.103	21.2	23.3	-1.7
1975	0.0272	3.746	0.102	2.939	0.091	14.5	27.4	-10.2
1976	0.0259	3.542	0.092	2.693	0.084	20.2	31.5	-8.7
1977	0.0279	3.326	0.093	2.514	0.078	11.6	32.3	-15.7
1978	0.0318	3.091	0.098	2.406	0.075	-2.0	28.5	-23.7
1979	0.0341	2.776	0.095	2.304	0.072	-8.7	20.5	-24.3
1980	0.0342	2.446	0.084	2.160	0.067	-9.0	13.2	-19.6
2006	0.0311	1.000	0.031	1.000	0.031	0.0	0.0	0.0

Sources: IMF, International Financial Statistics, various issues; ECB, Monthly Bulletin, March 2007; FOD Economie, Historiek Indexcijfer der consumptieprijzen (vanaf 1920); InflationData.com, Consumer Prices 1913 - 2006.Historical CPI-U data from 1913 tot the present; and National Bank of Belgium, Bulletin d'Information et de Documentation, Numero special "Statistiques economiques belges, 1929-1940, 1940.

1/ January-April for cost of living in Belgium and exchange rate.

Table 4.2 Yield on Long-Term Government Bonds in the US in Belgium, 1937-80

	Nominal Yields		Inflation		Real Yields	
	US	Belgium	US	Belgium	US	Belgium
	(percent per annum)		(percent per annum)		(percent per annum)	
1935						
1938	2.61	4.39	-2.08	3.57	4.69	0.82
1939	2.41	4.89	-1.42	1.15	3.83	3.74
1940 1/	2.26	4.81	0.72	11.10	1.54	-6.29
1941	2.05	...	5.00	...	-2.95	...
1944	...	3.82	...	...	...	...
1945	2.37	4.01	2.27	...	0.10	...
1946	2.19	4.18	8.33	-4.86	-6.14	9.04
1947	2.25	4.45	14.36	2.33	-12.11	2.12
1948	2.44	4.75	8.07	14.75	-5.63	-10.00
1949	2.31	4.61	-1.24	-3.27	3.55	7.88
1950	2.32	4.42	1.26	-0.85	1.06	5.27
1951	2.57	4.61	7.88	9.35	-5.31	-4.74
1952	2.68	5.10	1.92	0.90	0.76	4.20
1953	2.92	4.93	0.75	-0.29	2.17	5.22
1954	2.52	4.69	0.75	1.77	1.77	2.92
1955	2.80	4.61	-0.37	-0.50	3.17	5.11
1956	3.06	4.68	1.49	2.36	1.57	2.32
1957	3.54	5.99	3.31	3.16	0.23	2.83
1958	3.48	5.54	2.85	1.29	0.63	4.25
1959	4.13	4.99	0.69	1.23	3.44	3.76
1960	4.06	5.48	1.72	0.30	2.34	5.18
1961	3.92	5.90	1.01	0.95	2.91	4.95
1962	4.00	5.24	1.00	1.44	3.00	3.80
1963	4.05	4.98	1.32	2.15	2.73	2.83
1964	4.19	6.41	1.31	4.17	2.88	2.24
1965	4.27	6.44	1.61	4.06	2.66	2.38
1966	4.77	6.62	2.86	4.18	1.91	2.44
1967	5.01	6.70	3.09	2.85	1.92	3.85
1968	5.46	6.54	4.19	2.77	1.27	3.77
1969	6.33	7.20	5.46	3.74	0.87	3.46
1970	6.86	7.81	5.72	3.91	1.14	3.90
1971	6.12	7.35	4.38	4.34	1.74	3.01
1972	6.01	7.04	3.21	5.45	2.80	1.59
1973	7.12	7.44	6.22	6.96	0.90	0.48
1974	8.06	8.68	11.04	12.67	-2.98	-3.99
1975	8.19	8.50	9.13	12.77	-0.94	-4.27
1976	7.61	9.05	5.76	9.16	1.85	-0.11
1977	7.42	8.80	6.50	7.11	0.92	1.69
1978	8.41	8.45	7.59	4.47	0.82	3.98
1979	9.44	9.51	11.35	4.47	-1.91	5.04
1980	11.46	12.04	13.50	6.65	-2.04	5.39
1981	13.91	13.71	10.32	7.63	3.59	6.08

Source IMF Statistics

Annex 5 Was Franciscus-Alexius the son of Leopold I, first King of Belgium ?

In Chapter 4 I wrote that Franciscus-Alexius was probably raised by Catherine Elisabeth, a younger sister of Augustine Girardin. Catherine was married to Guillelmus Homble (or Humble). The family Homble lived in Lennik. When Franciscus-Alexius was in his early thirties, the farm on the Tuitenberg where he was brought up became too small; he looked for another farm. Franciscus-Alexius bought a farm from Simon Wauters-Borgenis located on the Lindenberg in Sint-Ulriks-Kapelle (see Chapter 4). The farm was built in 1845 and contained over 20 hectares of land around it. He rapidly started to expand it. In 1882 he opened a brewery on the Lindenberg.

Since Franciscus-Alexius was able to buy this farm, people quickly assumed that his father must have been well off. When later in the family a child was born with a handicap (a shorter arm), people made a quick connection with the Royal family where there was also a child born with a shorter arm.

Eugene Van den Broek wrote in *the Standard,* a Flemish newspaper, that Louise-Marie d'Orléans, oldest daughter of Louis-Philippe, King of France, brought with her to Brussels when she came to marry Leopold I, one of her court ladies from the Royal Palace in Orléans, whose name was Augustine Girardin, the mother of Franciscus-Alexius.

In 1996 other newspapers wrote about Franciscus-Alexius being the son of Leopold I: "De Scheve schaatsen van een koning" (The affairs of the King, published on January 11, 1996), "Allemaal familie van Leopold I" (We are all family of Leopold I, published on January 25, 1996), "Brabant wemelt van afstammelingen van Leopold I" (In Brabant there are many who descend from Leopold I, published January 31, 1996). Copies of these articles are provided at the end of this annex.

Jef van den Steen who wrote a book on *Gueuze and Cherry beer, the champagne beers,* repeated the story in 2006.[46] Jaak Ockeley, editor of *Eigenschoon and the Brabander,* wrote an article under the title: "The son of a King who became a brewer."[47] The reference was to one of the grandsons of Franciscus-Alexius Girardin, who is a brewer in Sint-Ulriks-Kapelle (Dilbeek). Marie-Louise Girardin, a granddaughter of Franciscus-Alexius maintained to her death that her godfather Franciscus was "de seune van de Keuning" (the son of the King).

None of these newspaper articles are validated by documents.[48] Many books have been written about the life of Leopold

---

46. Van den Steen, *Jef, Gueuze en Kriek, de champagne onder de bieren.* Davidsfonds, Leuven, 2006.

47. Ockeley Jaak: *Eeen Koningszoon die brouwer werd,* Randkrant, 2007

48. Neither was the marriage of Caroline Bauer and Leopold. Stockmar, the king's close friend and advisor, made sure that certain documents disappeared.

I as King of Belgium; much fewer have been written about his personal life. Henriette Claessens, wrote in 2002 about the love life of Leopold I. Based on her work the relationships of Leopold I with women have become public.

Where did Leopold I come from?

Leopold was the eighth child (and third son) of Franz Friedrich Anton, Duke of Saxen-Coburg-Saalfeld (which later through an exchange of territories became von Saxen-Coburg and Gotha, abbreviated S-C-G). Franz was married to Augusta, daughter of Heinrich XXIV von Reuss zu Ebersdorf. Leopold was born on December 16, 1790 in Coburg in Germany and was given the following names: *Leopold Georg Christian Friedrich.*

As a young boy Leopold was engaged in the Russian army. According to documents,[49] young Leopold became a captain in the Russian army in 1797 when he was seven years old. Leopold became Major General in 1803 at age 13.[50] The parents of young boys registered them in the army in order to obtain support. The Coburgs in those times were very poor and needed all the help they could get.

In 1807 at age 17 Leopold accompanied his brother Ernest, Duke of Coburg, to Paris to submit a petition to Napoleon to enlarge the Duchy of Coburg. Napoleon thought that the young Prince Leopold was one of *"the handsomest of all Europe."* He was not alone to notice this. Leopold managed to attract the attention of Empress Josephine and her daughter Hortense. Rumors were that Hortense managed to seduce the prince, but how close the relationship became is unknown. Hortense was seven years older than Leopold.[51]

One of Leopold's sisters married a Russian prince through whom the Saxen-Coburgs became well known in Saint Petersburg. Years later, Leopold would show great respect for Tsar Alexander I, son of Tsar Paul and grandson of Tsarina Catherina II.

After Napoleon invaded Saxen he demanded that all military titles be revoked. Hence Leopold was forced to resign from his military titles and honors. On May 5, 1811 Leopold wrote a letter to Tsar Alexander I to request that his military titles be restored. The Tsar recognized the sympathies that Leopold held towards the Russian court and agreed on condition that Leopold kept the arrangement secret for a year.

---

49. Documents provided by the Soviet Union at the time of the Exhibition on "Leopold and his time" in Belgium.

50. It was quite common to register young boys in the army, even as young as seven, because parents received a stipend for every boy registered in the military. The family was financially strapped and needed the money; they registered young Leopold early.

51. Leopold managed not to make too close of contact with Napoleon, which he would not regret because when Napoleon deceived Coburg, Leopold would fight in the Russian army for the retreat of Napoleon from Moscow.

Ancestors of Leopold I von Saxon-Coburg-Saalfled

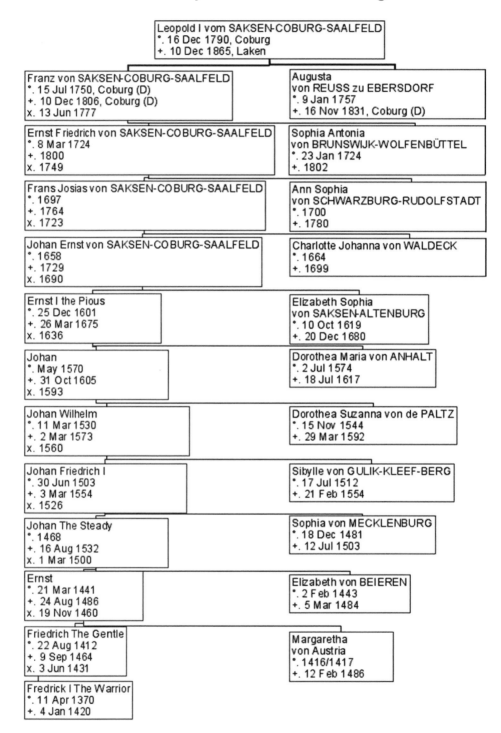

Figure 5.1 Ancestors of Leopold I von Saxon-Coburg-Saalfeld

Ancestors of Leopold I von Saxon-Coburg-Saalfled

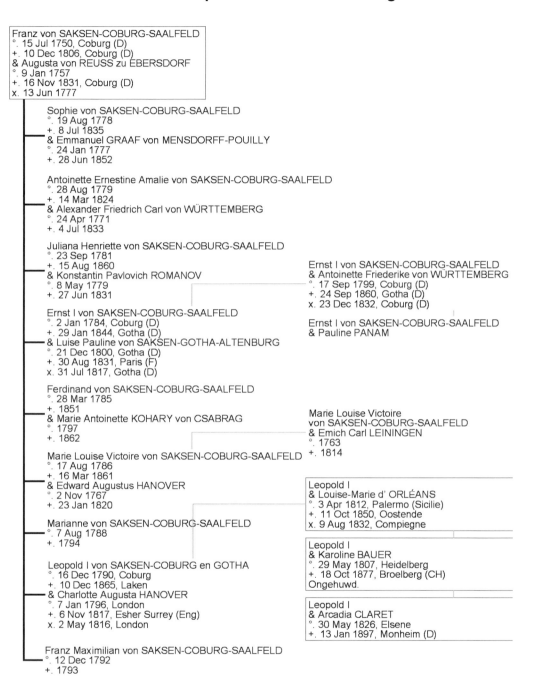

Figure 5.2 Family of Leopold I von Saxon-Coburg-Saalfeld

After a year Leopold's title was restored; Leopold was elevated to the command of the first division of the Russian cavalry against Napoleon. He was involved in several battles and pursued Napoleon on the retreat from Russia to France. He entered Paris with the Allies in 1814. For this he received in 1827 from the Russian government a silver medallion for his contribution to the liberation of Paris.

In 1816 Leopold married Charlotte, the only daughter of the future King George IV of Great Britain. A year after their marriage, Charlotte died in childbirth. Leopold continued to live in England as a widower and received from the British Government a pension.

Harald Sandner in his book on the *Saksen-Coburg und Gotha Dynasty* (1826-2001), written in German and commissioned by the current head of the family, Prince Andreas, claims that Leopold in 1819 may have fathered a child with Luise, Duchesse of S-C-G who was married to Duke Ernest III, later Ernest I of S-C-G. Luise and Ernest had two sons: first, Ernest, who was born on June 21, 1818 and secondly, Albert, who was born on August 26, 1819.[52]

In 1828, almost eleven years after the death of Princess Charlotte, Leopold was introduced to Caroline Philippine Aguste, also known as Lina Bauer. She was born in Heidelberg on May 29, 1807 and became an actress at the Prussian court. As daughter of Heinrich Bauer and Christine Stockmar she was the cousin of doctor Christian Stockmar, who was a personal friend, confidant, and physician of Leopold. At that time Leopold lived close to London in Claremont House.

In 1829 Caroline demanded to be married. Leopold hesitated (especially because a marriage could jeopardize his acceptance of the throne of Greece for which he was being considered). Stockmar orchestrated at Claremont a simulated marriage without witnesses, in which Leopold promised to Caroline the title of *"Comtesse de Montgomery"*. After a while Caroline realized that Leopold was only willing to make a limited commitment. According to *L'Intermediare des Chercheurs et des Curieux* (June 1999, Paris) she made a scene and left with her mother for Germany to take up again her career as theater actress. She died without

---

52. Sandner wrote *"Ihre in kurzer Folge geborenen Kinder sind grundvershieden, obwohl beiden im glichen Zimmer wohnen un vom gleichen Erzieher ausgebildet werden. Der charakterliche Unterschied wird sich spätter noch deutlicher ausprägen und es gibt Spekulationen, wonach der Vater von Prinz Albert nicht Herzog Ernest III, sonder sein Bruder Leopold, der später König der Belgier ist. Leopold war von September 1818 bis Mai 1819 in Coburg..."* (Their children born quickly after each other are totally different, although both live in the same house (room) and are trained by the same educator. The character differences will later become even more pronounced to the point where there is speculation that the father of Prince Albert was not Duke Ernest III, but his brother Leopold, who later became King of Belgium. Leopold was from September 1818 till May 1819 in Coburg...)

remarrying or having children but maintained till her death that Leopold did marry her.

In 1832, after accepting to become the King of Belgium, Leopold married Louise-Marie d'Orleans who was the daughter of King Louis-Philippe of France. With Louise-Marie d'Orleans Leopold had four children: Louis-Philippe, born in 1833, Leopold born in 1835, Philippe born in 1837 and Charlotte born in 1840.

Four years after Charlotte was born, Leopold was introduced to Arcadie Claret. It was at a concert of the Grand Harmonie. Arcadie made a big impression on the King. He wanted to see her again. Arcadie was however a minor; she was sixteen at the time; she was born on May 30, 1826. Leopold arranged for her to marry Frederick Meyer, who was his friend from Coburg.[53]

On the wedding day on June 30, 1845, Frederick Meyer departed for Coburg and never returned. The love affair between Arcadie and Leopold flourished and is documented in great detail in the books by H. Claessens and M. Kerkvoorde.[54]

Four years after her wedding in 1849 Arcadie gave birth to a son called Georg Fredrich Ferdinand Meyer. Christine Masuy wrote: *"Ce n'est pas, dit la rumeur, le premier enfant illégitime de Léopold. Mais, jusque-là, les amours adultères du Rois ont eu le bon goût de se faire discrètes."* In other words, rumor had it that this was not the first natural child of the King, but at least until then the other adulterous affairs of the King had been kept more discreet.[55]

Three years later another son was born. He was named Christian Freidrich Arthur Heinrich. Both Georg and Arthur were later recognized as sons of Leopold I.[56] Arcadie was elevated on June 21, 1863 to "Barones von Eppinghoven" and her sons become Barons von Eppinghoven.

Turning back to Augustine Girardin, who gave birth in 1847 to a son believed to be another natural child of Leopold. Conventional genealogy does not help to verify this because either the information is kept under lock in the Royal Archives or documents have been destroyed (as was the case regarding the affair of Leopold with Caroline Bauer). Nevertheless, there are some distinct patterns in the data about the relationships Leopold maintained

---

53. He took care of the royal horses and gave riding lessons to Leopold's children. He was a widower of 36 with one daughter, who both resided at the palace.

54. Mia Kerkvoorde "Marie-Louise d'Orleans" (chapter 31).

55. Christine Masuy: Princesses de Belgique: Laeken, les femmes de l'ombre, Editions Luc Pire, Bruxelles, 2001 , p 25.

56. V. Capron, who researched the natural descendants of Leopold, expressed surprise in one of his monograph that "four years passed by between the wedding and the first birth and nothing happened ("ce qui est etonnant" he writes on page 14) ".

with women. Leopold clearly preferred younger women and as he was growing older, this preference for younger women became one for under-aged girls! The evidence:

- **In 1816 Leopold married Charlotte.** She was 20; he was 26. This was the only relationship where the age difference was only 6 years.
- **If Leopold had an affair with Luise,** when Albert was conceived Luise was 18 and Leopold was 28.
- **Ten years later Leopold had an affair with Caroline Bauer.** She was 21 when the affair started; he was 38.
- **In 1832 Leopold married Louise-Marie;** she was 20, he was 42 years old; a difference of 22 years.
- **In 1842 Leopold met Arcadie Claret;** she was 16 when they first met; he was 52; a difference of 36 years.
- **If Augustine Girardin arrived in Brussels in 1832** the first time she could have met Leopold was when she was 26, Leopold was 42. Unless, of course, Leopold already met her at the Royal Palace in Orleans, where he claimed he had known Louise Marie since she was little…

In sum, in four documented relationships the age difference between Leopold and the women he had relations with varied from six to thirty-six years. In two others the age difference was between ten and six-teen years. The unconfirmed relationships fall within the observed general pattern. Leopold had a preference for women who were young and the older he became, the greater his preference for very young girls.

Arthur, a natural son of Leopold, married Anna Harris who was ten years younger. A grandson of Franciscus-Alexius, Louis Girardin married Jacqueline who was eight years younger. His son, Paul married Heidi who was eleven years younger. Could all of these be coincidental? A few years ago, when Jacqueline Girardin revealed these age differences, it became clear that this pattern is hardly coincidence. There are not many families where such age differences between married or love partners occur systematically. I have not found them in any of the other families discussed in this book.

Based on popular beliefs, circumstantial evidence, and patterns in the data it is therefore not unreasonable to claim that Leopold I was the father of Franciscus-Alexius. However, if no documents exist to prove this, only genetic genealogy can be deployed. The results of some preliminary findings to solve this family puzzle can be found in Chapter 9.

„Allemaal familie van Leopold I"

JULLIE gaan het in het buitenland zoeken, maar wij in het noordwesten van Brabant, wij hebben de afstammelingen van Leopold I voor het opscheppen. Het loopt hier vol afstammelingen van de eerste koning van dit land." Zo reageert lezer en oud-collega Eugeen Van Den Broeck uit Asse op het stuk *De scheve schaatsen van een koning* in Beknopt Verslag van 11 januari.

„Toen Louise-Marie in 1832 met Leopold I trouwde, bracht zij vanuit Parijs, haar hofhouding mee naar Brussel. Onder hen een zekere juffrouw Girardin, bij wie koning Leopold I een zoon verwekte: Franciscus-Alexius Girardin, geboren op 1 maart 1847 in Sint-Joost-ten-Node. Op zijn Brabants doodgewoon: Frans Girardin. Hij droeg dus als familienaam de naam van zijn moeder.

Frans Girardin werd uitbesteed bij een kinderloos landbouwersechtpaar in Sint-Ulriks-Kapelle, dat een grote boerderij bewoonde, een *kam*. Een *kam* was én boerderij én mouterij én brouwerij. Aangenomen zoon Frans volgde zijn pleegouders op en werd op de *kam* eveneens boer en brouwer met mouterij. Hier wordt nu nog bier van 't vat gebrouwd, lambiek en geuze. De geuze Girardin uit Sint-Ulriks-Kapelle wordt door kenners geprezen.

Frans Girardin trouwde met Antonia Smet. Uit dit huwelijk sproten zeven kinderen:

1. Justine Girardin (1876-1943) trouwde met Arnold Van den Houte. Van deze familienaam noteert men veel varianten in de schrijfwijze.
2. Maria Girardin (1878-1943), getrouwd met Alois De Rijck.
3. Louis Girardin (1879-1935), getrouwd met Philomena Wijns.
4. Henriëtte Girardin (1881)1968), getrouwd met Zacharie Carlier.

5. Elisabeth Girardin (1883-1946), getrouwd met Theophiel De Doncker.
6. Pelagie Girardin (1884-1958).
7. Jean Girardin (1888-1962), getrouwd met Josephine De Maeseneer.

Van deze zeven kinderen noteren wij tien getijpte bladzijden nakomelingen: de Girardins, de Van dèn Haute's, de De Rijckes, de Carliers, de De Donckers, de De Maeseneers. Bij hen voegen zich de Cantillons, de Janssens, de Balcaens, de De Vossen, de Wielantsen, de Schoukens, de Van Biesens, de De Keersmaekers, enzovoort, enzovoort.

Opgepast hé, wij in Brabant liggen daar niet van wakker. Maar het is toch curieus dat er tussen die afstammelingen hier en daar exemplaren zijn met lichamelijke afwijkingen: korte armen, twee verschillende ogen, het ene oog bruin en het andere blauw, en een lange, lichtjes gebogen haviksneus. Hebben zij dat van de koninklijke vader of van de adellijke moeder. Of van allebei?

En wees gerust: allemaal braaf, deftig en welstellend volk, alom geachte families. Als ge heden ten dage een begrafenis bijwoont van een Girardin of aanverwante, dan ziet ge ze allemaal samen, ondereen, hier en daar zelfs een gelaatssilhouet van de stamvader koning Leopold I. Niet te loochenen.

Er waren en er zijn boeren bij, brouwers, molenaars, veehandelaars, ingenieurs, garagehouders, geneesheren, herbergiers, hoveniers. Alle stielen en ambachten zijn vertegenwoordigd. Ook burgemeesters, zelfs een oorlogsburgemeester en een lid van de bestendige deputatie. Kristen-democraten, fervente liberalen en onverzettelijke Vlaams-nationalisten.

Ik herhaaal het: wij in het noordwesten van Brabant liggen daar niet van wakker.

Maar wanneer de koninklijke prinsen hun *matante* keizerin Charlotte van Mexico op het kasteel van Bouchout kwamen bezoeken, dan hielden de moeders uit Meise hun dochters binnenshuis. Zo wordt dat nu nog in de streek verteld. Maar dat is een ander koninklijk verhaal."

Tot zo ver het verhaal van Eugeen Van Den Broeck.

STEVEN

Dit is het pronkstuk van Roeselare en de blikvang. Oorspronkelijk een klooster van de paters Herei met Latijnse school, opgericht in 1635 en opgehe als onderwijsinstelling en sinds 1849 Klein Ser gevel van de kerk uit 1725 is getooid met het van Pfalz-Neuburg, heer van Roeselare.

"Het Nieuwsblad" januari 1996 (Eugene Van Den Broeck)

"La Libre"   26 januari 1996

LIVRES

L'autre famille du premier roi des Belges

Une jeune femme prénommée Arcadie. Elle eut deux fils de Léopold 1er. On retrouve sa descendance de Laeken à la Nouvelle-Zélande

Par Pierre Stéphany

Cobourg, dit-on, le prince Léopold adolescent composait des valses pour une demoiselle von Tubeuf dont il était épris. Le temps passant et l'ambition venant, ayant vu sa province natale, la Saxe, envahie par Napoléon, Léopold prit du service dans l'armée russe. Il était général. Après la défaite de l'Empereur, il se trouva à Paris dans le défilé des vainqueurs, descendant les Champs-Elysées, cavalier superbe, un manteau blanc sur sa cuirasse noire. Les femmes étaient folles de lui.

C'est cependant une frêle princesse aux yeux de myosotis, prénommée Charlotte, rencontrée dans un bal à Londres, qui lui fit battre le cœur. D'autant plus que, petite-fille du roi George III, elle était appelée à lui succéder. Ils se marièrent. Le jeune hobereau allemand sans fortune serait prince consort. Un an plus tard, Charlotte mourait en donnant le jour à un enfant qui ne survécut pas. Léopold avait 27 ans et il n'était plus que veuf. Plus jamais on ne le verrait rire.

Jusqu'à nos jours

Quatorze ans s'étaient écoulés depuis, quand les Belges fraîchement émancipés lui offrirent la Couronne. Il lui fallait aussi fonder une dynastie et, à cette fin, une épouse était nécessaire. Le sort tomba sur la plus jeune des filles du roi des Français, Louis-Philippe. Elle avait 19 ans, lui 42. Les siens la virent en sanglotant partir pour le sacrifice.

On sut bientôt que « *Monsieur Léopold* », comme il l'appelait dédaigneusement le roi de Hollande, était un grand monarque. Fut-il en outre un bon mari ? Il y eut toujours entre la Reine et lui beaucoup d'estime. Pourtant, quand Louise-Marie mourut, en 1850, Léopold avait fait la connaissance depuis quelque temps déjà, lors d'une fête officielle, d'une très jeune femme répondant au doux prénom d'Arcadie. Elle était fille d'un major de l'armée belge, Claret. Le Roi s'attacha à elle et, malgré la réprobation paternelle, la tendresse fut réciproque.

On la maria à un écuyer du Roi, déjà veuf et père de famille, Ferdinand Meyer, cabourgeois d'origine, qui, dit l'historien Carlo Bronne, « *eut le bel esprit de disparaître aussitôt après la cérémonie, de prendre congé de sa femme et de ne plus reparaître* », Arcadie, désormais, eut ses gens, sa voiture, sa livrée. C'est chez elle, souvent, vers la fin de l'après-midi, qu'un ministre apportait au Roi les dernières dépêches à signer. Discrète dans l'ombre du trône, « *elle employa toute sa grâce à mettre un peu de lumière dans cette vieillesse ombrageuse, un peu de douceur dans ce* ...

De cette liaison, naquirent deux garçons dont la descendance, pour l'un d'eux, s'est prolongée jusqu'à nos jours. Si bien qu'aujourd'hui, au Canada, en Angleterre, aux Etats-Unis et jusqu'en Nouvelle-Zélande, vivent des Locke, des Bowen, des Skelton, etc., eux-mêmes bien pourvus en progéniture, qui sont les arrière-arrière-petits-enfants naturels du premier roi des Belges.

On doit ces informations aux travaux d'un historien belge amateur, Victor Capron, juriste de son état, dont la patience dans la recherche pourrait rendre des points à bien des professionnels. Membre du Cercle d'Histoire de Laeken, Victor Capron est devenu un spécialiste, qui publie régulièrement -à ses frais- le résultat de ses veilles et qui mérite d'être connu (1).

Il a déjà donné, entre autres choses, un travail sur le domaine de Stuyvenberg, à Laeken, où la reine Fabiola doit s'installer. L'épouse de Baudouin Ier pourrait y rencontrer l'ombre d'Arcadie. Celle-ci acheta le château en 1850 moyennant 80.000 francs dont on a tout lieu de croire qu'ils provenaient de la cassette royale. Elle était déjà, à ce moment, mère d'un petit garçon, Georges (Meyer pour l'état-civil) et c'est à Stuyvenberg que naîtra le second, Arthur, en 1852. Bien qu'elle possédât d'autres biens où elle séjournait souvent, Arcadie resta propriétaire de Stuyvenberg pendant 38 ans, Léopold II, qui l'appelait avec hauteur, « une certaine donzelle », racheta le château, par l'intermédiaire d'hommes de paille, en 1889.

Léopold Ier mourut en 1865, torturé par des calculs urinaires. Il ne supportait auprès de lui, assure Carlo Bronne, d'autre présence que celle d'Arcadie, « *qui le soutenait avec dévouement* ». Le lendemain du décès du roi, la jeune femme en grand deuil, accompagnée de ses deux fils, quittait Laeken et prenait, pour toujours, la direction de l'Allemagne. Elle avait 39 ans.

Le divorce entre elle et Ferdinand Meyer avait été prononcé en 1861. En 1863, elle avait été faite baronne von Eppinghoven, sur intervention de Léopold Ier auprès de son neveu, Ernest II, duc régnant de Saxe-Cobourg-Gotha. Georges et Arthur furent anoblis de la même façon. Arcadie mourut en 1897.

Parmi sa descendance

La descendance de George devait être nombreuse. Il épousa Anna Brust, servante que ce mariage fit baronne, sur-le-champ, en 1904; Anna lui survécut près de quarante ans. Son fils, Georg, mort en 1988 à l'âge de 96 ans, avait servi en 1914-18 dans l'armée allemande, alors qu'une de ses filles, à laquelle il avait donné pour prénom Arcadie, épousait un officier anglais. A la génération suivante, la famille se dispersa.

Arthur avait épousé Anne Harris, fille du vice-consul britannique à Nice. Ils eurent une fille, Louise, restée célibataire. Il rentra en Belgique en 1924, et fut inscrit au registre de la population sous le nom de Meyer von Eppinghoven. Il décéda en 1940, sa femme en 1944, leur fille en 1966. Tous trois sont enterrés au cimetière de Laeken. La tombe n'est plus entretenue depuis longtemps. Les noms s'effacent peu à peu sur la pierre. A deux pas de là, dans la crypte de l'église Notre-Dame de Laeken, Léopold Ier repose pour toujours parmi sa descendance légitime.

■

Renseignements et brochures disponibles chez Victor Capron, Schependstraat, 39 b8, 1050 Bruxelles, tél. 02/640.27.63

Brabant wemelt van afstammelingen van Leopold

„Jullie gaan het in het buitenland zoe-en, maar wij in het noordwesten van rabant, wij hebben de afstammelingen an Leopold I voor het opscheppen. Het ›opt hier vol afstammelingen van de eer-:e koning van dit land". Zo reageert lezer n oud-kollega Eugeen Van Den Broeck it Asse op het stuk „De scheve schaatsen an een koning" in Courant van 12 janua-i.

„Toen Louise-Marie in 1832 met Leopold trouwde, bracht zij vanuit Parijs haar 1ofhouding mee naar Brussel. Onder hen :en zekere juffrouw Girardin, bij wie ko-1ing Leopold I een zoon verwekte: Fran-:iscus-Alexius Girardin, geboren op 1 maart 1847 in Sint-Joost-ten-Node. Op :ijn Brabants doodgewoon: Frans Girar-1in. Hij droeg dus als familienaam de 1aam van zijn moeder.

Frans Girardin werd uitbesteed bij een kinderloos landbouwersechtpaar in Sint-Ulriks-Kapelle, dat een grote boerderij be-woonde, een *kam*. Een *kam* was én boer-derij én mouterij én brouwerij. Aangeno-men zoon Frans volgde zijn pleegouders op en werd op de *kam* eveneens boer en brouwer met mouterij. Hier wordt nu nog bier van 't vat gebrouwd, lambiek en geu-ze. De geuze Girardin uit Sint-Ulriks-Ka-pelle wordt door kenners geprezen.

Frans Girardin trouwde met Antonia Smet. Uit dit huwelijk sproten zeven kin-deren:

1. Justine Girardin (1876-1943) trouwde met Arnold Van den Houte. Van deze fa-milienaam noteert men veel varianten in de schrijfwijze.

2. Maria Girardin (1878-1943), getrouwd met Alois De Rijck.

3. Louis Girardin (1879-1935), getrouwd met Philomena Wijns.

4. Henriëtte Girardin (1881)1968), ge-trouwd met Zacharie Carlier.

5. Elisabeth Girardin (1883-1946), ge-trouwd met Theophiel De Doncker.

6. Pelagie Girardin (1884-1958).

7. Jean Girardin (1888-1962), getrouwd met Josephine De Maeseneer.

Van deze zeven kinderen noteren wij tien getijpte bladzijden nakomelingen: de Gi-rardins, de Van den Haute's, de De Rijc-kes, de Carliers, de De Donckers, de De Maeseneers. Bij hen voegen zich de Can-tillons, de Janssens, de Balcaens, de De Vossen. de Wielantsen, de Schoukens, de van Biesens, de De Keersmaeckers, enzovoort, enzovoort.

Opgepast hé, wij in Brabant liggen daar niet van wakker. Maar het is toch curieus dat er tussen die afstammelingen hier en daar eksemplaren zijn met lichamelijke afwijkingen: korte armen, twee verschil-lende ogen, het ene oog bruin en het andere blauw, en een lange, lichtjes gebo-gen haviksneus. Hebben zij dat van de koninklijke vader of van de adellijke moe-der. Of van allebei?

En wees gerust: allemaal braaf, deftig en welstellend volk, alom geachte families. Als je heden ten dage een begrafenis bij-woont van een Girardin of aanverwante, dan zie je ze allemaal samen, onderen, hier en daar zelfs een gelaatssilhouet van de stamvader koning Leopold I. Niet te loochenen.

Er waren en er zijn boeren bij, brouwers, molenaars, veehandelaars, ingenieurs, ga-ragisten, geneesheren, herbergiers, hove-niers. Alle stielen en ambachten zijn verte-genwoordigd. Ook burgemeesters, zelfs een oorlogsburgemeester en een lid van de bestendige deputatie. Kristendemokraten, fervente liberalen en onverzettelijke Vlaams-nationalisten.

Ik herhaal het: wij in het noordwesten van Brabant liggen daar niet van wakker.

Maar wanneer de koninklijke prinsen hun *matante* keizerin Charlotte van Mexi-co op het kasteel van Boechout kwamen bezoeken, dan hielden de moeders uit Meise hun dochters binnenshuis. Zo wordt dat nu nog in de streek verteld. Maar dat is een ander koninklijk verhaal."

Tot zo ver het verhaal van Eugeen Van Den Broeck.

De scheve schaatsen van een koning

Waar zitten al die nakomelingen van Leopold, de eerste koning der Belgen? Hoe? Nakomelingen? Prinsen en prinsessen, koningen en koninginnen? Ekskuseer, de eerste koning der Belgen had niet alleen kinderen bij zijn eigen vrouw, koningin Louise Marie. Neen, onze eerste koning reed wel eens een scheve schaats. En daarmee doelen we niet op de Elfstedentocht.

In Brussel liet Leopold I zijn oog vallen op Arcadie Claret, de dochter van een officier uit het Belgisch leger. Arcadie was dan wel getrouwd met ene Frédéric Meyer, maar voor haar was dat geen bezwaar om voor de charmes van de koning te bezwijken.

Ook aan Leopold I schonk Arcadie twee zonen. Georges werd geboren in 1845 (het jaar waarin zijn ouders trouwden) en Arthur kwam in 1852 op de wereld.

Een geheim is dat niet en was het evenmin in de vorige eeuw. „Iedereen" wist dat Georges en Arthur wel Meyer heetten, maar eigenlijk Saksen-Coburgs waren. Dus verwonderde niemand zich erover dat in 1862 hertog Ernest II van Saksen-Coburg en Gotha, een neef van onze koning, zowel Georges als Arthur in de adelstand verhief. Voortaan gingen die jongens niet langer als meneer Meyer door het leven maar wel als Freiherr von Eppinghoven. In het Frans werd dat baron d'Eppinghoven.

Tot zo ver de algemeen bekende gechiedenis. Zo bekend dat die twee baronnen von Eppinghoven zelfs onder de hoofding „Belgisch vorstenhuis" vermeld staan in de Gotha, dat is het officiële naslagwerk van de Europese koninklijke adel.

En nu is er in Brussel ene meneer Capron die zich afvraagt of Georges en Arthur misschien op hun beurt ook afstammelingen zouden hebben gehad. Want als dat inderdaad het geval is, dan zijn die afstammelingen in feite afstammelingen van de eerste koning der Belgen. Volgt u nog?

Het resultaat van de onderzoekingen van meneer Capron is een geïllustreerde brochure, die helaas alleen maar in het Frans bestaat: *La descendance naturelle de Leopold Ier, Roi des Belges*. Te verkrijgen bij V. Capron, Postbus 28, 1050 Brussel 5.

En wat blijkt nu? Zowel in Canada, als in Engeland, als in Zuid-Afrika leven mannen en vrouwen die in hun stamboom teruggaan op Leopold, de eerste koning der Belgen. Daar zijn ingenieurs bij en dokters en boeren. Gewone mensen zonder geschie-

"Het Nieuwsblad" 11 januari 1996

Leopold I: nakomelingen over heel de wereld.   (RR)

denis, met als enige uitzondering dat zij een beetje koninklijk bloed in hun aderen hebben.

Mensen die nu namen dragen als Locke of Williams of Bowen of Skelon. Mensen die de wereld rondzwierven en die hun kinderen lieten geboren worden in Tanzania of in Egypte. Afstammelingen van Leopold I stierven gewoon in hun bed of debiel in een psychiatrische inrichting.

Nu nog lopen er op deze aardbol drie afstammelingen rond met de naam von Eppinghoven. Alarich Johannes von Eppinghoven werd geboren in Arusha in Tanzania en trouwde in Toronto met de Duitse Anna Margarete Ziggert. Zij zijn de ouders van de tweeling Armin Johannes en Ralph Georg von Eppinghoven. Twee broers van 36 jaar. Zonder nakomelingen.

"Het Nieuwsblad" 11 januari 1996 (b)

Glossary

Allele: Broadly, one of the alternative forms of a gene or genetic marker. More narrowly, the term allele value refers to a count of the number of repeats in an STR (pronounced ess-tee-are). A list of marker labels and their associated allele values constitutes an individual's haplotype.

Ancestral or Negative: The designation given a SNP when DNA testing determines that the SNP mutation is absent.

Anthrogenealogy: The tracing of human lineage beyond the limits of historical records through DNA testing through the use of SNP testing to determine haplogroups. The term is defined by Family Tree DNA in the document, *What is Anthrogenealogy?*

Anthropological Time Frame: A time frame of over 1000 to tens of thousands of years ago that predates recorded history and surnames for most people. The Y-DNA haplogroup tree traces SNP mutations over anthropological time.

Anthropology: The science of human beings, especially the study of human beings in relation to distribution, origin, and classification.

Base: A small chemical molecule which is the information portion of the nucleotides in DNA. The chemical bases are: A (Adenine), T (Thymine) C (Cytosine) and G (Guanine).

Base Pair (bp): A (Adenine) pairs with T (Thymine) and C (Cytosine) pairs with G (Guanine). These base pairs form the ladder of the DNA molecule.

Branch: A specific area on a haplogroup or phylogenetic tree that has associated SNPs. For example, E1, E2, and E3 are all branches of haplogroup E.

Chromosome: The self-replicating genetic structure of cells containing the cellular DNA that bears in its nucleotide sequence the linear array of genes. Chromosomes are normally found in pairs; human beings typically have 23 pairs of chromosomes.

Clade: From the Greek word klados, meaning branch. A clade on the Y chromosome tree is also called a haplogroup.

Confirmed SNP: See definition of confirmed SNP in Requirements for SNP Inclusion.

Deep Ancestry: Ancestry in an anthropological time frame of over 1000 to tens of thousands of years ago that predates recorded history and surnames for most people. The Y-DNA haplogroup tree traces SNP mutations to show deep ancestry.

Derived or Positive: The designation given a SNP when DNA testing determines that the SNP mutation is present.

DNA (deoxyribonucleic acid): The large molecule inside the nucleus of a cell that carries genetic instructions for making living organisms. See Y-DNA.

Downstream: A term used in association with a haplogroup or phylogenetic tree to designate the relationship between two SNPs or two branches or two clades, with downstream being the descriptor for the object that succeeds the first. The downstream item cannot exist without the existence of the upstream item.

Founder Effect: The effect of establishing a new population by a small number of individuals, carrying only a small fraction of the original population's genetic variation. As a result, the new population may be distinctively different, both genetically and phenotypically, from the parent population from which it is derived. In extreme cases the founder effect is thought to lead to the speciation and subsequent evolution of new species. The founder effect is a feature that can also occur in memetic evolution.

Gene: The fundamental physical and functional unit of heredity. A gene is an ordered sequence of nucleotides located in a particular position on a particular chromosome that encodes a specific functional product.

Genotype: The actual alleles present in an individual.

Genetic Genealogy: The tracing of human lineage within the time frame of historical records through DNA testing and comparison of haplotypes.

Genealogical Time Frame: A time frame within the last 500 up to 1000 years since the adoption of surnames and written family records. An individual's haplotype is useful within this time frame and is compared to others to help identify branches within a family.

Haplogroup: A population descended from a common ancestor, as evidenced by specific SNP mutations. Haplogroups are not cultural groups, although a haplogroup can be strongly represented by a cultural population such as American Indians. The Y Chromosome Consortium (YCC) has assigned hierarchical alphanumeric labels, which can be presented graphically in the form of a phylogenetic or haplogroup tree.

Haplogroup Tree: A diagram showing evolutionary lineages of organisms. See also Phylogenetic Tree.

Haplotype: Broadly, the complete set of results obtained from multiple markers located on a single chromosome. For the Y chromosome, the term is restricted by convention to allele values (number of repeats) obtained from microsatellite (STR) markers, as described by the Y Chromosome Consortium (YCC).

Human Genome Project: An international research project to map each human gene and to completely sequence human DNA, i.e., to sequence the entire human genome, the complete complement of all genetic material in the human species. The human genome sequencing was completed in 2003.

Locus: (plural-loci) a specific spot in the genome. A variable locus will have several possible alleles.

Long Interspersed Nucleotide Element (LINE): A Unique Event Polymorphism that is several thousand bases in length, with about 500,000 copies scattered over the human genome.

Marker: An identifiable physical location on a chromosome that is variable between individuals and whose inheritance can be monitored. A term commonly used along with allele values in describing an individual's haplotype. Marker labels, such as M173 or DYS388, have no intrinsic meaning.

Meiosis: The process of two consecutive cell divisions in the diploid progenitors of sex cells. Meiosis results in four rather than two daughter cells, each with a haploid set of chromosomes.

Microsatellite: Repetitive stretches of short sequences of DNA used as genetic markers to track inheritance in families. They are short sequences of nucleotides that are repeated over and over again a number of times in tandem. They are also called Short Tandem Repeats (STR) and Simple Sequence Repeats (SSRs)

Modal: Comes from the statistical term Mode, which means the value at which an absolute or maximum occurs in the frequency distribution of the variant.

Modal Haplotype (MH) Definition: any person who exactly matches the alleles found to be most common (Modal) among the descendants of a person. A person who matches 20 alleles while being 1 allele off in only 1 locus will be considered to be in the haplogroup, rather than in the family haplotype.

Mutation: A permanent structural alteration or change in the DNA sequence. Mutations in the sperm or egg are called germline mutations. Germline mutations in the Y chromosome of the male are passed on to all of his male-line descendants. Mutations that occur after conception are called somatic mutations; these mutations may be found in different tissues of the body and they are not passed on to offspring.

Negative or Ancestral: The designation given a SNP when DNA testing determines that the SNP mutation is absent.

NRY: Non-recombining Y, the large central portion of the Y chromosome that does not exchange material with the X chromosome.

Nucleotide: A sub-unit of DNA made of a molecule of sugar, a molecule of phosphoric acid, and a molecule called a base.

Nucleus: The central cell structure located in the center of the cell that houses DNA packaged in chromosomes.

Paternal Line of Descent: A direct line of descent from ancestral father to son to son to son along an all male line which is traced through Y-DNA.

Phylogenetic Tree: A diagram showing evolutionary lineages of organisms. See also Haplogroup Tree.

Phylogenetically Equivalent: A term used when describing the relationship between two or more SNPs; specifically, SNPs that belong on the same branch (or clade) of a haplogroup or phylogenetic tree, for example, Y-DNA haplogroup M is defined by the following SNPs: M4, M5, M106, M186, M189, P35, which are said to be phylogenetically equivalent.

Point Mutation: a change in a single base pair.

Polymorphism: A variation in the sequence of genetic information on a segment of DNA.

Population bottleneck: A population bottleneck (or genetic bottleneck) is an evolutionary event in which a significant percentage of a population or species is killed or otherwise prevented from reproducing; the population is reduced by 50% or more, often by several orders of magnitude. Population bottlenecks increase genetic drift, as the rate of drift is inversely proportional to the population size. They also increase inbreeding due to the reduced pool of possible mates. A slightly different sort of genetic bottleneck can occur if a small group becomes reproductively separated from the main population. This is called a founder effect.

Population Genetics: The study of the genetics of groups of individual organisms, often shown through the graphic of a haplogroup or phylogenetic tree.

Positive or Derived: The designation given a SNP when DNA testing determines that the SNP mutation is present.

Provisional SNP: See definition of provisional SNP in Requirements for SNP Inclusion.

Private SNP: See definition of private SNP in Requirements for SNP Inclusion.

Short Tandem Repeats (STR - pronounced ess-tee-are): Patterns in the DNA sequence which repeat over and over again in tandem, i.e., right after each other. Typically the repeat motif is less than six (6) base pairs long. By counting the repeats, one gets an allele value which is given in an individual's haplotype. They are also called microsatellites and Simple Sequence Repeats (SSRs).

Single Nucleotide Polymorphism (SNP which is pronounced 'snip'): Variation in the nucleotide allele at a certain nucleotide position in the human genome. When the change occurs it is called a polymorphism, and polymorphisms accumulate over time. A polymorphism can be very common (found in a significant fraction of global or localized populations) or very rare (found in a single individual). Common variations are used to track the evolution of the human genome over time (population genetics) and can be graphically represented in a haplogroup or phylogenetic tree.

Sister clade: A term used to describe clades that are on the same level of a haplogroup or phylogenetic tree. For example, R1b1c1, R1b1c2, R1b1c3, etc. would be considered sister clades.

STR (which is pronounced ess-tee-are): See Short Tandem Repeats.

Sub-branch: A term to describe the relationship between two branches with the sub-branch being downstream. See also Subclade.

Subclade: A term to describe the relationship between two clades with the subclade being downstream. See also Sub-branch.

TMRCA: this term used by population geneticists indicates the Time to the Most Recent Common Ancestor shared with another person.

UEP: See Unique Event Polymorphism.

Unique Event Polymorphism (UEP): A mutation that is treated as if it occurred only once in all of human history, so that all persons sharing the mutation descend from a common ancestor. Most UEPs are Single Nucleotide Polymorphisms (SNPs), while some are insertions or deletions (for examples, see LINE and YAP).

Upstream: A term used in association with a haplogroup or phylogenetic tree to designate the relationship between two SNPs or two branches or two clades, with upstream being the descriptor for the object that precedes the second. The upstream item must exist before the creation of the downstream item.

X chromosome: One of two types of sex determining chromosomes, the other being the Y chromosome. When two X chromosomes, one from each parents, are paired with each other in a fertilized egg cell, the resulting child will be female. If the fertilized egg cell contains both an X and a Y chromosome, the resulting child will be male. The X chromosomes become subject to cross-over effects during subsequent egg cell creation in the female offspring, and thus the homologous gene alleles and genetic marker alleles in both these X chromosomes can randomly swap positions in the next generations making it very difficult to track a particular X chromosome over more than a couple of generations. Determining a common ancestor for an X chromosome is very difficult beyond a couple of generations; therefore, the X chromosome is not a very useful tool for genetic genealogy purposes.

Y Alu Polymorphism (YAP): A Unique Event Polymorphism that is an insertion of a few hundred base pairs. There are about a million Alu inserts scattered throughout the human genome.

YCC: Y Chromosome Consortium, a committee formed to standardize haplogroup nomenclature.

Y chromosome: The Y chromosome is the chromosome that makes a person a male and can be passed by a male only to his sons. It differs from all other chromosomes that the majority of the chromosome is unique and does not recombine during meiosis (see NRY or non-combining Y). This means the historical pattern of mutations can easily be studied.

Y-DNA: The DNA in the Y chromosome that can be passed by a male only to his sons. This DNA can be tested to determine both haplotype and haplogroup of the individual.

Definitions adapted from the following References: 1. Avise, J.C. 1994. *Molecular Markers, Natural History and Evolution.* Chapman and Hall, New York. 2. Hartl, D. L. 2000. *A Primer of Population Genetics* (3rd ed.). Sinauer Associates, Sunderland, MA. 3. Kerchner, C. F. Jr. 2004. *Genetic Genealogy DNA Testing Dictionary.* C. F. Kerchner & Associates, Inc. Emmaus, PA. 4. National Human Genome Research Institute. 5. Family Tree DNA

Source: International Society of Genetic Genealogy (2007). Y-DNA Haplogroup Tree 2007, Version: 2.01, Date: January 12, 2007, http://www.isogg.org/ytree/ [March 25, 2007].

Useful Links

Genetic Genealogy

Flanders-Flemish DNA project
http://www.familytreeDNA.com/public/Flanders

Deboeck Surname Project
http://www.familyTreeDNA.com/public/Deboeck

Family Tree DNA
http://www.familytreedna.com/

Family Tree DNA Videos
http://www.ftdna.com/videoaudio.html

Y-chromosome Phylogenetic Tree
http://www.familytreedna.com/haplotree.htmlmutation

Relative Genetics
http://www.relativegenetics.com

Oxford Ancestors
http://www.oxfordancestors.com/

DNA 101
http://blairgenealogy.com/dna/dna101.html

DNA Heritage Tutorial
http://www.dnaheritage.com/tutorial1.asp

DNA Basics: cell chemistry, DNA Replication, DNA Sequencing etc
http://www.contexo.info/DNA_Basics/

DNA Master Class
http://www.dnaheritage.com/masterclass1.asp

National Geographic Project
https://www3.nationalgeographic.com/genographic/index.html

Yahoo Newbies
http://groups.yahoo.com/group/DNA-NEWBIE/

Chris Pomery DNA Page
http://freepages.genealogy.rootsweb.com/%7Eallpoms/genetics.html
http://www.DNAandFamilyHistory.com/

International Society for Genetic Genealogy
http://www.isogg.org/

The Sorenson Molecular Genealogy Foundation
http://www.smgf.org/

Ysearch Public Y-DNA Database
http://www.ysearch.org/

Ybase Public Y-DNA Database
http://www.y-base.org

Y chromosome Haplotype Reference Database
http://www.yhrd.org

Web-based Y-DNA Comparison Utility
http://www.mymcgee.com/tools/yutility.html

National Institute of Standards and Technology (NIST)
http://www.cstl.nist.gov/biotech/strbase/index.htm

National Center for Biotechnology Information
http://www.ncbi.nlm.nih.gov/BLAST/

mtDNA Public Database
http://www.mitosearch.org

Charles Kerchner's Genetic Genealogy Information
http://www.kerchner.com/dna-info.htm

Human Genome Project
http://www.ornl.gov/sci/techresources/Human_Genome/project/info.shtml

Genealogy DNA Listserv Archives
http://archiver.rootsweb.com/th/index/GENEAOLGY-DNA/

American Journal of Human Genetics
http://www.journals.uchicago.edy/AJHG/

Nature Genetics
http://www.nature.com/ng/

Dienekes' Anthopology Blog
http://dienekes.blogspot.com

Anthropology in the News
http://anthropology.tamu.edu/news.htm

John Hawks' Anthropology Weblog: Paleoanthropology, Genetics and Evolution
http://johnhawks.net/weblog

Genomics

Frontier Medicine Institute
http://fmiclinic.com/index.php

Personalized Medicine
http://www.ageofpersonalizedmedicine.org/

Genomic Testing
http://www.crlcorp.com/genomics/index.cfm

Genomic Tests Provided
http://www.genomeconsultation.com/id5.htm

123 Genomics: a genomics and bioinformatics knowledge base
http://123genomics.com

Institute Genomic Research
http://www.tigr.org/

Genovations: Predictive Genomics for Personalized Medicine
http://www.genovations.com/home/overview.html;

DNA Direct
http://genesanddrugs.dnadirect.com/

Conventional Genealogy

National Genealogy Society
http://www.ngsgenealogy.org/

Association of Professional Genealogists
http://www.apgen.org/

The US Library of Congress, Washington DC
http://www.loc.gov/index.html

Vital Records Information – State Index
http://vitalrec.com/index.html

Cyndi's List of Genealogy Sites on the Internet
http://www.cyndislist.com/

US GenWeb
http://www.usgenweb.org/

Belgian Americans
http://www.everyculture.com/multi/A-Br/Belgian-Americans.html

Flemish American Heritage
http://www.rootsweb.com/~gsfa/fahindex.html

The Belgian Researchers – Belgian laces
http://www.rootsweb.com/~inbr/belgian_laces.htm

History of Beer Brewing

Belgian Beer Society: Objectieve Bier Proevers
htpp://www.obp.be

HORAL: High Commission on Artisan Lambic Style Beers
http://welcome.to/horal

Belgian Beer Styles
http://belgianstyle.com/mmguide/

Beer & Health
http://www.bierandhealth.com/index.jsp

Belgian Brewers
http://www.beerparadise.be

Beer Message Board The Burgundian Babble Belt
http://www.cmg.net/belgium/clubhub/message/

Lambic
http://hbd.org/brewery/library/LmbicJL0696.html and
http://bergsman.org/jeremy/lambic/net.html

Gueuze
http://website.lineone.net/~beerrunners/Beer%20Runners/Pages/Gueuze.htm

Michael Jackson on Belgian Beers
http://www.beerhunter.com/

Belgian beer culture
http://www.globalbeer.com/

Bibliography

History

Aronson, Teo. *De Coburg van Belgie: Geschiedenis van een vorstenhuis (The Coburgs of Belgium).* Amsterdam: H.J. W. Brecht Uitgevermaatschappij NV, 1969.

Baye, Henry G. *The Belgians, First Settlers in New York and in the Middle States.* New York: New York University, 1924. Reprinted Bowie, MD: Heritage Books Inc., 1987.

Belien, Paul. *A Throne in Brussels.* U.K.: Imprint Academia, 2005.

Bilé, Elie. *Blankenberge: een rijk verleden en een schone toekomst* (Blankenberge a rich past and nice future). Blankenberge: Published by the City of Blankenberge, 1971.

Carson, Patricia. Flanders in Creative Contrasts. Tielt: Davidsfonds, 1990.

Claessens, Henriette. *Leven en liefde van Leopold I (Life and love affairs of Leopold I).* Tielt: Lanno, 2002.

Cook, John Steward. "*Belgian Americans.*" Gale Encyclopedia of Multicultural America, 2nd ed. Vol. 1. Gale, 2000. 3 vols.

Houthaeve, Robert. *Camille Cools en zijn Gazette van Detroit (Camilie Cools and his Gazet of Detroit).* Detroit: Flemish-American Heritage, 1989.

Dabney, Virginius. *Virginia: The New Dominion.* Charlottesville: University of Virginia, 1971.

Deboeck, Guido. "Kontakt van Beschavingen: een tragish dilemma" (Contact of Civilizations: a tragic dilemma?). Leuven: University Clearing on Development, 1967.

Deboeck, Guido. *Managing Information for Rural Development: Lessons from Eastern Africa.* Washington: World Bank Staff Working Paper no 379, March 1980.

Deboeck, Guido. *Monitoring Rural Development in Asia.* Washington: World Bank Staff Working Paper no 439, October 1980.

De Gronckel F.J. *Payottenland, gelijk het van oudtyds gestaen en gelegen is* (Pajottenland as it existed in the old days, a book of memories for all those who in this country live free and happy). Brussel. First edition 1846, third edition 1852.

De Goeyse, M. De *Liederen van de Brabantse omwenteling van 1789 (Songs of the Brabant Revolution of 1789).* Doctoral dissertation, 1933.

Das Fons, N.L. "Emigratie naar Frankrijk, Amerika en Argentinië te Wakken 1847-1900," in *Onze Voorouders,* sixth year nr. 1, Januari, 2003 and sixth year nr. 2, April, 2003.

De Lichtervelde, L. *Leopold First: The Founder of Modern Belgium.* New York: The Century Co., 1930.

Denis, Valentin. *Katholieke Universiteit te Leuven* 1425-1958 (Catholic University Leuven). Leuven: University Press, 1958.

Denys, Karel. "On the New World: Impressions of the 19th century Flemish Emigrants." *Flemish American Heritage,* Volume 2, number 2, July 1984.

Denys, Karel. "Belgians in Michigan," monograph, unpublished paper.

De Ridder, Paul. "History of Brussels, Linguistic usages in Brussels before 1794." Available online at http://www.paulderidder.be/history.htm.

De Ridder, Paul. *Brussels, History of a Brabant City.* Brussels: Vereniginv voor Brusselse Geschiedenis, seventh printing, 2001.

Demarrez, I. "Karel Verbeck's American Dream: From Meulebeke in Flanders to New Flanders in Pennsylvania," *Flemish-American Heritage,* vol. XXIV, issue 2, August 2006.

Goddyn, Reinout. *De kinderen van de koning: alle erfgenamen van Leopold I I (the children of the King).* Antwerp: The House of Books, 2002.

Gordon, John Steele. *An Empire of Wealth: The Epic History of American Economic Power,* New York: Harper Collins Publishers, 2004.

Haley, Alex. Roots. New York: Doubleday, and G K Hall & Co, 1976. Also available in paperback, June 2007.

Holton, Woody. *Forced Founders: Indians, Debtors, Slaves & the Making of the American Revolution in Virginia.* Williamsburg, Virginia: Omohundro Institute of Early American History and Culture, and Chapel Hill: University of North Carolina Press, 1999.

Kelen, Betty. *The Mistresses: Domestic Scandals of the 19th century Monarchs.* New York: Random House, 1966.

Kerckvoorde, Mia. *Louise van Orleans: het vergeten leven van Louise-Marie, eerste koninggin van Belgie,* (Louise of Orleans, the forgotten life of Louise-Maire, the first queen of Belgium) 1812-1850. Tielt: Lanno, 1998.

Masuy, Christine. *Princesses de Belgique: Laeken, les femmes de l'ombre. (Princesses of Belgium: Laeken the women in the dark).* Brussels: Editions Luc Pire, 2001.

Miller, James and Thompson, J. *Almanac of American History.* Washington: National Geographic Society, 2006.

Roosevelt, Theodore. *New York: A Sketch of the City's Social, Political and Commercial Progress from the First Dutch Settlement to Recent Times.* New York: Charles Scribner's Sons, 1906. Also available online at bartleby.com.

Peeters, J.P. *Bloei en verval van de Middeleeuwse stadsvrijheid Vilvoorde* (Growth and Depression in the Middle Ages of the freedom of Vilvoorde). Tielt: E. Veys Druk, 1975.

Post, M.J.H. *De Driebond van 1788 en de Brabantse Revolutie, (The partners of 1788 and the Brabant Revolution)* Bergen op Zoom: Wrappers, PhD. Dissertation, Universiteit van Nijmegen, 1961.

Sandner, Harald. *Das Haus Sachsen-Coburg und Gotha,* 1826 bus 2001 (The House of Saxen-Coburg and Gotha). Coburg: Neue Presse, 2001.

Stengers, Jean. *Brussel, Groei van een hoofdstad (Brussels Growth of a capital).* Antwerp: Mercatorfonds, 1979.

van Molle, L. and Pansaerts C. "Belgian Emigration to the United States," Washington D.C.: Belgian Embassy monograph, July, 1996.

Warners, David. *Chronicles of the Russian Tsars.* London: Thanes and Hudson, 1999.

550 Jaar Universiteit Leuven (550 Years of University of Leuven). Leuven: Stedelijk Museum, January 31- April 25, 1976.

History of Lace making

Claeys, Diane. "In Brugge herleeft het kantklossen" (In Bruges lace making is reviving). Brugge: *Libelle-Rosita,* nr 22, June 4, 1982.

Coene, Johan. *Lace Lexicon.* Waasmunster, July, 2002.

Deboeck, Guido. "Brief History of Lace Making in Flanders," in Belgian Laces, volume #29-111, 2007.

De Lantsheere, A. Carlier. *Les Dentelles Belges,* Bruxelles: Anc Ets A. Pauvrez, 1932.

Dpieser, C. and Legnazzi, M. E. *La Broderie and la mode.* Zurich: Editions Atelier Spieser, 1948.

Earnshaw, Pat. *The Identification of Lace.* Buckinghamshire: Shire Publications Ltd., 1980.

Kellog, Charlotte. *Bobbins of Belgium: a Book of Belgian Lace, Laceworkers, Lace-Schools and Lace Villages.* New York: Funk & Wagnalls Company, 1920.

Lauwers, Jos. *Van Lakenweverij tot kantwerk en wanttapijten, binnen de driehoek Brussel-Leuven-Mechelen* (From weaving to lace and wallcarpets in the triangle Brussel-Leuven-Mechelen). Nieuwkerken-Waas: Het Streekboek, 1999.

Reigate, Emity. *An Illustrated Guide to Lace.* Woodbridge: Antique Collector's Club, 1986.

Lissens, M. *Het ontstaan en enkele aspekten van de ontwikkeling van de machinale kant* (Origin and aspects of the development of mechanical lace). Brugge: Course Kantcentrum, 1985-88.

Paulis, L. *Pour connaître La Dentelle* (To know lace). Antwerp: Nederlandische Boekhandel, 1947.

Phannschmidt, Ernest Eric. *Twentieth-Century Lace.* London: Mills & Boon Limited, 1975.

Powys, Marian. *Lace and Lace Making.* New York: Dover Publications, Inc., Mineola, 2002.

Vannoppen, Henry. "Kant in Kortenberg en omgeving" (Lace in Kortenberg and environments), in *Cutemberg,* no 1-2, 1995-96.

Toomer, Heather. *Antique Lace, Identifying Types and Techniques.* Atglen, PA: Schiffer Publishing, 2001.

Van Noten, E. *Het Kantfabriek van Vilvoorde* (The lace factory of Vilvoorde). Leuven: Vlaamse Drukkerij, 1907.

Vincent, Margaret. *A Delicate Art: Flemish Lace,* 1700-1940. Allentown: Allenton Art Museum, 1986.

History of Beer Brewing

Buhner, Stephen Harrod. *Sacred and Herbal Healing Beers: The Secrets of Ancient Fermentation.* Boulder, Colorado: Brewers Publications, 1998.

Celis, Jos. *Het Land van de Geuze (The Land of the Geuze).* Roeselare: Roularta Books, 1996.

Deboeck, Guido. *Un"beer"ably Delicious: Recipes for Cooking with Artisan and Craft Beers.* Arlington: Dokus Publishing, 2002.

Eames, Alan D. *Secret Life of Beer: Legends, Lore & Little known Facts.* Pownal, Vermont: Storey Books, 1995.

Eckhardt, Fred. *Essentials of Beer Style.* Portland, Oregon: Fred Eckhardt Communications, 1989.

Fix, George J. and Fix, Laurie A. *An Analysis of Brewing Techniques.* Portland, Oregon: Brewers Publications, 1997.

Gordon, Enid. *A Taste of the Belgian Provinces.* Brussels: Midge Shirley, Tuesday Group, 1982.

Guinard, Jean-Xavier. *Lambic.* Boulder, Colorado: Brewers Publication, 1990.

Jackson, Michael. *The Great Beers of Belgium.* New York: Media Marketing Communications, 1997.

Perrier-Robert, Annie and Fontaine, Charles. *Beer by Belgium.* Esch/Alzette, Luxembourg: Schortgen, 1996.

Saunders, Lucy. *Cooking with Beer: Taste-tempting Recipes and Creative Ideas of Matching Beer and Food.* Alexandria, VA: Time Life Books, 1996.

Schermerhorn, Candy. *Great American Beer Cookbook.* Boulder, Colorado: Brewers Publications, 1993.

Smith, Gregg. *Beer in America: The Early Years 1587-1840.* Boulder, Colorado: Brewers Publications, 1998.

van den Steen, Jef. *Het Pajottenland en de Zennevallei Bakermat van Lambiek en Gueuze, (Pajottenland and the Senne Valley, sources of Lambic and Gueuze).* Pajottenland: HORAL and Province of Brabant, 2001.
van den Steen, Jef. Geuze en Kriek, de champagne onder de bieren (Gueuze and Cherrybeer, the champagne beers). Leuven: Davidsfonds, 2006.

van den Steen, Jef. Trappist: *Het Bier en de Monniken (Trappist, the beer and the monks).* Leuven: Davidsfonds, 2003.

van Herreweghen, Herman. *Geuze en Humanisme (Geuze and Humanism).* Brussels: De Bouwkroniek, 1955.

Conventional Genealogy

Deboeck, Rene. "Toestand van de Firma Deboeck Gebroeders" (Status of the Deboeck Brothers Ltd). Vilvoorde: internal document, October 19, 1966.

Demarrez, Iñez. *Meulebeke. Wel en wee tot 1850.* Tielt: Heemkundige Kring De Roede van Tielt, 2002.

Debrabandere, F. *Woordenboek van de familienamen in België en Noord-Frankrijk.* (Dictionary of family names in Belgium and North France). Amsterdam Antwerp: L.J. Veen, 2003.

De Clerq, Geert. *Ter Beurze, Geschiedenis van de aandelenhandel in Belgie 1300-1990* (Stock exchange: History of the stock exchange in Belgium from 1300-1990. Brugge: Uitgeverij Marc Van de Wile; also Antwerp: Uitgeverij Tijd, 1992.

Dermout, Jos. *De voorouders van Augustine Desiré Girardin (The ancestors of Augustine Desire Girardin).* Unpublished report, June 2005.

Dermout, Jos. *Stamboom gegevens Girardin* (Pedigree of Girardin family). Unpublished report, August 2005.

Dermout, Jos. *De nakomelingen van Ernest I van Saksen-Coburg-Saalfeld and Luise P. van Saksen-Gotha-Altenberg,* part I and II, (The descendants of Ernest I of Saxen-Coburg-Saalfeld). Unpublished report, August 2005.

Desmet, J. *Over café's gesproken (Talking about cafes).* Wakken: Heemkundige Kring Het Bourgondisch Erfgoed, 1982.

De Wever, E. "Rents and Selling Prices of Land at Zele, in Van der Wee," in Herman and van Cauwenberghe, E., eds., *Productivity of Lands and Agricultural Innovations in the Low Countries (1250-1800).* Leuven: Leuven University Press, 1978.

Goethals, Jozef. *A Forgotten Family: The Flemish Roots of General George Washington Goethals 1858-1928, Builder of the Panama Canal.* Baltimore, MD: Gateway Press Inc., 2004.

Goethals, Jozef. *Goethals: The ancestors of August Goethals and Elza Tavernier.* Baltimore, MD: Gateway Press Inc., 2006.

Lindemans, Jan. "Oude Brabantse Geslachten" (Old Brabant Families). *Eigen Schoon en De Brabander,* Year 34, number 5-6, 1952.

Lindemans, Jan. *Van Meiseniersbloed* (About Meisiniers blood). Gauw Vlaams Brabant: Vlaamse Vereniging voor Familiekunde, 1998.

Lindemans, L. "Genealogie de Bie uit Londerzeel," in: *L'Intermédiaire des Généalogistes,* nr. 297, May -June 1995.

Roelstraete, J. *Handleiding voor Genealogisch onderzoek in Vlaanderen* (Handbook of genealogical research in Flanders). Roeselaere: Vlaamse Vereniging voor Familiekunde, 1998

Van Elsen, J.A. "Geschiedenis der parochie Lippelo" (History of the parish of Lippelo), in *Eigen Schoon & De Brabander,* 1932.

Verheyden, A.L.E. *Vilvoordse scholen vroeger en nu* (Schools in Vilvoorde: past and present). Vilvoorde, 1974.

Volkstelling 1814 (Population counts) *Deel XXXVI, Oost-rozebeke-Meulebeke.* Brugge: Vlaamse Vereniging voor Familiekunde, 1998.

Wessman, Alice L. *A History of Elk County, Pennsylvania 1981.* Ridgway: Elk County Historical Society, 1982.

Genetic Genealogy

Bainbridge, David. *The X in Sex: How the X chromosome controls our lives.* Cambridge, MA: Harvard University Press, 2003.

Brandon, M. C., Lott, M. T., Nguyen, K. C., Spolim, S., Navathe, S. B., Baldi, P. & Wallace, D. C. "MITOMAP: a human mitochondrial genome database-- 2004 update." *Nucleic Acids Research 33,* Database Issue, D611-613, 2005. Also available at http://www.mitomap.org.

Behar, Doron M. "Is full mtDNA sequencing necessary?" Houston: Third International Conference on Genetic Genealogy, November 3-4, 2006.

Braveman, Eric R. *The Edge Effect: Reverse or Prevent Alzheimer's, Aging, Memory Loss, Weight Gain, Sexual Dysfunction and More.* New York: Sterling Publishing Co. Inc, 2004.

Fitzpatrick, C. & Yeiser, A. *DNA & Genealogy,* Rice Book Press, 2005.

Hart, Ann. *How to Interpret Your DNA Test Results for Family History and Ancestry.* New York: Writers Club Press, 2002.

Ingman, M. and Gyllensten, U. "mtDNA: Human Mitochondrial Genome Database, a Resource for Population Genetics and Medical Sciences." *Nucleic Acids Research 34,* D749-D751, 2006.

Johnson, Josephine. "Ethical Issues and Genetic Ancestry." Houston: Third International Conference on Genetic Genealogy, November 3-4, 2006.

Kalb, Claudia. "Peering into the Future: Genetic Testing – Health for Life." *Newsweek,* December 11, 2006. Available online at http://www.msnbc.msn.com/id/16006193/site/newsweek/.

Kurzweil, Ray, and Grossman, Terry. Fantastic Voyage: *Live Long enough to Live Forever.* Emmaus, PA: Rodale, 2004.

Logan, Ian. "The Medical Implications of Complete Mitochondrial DNA Sequencing." Available online at http://www.jogg.info/12/Logan.htm, November 2005.

MITOMAP: "A Human Mitochondrial Genome Database." http://www.mitomap.org, 2006.

Oppenheimer, Stephen. *The Real Eve: Modern Man's Journey out of Africa.* New York: Carroll & Graf Publishers, 2003.

Pomery, Chris. *DNA and Family History: How Genetic Testing Can Advance Your Genealogical Research.* Toronto: The Dundurn Group, 2004.

Rdley, Matt. *Genome: Autobiography of a Species in 23 Chapters.* New York: Perennial, Harper Collins Publishers, 1999.

Shawker, Thomas. *Unlocking Your Genetic History: A Step-by-Step Guide to Discovering Your Family's Medical and Genetic Heritage.* Nashville: Rutledge Hill Press, 2004.

Smolenyak Smolenyak, Megan and Turner, Ann. *Trace Your Roots with DNA: Using Genetic Tests to Explore Your Family Tree.* Emmaus, PA: Rodale, 2004.

Sykes, Brian. *The Seven Daughters of Eve.* New York: W.W. Norton Company, 2001.

Sykes, Brian. *Adam's Curse: The Science that Reveals our Genetic Destiny.* New York: W.W. Norton & Company, 2004.

Winter, P.C., Hickley, G.I., Fletcher, H.L. *Genetics.* Belfast: BIOS Scientific Publishers Ltd, 2002.

Wells, Spencer. *Deep Ancestry: Inside the Genographic Project.* Washington: National Geographic Society, 2007.

Name Index

Devisch, Virginia, 157-167
Doms, Anna, 50, 61
Dumon, Peronillia, 157-167
Duran, Paul, xxxiii, 26
Dusterhaus, Lynn, 58, 233-236

G

Geoffroy, Marie, 116
Girardin, Andre, 116
Girardin, Augustine, 111, 116-119, 121
Girardin, Augutine Desire 1806, 117, 334, 340
Girardin, Catherina Desire 1795, 117
Girardin, Catherine Elisabeth 1807, 117, 124
Girardin, Eustache, 116
Girardin, Florentine Antoinette, 126
Girardin, Franciscus-Alexius 1745, 116
Girardin, Franciscus-Alexius 1847, 27, 111,
    116-118, 122-123, 124, 131, 140, 276-279
Girardin, Henriette 1881, 125
Girardin, Jacobus Josephus 1778, 116
Girardin, Jacqueline (Mrs.), see
    van den Bossche
Girardin, Jean, 128, 143-144
Girardin, Jean (Joannes Baptist), 126, 127
Girardin, Jean Baptist 1774, 116
Girardin, Jean Francois 1770, 116
Girardin, Jean Francois 1799, 117
Girardin, Jean-Baptist, 1, 111, 113, 133,
    141-142
Girardin, Joanna 1904, 125
Girardin, Josephus Jean 1781, 116
Girardin, Justine 1876, 125
Girardin, Louis, 128, 130, 143
Girardin, Louis 1879, 125
Girardin, Louis Jr, 128, 144
Girardin, Lyne 1994, 128
Girardin, Madeleine Irma, 125
Girardin, Margareta 1906, 125
Girardin, Marguerite, 128, 130
Girardin, Maria 1878, 125
Girardin, Maria Adelaide 1804, 117
Girardin, Maria Elisabeth 1809, 117
Girardin, Maria Elisabeth 1875, 125
Girardin, Maria Elsabeth 1883, 126
Girardin, Maria Francoise 1800, 117
Girardin, Maria Josepha 1783, 116
Girardin, Maria Josephe 1796, 117
Girardin, Maria Philipinne 1769, 116
Girardin, Marie-Louise (Francisca), 57, 62,
    92, 111, 128, 130, 145-146, 334
Girardin, Marina, 128
Girardin, Michael Henricus 1786, 116
Girardin, Milly 1998, 128
Girardin, Paul, 128, 143-144
Girardin, Pelagie 1884, 126

Girardin, Pierre Jacques 1779, 116
Girardin, Pierre Joseph 1776, 116
Girardin, Pierre Josephe 1766, 116
Girardin, Pierre Josephe 1799, 117
Girardin, Yane 1996, 128
Girardin, Zelie Josephe 1798, 117
Goethals, George, 204
Goethals, Jozef, xxiii, 4, 150, 157, 211
Goossens, Catherina, 47, 61

H

Haley, Alex, 4
Hennepin, Antoine, 205
Hoemans, Johanna Maria, 255
Homble (Humble) , Guilelmus, 124, 334
Hondius, Jodcus, 188
Hudson, Henry, 187

J

Jacobs, Anne Maria, 49, 61, 65 ,
Jacobs, Anny, 166
Janssens, Joanna Catherina, 132
Jefferson, Thomas, 187
Johnson, Josephine, 5
Joos, Catherina, 41
Joos, Jan, 42

K

Kerremans, Rosallia Catharina, 255
Khan, Elizabeth, xxiii

L

Legrand, Henry, 78
Legrand, Louis-Alexander, 78, 82
Legrand, Roger, 78
Legrand, Vianney, 78
Leopold I, , 114, 121, 334-345
Lindemans, Jan, 13, 29, 42, 47, 49
Lopez, Olivia, 58, 232-235
Lord Baltimore, , 189
Louise-Maire d'Orleans, 332, 338
Louwye, Gratienne, 167

M

Mabesone, Joanne Cornelia, 157-167
Malou, Pieter, 206
Marcq, Maria Josepha, 116
Marynissen, Ann, 32
Meert, Maria, 42
Mehauden, Joanna, 44
Mergeay, George, 7
Mertens, Jan, 48
Meyer, Albert, 339
Meyer, George, 339
Minuit, Peter, 189

N

Nandrot, Ann, 116
Nobels, Joanna, 52, 55, 62, 65, 75, 77, 89, 92
Norga, Lea, 56

P

Pacquee, Anita, 166
Paridaen, Isabella, 157-167
Parmentier, Sylvia, 207
Pasteur, Louis, 137
Petrus, Stephen, 132
Pieters, Irma, 166
Plancius, Petrus, 188
Poirot, Hercules, 6

R

Rabaut, Louis C., 207
Raes, Irma, 157-167
Reinhardt, Jean Baptist, 208
Roelstraete, Johan, 7
Roets, Margaret, xxiii
Rogmans, Joanna, 41
Ruusbroec, Jan, 113

S

Sandner, Harald, 276, 336
Schaep, Joanna Francisca, 157-167
Schmidt, Robert, 107
Schumann, Klara Johanna, 258
Schunann, Klara Johanna, 167
Segers, Maria, 42
Seghers, Charles John, 208
Seifert, Sidonie August, 167, 258
Siegenbeek, Matthijs, 31
Smet, Antonia, 124
Smet, Dominicus, 124
Spanhoghe, Robert, 129
Spelier, Anne Maria, 162
Stappers, Marcel, xxiii, 14
Stas (Stasse), Jeanne, 117
Stuyvesant, Peter, 189

T

Tegethoff, Georges, 177-178
Twyffeloos, Franciscus, 112

V

Van Audenaerde, Pierre, 165
van Avermaet, Eddy, 149
van den Bossche, Jacqueline, 128,
    143-144, 340
van den Broecke, Anne-Marie, 157-167
van den Houte, Arnold 1873, 125
Van Depoele, Charles, 209

van der Wee, Herman, xxiii
Van Dingelen, Francesca, 166
van Dongelbergh, Anna Maria, 50, 61
Van Doorslaer, Joanna, 42
van Grasdorff, Stanny, xxiii, 33
van Grootven, Joannes, 42
Van Herp, Anne Maria Francisca, 51, 62
Van Hoecke, Livina, 157
Van Meteren, Emanuel, 188
van Praet, Joanna, 40
van Praet, Nicolas, 40
van Roy, Catherina, 124
van Ruysbroeck, Jan, 113
Vandenweghe, M.J., 30
vander Weyden, Roger, 113
Vandewiele, Maria, 157
Venter, Craig, 19
Verbruggen, Maria Ludovica, 255
Verhaegen, Gertrude, 52, 62, 65, 75
Verheyden, Maria, 47, 61
Verhoeven, Clemintine Ghislaine, 86
Vermeer, Jan, 69
Verstappen, Elisabeth, 44
Verstappen, Ursula, 42
Vertappen, Catherina, 41
Vetter, Jeannette, 120
von Saxen-Coburg, Leopold (see Leopold)

W

Wauters, Joseph, 132
Weiland, Petrus, 31
Wijns, Philomena 1878, 125

Y

Yoors, Jan, 209
Youcenar, Marguerite, 210

Z

Zehmisch, Emma, 168

Geographic Index

A

Antwerp   4, 19, 22, 23, 29, 32, 33, 34, 40, 45, 69
Austria   20-24, 69

B

Belgium   Kingdom of, 21-22, 114
Belgium   Pajottenland, 111, 138
Belgium   United States of-, 20, 22-24
Belgium - Cities/Villages,
    Blankenberge, 10, 25-26, 57, 150, 155, 174
    Brugge (Bruges), 151
    Brussels, market place-, 115, 174-175
    Dilbeek (see Sint-Ulriks-Kapelle), 93, 138
    Great Grimbergen, 2, 37
    Grimbergen, 2, 5, 8, 13-14, 29, 34-37, 49-51
    Lapscheure, 150, 154
    Lennick, 124
    Lippelo, 33-37, 43-47
    Londerzeel, 2, 14, 35-37, 44, 47-49
    Manderen, 35-36
    Moerkerke, 150-153
    Nieuwpoort
    Oppuurs, 33-35
    Puurs, 29, 33-35, 44
    Sint-Amands, 2, 10, 12-13, 25, 29, 33-34, 59-60
    Sint-Joost-ten-Noode, 120-124
    Sint-Ulriks-Kapelle, 93, 107, 122-128
    Vilvoorde, 1-2, 414, 16, 35-37, 50-53, 56-57, 63-65, 75-79, 81, 85-88, 93-93, 95, 107
    Westende (Lombardsijde), 149
Belgium - Provinces,
    Antwerp, 4, 19, 22, 23, 29, 32, 33, 34, 40, 45, 69
    Brabant (see Subject Index Brabant), 19-24
    East Flanders, 19
    Hinault, 114, 136
    Limburg, 19-22
    West Flanders, 9, 19, 25, 26, 151
Blankenberge 10, 25-26, 57, 150, 155, 174
Brabant (see Subject Index Brabant), 19-24
Brugge (Bruges) 151
Brussels, market place- 115, 174-175

D

Dilbeek (see Sint-Ulriks-Kapelle), 93, 138

E

East Flanders 19
England 5, 23, 70

F

Florida 186
France,
    general, 7, 14, 20-21, 24, 32-33, 67, 69, 70, 78, 84, 94, 105
    Nevers, 116
    Valenciennes, 30, 69, 70

G

Germany,
    Braunichswalde, 150, 167-174
    Dresden, 172
    East Germany, 25, 57, 98
    general, 25, 89, 90-91, 94, 97, 107
    POW camps, Stalag, 90-91
Great Grimbergen 2, 37
Grimbergen 2, 5, 8, 13-14, 29, 34-37, 49-51

H

Hinault 114, 136

I

Iberian peninsula 262
Indiana 197

L

Lapscheure 150, 154
Lennick 124
Limburg 19-22
Lippelo 33-37, 43-47
Londerzeel 2, 14, 35-37, 44, 47-49

M

Manderen 35-36
Maryland 8, 19, 189
Michigan - Detroit 194-197
Missouri 197
Moerkerke 150-153

N

    Netherlands,
    Austrian-, 20, 22, 69
    Burgundian, 20, 22

Subject Index

Gazette,
> of Detroit, 196
> of Moline, 195

genealogical society, of Flemish Americans, 195, 200

genealogy,
> advances, xx, 6
> etymology, 7

genetic clock, 242
genetic cousins, 266

genetic genealogy,
> general, xx, 4, 6, 17, 24, 237-296
> Genographic Project
> geographic project
> International Conference, 3, 238
> surname project, 30

genetic inheritance, 237-260
genetics, 4, 237
Genographic project, 269, 284 ,
genomics, 26, 301-303 ,
gentleman-farmer, 14
gentlewoman-farmer, 14
Geographical Project, 269
Geuzen, 152
Girardin brewery, 111, 132, 138-144

H

hand knitting, 71
health economics, , 218, 222, 224-226
health systems analyst, 224

history,
> Belgian federalism, 21
> Brabant, 22
> Brussels, 113-115
> computing, 83
> Flanders, 19

Hitlerjugend, 169
Holy Communion, 79
human genome, 238, 301
human-based trading, 229

I

Iberian peninsula, 262
Ice Age, 262, 264 ,
identity, , 4, 266
independence, true, xxi
independence, , 65, 71
Infiniti allele mutation model, 274
institutional data bases, , 227
international organizations, 230-232
intrapreneur, entrepreneur, 228, 297-298, 305, 308

investments,
> Brussels stock exchange, 106
> investment portfolio, 105

private -, 104, 145-146, 330-332
> see also trading

iron roads, 155

J

Jacquard machine, see embroidery
Japanese customs, xx

K

K.U.L. (see Catholic University Leuven)
kam, 139

L

lace,
> Binche -, 69
> Bobbin, continuous -, non-continuous 68, 69, 88
> Brugge, Bruges -, 72, 151
> Brussels -, 70, 72
> definition, 67
> Duchesse, Princess-, 71, 73
> embroidered -, 68
> English Honiton, Rosaline, Pearl-, 71, 73
> history of- , 67-74
> Italan -, 67
> kinds of -, 67-74
> Lille -, Chantilly-,, 69, 78
> macrame, 81, 102
> mechanical, 65
> Mechkin, 70
> needle, 68, 69, 72, 74
> pedigree of , 74
> pillow -, 68, 69, 74
> Point d'Angleterre, 70
> Point de Gaze, 71, 72
> Pointe de Flandre, 71
> Pottenkant, 69
> Rococo, 73
> The Lace Maker, 69
> Valenciennes, 69

land,
> see land measurements
> ownership, 13
> prices of, 38
> rents, 38

land measurement,
> bonnier, bunder, dagwaten, gemeten, 13
> hectare are, 315-316
> roede rod rood, 314, 315

langraviate, 22
language,
> Dietse taal, 113

space, Silver Snoopy Award, 233
Spain, see Geographic index
spinning, 70
stamp collecting, 106, 108
Statue of Liberty, 214
Stepwise mutation model, 274
stubborn, 33
surname project, 30, 59 ,
Surname Project, 269-275

T

taxes, 100e, 20e, 10e penning, 11, 38
taxes, on properties, 38
taxes, penning, 11
taxes, penningkohier, 12, 13
taxes, records of, 7
theater, drama, 84
to trace ancestry, 7
trading,
       changes in technology for -, 231
       day trading, 230
       deep market depression, 232
       electronic exchanges, 231
       human-based trading, 229
       machine-learning techniques, 229
       Trading Analytics Lab, 229

trading room,
       daytrading, 230
       Trading Analytics Lab, 229
transmission events, 242
Trappist, 136
travel back in time, 7, 237, 297
Tscany of the North, 112

U

United Provinces, xx, 20
University of Arizona, , 3
universtiy,
       Catholic University Leuven (K.U.L.),
         1, 140, 149, 216-217
       Clark -, 220-224
       cost of university education, 224

W

weaving, 70
welfare state, 214
Western Atlantic Modal Haplotype (WAMH),
248
Windows of Flanders, 100
World Bank, 226-230

Y

youth ministry, 235-236

About the Author

Guido Deboeck is an amateur genealogist who has collected information
about his family for the past twenty-
five years. On Father's Day of 2006 at
the Wine and Food Festival in Aspen
(photo left) he decided to assemble
all of it in a book. For close to a year
his genealogy interests took pre-
cedence over all his other interests
including investing, oenology, beer
brewing, cooking, photography and
eco-tourism. In addition to conventional genealogy he explored genetic
genealogy over the last few years and
has launching in 2005 the Flanders-
Flemish DNA Project. This project
was setup to collect and analyze DNA
in one place on the web from anyone
with Flemish roots.

The author started his career
as a health economist in the World
Health Organization, worked on rural
development projects around the world and eventually became an advisor and manager
of investment technology at the World Bank. He published several articles and books
including *Visual Explorations in Finance: using self-organizing maps* (1998) that was
translated in Japanese and Russian; and *Trading on the Edge: Neural, Genetic and
Fuzzy Systems for Chaotic Financial Markets* (1994). He also published a cookbook
titled *Un'beer'ably Delicious: recipes for cooking with artisan and craft beers* (Dokus
Publishing, Arlington, 2001). Besides being an avid genealogist and home beerbrewer,
he writes investment columns for Bella On-line, the Women's Voice on the Internet
(www.bellaonline.com/investing)

L'AMERIQUE SEPTENTRIONALE DIVISEÉ EN SES PRINCIPALES PARTIES *sçavoir* LES TERRES ARCTICQUES, LE CAN...
ANTILLES *ou sont distingueés les uns des autres* LES ESTATS COMME ILS SONT POSSEDES PRESENTEMENT PAR LES FRANÇOIS, CASTILLANS, A...